BRUNEI

T0291368

INVESTMENT, TRADE
STRATEGY AND AGREEMENTS
HANDBOOK
VOLUME 1
STRATEGIC INFORMATION AND DEVELOPMENTS

International Business Publications, USA
Washington DC, USA - Bandar Seri Begawan

BRUNEI
INVESTMENT, TRADE STRATEGY AND AGREEMENTS HANDBOOK
VOLUME 1 STRATEGIC INFORMATION AND DEVELOPMENTS

UPDATED ANNUALLY

We express our sincere appreciation to all government agencies and international organizations which provided information and other materials for this handbook

Cover Design: International Business Publications, USA

International Business Publications, USA. *has used its best efforts in collecting, analyzing and preparing data, information and materials for this unique handbook. Due to the dynamic nature and fast development of the economy and business environment, we cannot warrant that all information herein is complete and accurate. IBP does not assume and hereby disclaim any liability to any person for any loss or damage caused by possible errors or omissions in the handbook.*
This handbook is for individual use only. Use this handbook for any other purpose, included but not limited to reproducing and storing in a retrieval system by any means, electronic, photocopying or using the addresses or other information contained in this handbook for any commercial purposes requires a special written permission from the publisher.

2018 Edition Updated Reprint International Business Publications, USA
ISBN 978-1-5145-2140-3

For additional analytical, business and investment opportunities information,
please contact Global Investment & Business Center, USA
at (703) 370-8082. Fax: (703) 370-8083. E-mail: ibpusa3@gmail.com
Global Business and Investment Info Databank - www.ibpus.com

Printed in the USA

For additional analytical, business and investment opportunities information,
please contact Global Investment & Business Center, USA
at (703) 370-8082. Fax: (703) 370-8083. E-mail: ibpusa3@gmail.com
Global Business and Investment Info Databank - www.ibpus.com

BRUNEI
INVESTMENT, TRADE STRATEGY AND AGREEMENTS HANDBOOK
VOLUME 1
STRATEGIC INFORMATION AND DEVELOPMENTS

For additional analytical, business and investment opportunities information,
please contact Global Investment & Business Center, USA
at (703) 370-8082. Fax: (703) 370-8083. E-mail: ibpusa3@gmail.com
Global Business and Investment Info Databank - www.ibpus.com

**For additional analytical, business and investment opportunities information,
please contact Global Investment & Business Center, USA
at (703) 370-8082. Fax: (703) 370-8083. E-mail: ibpusa3@gmail.com
Global Business and Investment Info Databank - www.ibpus.com**

For additional analytical, business and investment opportunities information,
please contact Global Investment & Business Center, USA
at (703) 370-8082. Fax: (703) 370-8083. E-mail: ibpusa3@gmail.com
Global Business and Investment Info Databank - www.ibpus.com

**For additional analytical, business and investment opportunities information,
please contact Global Investment & Business Center, USA
at (703) 370-8082. Fax: (703) 370-8083. E-mail: ibpusa3@gmail.com
Global Business and Investment Info Databank - www.ibpus.com**

**For additional analytical, business and investment opportunities information,
please contact Global Investment & Business Center, USA
at (703) 370-8082. Fax: (703) 370-8083. E-mail: ibpusa3@gmail.com
Global Business and Investment Info Databank - www.ibpus.com**

STRATEGIC AND BUSINESS PROFILE

BRUNEI DARUSSALAM

Capital and largest city	Bandar Seri Begawan 4°53.417'N 114°56.533'E4.890283°N 114.942217°E
Official languages	Malay
Recognised	English
Other languages	• Brunei Malay • Tutong • Kedayan • Belait • Murut • Dusun • Bisaya • Melanau • Iban • Penan
Ethnic groups (2004)	• 66.3% Malays • 11.2% Chinese • 3.4% Indigenous • 19.1% other
Demonym	Bruneian
Government	Unitary Islamic absolute monarchy
- Sultan	Hassanal Bolkiah
- Crown Prince	Al-Muhtadee Billah
Legislature	Legislative Council
	Formation
- Sultanate	14th century
- British protectorate	1888
- Independence from the United Kingdom	1 January 1984
	Area
- Total	5,765 km^2 (172nd) 2,226 sq mi
- Water (%)	8.6
	Population
- Jul 2013 estimate	415,717 (175th)
- Density	67.3/km^2 (134th) 174.4/sq mi
GDP (PPP)	2012 estimate
- Total	$21.907 billion
- Per capita	$50,440
GDP (nominal)	2012 estimate
- Total	$17.092 billion
- Per capita	$39,355
HDI (2013)	▲0.855 very high · 30th
Currency	Brunei dollar (BND)
Time zone	BDT (UTC+8)
Drives on the	left

For additional analytical, business and investment opportunities information, please contact Global Investment & Business Center, USA at (703) 370-8082. Fax: (703) 370-8083. E-mail: ibpusa3@gmail.com Global Business and Investment Info Databank - www.ibpus.com

Calling code	+673
ISO 3166 code	BN
Internet TLD	.bn

Brunei officially the **Nation of Brunei, the Abode of Peace** is a sovereign state located on the north coast of the island of Borneo in Southeast Asia. Apart from its coastline with the South China Sea, it is completely surrounded by the state of Sarawak, Malaysia; and it is separated into two parts by the Sarawak district of Limbang. It is the only sovereign state completely on the island of Borneo; the remainder of the island's territory is divided between the nations of Malaysia and Indonesia. Brunei's population was 408,786 in July 2012.

At the peak of Bruneian Empire, Sultan Bolkiah (reigned 1485–1528) is alleged to have had control over the northern regions of Borneo, including modern-day Sarawak and Sabah, as well as the Sulu archipelago off the northeast tip of Borneo, Seludong (modern-day Manila), and the islands off the northwest tip of Borneo. The maritime state was visited by Spain's Magellan Expedition in 1521 and fought against Spain in 1578's Castille War.

During the 19th century the Bruneian Empire began to decline. The Sultanate ceded Sarawak to James Brooke as a reward for his aid in putting down a rebellion and named him as rajah, and it ceded Sabah to the British North Borneo Chartered Company. In 1888 Brunei became a British protectorate and was assigned a British Resident as colonial manager in 1906. After the Japanese occupation during World War II, in 1959 a new constitution was written. In 1962 a small armed rebellion against the monarchy was ended with the help of the British.

Brunei regained its independence from the United Kingdom on 1 January 1984. Economic growth during the 1990s and 2000s, averaging 56% from 1999 to 2008, has transformed Brunei into a newly industrialised country. It has developed wealth from extensive petroleum and natural gas fields. Brunei has the second-highest Human Development Index among the South East Asia nations after Singapore, and is classified as a developed country. According to the International Monetary Fund (IMF), Brunei is ranked fifth in the world by gross domestic product per capita at purchasing power parity. The IMF estimated in 2011 that Brunei was one of two countries (the other being Libya) with a public debt at 0% of the national GDP. *Forbes* also ranks Brunei as the fifth-richest nation out of 182, based on its petroleum and natural gas fields

Brunei can trace its beginnings to the 7th century, when it was a subject state of the Srivijayan empire under the name Po-ni. It later became a vassal state of Majapahit before embracing Islam in the 15th century. At the peak of its empire, the sultanate had control that extended over the coastal regions of modern-day Sarawak and Sabah, the Sulu archipelago, and the islands off the northwest tip of Borneo. The thalassocracy was visited by Ferdinand Magellan in 1521 and fought the Castille War in 1578 against Spain. Its empire began to decline with the forced ceding of Sarawak to James Brooke and the ceding of Sabah to the British North Borneo Chartered Company. After the loss of Limbang, Brunei finally became a British protectorate in 1888, receiving a resident in 1906. In the post-occupation years, it formalised a constitution and fought an armed rebellion. Brunei regained its independence from the United Kingdom on 1 January 1984. Economic growth during the 1970s and 1990s, averaging 56% from 1999 to 2008, has transformed Brunei Darussalam into a newly industrialised country.

Brunei has the second highest Human Development Index among the South East Asia nations, after Singapore and is classified as a Developed Country. According to the International Monetary Fund (IMF), Brunei is ranked 4th in the world by gross domestic product per capita at purchasing power parity.

According to legend, Brunei was founded by Awang Alak Betatar. His move from Garang [location required] to the Brunei river estuary led to the discovery of Brunei. His first exclamation upon landing on the shore, as the legend goes, was "Baru nah!" (Which in English loosely-translates as "that's it!" or "there") and thus, the name "Brunei" was derived from his words.

It was renamed "Barunai" in the 14th Century, possibly influenced by the Sanskrit word varunai (वरुण   ), meaning "seafarers", later to become "Brunei". The word "Borneo" is of the same origin. In the country's full name "Negara Brunei Darussalam" "Darussalam" means "Abode of Peace" in Arabic, while "Negara" means "Country" in Malay. "Negara" derives from the Sanskrit Nagara , meaning "city".

Brunei Darussalam, the host of the 1995 BIMP-EAGA EXPO is a stable and prosperous country which offers not only a well-developed infrastructure but also a strategic location within the Asean region. The country is chugging full steam ahead to diversify its economy away from an over-dependence on oil and gas, and has put in place flexible and realistic policies to facilitate foreign and local investment. The cost of utilities are the lowest in the region, while political stability, extensive economic and natural resources and a business environment attuned to the requirements of foreign investors go towards making Brunei an excellent investment choice

At present the country's economy is dominated by the oil and liquefied natural gas industries and government expenditure patterns. Brunei exports crude oil, petroleum products and LNG mainly to Japan, the United States and the Asean countries. The second most important industry is construction, a direct result of the government's investment in development and infrastructure projects. Gearing up towards putting on the mantle of a developed country in January 1996, Brunei allocated in its 1991-95 Five Year Plan a hefty B$5 billion for national development, over a billion dollars more than in the previous budget. About B$510 million was allotted for 619 projects while B$550 million or 10 percent of the development budget went to industry and commerce. Some B$100 million alone was reserved for industrial promotion and development.

STABLE, CONDUCIVE ENVIRONMENT

The oil-rich country, lying on the north-western edge of the Borneo island, has never experienced typhoons, earthquakes or severe floods. Profitable investment can be had as the country levies no personal income tax, no sales tax, payroll, manufacturing or export tax.

Competitive investment incentives are available for investors throughout the business cycle marked by the start up, growth, maturity and expansion stages. The tax advantages at start up and the on-going incentives during growth and expansion are among the most competitive around. There is no difficulty in securing approval for foreign workers, from labourers to managers. With a small labour pool of 284,500 Brunei people and Bruneians showing a marked preference for the public sector as employer, the country has had to rely on foreign workers. These make up a third of its work force.

In line with moves to promote the private sector, it is encouraging to note the contribution from the non-oil and gas sector of the economy has risen, contributing about 25 percent to GDP compared to the oil and gas sector's 46 percent. In terms of infrastructure, Brunei is ready for vigorous economy activity. At its two main ports at Muara and Kuala Belait, goods can be shipped direct to Hong Kong, Singapore and other Asian destinations. Muara, a deep-water port 29 km away from the capital of Bandar Seri Begawan, has seen continual increase in container traffic over the past two decades.

The Brunei International Airport at Bandar offers expanded passenger and cargo facilities. Its new terminal can accommodate 1.5 million passengers and 50,000 tonnes of cargo a year, which is expected to suffice till the end of the decade. A 2,000-km road network serving the whole country

For additional analytical, business and investment opportunities information,
please contact Global Investment & Business Center, USA
at (703) 370-8082. Fax: (703) 370-8083. E-mail: ibpusa3@gmail.com
Global Business and Investment Info Databank - www.ibpus.com

undergoes continual expansion. A main highway runs the entire length of its coastline, linking Muara, the port entry point at one end, and Belait, the oil-production centre, at another end.

Telecommunications-wise, Brunei has one of the best systems in the region with plans for major upgrading. Telephone availability is about one to every three people.

Two earth satellite stations provide direct telephone, telex and facsimile links to most parts of the world. Operating systems include an analogue telephone exchange, fibreoptic cable links with Singapore and Manila, a packet switching exchange for access to high-speed computer bases overseas, cellular mobile telephone and paging systems. Direct phone links are also available in the more remote parts of the country via microwave and solar-powered telephones.

PIONEER INDUSTRY INCENTIVES

Companies granted pioneer status enjoy tax holidays of up to eight years. Brunei's regulations governing foreign participation in equity are the most flexible in the region, with 100 percent foreign ownership permitted. A pioneer company is also exempt from customs duty on items to be installed in the pioneer factory and from paying import duties on raw materials not available locally or produced in Brunei for the manufacture of pioneer products.

GEOGRAPHY

Location: Southeastern Asia, bordering the South China Sea and Malaysia
Geographic coordinates: 4 30 N, 114 40 E
Map references: Southeast Asia

Area:
total: 5,770 sq km
land: 5,270 sq km
water: 500 sq km

Area—comparative: slightly smaller than Delaware

Land boundaries:
total: 381 km
border countries: Malaysia 381 km

Coastline: 161 km
Land use:
arable land: 1%
 other: 12%

permanent crops: 1%
permanent pastures: 1%
forests and woodland: 85%

For additional analytical, business and investment opportunities information,
please contact Global Investment & Business Center, USA
at (703) 370-8082. Fax: (703) 370-8083. E-mail: ibpusa3@gmail.com
Global Business and Investment Info Databank - www.ibpus.com

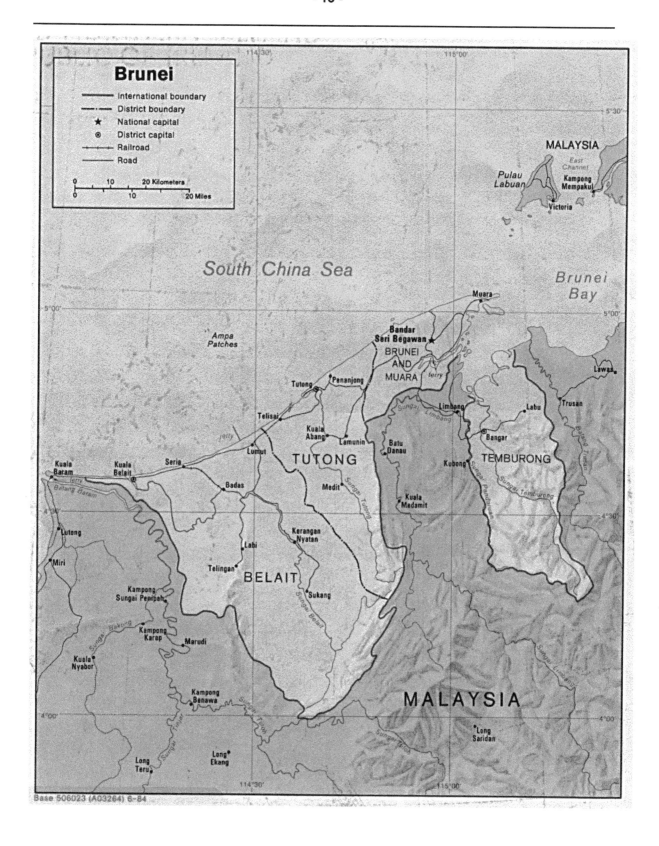

Irrigated land: 10 sq km

Natural hazards: typhoons, earthquakes, and severe flooding are very rare
Environment—current issues: seasonal smoke/haze resulting from forest fires in Indonesia

Environment—international agreements:
party to: Endangered Species, Law of the Sea, Ozone Layer Protection, Ship Pollution
signed, but not ratified: none of the selected agreements

Geography—note: close to vital sea lanes through South China Sea linking Indian and Pacific Oceans; two parts physically separated by Malaysia; almost an enclave of Malaysia

PEOPLE

Population: 322,982

Age structure:
0-14 years: 33% (male 54,154; female 51,766)
15-64 years: 63% (male 106,492; female 95,921)
65 years and over: 4% (male 7,945; female 6,704)

Population growth rate: 2.38%
Birth rate: 24.69 births/1,000 population
Death rate: 5.21 deaths/1,000 population
Net migration rate: 4.35 migrant(s)/1,000 population

Sex ratio:
at birth: 1.06 male(s)/female
under 15 years: 1.05 male(s)/female
15-64 years: 1.11 male(s)/female
65 years and over: 1.19 male(s)/female
total population: 1.09 male(s)/female

Infant mortality rate: 22.83 deaths/1,000 live births

Life expectancy at birth:
total population: 71.84 years
male: 70.35 years
female: 73.42 years

Total fertility rate: 3.33 children born/woman

Nationality:
noun: Bruneian(s)
adjective: Bruneian

Ethnic groups: Malay 64%, Chinese 20%, other 16%
Religions: Muslim (official) 63%, Buddhism 14%, Christian 8%, indigenous beliefs and other 15% (1981)
Languages: Malay (official), English, Chinese

Literacy:
definition: age 15 and over can read and write

total population: 88.2%
male: 92.6% *female:* 83.4%

GOVERNMENT

Country name:
conventional long form: Negara Brunei Darussalam
conventional short form: Brunei

Data code: BX
Government type: constitutional sultanate
Capital: Bandar Seri Begawan

Administrative divisions: 4 districts (daerah-daerah, singular—daerah); Belait, Brunei and Muara, Temburong, Tutong

Independence: 1 January 1984 (from UK)
National holiday: National Day, 23 February (1984)

Constitution: 29 September 1959 (some provisions suspended under a State of Emergency since December 1962, others since independence on 1 January 1984)

Legal system: based on English common law; for Muslims, Islamic Shari'a law supersedes civil law in a number of areas

Suffrage: none

Executive branch:
Brunei

Sultan	HASSANAL Bolkiah, Sir
Prime Minister	HASSANAL Bolkiah, Sir
Min. of Communications	Awang ABU BAKAR bin Apong
Min. of Culture, Youth, & Sports	MOHAMMAD bin Daud, Gen. (Ret.)
Min. of Defense	HASSANAL Bolkiah, Sir
Min. of Development	ABDULLAH bin Begawan
Min. of Education	Abdul RAHMAN bin Mohamed Taib
Min. of Energy	YAHYA bin Begawan
Min. of Finance	HASSANAL Bolkiah, Sir
Min. of Finance II	ABDUL RAHMAN bin Ibrahim
Min. of Foreign Affairs	MOHAMED Bolkiah, Prince
Min. of Foreign Affairs II	LIM Jock Seng
Min. of Health	SUYOI bin Osman
Min. of Home Affairs	ADANAN bin Begawan
Min. of Industry & Primary Resources	AHMAD bin Jumat, Dr.
Min. of Religious Affairs	MOHD ZAIN bin Serudin, Dr.
Senior Min. in the Prime Minister's Office	Al Muhtadee BILLAH, Crown Prince
Ambassador to the US	PUTEH ibni Mohammad Alam
Permanent Representative to the UN, New York	SHOFRY bin Abdul Ghafor

Legislative branch: unicameral Legislative Council or Majlis Masyuarat Megeri (a privy council that serves only in a consultative capacity; NA seats; members appointed by the monarch)
elections: last held in March 1962
note: in 1970 the Council was changed to an appointive body by decree of the monarch; an elected Legislative Council is being considered as part of constitutional reform, but elections are unlikely for several years

Judicial branch: Supreme Court, chief justice and judges are sworn in by the monarch for three-year terms

Political parties and leaders: Brunei Solidarity National Party or PPKB in Malay [Haji Mohd HATTA bin Haji Zainal Abidin, president]; the PPKB is the only legal political party in Brunei; it was registered in 1985, but became largely inactive after 1988; it has less than 200 registered party members; other parties include Brunei People's Party or PRB (banned in 1962) and Brunei National Democratic Party (registered in May 1985, deregistered by the Brunei Government in 1988)

International organization participation: APEC, ASEAN, C, CCC, ESCAP, G-77, IBRD, ICAO, ICRM, IDB, IFRCS, IMF, IMO, Inmarsat, Intelsat, Interpol, IOC, ISO (correspondent), ITU, NAM, OIC, OPCW, UN, UNCTAD, UPU, WHO, WIPO, WMO, WTrO

Diplomatic representation in the US:
chief of mission: Ambassador Pengiran Anak Dato Haji PUTEH Ibni Mohammad Alam
chancery: Watergate, Suite 300, 3rd floor, 2600 Virginia Avenue NW, Washington, DC 20037
telephone: (202) 342-0159
FAX: (202) 342-0158

Diplomatic representation from the US:
chief of mission: Ambassador Glen Robert RASE
embassy: Third Floor, Teck Guan Plaza, Jalan Sultan, Bandar Seri Begawan
mailing address: PSC 470 (BSB), FPO AP 96534-0001
telephone: [673] (2) 229670 *FAX:* [673] (2) 225293

Flag description: yellow with two diagonal bands of white (top, almost double width) and black starting from the upper hoist side; the national emblem in red is superimposed at the center; the emblem includes a swallow-tailed flag on top of a winged column within an upturned crescent above a scroll and flanked by two upraised hands

ECONOMY

Brunei is an energy-rich sultanate on the northern coast of Borneo in Southeast Asia. Brunei boasts a well-educated, largely English-speaking population; excellent infrastructure; and a stable government intent on attracting foreign investment. Crude oil and natural gas production account for approximately 65% of GDP and 95% of exports, with Japan as the primary export market.

Per capita GDP is among the highest in the world, and substantial income from overseas investment supplements income from domestic hydrocarbon production. Bruneian citizens pay no personal income taxes, and the government provides free medical services and free education through the university level.

The Bruneian Government wants to diversify its economy away from hydrocarbon exports to other industries such as information and communications technology and halal manufacturing, permissible under Islamic law. Brunei's trade in 2016 was set to increase following its regional economic integration in the ASEAN Economic Community, and the expected ratification of the Trans-Pacific Partnership trade agreement.

GDP (purchasing power parity):

$32.54 billion (2016 est.)

$33.6 billion (2015 est.)
$33.74 billion (2014 est.)
note: data are in 2016 dollars
country comparison to the world: 125

GDP (official exchange rate):
$11.18 billion (2016 est.)

GDP - real growth rate:
-3.2% (2016 est.)
-0.4% (2015 est.)
-2.5% (2014 est.)
country comparison to the world: 189

GDP - per capita (PPP):
$76,900 (2016 est.)
$80,600 (2015 est.)
$81,900 (2014 est.)
note: data are in 2016 dollars
country comparison to the world: 10

Gross national saving:
44.2% of GDP (2015 est.)
55.1% of GDP (2014 est.)
60.5% of GDP (2013 est.)
country comparison to the world: 4

GDP - composition, by end use:
household consumption: 21.7%
government consumption: 23.6%
investment in fixed capital: 37.6%
investment in inventories: 0%
exports of goods and services: 50.8%
imports of goods and services: -33.7% (2016 est.)

GDP - composition, by sector of origin:
agriculture: 1.1%
industry: 60.4%
services: 38.5% (2016 est.)

Agriculture - products:
rice, vegetables, fruits; chickens, water buffalo, cattle, goats, eggs

Industries:
petroleum, petroleum refining, liquefied natural gas, construction, agriculture, transportation

Industrial production growth rate:
1% (2016 est.)
country comparison to the world: 148

Labor force:
203,600 (2014 est.)
country comparison to the world: 168

Labor force - by occupation:
agriculture: 4.2%
industry: 62.8%
services: 33% (2008 est.)

Unemployment rate:
6.9% (2014 est.)
9.3% (2011 est.)
country comparison to the world: 84

Budget:
revenues: $2.958 billion
expenditures: $4.618 billion (2016 est.)

Taxes and other revenues:
28.3% of GDP (2016 est.)
country comparison to the world: 85

Budget surplus (+) or deficit (-):
-15.9% of GDP (2016 est.)
country comparison to the world: 213

Fiscal year:
1 April - 31 March

Inflation rate (consumer prices):
-0.7% (2016 est.)
-0.4% (2015 est.)
country comparison to the world: 31

Commercial bank prime lending rate:
5.5% (31 December 2016 est.)
5.5% (31 December 2015 est.)
country comparison to the world: 132

Stock of narrow money:
$3.467 billion (31 December 2016 est.)
$3.31 billion (31 December 2015 est.)
country comparison to the world: 111

Stock of broad money:
$10.29 billion (31 December 2016 est.)
$10.16 billion (31 December 2015 est.)
country comparison to the world: 106

For additional analytical, business and investment opportunities information,
please contact Global Investment & Business Center, USA
at (703) 370-8082. Fax: (703) 370-8083. E-mail: ibpusa3@gmail.com
Global Business and Investment Info Databank - www.ibpus.com

Stock of domestic credit:
$6.909 billion (31 December 2016 est.)
$5.323 billion (31 December 2015 est.)
country comparison to the world: 115

Current account balance:
$1.061 billion (2016 est.)
$2.072 billion (2015 est.)
country comparison to the world: 43

Exports:
$5.315 billion (2016 est.)
$7.235 billion (2015 est.)
country comparison to the world: 105

Exports - commodities:
mineral fuels, organic chemicals

Exports - partners:
Japan 36.1%, South Korea 14.9%, Thailand 10.9%, India 9.3%, NZ 5.6%, Australia 5%

Imports:
$3.648 billion (2016 est.)
$3.359 billion (2015 est.)
country comparison to the world: 132

Imports - commodities:
machinery and mechanical appliance parts, mineral fuels, motor vehicles, electric machinery

Imports - partners:
Singapore 27.9%, China 25.3%, Malaysia 12.3%, UK 10.6%, South Korea 4.9% (2015)

Debt - external:
$0 (2014)
$0 (2013)
note: public external debt only; private external debt unavailable
country comparison to the world: 204

Exchange rates:
Bruneian dollars (BND) per US dollar -
1.39 (2016 est.)
1.37 (2015 est.)
1.37 (2014 est.)
1.27 (2013 est.)
1.25 (2012 est.)

ENERGY

Electricity - production:
3.723 billion kWh (est.)
country comparison to the world: 126

Electricity - consumption:
3.391 billion kWh (est.)

For additional analytical, business and investment opportunities information,
please contact Global Investment & Business Center, USA
at (703) 370-8082. Fax: (703) 370-8083. E-mail: ibpusa3@gmail.com
Global Business and Investment Info Databank - www.ibpus.com

country comparison to the world: 127

Electricity - exports:
0 kWh (est.)
country comparison to the world: 111

Electricity - imports:
0 kWh (est.)
country comparison to the world: 123

Electricity - installed generating capacity:
759,000 kW (est.)
country comparison to the world: 129

Electricity - from fossil fuels:
100% of total installed capacity (est.)
country comparison to the world: 9

Electricity - from nuclear fuels:
0% of total installed capacity (est.)
country comparison to the world: 57

Electricity - from hydroelectric plants:
0% of total installed capacity (2010 est.)
country comparison to the world: 161

Electricity - from other renewable sources:
0% of total installed capacity (est.)
country comparison to the world: 162

Crude oil - production:
141,000 bbl/day (est.)
country comparison to the world: 45

Crude oil - exports:
147,900 bbl/day (est.)
country comparison to the world: 35

Crude oil - imports:
0 bbl/day (est.)
country comparison to the world: 166

Crude oil - proved reserves:
1.1 billion bbl (1 January 2013 est.)
country comparison to the world: 41

Refined petroleum products - production:
13,500 bbl/day (est.)
country comparison to the world: 101

For additional analytical, business and investment opportunities information,
please contact Global Investment & Business Center, USA
at (703) 370-8082. Fax: (703) 370-8083. E-mail: ibpusa3@gmail.com
Global Business and Investment Info Databank - www.ibpus.com

Refined petroleum products - consumption:
14,640 bbl/day (est.)
country comparison to the world: 144

Refined petroleum products - exports:
0 bbl/day (est.)
country comparison to the world: 159

Refined petroleum products - imports:
3,198 bbl/day (est.)
country comparison to the world: 169

Natural gas - production:
12.44 billion cu m (est.)
country comparison to the world: 38

Natural gas - consumption:
2.97 billion cu m (est.)
country comparison to the world: 73

Natural gas - exports:
9.42 billion cu m (est.)
country comparison to the world: 25

Natural gas - imports:
0 cu m (est.)
country comparison to the world: 167

Natural gas - proved reserves:
390.8 billion cu m (1 January 2013 est.)
country comparison to the world: 35

Carbon dioxide emissions from consumption of energy:
8.656 million Mt (2011 est.)

COMMUNICATION

Telephones - main lines in use:
70,933
country comparison to the world: 154

Telephones - mobile cellular:
469,700
country comparison to the world: 170

Telephone system:
general assessment: service throughout the country is good; international service is good to Southeast Asia, Middle East, Western Europe, and the US
domestic: every service available

For additional analytical, business and investment opportunities information,
please contact Global Investment & Business Center, USA
at (703) 370-8082. Fax: (703) 370-8083. E-mail: ibpusa3@gmail.com
Global Business and Investment Info Databank - www.ibpus.com

international: country code - 673; landing point for the SEA-ME-WE-3 optical telecommunications submarine cable that provides links to Asia, the Middle East, and Europe; the Asia-America Gateway submarine cable network provides new links to Asia and the US; satellite earth stations - 2 Intelsat (1 Indian Ocean and 1 Pacific Ocean)

Broadcast media:
state-controlled Radio Television Brunei (RTB) operates 5 channels; 3 Malaysian TV stations are available; foreign TV broadcasts are available via satellite and cable systems; RTB operates 5 radio networks and broadcasts on multiple frequencies; British Forces Broadcast Service (BFBS) provides radio broadcasts on 2 FM stations; some radio broadcast stations from Malaysia are available via repeaters (2009)

Internet country code:
.bn

Internet hosts:
49,457
country comparison to the world: 96

Internet users:
314,900
country comparison to the world: 128

TRANSPORTATION

Railways:
total: 13 km (private line)
narrow gauge: 13 km 0.610-m gauge

Highways:
total: 1,150 km *paved:* 399 km *unpaved:* 751 km

Waterways: 209 km; navigable by craft drawing less than 1.2 m
Pipelines: crude oil 135 km; petroleum products 418 km; natural gas 920 km
Ports and harbors: Bandar Seri Begawan, Kuala Belait, Muara, Seria, Tutong
Merchant marine:
total: 7 liquefied gas tankers (1,000 GRT or over) totaling 348,476 GRT/340,635 DWT

Airports: 2

Airports—with paved runways:
total: 1
over 3,047 m: 1
Airports—with unpaved runways:
total: 1 *914 to 1,523 m:* 1 **Heliports:** 3

MILITARY

Military branches: Land Forces, Navy, Air Force, Royal Brunei Police
Military manpower—military age: 18 years of age
Military manpower—availability:
males age 15-49: 88,628

Military manpower—fit for military service:
males age 15-49: 51,270
Military manpower—reaching military age annually:
males: 3,078
Military expenditures—dollar figure: $343 million
Military expenditures—percent of GDP: 6%

TRANSNATIONAL ISSUES

Disputes—international: possibly involved in a complex dispute over the Spratly Islands with China, Malaysia, Philippines, Taiwan, and Vietnam; in 1984, Brunei established an exclusive fishing zone that encompasses Louisa Reef in the southern Spratly Islands, but has not publicly claimed the island.

IMPORTANT INFORMATION FOR UNDERSTANDING BRUNEI

PROFILE
OFFICIAL NAME: Negara Brunei Darussalam

Geography
Area: 5,765 sq. km. (2,226 sq. mi.), slightly larger than Delaware.
Cities: *Capital*--Bandar Seri Begawan.
Terrain: East--flat coastal plain rises to mountains; west--hilly lowland with a few mountain ridges.
Climate: Equatorial; high temperatures, humidity, and rainfall.

People
Nationality: *Noun and adjective*--Bruneian(s).
Population : 383,000.
Annual growth rate: 3.5%.
Ethnic groups: Malay, Chinese, other indigenous groups.
Religion: Islam.
Languages: Malay, English, Chinese; Iban and other indigenous dialects.
Education: *Years compulsory*--9. *Literacy* (2006)--94.7%.
Health: *Life expectancy (years)*--74.4 (men), 77.4 (women) yrs. *Infant mortality rate* --12.25/1,000.

Government
Type: Malay Islamic Monarchy.
Independence: January 1, 1984.
Constitution: 1959.
Branches: *Executive*--Sultan is both head of state and Prime Minister, presiding over a fourteen-member cabinet. *Legislative*--a Legislative Council has been reactivated after a 20-year suspension to play an advisory role for the Sultan. *Judicial* (based on Indian penal code and English common law)--magistrate's courts, High Court, Court of Appeals, Judicial Committee of the Privy Council (sits in London).
Subdivisions: *Four districts*--Brunei-Muara, Belait, Tutong, and Temburong.

Economy
Natural resources: Oil and natural gas.
Trade: *Exports*--oil, liquefied natural gas, petroleum products, garments. Major markets--Japan, Korea, ASEAN, U.S. *Imports*--machinery and transport equipment, manufactured goods. *Major suppliers*--ASEAN, Japan, U.S., EU.

PEOPLE

Many cultural and linguistic differences make Brunei Malays distinct from the larger Malay populations in nearby Malaysia and Indonesia, even though they are ethnically related and share the Muslim religion.

Brunei has hereditary nobility, carrying the title Pengiran. The Sultan can award to commoners the title Pehin, the equivalent of a life peerage awarded in the United Kingdom. The Sultan also can award his subjects the Dato, the equivalent of a knighthood in the United Kingdom, and Datin, the equivalent of damehood.

Bruneians adhere to the practice of using complete full names with all titles, including the title Haji (for men) or Hajah (for women) for those who have made the Haj pilgrimage to Mecca. Many Brunei Malay women wear the tudong, a traditional head covering. Men wear the songkok, a traditional Malay cap. Men who have completed the Haj can wear a white songkok.
The requirements to attain Brunei citizenship include passing tests in Malay culture, customs, and language. Stateless permanent residents of Brunei are given International Certificates of Identity, which allow them to travel overseas. The majority of Brunei's Chinese are permanent residents, and many are stateless. An amendment to the National Registration and Immigration Act of 2002 allowed female Bruneian citizens for the first time to transfer their nationality to their children.

Oil wealth allows the Brunei Government to provide the population with one of Asia's finest health care systems. Malaria has been eradicated, and cholera is virtually nonexistent. There are five general hospitals--in Bandar Seri Begawan, Tutong, Kuala Belait, Bangar, and Seria--and there are numerous health clinics throughout the country.

Education starts with preschool, followed by 6 years of primary education and up to 7 years of secondary education. Nine years of education are mandatory. Most of Brunei's college students attend universities and other institutions abroad, but approximately 3,674 (2005) study at the University of Brunei Darussalam. Opened in 1985, the university has a faculty of more than 300 instructors and is located on a sprawling campus overlooking the South China Sea.
The official language is Malay, but English is widely understood and used in business. Other languages spoken are several Chinese dialects, Iban, and a number of native dialects. Islam is the official religion, but religious freedom is guaranteed under the constitution.

HISTORY

Historians believe there was a forerunner to the present Brunei Sultanate, which the Chinese called Po-ni. Chinese and Arabic records indicate that this ancient trading kingdom existed at the mouth of the Brunei River as early as the seventh or eighth century A.D. This early kingdom was apparently conquered by the Sumatran Hindu Empire of Srivijaya in the early ninth century, which later controlled northern Borneo and the Philippines. It was subjugated briefly by the Java-based Majapahit Empire but soon regained its independence and once again rose to prominence.

The Brunei Empire had its golden age from the 15th to the 17th centuries, when its control extended over the entire island of Borneo and north into the Philippines. Brunei was particularly powerful under the fifth sultan, Bolkiah (1473-1521), who was famed for his sea exploits and even briefly captured Manila; and under the ninth sultan, Hassan (1605-19), who fully developed an elaborate Royal Court structure, elements of which remain today.

After Sultan Hassan, Brunei entered a period of decline due to internal battles over royal succession as well as the rising influences of European colonial powers in the region that, among other things, disrupted traditional trading patterns, destroying the economic base of Brunei and many other Southeast Asian sultanates. In 1839, the English adventurer James Brooke arrived in Borneo and helped the Sultan put down a rebellion. As a reward, he became governor and later "Rajah" of Sarawak in northwest Borneo and gradually expanded the territory under his control.

Meanwhile, the British North Borneo Company was expanding its control over territory in northeast Borneo. In 1888, Brunei became a protectorate of the British Government, retaining internal independence but with British control over external affairs. In 1906, Brunei accepted a further measure of British control when executive power was transferred to a British resident, who advised the ruler on all matters except those concerning local custom and religion.

In 1959, a new constitution was written declaring Brunei a self-governing state, while its foreign affairs, security, and defense remained the responsibility of the United Kingdom. An attempt in 1962 to introduce a partially elected legislative body with limited powers was abandoned after the opposition political party, Parti Rakyat Brunei, launched an armed uprising, which the government put down with the help of British forces. In the late 1950s and early 1960s, the government also resisted pressures to join neighboring Sabah and Sarawak in the newly formed Malaysia. The Sultan eventually decided that Brunei would remain an independent state.

In 1967, Sultan Omar abdicated in favor of his eldest son, Hassanal Bolkiah, who became the 29th ruler. The former Sultan remained as Defense Minister and assumed the royal title Seri Begawan. In 1970, the national capital, Brunei Town, was renamed Bandar Seri Begawan in his honor. The Seri Begawan died in 1986.

On January 4, 1979, Brunei and the United Kingdom signed a new treaty of friendship and cooperation. On January 1, 1984, Brunei Darussalam became a fully independent state.

GOVERNMENT AND POLITICAL CONDITIONS

Under Brunei's 1959 constitution, the Sultan is the head of state with full executive authority, including emergency powers since 1962. The Sultan is assisted and advised by five councils, which he appoints. A Council of Ministers, or cabinet, which currently consists of 14 members (including the Sultan himself), assists in the administration of the government. The Sultan presides over the cabinet as Prime Minister and also holds the positions of Minister of Defense and Minister of Finance. His son, the Crown Prince, serves as Senior Minister. One of the Sultan's brothers, Prince Mohamed, serves as Minister of Foreign Affairs.

Brunei's legal system is based on English common law, with an independent judiciary, a body of written common law judgments and statutes, and legislation enacted by the sultan. The local magistrates' courts try most cases. More serious cases go before the High Court, which sits for about 2 weeks every few months. Brunei has an arrangement with the United Kingdom whereby United Kingdom judges are appointed as the judges for Brunei's High Court and Court of Appeal. Final appeal can be made to the Judicial Committee of the Privy Council in London in civil but not criminal cases. Brunei also has a separate system of Islamic courts that apply Sharia law in family and other matters involving Muslims.
The Government of Brunei assures continuing public support for the current form of government by providing economic benefits such as subsidized food, fuel, and housing; free education and medical care; and low-interest loans for government employees.

The Sultan said in a 1989 interview that he intended to proceed, with prudence, to establish more liberal institutions in the country and that he would reintroduce elections and a legislature when he "[could] see evidence of a genuine interest in politics on the part of a responsible majority of Bruneians." In 1994, a constitutional review committee submitted its findings to the Sultan, but these have not been made public. In 2004 the Sultan re-introduced an appointed Legislative Council with minimal powers. Five of the 31 seats on the Council are indirectly elected by village leaders.

For additional analytical, business and investment opportunities information, please contact Global Investment & Business Center, USA at (703) 370-8082. Fax: (703) 370-8083. E-mail: ibpusa3@gmail.com Global Business and Investment Info Databank - www.ibpus.com

Brunei's economy is almost totally supported by exports of crude oil and natural gas. The government uses its earnings in part to build up its foreign reserves, which at one time reportedly reached more than $30 billion. The country's wealth, coupled with its membership in the United Nations, Association of Southeast Asian Nations (ASEAN), the Asia Pacific Economic Cooperation (APEC) forum, and the Organization of the Islamic Conference give it an influence in the world disproportionate to its size.

Principal Government Officials

Sultan and Yang di-Pertuan, Prime Minister, Minister of Defense, and Minister of Finance--His Majesty Sultan Hassanal Bolkiah
Senior Minister--His Royal Highness Crown Prince Billah
Minister of Foreign Affairs--His Royal Highness Prince Mohamed Bolkiah
Ambassador to the United States--Pengiran Anak Dato Haji Puteh
Ambassador to the United Nations--Dr. Haji Emran bin Bahar
Brunei Darussalam maintains an embassy in the United States at 3520 International Court, NW, Washington, DC 20008; tel. 202-237-1838.

ECONOMY

Currency	Brunei dollar BND
Fixed exchange rates	1 Brunei dollar = 1 Singapore dollar
Fiscal year	1 April – 31 March (from April 2009)
Trade organisations	APEC, ASEAN, WTO. BIMP-EAGA
	Statistics
GDP	$20.38 billion PPP Rank: 123rd
GDP growth	2.8% Q1
GDP per capita	$51,600
GDP by sector	agriculture (0.7%), industry (73.3%), services (26%)
Inflation (CPI)	1.2%
Population below poverty line	1000 person
Labour force	188,800
Labour force by occupation	agriculture 4.5%, industry 63.1%, services 32.4%
Unemployment	3.7%
Main industries	petroleum, petroleum refining, liquefied natural gas, construction
Ease-of-doing-business rank	83rd
	External
Exports	$10.67 billion
Main export partners	Japan 46.5% South Korea 15.5% Australia 9.3% India 7.0% New Zealand 6.7% (est.)
Imports	$12.055 billion c.i.f.
Main import partners	Singapore 26.3% China 21.3% United Kingdom 21.3% Malaysia 11.8%
	Public finances
Public debt	$0
Revenues	$10.49 billion

| Expenses | $5.427 billion |
| Credit rating | Not rated |

Main data source: CIA World Fact Book *All values, unless otherwise stated, are in US dollars.*

Brunei is a country with a small, wealthy economy that is a mixture of foreign and domestic entrepreneurship, government regulation and welfare measures, and village tradition. It is almost totally supported by exports of crude oil and natural gas, with revenues from the petroleum sector accounting for over half of GDP. Per capita GDP is high, and substantial income from overseas investment supplements income from domestic production. The government provides for all medical services and subsidizes food and housing. The government has shown progress in its basic policy of diversifying the economy away from oil and gas. Brunei's leaders are concerned that steadily increased integration in the world economy will undermine internal social cohesion although it has taken steps to become a more prominent player by serving as chairman for the 2000 APEC (Asian Pacific Economic Cooperation) forum. Growth in 1999 was estimated at 2.5% due to higher oil prices in the second half.

Brunei is the third-largest oil producer in Southeast Asia, averaging about 180,000 barrels per day (29,000 m^3/d). It also is the fourth-largest producer of liquefied natural gas in the world.

Brunei is the fourth-largest oil producer in Southeast Asia, averaging about 219,000 barrels a day in 2006. It also is the ninth-largest exporter of liquefied natural gas in the world. Like many oil producing countries, Brunei's economy has followed the swings of the world oil market. Economic growth has averaged around 2.8% in the 2000s, heavily dependent on oil and gas production. Oil production has averaged around 200,000 barrels a day during the 2000s, while liquefied natural gas output has been slightly under or over 1,000 trillion btu/day over the same period. Brunei is estimated to have oil reserves expected to last 25 years, and enough natural gas reserves to last 40 years.

Brunei Shell Petroleum (BSP), a joint venture owned in equal shares by the Brunei Government and the Royal Dutch/Shell group of companies, is the chief oil and gas production company in Brunei. It also operates the country's only refinery. BSP and four sister companies--including the liquefied natural gas producing firm BLNG--constitute the largest employer in Brunei after the government. BSP's small refinery has a distillation capacity of 10,000 barrels per day. This satisfies domestic demand for most petroleum products.

The French oil company Total (then known as ELF Aquitaine) became active in petroleum exploration in Brunei in the 1980s. The joint venture Total E&P Borneo BV currently produces approximately 35,000 barrels per day and 13% of Brunei's natural gas.

In 2003, Malaysia disputed Brunei-awarded oil exploration concessions for offshore blocks J and K (Total and Shell respectively), which led to the Brunei licensees ceasing exploration activities. Negotiations between the two countries are continuing in order to resolve the conflict. In 2006, Brunei awarded two on-shore blocks--one to a Canadian-led and the other to a Chinese-led consortium. Australia, Indonesia, and Korea were the largest customers for Brunei's oil exports, taking over 67% of Brunei's total crude exports. Traditional customers Japan, the U.S., and China each took around 5% of total crude exports.

Almost all of Brunei's natural gas is liquefied at Brunei Shell's Liquefied Natural Gas (LNG) plant, which opened in 1972 and is one of the largest LNG plants in the world. Some 90% of Brunei's LNG produced is sold to Japan under a long-term agreement renewed in 1993.

The agreement calls for Brunei to provide over 5 million tons of LNG per year to three Japanese utilities, namely to TEPCo, Tokyo Electric Power Co. (J.TER or 5001), Tokyo Gas Co. (J.TYG or 9531) and Osaka Gas Co. (J.OSG or 9532). The Japanese company, Mitsubishi, is a joint venture partner with Shell and the Brunei Government in Brunei LNG, Brunei Coldgas, and Brunei Shell

Tankers, which together produce the LNG and supply it to Japan. Since 1995, Brunei has supplied more than 700,000 tons of LNG to the Korea Gas Corporation (KOGAS) as well. In 1999, Brunei's natural gas production reached 90 cargoes per day. A small amount of natural gas is used for domestic power generation. Since 2001, Japan remains the dominant export market for natural gas. Brunei is the fourth-largest exporter of LNG in the Asia-Pacific region behind Indonesia, Malaysia, and Australia.

The government sought in the past decade to diversify the economy with limited success. Oil and gas and government spending still account for most of Brunei's economic activity. Brunei's non-petroleum industries include agriculture, forestry, fishing, aquaculture, and banking. The garment-for-export industry has been shrinking since the U.S. eliminated its garment quota system at the end of 2004. The Brunei Economic Development Board announced plans in 2003 to use proven gas reserves to establish downstream industrial projects. The government plans to build a power plant in the Sungai Liang region to power a proposed aluminum smelting plant that will depend on foreign investors. A second major project depending on foreign investment is in the planning stage: a giant container hub at the Muara Port facilities.

The government regulates the immigration of foreign labor out of concern it might disrupt Brunei's society. Work permits for foreigners are issued only for short periods and must be continually renewed. Despite these restrictions, the estimated 100,000 foreign temporary residents of Brunei make up a significant portion of the work force. The government reported a total work force of 180,400 in 2006, with a derived unemployment rate of 4.0%.

Oil and natural gas account for almost all exports. Since only a few products other than petroleum are produced locally, a wide variety of items must be imported. Nonetheless, Brunei has had a significant trade surplus in the 2000s. Official statistics show Singapore, Malaysia, Japan, the U.S., and the U.K. as the leading importers in 2005. The United States was the third-largest supplier of imports to Brunei in 2005.

Brunei's substantial foreign reserves are managed by the Brunei Investment Agency (BIA), an arm of the Ministry of Finance. BIA's guiding principle is to increase the real value of Brunei's foreign reserves while pursuing a diverse investment strategy, with holdings in the United States, Japan, Western Europe, and the Association of Southeast Asian Nations (ASEAN) countries.

The Brunei Government encourages more foreign investment. New enterprises that meet certain criteria can receive pioneer status, exempting profits from income tax for up to 5 years, depending on the amount of capital invested. The normal corporate income tax rate is 30%. There is no personal income tax or capital gains tax.

One of the government's priorities is to encourage the development of Brunei Malays as leaders of industry and commerce. There are no specific restrictions of foreign equity ownership, but local participation, both shared capital and management, is encouraged. Such participation helps when tendering for contracts with the government or Brunei Shell Petroleum.

Companies in Brunei must either be incorporated locally or registered as a branch of a foreign company and must be registered with the Registrar of Companies. Public companies must have a minimum of seven shareholders. Private companies must have a minimum of two but not more than 50 shareholders. At least half of the directors in a company must be residents of Brunei.

The government owns a cattle farm in Australia through which the country's beef supplies are processed. At 2,262 square miles, this ranch is larger than Brunei itself. Eggs and chickens are largely produced locally, but most of Brunei's other food needs must be imported. Agriculture, aquaculture, and fisheries are among the industrial sectors that the government has selected for highest priority in its efforts to diversify the economy.

Recently the government has announced plans for Brunei to become an international offshore financial center as well as a center for Islamic banking. Brunei is keen on the development of small and medium enterprises and also is investigating the possibility of establishing a "cyber park" to develop an information technology industry. Brunei has also promoted ecotourism to take advantage of the over 70% of Brunei's territory that remains primal tropical rainforest.

DEFENSE

The Sultan is both Minister of Defense and Supreme Commander of the Armed Forces (RBAF). All infantry, navy, and air combat units are made up of volunteers. There are two infantry battalions equipped with armored reconnaissance vehicles and armored personnel carriers and supported by Rapier air defense missiles and a flotilla of coastal patrol vessels armed with surface-to-surface missiles. Brunei has ordered, but not yet taken possession of, three offshore patrol vessels from the U.K.

Brunei has a defense agreement with the United Kingdom, under which a British Armed Forces Ghurka battalion (1,500 men) is permanently stationed in Seria, near the center of Brunei's oil industry. The RBAF has joint exercises, training programs, and other military cooperation with the United Kingdom and many other countries, including the United States. The U.S. and Brunei signed a memorandum of understanding (MOU) on defense cooperation in November 1994. The two countries conduct an annual military exercise called CARAT.

FOREIGN RELATIONS

Brunei joined ASEAN on January 7, 1984--one week after resuming full independence--and gives its ASEAN membership the highest priority in its foreign relations. Brunei joined the UN in September 1984. It also is a member of the Organization of the Islamic Conference (OIC) and of the Asia-Pacific Economic Cooperation (APEC) forum. Brunei hosted the APEC Economic Leaders' Meeting in November 2000 and the ASEAN Regional Forum (ARF) in July 2002.

U.S.-BRUNEI RELATIONS

Relations between the United States and Brunei date from the 1800s. On April 6, 1845, the U.S.S. Constitution visited Brunei. The two countries concluded a Treaty of Peace, Friendship, Commerce and Navigation in 1850, which remains in force today. The United States maintained a consulate in Brunei from 1865 to 1867.

The U.S. welcomed Brunei Darussalam's full independence from the United Kingdom on January 1, 1984, and opened an Embassy in Bandar Seri Begawan on that date. Brunei opened its embassy in Washington in March 1984. Brunei's armed forces engage in joint exercises, training programs, and other military cooperation with the U.S. A memorandum of understanding on defense cooperation was signed on November 29, 1994. The Sultan visited Washington in December 2002.

Principal U.S. Embassy Officials
Ambassador-- Craig Allen
Ambassador Craig Allen was sworn in as the United States ambassador to Brunei Darussalam on December 19, 2014.
Deputy Chief of Mission--John McIntyre
Management Officer--Michael Lampel

The U.S. Embassy in Bandar Seri Begawan is located on the third & fifth floors of the Teck Guan Plaza, at the corner of Jalan Sultan and Jalan MacArthur; tel: 673-2229670; fax: 673-2225293; e-mail: usembassy_bsb@state.gov

TRAVEL AND BUSINESS INFORMATION

The U.S. Department of State's Consular Information Program advises Americans traveling and residing abroad through Consular Information Sheets, Public Announcements, and Travel Warnings. **Consular Information Sheets** exist for all countries and include information on entry and exit requirements, currency regulations, health conditions, safety and security, crime, political disturbances, and the addresses of the U.S. embassies and consulates abroad. **Public Announcements** are issued to disseminate information quickly about terrorist threats and other relatively short-term conditions overseas that pose significant risks to the security of American travelers. **Travel Warnings** are issued when the State Department recommends that Americans avoid travel to a certain country because the situation is dangerous or unstable.

For the latest security information, Americans living and traveling abroad should regularly monitor the Department's Bureau of Consular Affairs Internet web site at http://www.travel.state.gov, where the current Worldwide Caution, Public Announcements, and Travel Warnings can be found. Consular Affairs Publications, which contain information on obtaining passports and planning a safe trip abroad, are also available at http://www.travel.state.gov. For additional information on international travel, see http://www.usa.gov/Citizen/Topics/Travel/International.shtml.

The Department of State encourages all U.S citizens traveling or residing abroad to register via the State Department's travel registration website or at the nearest U.S. embassy or consulate abroad. Registration will make your presence and whereabouts known in case it is necessary to contact you in an emergency and will enable you to receive up-to-date information on security conditions.

Emergency information concerning Americans traveling abroad may be obtained by calling 1-888-407-4747 toll free in the U.S. and Canada or the regular toll line 1-202-501-4444 for callers outside the U.S. and Canada.

The National Passport Information Center (NPIC) is the U.S. Department of State's single, centralized public contact center for U.S. passport information. Telephone: 1-877-4USA-PPT (1-877-487-2778). Customer service representatives and operators for TDD/TTY are available Monday-Friday, 7:00 a.m. to 12:00 midnight, Eastern Time, excluding federal holidays.

Travelers can check the latest health information with the U.S. Centers for Disease Control and Prevention in Atlanta, Georgia. A hotline at 877-FYI-TRIP (877-394-8747) and a web site at http://www.cdc.gov/travel/index.htm give the most recent health advisories, immunization recommendations or requirements, and advice on food and drinking water safety for regions and countries. A booklet entitled "Health Information for International Travel" (HHS publication number CDC-95-8280) is available from the U.S. Government Printing Office, Washington, DC 20402, tel. (202) 512-1800.

EU-BRUNEI RELATIONS

Official Name	Negara Brunei Darussalam
Population	0.38 million
Area	6000 km²
Gross Domestic Product	5 bn euros
GDP Per Capita	14.173 €
Real GDP (% growth)	3.0 %
Exports GDP %	0.85
Imports GDP %	0.27
Exports to Brunei from EU (mn €, 2001)	108 EU imports from Brunei (mn €)
Imports to EU from Brunei (mn €, 2001)	72

Human Development Index (rank of 175°)	33
Head of State	HM Paduka Seri Baginda Sultan Haji Hassanal Bolkiah Mu'izzadddin Waddaulah (Sultan, prime minister, minister of finance and defence)

FRAMEWORK

The framework for co-operation dialogue with Brunei is the EC-ASEAN Agreement of 1980. There is no bilateral cooperation agreement.

POLITICAL CONTEXT

Brunei Darussalam became independent from the United Kingdom on 1 January 1984, and a week later joined the Association of South-East Asian Nations (ASEAN). Brunei is a constitutional monarchy with the Sultan Yang Di-Pertuan – Hassanal Bolkiah as the Head of State, Prime Minister, Defence Minister, as well as Minister for Finance. The Sultan presides over a 10-member cabinet which he appoints himself. Five councils advise the Sultan on policy matters: the Religious Council, the Privy Council, the Council of Succession, the Legislative Council and the Council of Ministers (the cabinet). Since 1962 the Sultan has ruled by decree. Thus, the system of government revolves around the Sultan as the source of executive power.

On 25 September 2004, the Legislative Council met for the first time in 20 years, with 21 members appointed by the Sultan. It passed constitutional amendments, calling for a 45-seat council with 15 elected members. In a move towards political reform an appointed parliament was revived in 2004. The constitution provides for an expanded house with up to 15 elected MPs. However, no date has been set for elections.

Brunei is a Muslim country, with a Ministry of Religious Affairs established to foster and promote Islam. Brunei continues to play a peacekeeping role in the Philippines, and is taking part in efforts to monitor peace in the Indonesian region of Aceh.

EUROPEAN COMMUNITY ASSISTANCE

By virtue of its advanced level of economic development Brunei does not benefit from bilateral development or economic projects.

EC co-operation with Brunei has for the greater part been limited to joint EC- ASEAN projects.

The EC has given financial support to the ASEAN-EC Management Centre (AEMC), located in Brunei, the contract for which has come to an end.

TRADE AND ECONOMIC

Since 1929, when oil was discovered in Brunei, the country has flourished. During 1998 and as a consequence of the Asia crisis, however, both exports and imports decreased in comparison with previous years.

· **Key role of oil and gas**: Brunei suffered little directly from the Asian financial crisis of 1997. But, in 1998, the Sultanate was hit by the sharp fall in oil sales and the bankruptcy of a locally-owned oil and gas company, resulting in a contraction in GDP of 4%. Subsequently, economic activity recovered in step with the resumption of oil and gas extraction and, in recent years, the sharp rise in the oil price. The latest available data for GDP shows real annual growth around 3%. Oil reserves are officially estimated at 25 years, but, great hopes are placed in two new drilling concessions.

Economic structure: Almost everything the country needs is imported. Even the industrial labour force comes from abroad, mainly from India, the Philippines, Indonesia and Bangladesh as most of Brunei's citizens are employed as civil servants (60% of the population) and prefer the status related to that occupation. This also explains the apparent contradiction between the necessity to employ foreign manpower and the rising unemployment rate (officially at 4.7% but estimated at 9%).

· At the beginning of 2000, the government of the Sultanate announced an ambitious programme of **economic reforms** in order to reduce the dependence on oil and gas. Two initiatives have been taken up till know– to develop tourism and to support the creation of an off-shore financial centre in developing Islamic banking business.

· The tourism industry is, however, handicapped by the shortage of quality infrastructure, and the geographical insulation of the Sultanate.

Brunei's trade surplus fell by an estimated 74% in US dollar terms in 1999 as the price of oil and gas collapsed. A strengthening oil price and long-term contracts for natural gas, paid in US dollars, should, however, ensure that Brunei's trade position remains healthy.

At present Brunei produces oil and gas almost to the exclusion of other products. The government is trying hard, however, to develop manufactured exports, in particular cement and roofing (tiles) which are both protected sectors. The garment industry is struggling after the abolition of global quotas on the textile trade. The Sultan has announced financial reforms.

Brunei has signed a free-trade pact with New Zealand, Singapore and Chile. A Brunei Tourism Board has been set up

The domestic economy: Brunei's economic growth remains fairly sluggish, at 2.6% year on year but a recovery is likely to have taken place in the second quarter of 2005. The non-oil and gas sector is expanding more rapidly than the energy sector. High global oil prices have lifted transport prices, but overall inflation remains low.

Foreign trade and payments: High oil prices lay behind an increase in the merchandises-trade surplus in the first quarter of 2005. The oil and gas sector continues to account for the bulk of exports; garments exports were much lower than in the year-earlier period.

The investment policy in Brunei is largely open to foreign investors, as indicated by a favourable legal environment and a policy allowing full foreign ownership in a majority of economic sectors. Foreign investments have been more particularly in the last years as they are considered by the government as a key element to contribute to the targeted diversification of the country's economy.

As part of this strategy to attract foreign investments, an Economic Development Board (EDB) was created in 2001. The main sectors and projects promoted by the EDB and susceptible to attract foreign investments include port infrastructure, industry, communication (aviation hub), eco-tourism, and financial services. In parallel with the creation of the EDB, major policy changes have been made in the last years to promote foreign investments. August 2000 saw the introduction of an offshore legislation in Brunei. New laws were drafted covering international banking, insurance, offshore companies, trusts, limited partnerships and registered agents.

Changes in the legislation are too recent analyze its effects. The volume of FDI has doubled between 2001 and 2002, while the figures available until mid 2003 include that the trend is positive and that investments do not only target natural resources but also services.

For additional analytical, business and investment opportunities information,
please contact Global Investment & Business Center, USA
at (703) 370-8082. Fax: (703) 370-8083. E-mail: ibpusa3@gmail.com
Global Business and Investment Info Databank - www.ibpus.com

INVESTMENT, TRADE AND BUSNESS DEVELOPMENT STRATEGY - IMPORTANT DEVELOPMENTS

The economy of Brunei Darussalam remains highly dependent on oil and gas, which accounts for about two-thirds of output, and over 90% of merchandise exports and government revenues. This makes Brunei particularly vulnerable to an eventual depletion of its petroleum resources, and remains a cause for concern due to fluctuating international energy prices. The Government is thus implementing an ambitious diversification strategy and promoting private-sector participation in the economy, which remains limited.

Brunei's economy grew at an average annual rate of 0.2% during 2008-13 mainly due to lower oil and gas production. Real GDP growth of 5.3% is expected in 2014 as large energy-related projects begin production. Under its National Vision 2035, Brunei aims to achieve annual real GDP growth rates of 5-6% which may require increasing overall productivity, particularly in the government sector (including state-owned enterprises) being the largest employer.

Sizable hydrocarbon exports and the steady accumulation of long-term foreign assets over many years have provided Brunei with a comfortable balance of payments position, which also reflects the big gap between savings and investment. The external current account surplus, as percentage of GDP, fell from 48.9% in 2008 to 31.5% in 2013 because of the important reduction in oil and gas export revenues and, consequently, Brunei's trade balance surplus decreased from US$7,867 million in 2008 to US$6,916 million in 2013.

Petroleum and natural gas represented 96.5% of total merchandise exports in 2013 (97.8% in 2008) . The remaining exports are manufactures, mostly machinery and transport equipment. Brunei's exports are mainly destined to Japan and other countries in East Asia. Machinery and transport equipment are Brunei's most important import category, accounting for 37% of total imports in 2013 (44% in 2008) . Its merchandise imports also originate mainly in East Asia, led by Malaysia. Brunei is, increasingly, a net importer of services.

FDI inflows have increased during the last years but remain relatively small averaging some US$600 million per year in 2008-13. Success in attracting larger FDI inflows has been hampered by increased competition from neighbouring economies. Brunei would benefit from further improvement of its business climate, and its FDI policies could also be more transparent, particularly with respect to limits on foreign equity participation, partnership requirements, and identification of sectors in which FDI is restricted. Full foreign investment may be allowed in most activities, except in those that use natural resources, relate to food security, and are located in industrial sites for which 30% minimum local equity participation is required.

Brunei has eight RTAs encompassing 16 partners: the other nine parties of ASEAN; six countries that have negotiated agreements with ASEAN (Australia and New Zealand, China, Japan, Republic of Korea, and India), and Chile in the context of the Trans-Pacific Strategic Economic Partnership (TPSEP) . Five RTAs entered into force during the review period: four are RTAs negotiated in the context of ASEAN, and one bilateral arrangement with Japan. Brunei's RTAs have been notified to the WTO.

Brunei is an original Member of the WTO, and grants at least MFN treatment to all its Members. It has never been involved in any trade dispute. During the review period, Brunei made a number of notifications to the WTO, but some remain outstanding, particularly in agriculture and import licensing. Since 2008, Brunei has adopted new trade-related legislation in the areas of business environment, financial services, fisheries, intellectual property, and TBT. Additional legislation on standards and competition is being drafted. Brunei has no legislation pertaining to contingency trade remedies. It does not participate in the Information Technology Agreement.

During the review period, Brunei took steps to further facilitate trade, such as e-Customs which has been fully operational since 2008 allowing traders to submit applications electronically, and Brunei Darussalam National Single Window (BDNSW) which began to operate, in phases, in January 2014 and will allow applications for several trade procedures (e.g. certificates of origin and import permits) . BDNSW is expected to be integrated into a wider ASEAN level single window system in the future. Brunei has no customs fees for import/export procedures or registration.

Goods imported into Brunei may be subject to import and excise duties (there is no VAT) . Since its last TPR, Brunei has introduced new excise duties on liquors, tobacco, vehicles, nuclear reactors, boilers, machinery, and mechanical appliances, and medical or surgical instruments. The authorities informed that these new excise duties are levied for fiscal, social, health, and environmental considerations. The authorities also indicated that goods subject to excise duties are not manufactured in Brunei.

Brunei applies relatively very low tariffs. With the adoption of the 2012 ASEAN Harmonized Tariff Nomenclature, the number of Brunei's tariff lines (at the HS ten-digit level) was reduced from 10,689 in 2007 to 9,916 lines in 2014, and the simple average applied MFN rate decreased from 4.8% in 2007 to 1.7% in 2014. Specific tariff lines were reduced from 131 in 2007 to 55 in 2014 which enhances transparency.

The coverage of Brunei's bound tariff lines went from 92.8% in 2007 to 89.1% in 2014 also because of the changes in HS nomenclature. There remains a significant gap between the overall bound average of 25.4% and Brunei's applied MFN tariff of 1.7% which undermines predictability. The difference is even larger in agriculture where the bound average tariff is 23.1% and the MFN tariff rate is zero.

Import and export prohibitions, restrictions, and licensing requirements apply on various products for safety, health, and moral grounds. In some cases, Brunei maintains export restrictions on certain goods, such as sugar, rice, paddy and products thereof, to ensure adequate domestic supply and price stability.

In 2010, the National Standards Council, under the Ministry of Industry and Primary Resources, was established as the body responsible to monitor and strengthen standards and conformance activities in Brunei. There are no technical regulations in Brunei. It has 83 national standards, mainly on construction and electrical-related products; 53 have been directly adopted from international standards. Brunei is still to notify its enquiry point to the WTO Committee on Technical Barriers to Trade.

In order to encourage investment in priority sectors and production for export, Brunei continues to use extensive tax and other incentives. During the review period, Brunei changed the Income Tax Act to reduce tax liabilities of enterprises, with the exception of those engaged in petroleum activities. The income tax rate decreased from 27.5% in 2008 to 20% in 2014, and will be further reduce to 18.5% as from 2015. Also, tax thresholds were introduced in 2008 to further reduce corporate tax burden.

Since 2008, three grant and loan schemes have been created and two more revised to help micro, small, and medium sized enterprises grow, consolidate, and internationalize. Three grant schemes have also been established to support start-ups and innovation. Under the 10th National Development Plan 2012-17, Brunei has allocated 1% of GDP (B$200 million) to R&D and innovation to help achieve economic diversification.

For additional analytical, business and investment opportunities information,
please contact Global Investment & Business Center, USA
at (703) 370-8082. Fax: (703) 370-8083. E-mail: ibpusa3@gmail.com
Global Business and Investment Info Databank - www.ibpus.com

In line with commitments under the ASEAN Economic Community, since 2011 Brunei has been drafting comprehensive competition legislation. At present, competition issues are addressed on a sector-by-sector basis and tackled by its respective regulator. Competition regulations exist in telecommunications, financial services, and energy, although in limited forms.

Goods subject to price control increased substantially during the review period. Currently, there are 19 categories of products for which maximum retail prices are set (e.g. rice and sugar) . Prices/tariffs of housing, petroleum products, utilities, healthcare, and telecom services continue to be subsidized in Brunei. Fuel subsidy reform over the medium term could provide fiscal space to maintain development expenditures and reduce distortions that could limit diversification efforts.

The public sector continues to exert a direct influence on the economy, mainly through state-owned enterprises. Some of these still operate under monopoly or hold exclusive rights in sectors such as oil and gas, manufacturing, banking, telecom, and air transport. Brunei's Privatization Master Plan is in the process of being completed.

As the Government is the largest operator in the economy, procurement also plays an important role. Some changes have recently been made to the legal framework, including adjusting the thresholds under the different procurement methods. Brunei is not a party to the WTO Agreement on Government Procurement.

Main changes to Brunei's IPR regime since its last TPR include the restructuring of the administrative system, notably the establishment of the Brunei Intellectual Property Office, as well as the entry into force of a new patent law in 2011 which, *inter alia*, established a national patent system. Brunei has made concerted efforts to improve IPR enforcement, in particular to curb copyright piracy through, for example, an increase in fines and prison sentences. During the review period, Brunei acceded to three additional WIPO-administered treaties and is considering acceding to others.

Under its National Vision 2035, Brunei has identified the following activities that may increase value-added, exports, and jobs creation: agri-food; downstream oil and gas and energy-intensive industries; information and communication technology; life sciences (pharmaceutical, cosmetics, and functional health food and health supplements); light manufacturing; services, such as financial services and tourism; and other activities that may be technology driven.

Despite its relatively small share of total real GDP (1%), agriculture and related activities is of key importance in the economy because of Brunei's food security and self-sufficiency objectives. As a net importer of agricultural products, food security is mainly promoted through zero applied MFN and preferential tariffs. The agri-food processing industry has increased its participation in agricultural production supported by growing domestic demand in halal food and the authorities' efforts to market the "Brunei Halal brand" at regional and international level. Brunei maintains a system of subsidy for rice and sugar to protect consumers from increases in commodity prices.

The energy sector, mainly oil and gas, remains the backbone of Brunei's industrial output and trade. However, oil and gas production shrunk at an annual average rate of -1.8% during 2008-13 partly due to maintenance works. The largest oil and gas operator and producer remains the state-owned Brunei Shell Petroleum (BSP) by virtue of its control of the major oil and natural gas fields. While BSP operates a concession, the exploration and development of a number of new onshore and offshore blocks have been offered on production sharing basis.

Brunei has the lowest electricity rate and the highest energy intensity of all ASEAN countries. The Government spends some B$40 million per year on its electricity subsidy, out of a total annual energy subsidy of about B$1 billion. Steps are being taken to reduce 45% of its energy intensity by 2035 and

**For additional analytical, business and investment opportunities information,
please contact Global Investment & Business Center, USA
at (703) 370-8082. Fax: (703) 370-8083. E-mail: ibpusa3@gmail.com
Global Business and Investment Info Databank - www.ibpus.com**

improve efficiency. In 2012, a progressive electricity tariff structure was introduced to reduce the government power subsidy by more than half.

Overall, the performance of the manufacturing sector has been weak in recent years partly due to the relatively high cost of doing business, shortage of skilled and unskilled workers, and lack of competitiveness of local products. To encourage private participation, manufacturing companies are eligible to receive financial support, incentives, and other measures. The Government also invests directly, mainly through its company Semaun Holdings which still dominates manufacturing. In addition, the Government is promoting and managing large-scale industrial sites, including industrial parks that cater to downstream petrochemicals plants.

Since its establishment in 2011, the Autoriti Monetari Brunei Darussalam, a statutory body acting as the central bank, has been responsible for the supervision and regulation of the financial system. Brunei aims to become a regional financial centre for Islamic financial services. In terms of banking, the main change over the review period was the adoption of the Islamic Banking Order 2008 which harmonized Islamic and conventional banking regulations. Brunei does not have its own stock exchange and the capital market still is in an infant stage. It is not a signatory to the Fifth Protocol to the GATS (on financial services) .

A complete review of the telecoms regulatory framework is being undertaken so as to have a single converged regulator for telecoms and broadcasting by 2015. Moreover, a Telecommunications and Broadcasting Competition Code, Brunei's first-sector specific competition code, is expected to be implemented in 2015. A new Tariff Regulation Code of Practice will be also introduced to regulate retail and wholesale tariffs for telecoms and broadcasting infrastructure and services. Currently, there are two mobile operators, and the state-owned Telekom Brunei continues to have the monopoly over the fixed-line market.

28. Brunei has liberalized international air transport through bilateral, regional, and plurilateral agreements. It has signed 36 bilateral air agreements of which five integrate open sky arrangements. Since 2009, three regional open sky agreements came into force with a view to establish the ASEAN Single Aviation Market. Most of Brunei's international waterborne trade is carried by foreign vessels.

ECONOMIC ENVIRONMENT

RECENT ECONOMIC DEVELOPMENTS

At the time of the second TPR of Brunei Darussalam in 2008, economic growth had resumed following the recession of the late 1990s. Nonetheless, its modest annual average GDP growth rate of 2.5% during 2002-06 was insufficient to generate enough jobs for Brunei's growing labour force, a cause of concern among Bruneians. Moreover, the prospect of an eventual depletion of its abundant petroleum and natural gas resources had prompted the Government to continue pursuing an active industrial policy to encourage economic diversification and boost non energy output and employment.[1]

Since then, Brunei experienced an important contraction in economic activity in 2008-09 mainly due to the global financial crisis. From 2010 to 2012, its GDP growth rates were positive with the non-energy sector, led by services, growing in general faster than the energy sector.[2] In 2013, the economy contracted again (-1.8%) as the energy sector GDP declined 7.2% due to lower oil and gas production (section 4.2.1.1) . In 2013, the non-energy sector GDP grew by 2.7% driven by public development expenditure and property financing.[3]

The "Bruneization" policy which encourages companies to give preference to Bruneians in their employment policies has continued. It is estimated that 56% of working citizens and permanent residents are employed by the Government.[4] In the private sector, chronic labour shortages, in professional and unskilled areas, have been alleviated by more recruitment of foreign workers, who now make up almost half of the total working population. According to the latest census figures, the unemployment rate was 9.3% in 2011.

On 1 January 2011, the Autoriti Monetari Brunei Darussalam (AMBD), a statutory body acting as the central bank, was established and replaced the Brunei Currency and Monetary Board.[5] The AMBD has four main objectives: to achieve and maintain domestic price stability; to ensure the stability of the financial system, in particular by formulating financial regulations and prudential standards; to assist in the establishment and functioning of an efficient payment system; and foster and develop a sound and progressive financial services sector (section 4.4.2) .[6]

The annual average inflation rate in Brunei was 0.7% over 2008-13 supported by the pegged exchange rate between the Brunei dollar (B$) and the Singapore dollar at par.[7] According to the IMF, the AMBD has been successful in managing such currency board arrangement and the real exchange rate appears to be broadly in line with fundamentals.[8] Inflation has also been subdued by price controls on basic commodities and selected goods (section 3.3.2.3), as well as subsidies, *inter alia*, on petrol and electricity (sections 4.2.1 and 4.2.2) . For 2014 and 2015, the IMF expects average inflation rates of 0.4% and 0.5%, respectively.[9]

Brunei's overall fiscal surplus, as percentage of GDP, fell from 40% in 2008 to 16.6% in 2013 as oil and gas revenues declined (Table 1.1) . Corporate taxes levied on oil and gas companies represent over 90% of total government revenues. Prices of housing, petroleum products, utilities, education, healthcare, and telecom services continue to be subsidized in Brunei. In addition, the State absorbs unpaid consumers' bills (section 3.3.1.2) . During the next few years, Brunei aims to foster non-oil revenues, contain the size of the government and public sector wage bill, and reduce subsidies including through a progressive electricity tariff structure introduced in 2012 (section 4.2.2) . The IMF has pointed out that Brunei's long-term fiscal sustainability could be further strengthened by improving public financial management, including through the governance framework for oil-related funds (section 1.3) .[10]

TRADE PERFORMANCE AND INVESTMENT

TRADE IN GOODS AND SERVICES

Sizable hydrocarbon exports and the steady accumulation of long-term foreign assets over many years have provided Brunei with a comfortable balance of payments position (Table 1.2), which also reflects the big gap between savings and investment. Nonetheless, the external current account surplus, as percentage of GDP, fell from 48.9% in 2008 to 31.5% in 2013 (Table 1.1) because of the important reduction in oil and gas export revenues and consequently in Brunei's trade balance during the period. For 2014 and 2015, the IMF expects a current account surplus of 31.6% and 30.1% of GDP, respectively.[11]

Brunei's ratio of merchandise trade (exports and imports) to GDP reached 104.1% in 2013, up from 91.1% in 2008 (Table 1.1) . In 2013, Brunei ranked 63rd among world merchandise exporters and 112th among importers (considering EU member States as one and excluding intra-EU trade) . In services trade, Brunei ranked 94th as exporter and 93rd as importer.[12]

Brunei's merchandise exports amounted to US$11,432 million in 2013 (compared with US$10,543 million in 2008) . Imports went up from US$2,574 million in 2008 to US$3,612 million in

2013 (Charts 1.1 and 1.2; and Tables A1.1 and A1.2) . Mineral fuels, which includes petroleum and natural gas, represented 96.5% of total merchandise exports in 2013 (down from 97.8% in 2008) . The remaining exports are manufactures, led by machinery and transport equipment (1.1% of total merchandise exports in 2013) and chemicals (0.8%) (Table A1.1) .

Brunei's merchandise exports are mainly destined for the East Asian region. Japan remains Brunei's largest export partner, with a share of 39.8% in 2013 (43.2% in 2008), followed by the Republic of Korea (16.3%) . ASEAN's share declined from 24.2% in 2008 to 23.2% in 2013, with a significant reduction in the participation of Indonesia from 20% to 4.7% in the period. Outside the East Asian region, the share of India increased from 3.2% to 7.6%, whereas the participation of China has fluctuated over the recent years. The share of the EU and the United States in Brunei's merchandise exports is negligible (Table A1.2) .

Manufactures continue to dominate Brunei's imports; machinery and transport equipment remained Brunei's most important merchandise import category, accounting for 36.6% of total imports in 2013 (compared with 43.8% in 2008), followed by other manufactured imports such as chemicals. The share of food imports in total merchandise imports increased from 12.3% in 2008 to 13.3% in 2013, while that of mineral fuels also increased from 2.6% to 7.5% during the same period (Table A1.1) .

Brunei's merchandise imports also originate mainly in East Asia. Malaysia has become the largest source of imports, increasing its share from 18.7% in 2008 to 21.9% in 2013, while Singapore's participation went from 20.4% to 19.1% in the same period. Imports from ASEAN countries represented 50.9% in 2013 (47.9% in 2008) . Overall, Asian countries have further increased their share of Brunei's imports during 2008-13 partly at the expense of the United States and the EU

Balance of payments data indicate that Brunei is a net importer of services with a deficit that increased from US$642 million in 2008 to US$2,365 million in 2013 (Table 1.2) . Net outflows have occurred in the form of payments for foreign travel, trade-related transport, and occasionally high professional fees in the oil and gas sector.

FOREIGN DIRECT INVESTMENT

1.14. Brunei's FDI inflows averaged some US$600 million per year during 2008-13 (up from US$328 million over 2005-07) . Over the review period about 90% of FDI flows have been allocated to the mining and quarrying sector (i.e. oil and gas industry), followed by manufacturing and services, particularly wholesale and retail trade (Table 1.3) . Traditionally, FDI inflows have been dominated by investment from the EU, notably from the United Kingdom and the Netherlands. Hong-Kong, China is also an important investor in Brunei.

Success in attracting significant FDI inflows has been hampered by increased competition from neighbouring economies. In addition, external sources indicate that while positive steps have been taken, there remains considerable scope for Brunei to improve its business climate.[13] Moreover, Brunei's FDI policies could be more transparent, particularly with respect to limits on foreign equity participation, partnership requirements, and the identification of sectors in which FDI is restricted (section 2.4.1) .[14]

ECONOMIC AND BUSINESS TRENDS

Brunei's economy remains highly dependent on oil and gas production, which accounts for about two-thirds of output[15], and over 90% of merchandise exports and government revenues. This makes Brunei particularly vulnerable to an eventual depletion of resources over the next decades, and remains a cause for concern for the authorities due to fluctuating international energy prices. With the objective of ensuring inter-generational economic equity in the exploitation of its non-renewable natural wealth, Brunei has the General Reserve Fund (GRF), a sovereign fund administered by the autonomous Brunei Investment Agency (BIA) containing savings set aside for future generations.[16]

Under its National Vision 2035 (*Wawasan* 2035), Brunei aims to achieve an annual average real GDP growth of 5%-6%. According to the IMF, Brunei's economic outlook remains favourable as planned large petrochemical and refinery projects begin production; real GDP growth is expected to reach 5.3% in 2014 and 3% in 2015.[17] Over the medium term, acceleration in the non-energy sector due to infrastructure and downstream projects is expected to support economic growth.[18] Nonetheless, sustaining high growth rates on an ongoing basis will require the successful implementation of Brunei's ambitious diversification strategy, and on enhancing private-sector participation in the economy.[19]

Brunei's economic strategy targets investment in sectors that may bring value-added activities, have a potential for exports, and create jobs. These sectors are: agri-food (section 4.1.1); downstream oil and gas and energy-intensive industries (section 4.2.1); information and communication technology (ICT) (section 4.4.3); life sciences (pharmaceutical, cosmetics, and functional health food and health supplements); light manufacturing (section 4.3); services such as financial services (section 4.4.2), logistics, and tourism (section 4.4.5); and activities that may be driven by technology development (section 2.2) .[20] In addition, there is room to improve productivity throughout the economy and particularly in the government sector. Fuel subsidy reform over the medium term could provide fiscal space to maintain development expenditures and reduce distortions that could limit diversification efforts.[21]

TRADE REGIME

GENERAL INSTITUTIONAL AND LEGAL FRAMEWORK

There have been no changes to the institutional framework in Brunei Darussalam since its last Trade Policy Review in 2008. Under the Constitution, the Sultan is the head of State and serves as Prime Minister, Minister of Finance, and Minister of Defence. The power to promulgate laws is also vested in the Sultan. He is assisted by the Council of Ministers[22] which handles executive matters and the Legislative Council in which policies under consultation or implementation are debated.[23] Other councils advise the Sultan on constitutional, religious, and customs and tradition issues.

Brunei's legal system is based on the common law and the Sharia law.[24] On 1 May 2014, a new Sharia Penal Code entered into force applicable to both Muslims and non-Muslims.[25]

TRADE POLICY OBJECTIVES

Formulating and implementing Brunei's trade policy lies with the Ministry of Foreign Affairs and Trade (MOFAT) in cooperation with other ministries and trade-related agencies. MOFAT is also responsible for: WTO issues, negotiating and implementing Regional Trade Agreements (RTAs), and promoting trade and investment. MOFAT holds consultations with the private sector in the formulation of Brunei's trade policy on *ad hoc* basis, including organizing briefings on RTA negotiations.

Brunei aims to achieve three key objectives: have more highly skilled people; an economy that is sustainable, dynamic and diversified; and high quality of life for its population. These objectives are contained in Brunei's long-term development plans: the National Vision 2035 (*Wawasan* 2035) launched in 2008, the First Outline of Strategies and Policy Directions (OSPD) 2007-17, and its 10th National Development Plan 2012-17.

Brunei's economic strategy targets investment in sectors that may bring value-added activities, have a potential for exports, and create jobs. These sectors are: agri-food; downstream oil and gas, and energy-intensive industries; information and communications technology (ICT); life sciences (pharmaceutical, cosmetics, and functional health food and health supplements); light manufacturing; services (financial services, logistics, and tourism); and activities that may be driven by technology development.[26] Better assisting SMEs in increasing competitiveness and venturing in overseas markets would also help Brunei's efforts for economic diversification.

Since 2008, new trade-related legislation has been introduced in the areas of business environment, competition, financial services, fisheries, intellectual property, and TBT (Table A2.1) .[27] Additional legislation on standards (section 3.1.7) and competition (section 3.3.2.1) is being drafted.

TRADE AGREEMENTS

WTO

Brunei is an original Member of the WTO, and grants MFN treatment to all its Members. Brunei is neither a party to the Information Technology Agreement nor to the plurilateral agreements on government procurement and trade in civil aircraft. Brunei fully supports the multilateral trading system and endorses the Bali Package, in particular the Agreement on Trade Facilitation.[28] It has never been involved in any trade dispute. During the review period, Brunei made regular notifications to the WTO (Table 2.1); however, by March 2014, it had 45 outstanding notifications, including on agriculture and import licensing.[29]

REGIONAL TRADE AGREEMENTS

Brunei is of the view that regional integration, based on open regionalism, is a complementary approach to multilateralism. It considers that its RTAs will help increase market access and investment inflows in support of its economic diversification efforts.[30]

2.9.   Brunei has eight RTAs encompassing 16 partners. Five RTAs entered into force during the review period: four are regional agreements negotiated in the context of ASEAN (with Australia and New Zealand; India; Japan; and the Republic of Korea), and one was negotiated bilaterally with Japan (Table A2.2) .[31] Brunei's RTAs have been notified to the WTO; the Brunei-Japan Economic Partnership Agreement and the Trans-Pacific Strategic Economic Partnership (TPSEP) have been reviewed by the Committee on Regional Trade Agreements.

In 2013, merchandise trade with RTA partners accounted for about 75% of Brunei's total imports and 99.6% of total exports.

ASEAN

During the review period, the ASEAN member States worked to achieve regional economic integration by 2015 when the ASEAN Economic Community (AEC) is to be established. AEC converts ASEAN into a single market and production base, in which there is a free flow of goods, services, investment, capital, and skilled labour.

2.12.   The ASEAN Trade in Goods Agreement (ATIGA) entered into force in 2010 to consolidate into a comprehensive document existing commitments on trade in goods. ATIGA supersedes the 1992 Common Effective Preferential Tariffs Agreement for the ASEAN Free-Trade Area (CEPT-AFTA) and 11 economic integration agreements.[32] However, the Protocol to Provide Special Consideration for

Rice and Sugar, which allows ASEAN member States to temporarily waive their obligations, continues to apply.[33]

Compared with CEPT-AFTA, ATIGA introduces a broader coverage for trade in goods. It incorporates enhanced measures for NTBs elimination and trade facilitation. In addition, ATIGA contributes to a more transparent and predictable tariff regime by consolidating tariff liberalization/reduction for each ASEAN member into a single schedule.[34] Intra-ASEAN trade was liberalized in 2010 among ASEAN-6. Cambodia, Lao PDR, Myanmar, and Viet Nam will complete tariff liberalization in 2015, with flexibility until 2018. Under ATIGA, Brunei has only one dutiable tariff line (Table 3.4) .

During the review period, ASEAN member States continued to liberalize progressively trade in services under the ASEAN Framework Agreement on Services (AFAS) to cover all sectors and modes of supply. To date, 9 out of 10 packages of commitments have been signed. Liberalization in financial and air transport services is carried out in separate packages.[35] For each new package of commitments, the number of subsectors to be liberalized increases and member States are committed to: (i) remove restrictions for cross-border supply and consumption abroad; and (ii) increase foreign (ASEAN) equity participation and remove other market access limitations for commercial presence.[36]

To liberalize trade in services further, ASEAN member States have signed mutual recognition arrangements for greater mobility of qualified workers in accountancy, architectural, dental, engineering, medical, nursing, surveying, and tourism services. In addition to the AFAS packages on air transport, three mutual agreements allow unlimited air passenger and cargo services within the region[37]; these agreements have been ratified by Brunei.[38]

The ASEAN Comprehensive Investment Agreement (ACIA), a new legal framework for investment, entered into force in 2012 to replace the ASEAN Investment Area (AIA) and the ASEAN Investment Guarantee Agreement (IGA) . ACIA reaffirms relevant AIA/IGA provisions (i.e. obligation of national and MFN treatments); covers direct and portfolio investment; and benefits to ASEAN investors and ASEAN-based foreign investors. Under ACIA, protection is granted to investment made in all sectors and a more comprehensive investor-State dispute mechanism has been introduced. In addition, liberalization applies to manufacturing, agriculture and fisheries, forestry, mining and quarrying, and services related to these sectors. Reservations may be maintained on national treatment and nationality requirements for senior management but are required to be reduced or eliminated gradually.[39] The Protocol to amend the ASEAN Comprehensive Investment Agreement is still to be signed.

Integration into the world economy is a core element to establish the AEC. To this end, ASEAN has signed RTAs with six dialogue partners, referred to as ASEAN+1. During the review period, agreements entered into force with Australia and New Zealand; India; Japan; and the Republic of Korea (Table A2.2) . The ASEAN-Australia-New Zealand agreement was negotiated as a single undertaking to cover trade in goods, services, and investment. Trade in services and investment was subsequently negotiated with China (signed 2007/entry into force 2007)[40], the Republic of Korea (2008/2009), and India (2014/not yet in force) (Table A2.2) . Negotiations with Japan are still ongoing.[41]

ASEAN is also engaged in expanding the ASEAN+1 network. FTA negotiations are ongoing with the EU and Hong Kong, China. In addition, ASEAN seeks further economic integration with its six RTA partners in an effort to broaden and deepen current engagements. To this end, negotiations for a Regional Comprehensive Economic Partnership (RCEP), which cover trade in goods, services, and investment, began in 2012. The RCEP is built upon two initiatives for regional economic integration in which ASEAN member States and RTA partners are also engaged, the ASEAN+3[42] East Asia Free

For additional analytical, business and investment opportunities information,
please contact Global Investment & Business Center, USA
at (703) 370-8082. Fax: (703) 370-8083. E-mail: ibpusa3@gmail.com
Global Business and Investment Info Databank - www.ibpus.com

Trade Agreement (EAFTA) and the ASEAN+6 Comprehensive Economic Partnership for East Asia (CEPEA).[43]

Trans-Pacific Strategic Economic Partnership (TPSEP) Agreement

Brunei, Chile, Singapore, and New Zealand signed the TPSEP Agreement in 2005. The agreement entered in Brunei into force fully in 2009 after it had finalized its schedules on services and government procurement.[44] Brunei was given extra time to negotiate these schedules as this was the first time Brunei drafted a negative list on services and provided market access for government procurement. In the meantime, Brunei did not benefit from the other parties' commitments.[45] Brunei's schedule for procurement of goods and services applies to some entities listed in its schedule and contracts valued at or above B$250,000.[46]

The TPSEP Agreement provides for complete trade liberalization among the parties, except for alcohol, tobacco, and firearms which Brunei excludes to safeguard public morals, human health, and security.

BILATERAL AGREEMENTS

2.22.   The Economic Partnership Agreement between Brunei and Japan entered into force on 31 July 2008. Japan is among the main trading partners for Brunei in terms of exports (section 1.2). Under the agreement, Brunei's tariff liberalization excludes a small number of products such as prepared food, chemicals, and minerals[49]; these products accounted for 0.1% of Brunei's total imports from Japan over the 2008-13 period. The Agreement incorporates specific provisions for the energy sector according to which measures affecting trade in oil and natural gas may be notified among the parties. However, contracts signed prior to the introduction of new measures, will have to be fulfilled.[50] Liberalization in trade in services excludes measures affecting air traffic rights[51]; government procurement; cabotage in maritime transport services; subsidies; and measures affecting job seekers or measures on nationality, residence or employment on a permanent basis (Table A2.2).

Brunei and Pakistan are exploring ways to enhance trade, investment and economic cooperation.

Other arrangements

2.24.   During the review period, Brunei received GSP treatment from Belarus/Kazakhstan/Russian Federation; Canada; the European Union; Norway; and Turkey.[52]

INVESTMENT REGIME

LEGAL FRAMEWORK

There is no specific framework to regulate domestic and foreign investment in Brunei. The main investment legislation is the Investment Incentives Order 2001 which provides tax incentives to investors (section 2.4.1.1). No changes were made to this legislation during the review period.

The Ministry of Foreign Affairs and Trade (MOFAT) is responsible for maintaining a conducive investment climate to attract FDI. The Brunei Economic Development Board (BEDB), under the Prime Ministers' Office, is in charge of promoting Brunei as an attractive destination for FDI. BEDB markets Brunei in sectors of interest for economic diversification (section 2.2). To attract foreign investors, BEDB has identified 12 industrial sites for which it is in charge of infrastructure development, marketing, operation, and maintenance. During the review period, BEDB's efforts in securing industrial land with a complete infrastructure package attracted investors in large-scale downstream oil and gas and manufacturing projects.[53] The Brunei Industrial Development Authority (BINA), under the Ministry of Industry and Primary Resources, manages nine industrial estates in which small-and-medium size projects have established (section 4.3) . The Autoriti Monetari Brunei Darussalam (AMBD) is in charge of, *inter alia*, attracting financial institutions to convert Brunei into a new centre for international financial services (section 4.4.2) .

Brunei prohibits domestic and foreign investment in the manufacture of liquor and armaments. Full foreign participation may be allowed in most activities, except in those that use natural resources, relate to national food security, and are located in industrial sites for which 30% minimum local equity participation is required. In addition, domestic and foreign investment in sectors for which the State is the major service provider (e.g. telecom, energy) is subject to approval by the relevant regulatory authority. Market concentration and nationality requirement may also restrict the participation of domestic and foreign investors. In retail trade, foreigners are allowed on a case-by-case basis.[54]

No minimum level of investment is required to invest in Brunei. There are no restrictions on repatriation of capital, remittance of profits or royalties abroad, and exchange control. However, pursuant to measures against money laundering introduced in 2011, cross-border movements of cash exceeding B$15,000 must be reported to Customs on arrival and the Immigration and National Registration Department on departure. Financial institutions must declare suspicious transactions to the Financial Intelligence Unit under the AMBD.[55] There is no record of expropriation in Brunei.[56]

Previously, permanent residents and foreigners were able to purchase land and property through power of attorney or trust deeds. However, in 2012, the Government announced it intended to revoke such procedure and convert land and property purchases into 60-year leases. The authorities are still drafting the relevant amendment to the Land Code (Chapter 40) .[57]

Foreigners may own strata titles in commercial and residential multi-storey buildings, on leasehold for up to 99 years (up from 60 years effective since 2010) .[58] In addition, long-term agreements may be signed for lease of industrial land (30 years) and commercial property (60 years); leases exceeding seven years must be registered and approved by the Sultan. Temporary occupation licences (TOL) are issued for temporary use of state-owned land. Since 2011, new TOL for land are only issued for, *inter alia*, commercial and educational use (schools) .[59]

In 2010, new legislation for domestic and international arbitration entered into force (Table A2.1) based on model laws from the United Nations Commission on International Trade Law (UNCITRAL) . The new international arbitration legislation allows courts in Brunei to support but not interfere in arbitration proceedings. The Attorney General's Chambers and the Arbitration Association of Brunei Darussalam are working to enhance infrastructure and capacity building for arbitration in Brunei.[60]

Brunei has 8 bilateral investment treaties (BITs)[61], 16 double taxation agreements (DTAs)[62], and 10 tax information exchange agreement (TIEA) .[63] Brunei is also a signatory to the ASEAN Comprehensive Investment Agreement (ACIA) (section 2.3.2.1), and a contracting party to the International Centre for Settlement of Investment Disputes (ICSID) .

INCENTIVES

During the review period, no substantial changes were introduced to the incentives granted to domestic and foreign investors under the Investment Incentives Order 2001 (S 48/01) .[64] Investors may apply for an incentive certificate to the Ministry of Industry and Primary Resources (MIPR) .[65] Incentives are aimed at encouraging enterprises to manufacture pioneer products or provide pioneer services, engage in export activities, and invest in new productive equipment to increase production or profitability (Table 2.2) . Pioneer status in manufacturing is granted to activities that are innovative and have significant development prospects to contribute to economic diversification, exports, and job creation.[66] Brunei has declared 28 manufacturing activities eligible for pioneer status.[67] In 2013, two manufacturing companies were granted pioneer status in production of animal feeds, and canning/bottling/packaging.

Investment incentives

	Incentive	Tax relief period (not exceeding)
Pioneer industries	Exemption from income tax Carry forward of losses and allowances Exemption from customs and import duties	5-8 years (11 years), depending on the amount of fixed capital expenditure 11 years (20 years) for industries established in high tech park
Pioneer service companies	Exemption from income tax Carry forward of losses and allowances Exemption from customs and import duties	8 years (11 years) 5 years (10 years) for financial services
Post-pioneer companies	Exemption from income tax Deduction of losses Adjustment of capital allowances and losses	6 years (11 years)
Expansion of established enterprises	Exemption from income tax	3-5 years (15 years), depending on the amount of new capital expenditure
Expanding service companies	Exemption from income tax	11 years (20 years)
Production for export	Exemption from income tax	6 years (11 years) for pioneer enterprises, depending on sales volume 8 years for the remaining enterprises, depending on sales volume 15 years, depending on the amount of fixed capital expenditure
Export of services	Exemption from income tax Deduction of allowances and losses	11 years (20 years)
International trade incentives	Exemption from income tax	8 years
Foreign loans for productive equipment	Exemption from withholding tax on interests paid to non-resident lenders	Depends on the financial agreement with the foreign lender
Investment allowances	Exemption from income tax	5 years 11 years for tourism
Warehousing and servicing incentives	Exemption from income tax	11 years (20 years)
Investment in new technology companies	Deduction of losses	
Overseas investment and venture	Deduction of losses	

capital incentives		

Source: Investment Incentives Order 2001, as amended by S 15/10 and S 5/11.

Incentives are mainly in the form of income tax exemption for specific periods of time that may be extended further (Table 2.2) . Tax relief period for pioneer industries is determined by the amount of expenses in fixed capital (minimum B$500,000) or the location. Providers of pioneer services are granted an eight-year tax relief period except for those providing financial services for which a five-year tax relief period was introduced in 2010.

2.35.   Enterprises manufacturing pioneer products or export products are also exempt from import duties on capital goods and raw materials only if these are not on sale in Brunei.[68]

STARTING A BUSINESS

Business entities are registered in Brunei under the Companies Act (Chapter 39)[69] or the Business Names Act (Chapter 92) .[70] The Companies Act sets guidelines for the incorporation of companies and the registration of foreign branches of companies. All businesses must register at the Registry of Companies and Business Names Division under the Ministry of Finance.[71] The cost of name search is B$5 per name. The registration fees for companies are based on a flat fee of B$300. The registration fee for sole proprietorship or partnerships is B$30. Foreigners are not allowed to establish as sole proprietors. In 2014, there were 9,822 companies incorporated in Brunei and 822 branches of foreign companies.

Regulated activities (e.g. financial services, telecom) are also required to be licensed by or registered with the regulatory authority prior to operations with a view to protect consumers' interest. In addition, shops are subject to licensing under the Miscellaneous Licences Act (Table 2.3) . Miscellaneous licences may be applied (and paid) online through the Business Licensing System (OneBiz)[72]; licences are collected at the Business Facilitation Center (BFC) .[73] OneBiz was launched in 2013 by the Ministry of Industry and Primary Resources to streamline procedures in starting and operating a business.[74] To date, OneBiz is partly operational; there is no timing for its full implementation. According to the authorities, about 4,000 miscellaneous licences were processed online in 2013.

Miscellaneous licences

Activity	Regulatory authority
Beauty and health establishment[a]	Municipal Board or District Licensing Board
Coffee shops, restaurants, boarding house, lodging house, and places for public resort and entertainment	Municipal Board or District Licensing Board
Hawkers	District Licensing Board
Motor vehicle dealer	Ministry of Industry and Primary Resources
Petrol station, including storage places for petrol and inflammable materials	Ministry of Industry and Primary Resources
Retail shop	Municipal Board or District Licensing Board
Timber store and furniture factories	Municipal Board or District Licensing Board
Workshop	Municipal Board or District Licensing Board

a Included in 2011.
Source: Miscellaneous Licences Act (Chapter 127), as amended by S 43/08, S 85/08, and S 69/11.

Companies may be incorporated in Brunei as public or private companies with limited or unlimited liabilities[75]; 90% of the companies were incorporated as private limited companies in 2014.[76] Private

companies must, *inter alia*, have at least two but not more than 50 shareholders and at least two directors.[77] Shareholders may be of any nationality; however, participation of national shareholders may be required in companies subject to licensing. In 2010, the nationality restriction of having at least half the board of directors to be Brunei nationals was removed[78]; private companies must now have one of the two directors or at least two where there are more than two directors, to be ordinarily resident.[79] There is no minimum paid-up capital requirement for the incorporation of companies (or registration of foreign branches) except for financial institutions as criteria for licensing (section 4.4.2)
.

A branch of a foreign company must have a registered office in Brunei and, effective from 2010, at least two local authorized agents. It has the same powers and authority as a local company.[80]

2.40.   Foreigners may also participate in partnerships which are exempt from income tax.[81] Brunei allows limited liability partnerships to be established but the Limited Liability Partnership Order 2010 has yet to enter into force.

International business companies (IBCs) and international limited partnerships (ILPs) generally conduct business outside Brunei, but they may also conduct business in Brunei. They are governed by the International Business Companies Order (IBCO) 2000 and International Limited Partnerships Order 2000, respectively. IBCs and ILPs may incorporate in Brunei only through agents licensed by the AMBD under the Registered Agents and Trustees Licensing Order 2000.

To date, there are 11 licensed agents. Registration with AMBD is also compulsory for IBCs and ILPs.[82] There were some 11,000 companies incorporated as IBCs in 2013. IBCO 2000 provides tax-free corporate facilities for both IBCs and foreign international companies (FICs) . Companies incorporated under the IBCO wishing to provide international financial services must be licensed under the relevant international banking and insurance orders (section 4.4.2) .

Expat employment is controlled by the Labour Department through a labour quota system and the Department of Immigration and National Registration through the issuance of employment visas and/or work permits (employment passes) . Employers must be licensed by the Labour Department prior to recruiting foreign workers. They must also obtain a bank guarantee to cover repatriation and insurance costs for each foreign worker they intend to hire. Employment visas may be granted by Brunei's diplomatic missions overseas and are required prior to the entry into Brunei. Work permits may be subject to laws, regulations, and policies enforced from time to time.

For additional analytical, business and investment opportunities information,
please contact Global Investment & Business Center, USA
at (703) 370-8082. Fax: (703) 370-8083. E-mail: ibpusa3@gmail.com
Global Business and Investment Info Databank - www.ibpus.com

TRADE POLICIES AND PRACTICES BY MEASURE

MEASURES AFFECTING IMPORTS

CUSTOMS PROCEDURES AND REQUIREMENTS

Since its last Review in 2008, Brunei has taken steps to further facilitate customs procedures particularly at the regional level. Under the ASEAN Trade in Goods Agreement (ATIGA) (section 2.3.2.1), an ASEAN Single Window (ASW) to process trade documents electronically will integrate the national single windows of ASEAN member States.[83] Brunei Darussalam National Single Window (BDNSW) began to operate, in phases, in January 2014. BDNSW will allow applications for several trade procedures, such as certificates of origin and import permits. In addition, a new ASEAN Agreement on Customs was signed in 2012 (replacing the 1997 ASEAN Agreement on Customs) to streamline customs procedures. For Brunei, the agreement entered into force on 1 April 2013. Also, progress has been achieved in establishing the ASEAN Customs Transit System.[84]

Brunei's e-Customs system has been fully operational since 2008 and allows traders to submit applications electronically.[85] Merchandise imports into (and exports from) Brunei continue to be governed under the Customs Order (2006) administered by the Royal Customs and Excise Department (RCED) under the Ministry of Finance.

All imports into Brunei shall be declared through electronic submission via the e-Customs system. Bill of lading or airway bill and commercial invoice, and any supporting documents must be presented during customs clearance. If applicable, preferential tariff treatment under a regional trade agreement (RTA) may be given when the certificate of origin is endorsed by a trade officer at the Certificate of Origin Office of the Ministry of Foreign Affairs and Trade (MOFAT) .

Estimates for 2014 indicate that import procedures take 15 days and cost US$770 per container.[86] According to a Time Release Study by RCED, the average time from submission of customs declaration to customs clearance was 10 hours and 18 minutes in 2012.

The RCED classifies risk based on an internal process which includes analyzing past record of companies, importation of controlled and dutiable items, and high value items.

3.6.   There are no customs fees for import procedures or registration; goods in transit via Brunei are subject to fees ranging from B$10 to B$100 depending on their type or nature.

Importers must register with the RCED and appoint registered forwarding agents to log into the e-Customs system, and submit all required documentation for import/export. Import permits are required for some products, including plants, animals, birds, fish, salt, sugar, rice, drugs, gambling machines, and used motor vehicle. These are available from the relevant government ministries and departments. In some cases, including for plants, animals and animal products, birds, and fish, import licences must be accompanied by SPS certificates from the exporting country. All other goods, unless prohibited, may be imported under open general licences.

Customs decisions may be appealed under section 153 of the Customs Order 2006. Authority for all customs decisions lies with the Controller of Customs; unless it is specifically stated that such decisions may only be made at the absolute discretion of the Controller, appeals may be made to the Minister of Finance, whose decision is final.

For additional analytical, business and investment opportunities information,
please contact Global Investment & Business Center, USA
at (703) 370-8082. Fax: (703) 370-8083. E-mail: ibpusa3@gmail.com
Global Business and Investment Info Databank - www.ibpus.com

3.9.   Brunei has no laws pertaining to pre-shipment inspection for customs valuation and classification, and no company has ever provided pre-shipment inspection services in Brunei.

3.10.   Brunei is a member of the World Customs Organization since 1996, and became party to the Harmonized System Convention on 1 June 2014. Brunei is currently doing gap analysis on the International Convention on the Simplification and Harmonization of Customs Procedures (Revised Kyoto Convention) .

3.11.   Brunei has already made its notification of Category A commitments under the Agreement on Trade Facilitation.[87]

CUSTOMS VALUATION

Brunei's legislation on customs valuation has not changed during the review period. It is still based on Customs (Valuation of Imported Goods) Rules 2001.[88] Customs value is primarily assessed based on the transaction value which must also reflect costs incurred by the buyer when appropriate (e.g. packing fees, transport charges[89]) . If the transaction value method may not be used, five methods apply in sequential order: (i) transaction value of identical goods; (ii) transaction value of similar goods; (iii) deductive value; (iv) computed value; and (v) residual valuation (flexible and reasonable method) .[90] At the request of the importer, computer and residual methods may be applied reversely.[91] According to the authorities, most goods were assessed under the transaction value in 2013.

Customs value must be determined within 30 days of the date of the customs declaration. If the value is objected by the importer, goods may be released from Customs' control provided the importer deposits a guarantee equivalent to the amount of the duty due. Importers have also the right to appeal on the value determined by RCED.[92]

RULES OF ORIGIN

Brunei has notified the WTO that it does not have non-preferential rules of origin.

Brunei applies preferential rules of origin under its eight RTAs in force (section 2.3.2), i.e. Association of Southeast Asian Nations (ASEAN-ATIGA)[94]; ASEAN-Australia-New Zealand; ASEAN-China; ASEAN-India; ASEAN-Japan; ASEAN-Korea; Trans-Pacific Strategic Economic Partnership[95]; and Brunei-Japan.[96] In general, the basic rule is a product wholly obtained or that has undergone substantial transformation in the country of export. Substantial transformation is defined as a change in tariff classification, value-added threshold, and specific process, which vary across agreements. The revision of the ASEAN rules of origin has introduced, so far, other origin criteria as an alternative to the long-standing regional value content of at least 40%.[97]

Co-equal and dual rules of origin are used across ASEAN agreements to determine if goods not wholly obtained or produced in the exporting party qualify for tariff preferences (Table 3.1) . When co-equal rule applies, tolerance in change in tariff classification (CTC) may allow final products to contain a percentage of non-originating inputs that have not undergone a change in tariff classification. In addition, cumulation of regional value content is permitted under ASEAN agreements. ATIGA allows also inputs that have at least 20% but less than 40% regional value content to qualify for partial cumulation; these inputs are, however, not eligible for tariff preferences.[98] Product-specific rules have also been established with the exception of the agreement ASEAN-India for which they are being negotiated. Brunei has appointed certified exporters to participate in the test for the ASEAN Self-Certification System which is aimed at replacing ATIGA certificate of origin in paper form; the System is being tested until 31 December 2015.

TARIFFS AND EXCISE DUTIES

MFN applied tariff

3.17.   Brunei applies relatively very low tariffs. Goods imported into Brunei may be subject to import and excise duties. There is no VAT.

3.18.   With the adoption of the 2012 ASEAN Harmonized Tariff Nomenclature (the AHTN Protocol)[100], Brunei's tariff was simplified and now comprises 9,916 lines at the national tariff line HS ten-digit level, compared with 10,689 in 2007 (Table 3.2). Specific tariff lines have been reduced from 131 in 2007 to 55 in 2014 which enhances transparency.[101]

Brunei does not maintain any tariff quotas, and there are no seasonal tariffs. Overall, 94.6% of tariff lines are within the range >0-5%. The share of duty-free imports increased from 68.1% in 2007 to 76.9% in 2014

The simple average applied MFN rate is 1.7% (down from 4.8% in 2007). The reduction is mainly due to changes in tariff nomenclature. Tariffs are zero on agriculture (WTO definition[102]), and 2% on non-agricultural products (5.4% in 2007). Tariff rates range from zero to 30%, with chemicals and products thereof subject to the highest tariff protection (Table 3.3). By HS section, the highest tariff rates are on footwear and headgear, followed by machinery, and wood and products thereof (Chart 3.2).

Brunei does not participate in the Information Technology Agreement (ITA).

BOUND TARIFF

The coverage of Brunei's bound tariff lines went from 92.8% in 2007 to 89.1% in 2014 also because of the changes made in HS nomenclature. There remains a significant difference between the overall bound average of 25.4% and Brunei's applied MFN tariff of 1.7% (Table 3.2 and Chart 3.2). The difference is even larger in agriculture where the bound average tariff is 23.1% compared with an MFN average of zero.

Greater coverage of bindings could increase tariff predictability. According to the authorities, applied rates have not been raised during the review period and the gap also provides some flexibility to policymakers. Regarding agricultural products, the authorities maintain that the difference is necessary to address food security concerns and that it would consult with, and notify, all affected parties in advance, should tariffs be raised.

Preferential tariff

Brunei has preferential trading agreements with 16 partners: the other nine parties of ASEAN[103]; seven countries that have negotiated agreements with ASEAN (Australia and New Zealand; China; Japan[104]; Republic of Korea, and India); as well as Chile in the context of the TPSEP.[105] Brunei is committed to achieving free trade by specific dates under some of these RTAs (Table A2.2).

In 2014, the average preferential tariff (on all products) under Brunei's RTAs ranged from zero (ASEAN Trade in Goods Agreement and Brunei-Japan Economic Partnership Agreement) to 1.4% (ASEAN India Free Trade Agreement). Simple average tariff rates under those RTAs are lower than the simple average applied MFN rates of 1.7% (Table 3.4). Tariffs, both MFN and preferential, are zero on agriculture (WTO definition).

EXCISE DUTIES

3.26.   Brunei's legislation on excise taxes is contained in the Excise Order 2006, which allows the Minister of Finance to impose and revoke excise taxes on any goods deemed appropriate. Until 31 December 2007, excise duties were levied only on *Samsu* liquor (included medicated *Samsu* liquor) . Since 1 January 2008, excise duties are levied on liquors (Chapter 22); tobacco (Chapter 24); vehicles (Chapter 87); and, effective from 1 April 2012, excise duties are also applied on nuclear reactors, boilers, machinery, and mechanical appliances (Chapter 84), and medical or surgical instruments (Chapter 90) .[106] The authorities informed that these new excise duties are levied for fiscal, social, health, and environmental considerations.[107] The authorities also indicated that all goods subject to excise duty were not manufactured in Brunei. Import duties on products subject to excise duties have been eliminated.

According to the authorities, 10.3% of total tariff lines (1,021 tariff lines at HS ten-digit level) were subject to excise duties in 2014, of which: 633 lines relate to vehicles; 276 to nuclear reactors, boilers, machinery, and mechanical appliances; 42 to liquors; 39 to medical or surgical instruments; and 31 to tobacco. Over the 2008-13 period, excise revenue from imports amounted to B$883 million.

Excise rates are set as a percentage of the value of the goods with the exception of liquors and tobacco (Table 3.5) . In 2012, changes were introduced to the rate applied to passengers' vehicles in an effort to encourage the use of energy-efficient and environmentally-friendly vehicles. Originally set at 20%, the rate is now based on the engine capacity and is divided in five tiers ranging from 15% for vehicles with engine capacity not exceeding 1,700 cc to 35% for those with engine capacity exceeding 3,500 cc. Diesel vehicles are also charged an additional 5% on the applied excise rate and hybrid vehicles (petrol or diesel) are granted a 5% reduction. The rate for vehicles used for public transport was reduced from 20% to 15%, while that for other vehicles remains unchanged (20%) . The rate is set at 5% for nuclear reactors, boilers, machinery, and mechanical appliances, and medical or surgical instruments.

Specific excise duties, 2014(B$)

Goods	Excise duty
Liquors and vinegar (per 10 litres or decalitres)	
Beer made from malt	30
Sparkling wine	120
Wine and grape must	
Alcohol content < 15%	55
Alcohol content > 15%	90
Vermouth and other wine of fresh grapes flavoured with plants or aromatic substances	
Alcohol content < 15%	55
Alcohol content > 15%	90
Other fermented beverages	
Cider, shandy, other rice wine	30
Sake, toddy	90
Undernatured ethyl alcohol of ≥ 80% alcohol content	250
Spirits, liqueurs, and other spirituous beverages	
Spirits and liqueurs	250
Samsu (including medicated Samsu), arrack, and pineapple spirit	
Alcohol content < 40%	90

Alcohol content > 40%	120
Bitters and similar beverages	250
Other	120
Tobacco and manufactured tobacco substitutes (per kg.)	
Unmanufactured tobacco	60
Cigars	200
Cigarettes	
Beedies	120
Clove cigarettes (per stick)	0.25
Other manufactured tobacco	120

IMPORT PROHIBITIONS, RESTRICTIONS, AND LICENSING

IMPORT PROHIBITIONS

Import prohibitions are mainly in place for security, health, protection of wild life, and moral reasons (Table 3.6) . During the review period, Brunei incorporated the following products to the list of prohibited imports: cigarettes without health warning written on their packages; fabric of tissue bearing the imprint of any currency or bank notes or coin; salk polio vaccine; and shark products (section 4.1.2) . Only vaccines for human medicine manufactured in countries with good manufacturing practices and authorized by the Ministry of Health, may be imported.[108] The Customs Order 2006 (Section 31) allows the Minister of Finance to prohibit imports or exports.

3.30.   Although sale of alcohol is prohibited in Brunei, permission is granted to non-Muslims who may import 12 cans of beer and 2 litres of liquors duty free for personal consumption. Imports must be declared to Customs on arrival and a 48-hour gap is required between imports.[109] The authorities indicated that import prohibited goods are not manufactured in Brunei.[110]

Prohibited imports, 2014

Product	Reason for prohibition
1. Dangerous drugs (e.g. opium, heroin, morphine)	Health and moral
2. Java sparrows	CITES
3. Live animals from countries with Foot and Mouth Disease (FMD)	Health
4. Fire crackers (known as double bangers)	Safety and security
5. Salk polio vaccine	Health
6. Vaccines of Chinese Taipei origin	Health and security
7. Arms and ammunition	Security
8. Fabric of tissue bearing the imprint of any currency or bank notes/coins	Security
9. Cigarettes without health warning written on packaging	Health
10. Shark products	Food security and environment

Source: Information provided by the authorities.

3.1.5.2   Import restrictions and licensing

For additional analytical, business and investment opportunities information,
please contact Global Investment & Business Center, USA
at (703) 370-8082. Fax: (703) 370-8083. E-mail: ibpusa3@gmail.com
Global Business and Investment Info Databank - www.ibpus.com

3Brunei maintains various import restrictions mainly for health, sanitary and phytosanitary, and moral reasons, and in some cases to ensure adequate supply and stable prices (Table 3.7) . Since the last review in 2008, Brunei added separated skimmed or filled milk to the list.

Importers must refer to the relevant governmental agency to obtain an import permit prior to apply for an approval permit (AP) with RCED. Only importers registered with RCED and domiciled in Brunei may apply for APs. RCED requires 3 to 10 working days to process APs; no fees are charged. RCED is responsible for informing the Customs office where goods with APs are to be released. Applications must also be accompanied with the packing list and any relevant documents, e.g. veterinary health certificate (if required) . Import licences are then issued for six months (with possible extension) and may not be transferred to another importer.[111]

Restricted imports, 2014

Product	Reason for restriction	Authorizing agency
Eggs for hatching purposes and fresh eggs unless clearly stamped in non-erasable ink or similar substance with the word "IMPORTED" on the shell of each egg	Health. To prevent introduction of zoonotic poultry diseases (e.g. Avian Influenza)	Department of Agriculture and Agrifood (DOAA)
Any living plant or planting material, plant products and soil	To prevent the introduction of exotic plant pest and diseases	DOAA
Live animals (e.g. cattle, sheep, goats, poultry, and birds)	To prevent the introduction of animal diseases	DOAA
Pin tables, fruit machines, slot machines and any other machines of like nature whether involving an element of chance or not	To prevent illegal gambling activities	Ministry of Home Affairs
Poisons and deleterious drugs	Health	Narcotics Control Bureau
Rice paddy and the products thereof, and separated, skimmed or whole milk	Security of supply and price stability	Supply and State Stores Department (SSSD)
Separated skimmed of filled milk	Food safety and health	Ministry of Health
Persian glue	Health	Ministry of Health
Poh Ka, Poh Kah or Poh Kau; Koyoh or Koyok; Liow Ko, Ch'ow Ko	To prevent illegal gambling activities	Ministry of Home Affairs
Sugar, salt	Security of supply and price stability	SSSD
Converted timber	Security of supply and price stability	Forestry Department
Used and reconditioned vehicles (5 years or older) including motorcars, motorcycles, lorries, omnibuses, tractors and trailers	Safety	RCED, Land Transport Department
Any radio-active materials	Safety	Ministry of Health
Rhinoceros horn and all other parts of or products derived from the carcass of a rhinoceros	CITES	DOAA

Beef, including the carcass of the animal or any part thereof, the meat (whether frozen, chilled or fresh), bones, hide, skin, hooves, horns, offal or any other part of the animal or any portion thereof, unless it has been slaughtered in an abattoir approved in writing by the Minister of Religious Affairs	Religious and health	Ministry of Religious Affairs; DOAA
Turtle eggs	CITES	DOAA
Broadcasting equipment	Security	Authority for Info-Communication Technology Industry (AITI)
Cigarettes unless with Ministry of Health approved health warning written on the packages	Health	Ministry of Health
Poultry, including the carcass of the bird or any part thereof, the meat (whether frozen, chilled or fresh), bones, skin, offal or any other part of the animal or any portion thereof, unless it has been slaughtered in an approved abattoir	Religious and health	Ministry of Religious Affairs; DOAA
Alcoholic beverages	Religious	RCED
Cough mixture containing codeine	Health	RCED
Pens and other articles resembling syringes	Safety and security	RCED

Source: Information provided by the authorities.

In addition to prohibited and restricted imports, Brunei also has some controlled goods which require a special permit from relevant agencies to be imported (with prior approval from RCED) (Table 3.8) .

Licensed imports

Product	Reason for licence	Authorizing agency
Publication materials, prints, films, CDs, DVDs, etc.	Security and moral	Royal Brunei Police Force
Recital of Al-Quran, Hadith, religious books	Religion and moral	Islamic Dakwah Center
Talisman goods (e.g. clothing with dubious photos)	Moral	Internal Security Department
Halal meat and meat products (fresh, cold, frozen)	Religion	Halal Import Permit Issuing Board
Firearms, explosives, dangerous weapons	Safety	Royal Brunei Police Force
Scrap metal	Safety	Royal Brunei Police Force
Plants, crops, live animals, vegetables, fruits, eggs	Safety	Department of Agriculture
Fish, prawns, shells, water organisms, fishing equipment, etc.	Safety	Fisheries Department

Chemical, poison and radioactive materials	Safety	Ministry of Health
Medicines, herbal, health foods, soft drinks, snacks	Safety	Ministry of Health
Radio transmitter and receiver and communications equipment, and broadcasting equipment	Security	Authority for Info-Communication Technology Industry (AITI)
Used vehicles, e.g. cars, motorcycles, mini buses, trucks, trailers, bicycles	Safety	RCED, Land Transport Department
Timber and products thereof	Primary resources	Forestry Department
Badges, banners, souvenirs of government flags and emblems, royal regalia, government flags and crests	Security	Adat Istiadat Department
Antiques made or found in Brunei	Historical	Museums Department
Mineral water	Safety	Ministry of Industry and Primary Resources
Building construction material, e.g. cement	Safety	Ministry of Industry and Primary Resources
Rice, sugar and salt	Security of supply and price stability	Supply and State Stores Department (SSSD)

CONTINGENCY TRADE MEASURES

Brunei does not have legislation or regulations on antidumping, subsidies and countervailing, and on safeguard measures. No anti-dumping, countervailing or safeguard measures have been taken during the review period or are currently in force.

Standards and other technical requirements

In 2010, the National Standards Council (NSC), under the Ministry of Industry and Primary Resources (MIPR), was established as the body responsible to monitor and strengthen standards and conformance activities in Brunei.[112] It also provides policy direction with the aim of creating industries that are able to stimulate sustainable economic growth, and promotes awareness on consumer safety issues. Up to September 2014, the following five Standards Committees had been formed: Construction, Halal, Food, Management Systems, and Electrical. Other three Standards Committees are envisaged for Energy, Pharmacy and Medicines, and Tourism and Handicraft. As of 1 January 2014, the National Standards Centre, also under the MIPR, is in charge of developing quality infrastructure in Brunei. Previously, this was the responsibility of the Authority for Building Control and Construction Industry (ABCi) Division in the Ministry of Development.

Brunei is still to notify its WTO enquiry point. So far, it has made three notifications to the WTO Committee on Technical Barriers to Trade, one during the review period (Table 2.1) .

In Brunei all standards are voluntary. National standards, which are prepared by technical committees, are submitted for approval to the Standards Committees, which are chaired by the relevant Minister. Technical committees currently exist for the construction sector and for food-related standards. Technical Committees adopt international standards where relevant, and the alignment of national standards with existing relevant international standards is reviewed in line with the ISO/IEC Guide 25. Following examination by the Standards Committees, a standard is sent to the Standards Secretariat at the National Standards Centre for public comment (usually for six weeks); any comments are forwarded to the Technical Committees. For transparency, the Ministry of Development publishes a directory of certified products, companies, and accredited laboratories.[113]

Currently, there are no mandatory standards (technical regulations) in Brunei. It has 83 national standards, mainly on construction and electrical-related products; 53 have been directly adopted from international standards. They cover use of the metric system in construction, quality management, steel reinforcement, cement, concrete, timber, and roads. Standards for electrical and electronic goods, gas appliances, and fire equipment are voluntary and based on ISO or IEC standards (for electrical/electronic products), where international equivalents exist. Both under ASEAN and APEC, Brunei participates on the harmonization of standards with international standards in areas such as: electrical and electronic, rubber-based products, medical devices, wood products, automotive, and cosmetics.

Since April 2010, the Accreditation Division, under the National Standards Centre, has been the national accreditation service provider. Currently, there are eight conformity assessment bodies registered under NSC. The Accreditation Division offers three accreditation schemes: Management System Accreditation Scheme, Laboratory Accreditation Scheme, and Inspection Bodies Accreditation Scheme.

Since 1 July 2012, the Measurement Standards Division, under the National Standards Centre, has been the custodian of measurement standards in Brunei on the basis of the International System of Units (SI) . Measurement and metrology facilities in Singapore (PSB) and Malaysia (SIRIM) are used frequently by Brunei's laboratories in calibration activities. Currently, laboratory accreditation for the construction sector is covered by the Ministry of Development Laboratory Accreditation Scheme; all other sectors are covered by the Brunei-Singapore SAC MoU on accreditation.

Brunei is a member of several international and regional standard-setting fora, including the ISO, Pacific Area Standards Congress, Codex Alimentarius, ASEAN Consultative Committee on Standards and Quality[114], Pacific Accreditation Cooperation, APEC Sub-Committee on Standards and Conformance, and Asia-Pacific Laboratory Accreditation Cooperation scheme. Brunei participates in the IEC Affiliate Member programme, participates in the APEC E/E MRA, and signed the TEL MRA with Singapore in telecommunications; the scope of these MRAs concerns acceptance of test and certification. To reduce business compliance costs, Brunei unilaterally accepts certificates of conformity from such recognized bodies, and therefore does not require re-certification or testing. Under ASEAN, MRAs for recognition and acceptance of conformity assessment results have been developed and implemented for electrical, electronic equipment, and medicinal products/pharmaceuticals.[115]

SANITARY AND PHYTOSANITARY REQUIREMENTS

Brunei's national notification authority for SPS measures is the Department for Trade Development in the Ministry of Foreign Affairs and Trade.[116] Three institutions, under MIPR, deal with SPS measures: the Department of Agriculture and Agrifood (DOAA) for plants and plant products, live animals, and eggs and other fresh animal (non-halal) products; the Department of Fisheries for fish and fisheries products; and the Department of Forestry for forestry products. In addition, the Ministry of Religious Affairs is responsible for halal products.

Since 2008, Brunei has made only one SPS notification of emergency measures, regarding the temporarily ban of imports of fresh agricultural and fish products (and processed foods) from certain regions of Japan due to possible radioactive contaminants.[117] Brunei also prohibits the importation of live animals from countries with FMD (Table 3.6) .

Restricted/licensed live animals, animal products, fruits, vegetables, plants and plant products are listed in Tables 3.6 and 3.7, respectively.

Brunei is member of the Codex Alimentarius Commission and the World Organization for Animal Health (OIE) .[118] Brunei is not yet a member of the International Plant Convention (IPPC) but, according to the authorities, it complies with the IPPC.

Phytosanitary regulations are implemented by the DOAA Plant Quarantine Unit, under the Agricultural Pests and Noxious Plants Act, revised in 1984. Under the Act, imports of all plants and plant materials require import permits, issued by the DOAA, and phytosanitary certificates, issued by the legal issuing authority in the country of origin, certifying the phytosanitary status of the plants.[119] Imports of a number of plants and materials from specific regions or countries may be prohibited to prevent entry of dangerous pests and diseases. All plant imports are subject to inspection by the DOAA on arrival in Brunei. Imports of soil (including attached to plant roots), are prohibited. Phytosanitary certificates for exports of agricultural materials may be obtained from the DOAA.

The Quarantine and Prevention of Disease (Animals) Regulations allow for the prohibition of import, detention of animals for treatment and examination, and for the investigation of imported products. Imports and exports of animals or their products must be declared at the port of entry or exit for quarantine inspection; and must be accompanied by an import permit, issued by the DOAA, and a veterinary health certificate, issued by a veterinarian authorized in the country concerned within seven days before departure. Exports of live animals and poultry must be accompanied by a veterinary health certificate. When a certificate is required for exports of products derived from animals, an Animal Health Certificate may be obtained from the relevant veterinary office.[120]

Imports of beef and poultry are subject to import restrictions under the Second Schedule of the Customs (Prohibition and Restriction on Imports and Exports) Order, unless they have been slaughtered in a foreign abattoir approved in writing by the Minister of Religious Affairs. The Government maintains a list of approved abattoirs from which meat or poultry may be imported by holders of halal import permits issued under the Halal Meat Act (Chapter 183) and the Halal Certificate and Halal Label Order 2005. Under the Halal Meat Act, the Board for Issuing Halal Import Permits grants the permit if the slaughterhouse is already on a list approved by the Brunei Islamic Religious Council (Majlis Ugama Islam)[121]; for slaughterhouses not on the list, an inspection committee, including representatives from the Ministry of Religious Affairs, the Majlis, and the DOAA is required to inspect and approve the abattoir. The Board forwards the application to the Majlis who makes the final decision on issuing the import permit.[122] Authorized officers from the DOAA examine all imports of halal meat and certify it fit for human consumption. Currently, halal meat and poultry may be imported only from Australia, China, India, Indonesia, Jordan, Malaysia, and the Philippines. Brunei imports live cattle from Australia and Malaysia (Sabah and Sarawak) for slaughter at local abattoirs.

Other sanitary and health restrictions are maintained under the Poisons Act and the Misuse of Drugs Regulations, which are enforced by the Pharmaceutical Enforcement Services, in the Ministry of Health. This includes regulation of all imports and exports of pharmaceuticals, chemicals, agri-chemicals, pesticides, etc. in collaboration with Customs. Regular inspections are also conducted on pharmaceutical wholesalers, clinics, and retailers in Brunei. Imported veterinary pharmaceuticals, animal vaccines, and agri-chemicals are controlled and approved by the DOAA, through the Ministry of Health under the Poisons Act. The Drug Quality Control Service also inspects all drugs, both locally produced and imported, to ensure quality.

The Department of Health Services under the Ministry of Health ensures food imported and distributed in Brunei is safe. Food importers are required to comply with the Public Health Order

(Food) 1998, Public Health (Food) (Amendment) Order 2002 and its Regulations 2000, which protect consumers from dangerous adulterated or poor quality foods. Food importers are required to submit the customs declaration form together with relevant documents (including health certificates) to the Food safety and Quality Control Division, Department of Health Services, for endorsement.

LABELLING AND MARKING

Brunei's legislation on food labelling requirements is contained in the Public Health (Food) Order, 1998. Labels for food products must contain the following information either in Malay or English: name of food, list of ingredients, net/drained content, name and address of manufacturer, packer, wholesaler, importer and distributor, the country of origin, lot identification, date and storage instructions, and instructions and date for use. Where a suitable common name for the food product is not available, a description to indicate the nature of the food is required. All imports of meat and products containing meat must conform to labelling requirements approved by the Board for Issuing Halal Import Permits.[123] For food with animal or alcohol content, the origin of the animal or alcohol product must also be indicated. In addition, the contents of all meat products should be clearly mentioned on the label.

Since 1 January 2002, 25 categories of food and beverage products require date marking and must be registered with the Food Safety and Quality Control Division before importation into Brunei. The products include cream, milk and milk products, pasteurised fruit and vegetable juice, soya bean curd, chilled food, sauces, peanut butter, flour and flour products, egg products, raisins and sultanas, chocolate, edible fats and oils, food additives, margarine, meat products, and nutrient supplements.

Labelling requirements on imported tobacco are set out in the Tobacco (Labelling) Regulations, 2007 and the Tobacco Order, 2005 (S/49/05) . Labels must include a printed health warning in English on one surface and in Malay on the other surface, and conform to the specifications set out in the specific schedules in the Tobacco (Labelling) Regulations, 2007.

3.54.   No genetically-modified labelling requirements are currently in force in Brunei.

MEASURES DIRECTLY AFFECTING EXPORTS

EXPORT PROCEDURES AND REQUIREMENTS

Exporters must be registered with the Royal Customs and Excise Department (RCED) and must appoint a forwarding agent who should also be registered with the RCED. All exports from Brunei shall be declared through electronic submission via e-Customs system. Invoices and other related documents shall be presented during customs clearance. However, for restricted and/or controlled items, supporting documents, such as export permit(s) from relevant government agencies may be required.

During the review period, two IT applications were implemented to make export procedures paperless: (i) the Brunei's e-Customs[124] in 2008; and (ii) the Brunei Darussalam National Single Window (BDNSW) to process several trade-related requests, including certificates of origin. At the regional level, Brunei has appointed ten certified exporters to participate in the pilot project for the ATIGA Self-Certification System.[125] The System allows certified exporters to self-certify that export products comply with ASEAN rules of origin. The declaration of origin is made on the invoice or any commercial document. The test period ends on 31 December 2015.[126]

According to the latest estimates from the World Bank, export procedures in Brunei take 19 days and cost US$705 per container (27 days and US$515 per container in 2008) .[127] There are no customs fees for export procedures or registration; goods in transit via Brunei have fees ranging from B$10 to B$100 depending on their type or nature.

EXPORT TAXES, CHARGES, AND LEVIES

3.58.   Brunei does not have export taxes, charges, levies or minimum export prices.

Export prohibitions, restrictions, and licensing

The Customs Order 2006 (Section 31) allows the Minister of Finance to prohibit imports or exports. Brunei prohibits exports of prawn refuse and copra cake, stone and gravel, and round timber of logs and sawn timber.

Brunei maintains export restrictions on certain goods, such as sugar, rice, paddy and products thereof, to ensure adequate domestic supply and price stability. Before restricted goods may be exported, an export permit from the relevant authorizing agency and Customs' approval are required (Table 3.9) .[128]

Restricted exports, 2014

Goods	Reason	Authorizing agency
Articles of antique or historical nature made or discovered in Brunei	Cultural heritage	Department of Museums
Cigarettes	Health	Ministry of Health
Automotive gas oil (diesel)	Supply and price stability	Energy Department
Gasoline (premium and regular)	Supply and price stability	Energy Department
Kerosene	Supply and price stability	Energy Department
Rice, paddy, and products thereof	Supply and price stability	Supply and State Stores Department (SSSD)[a]
Sugar	Supply and price stability	SSSD[a]
Highly processed timber	Supply and price stability	Department of Forestry
Elaeis Quineesis (oil palm)	Supply and price stability	SSSD[a]
Derris species (tuba)	Wildlife	Department of Agriculture and Agrifood (DOAA)

Some other products are subject to export licences which may be obtained upon fulfilment of certain conditions (Table 3.10), including local content and packaging and labelling requirements.

Licensed exports

Goods	Authorizing agency
Badges, banners, and souvenirs	Department of Adat Istiadat
Eggs, crops, fruits, live animals, plants, vegetables	Department of Agriculture and Agrifood (DOAA)
Fishes, prawns, shells, water organisms, and fishing equipment	Department of Fisheries
Halal meat and meat products (fresh, cold, and frozen)	Halal Import Permit Issuing Board
Radio transmitter and receiver, communications equipment	Info-Communication Technology Industry

Salt	Supply and State Stores Department (SSSD)
Vehicles	Land Transport Department
Poison, chemicals, and radioactive materials	Ministry of Health
Broadcasting equipment	Authority of Info-Communication Technology Industry (AITI)
Firearms, explosives, fire crackers, dangerous weapons, publication materials, prints, films, CDs, scrap metal	Royal Brunei Police Force

EXPORT SUPPORT

Duty drawback

There was no change to the duty drawback system during the review period.[129] Duty drawback may be claimed on goods that are re-exported without transformation within 12 months of import duty payment. In addition, re-export consignments must bear a minimum value of B$500. Drawback is set at nine tenth of the import duties paid. Exporter manufacturers are also entitled to claim duty drawback on inputs imported by them and used in the manufacture of export goods providing production takes place in premises approved by Customs and inputs are re-exported within 12 months of import duty payment. Drawback is permitted for re-exportation of imported goods not used or sold in Brunei. According to the authorities, the amount of duty drawback is negligible.

Tax exemption

Exporters may claim income tax exemption under Part VII of the Investment Incentives Order 2001 (S 48/01)[130] (section 2.4.1.1 and Table 2.2) . Claims are made to the Ministry of Primary Resources and Industry (MIPR) . Eligible exporters are those that manufacture and export agricultural, forestry, fishery, and manufacturing goods. The grant of income tax exemption is subject to the exporter manufacturers giving evidence of: (a) incurred fixed capital expenditure of at least B$500,000[131] ; or (b) export sales of at least 20% of total sales and not less than B$20,000 in the first year of assessment and not less than B$20,000 in subsequent years.[132] Income tax exemption is granted for up to 15 years. According to the authorities, there is no data on revenue forgone from tax incentives granted to exporters. Also, exporter manufacturers are allowed to duty-free imports of capital goods and raw materials providing these are not on sale in Brunei.[133]

Enterprises engaged in overseas services projects and international trading companies may also claim income tax exemption under the Investment Incentives Order 2011

EXPORT FINANCE, INSURANCE, AND PROMOTION

3.66.   The MIPR launched the Export Refinancing Scheme (ERS) in 2010 in collaboration with the state-owned Bank Islam Brunei Darussalam (BIBD) .[134] ERS is a loan scheme aimed at helping enterprises to internationalize and increase competitiveness. Eligible exporters are direct and indirect exporters exporting "promoted products", i.e. agricultural and fishery products, downstream forestry products, manufacturing, and ICT products.[135] ERS loans are used to finance pre- and post-shipment costs, i.e. raw materials, packing, storage, transport, and delivery expenses. The amount of loans ranges from B$50,000 to B$500,000, at a 4% interest rate. Guarantee is required in the form of letters of credit and purchase orders.[136] No exporters have yet applied to ERS; the authorities are in the process of reviewing procedures and eligibility criteria.

The MIPR is also engaged in export promotion through sponsorship and certification programmes. Costs associated with exporters' participation in overseas trade fairs and exhibitions, are sponsored by MIPR. These cost include registration, booth, advertisement, interpretation service, shipment of material (not exceeding 150 kg per company), and transport or accommodation (whichever is higher and for one person per enterprise) . In addition, to ensure compliance of export goods with standards in overseas markets, MIPR covers the full cost of certification for food and manufactured products providing export goods are manufactured in factories approved by the relevant governmental authorities. To apply to MIPR programmes, export enterprises are required a minimum 30% local equity participation.[137]

3.68.   In 2010, Brunei's first B2B online portal, Buy Brunei[138] , was launched to promote trade and partnerships between local and international traders.[139] Buy Brunei is a BEDB initiative co-financed with AMIR consortium which was awarded web development.[140]

Brunei does not have export insurance schemes.

MEASURES AFFECTING PRODUCTION AND TRADE

TAX INCENTIVES

During the review period, Brunei introduced several changes to the Income Tax Act (Chapter 35) with the view to reducing tax liabilities of enterprises, with the exception of those engaged in petroleum activities (see below) .

3.71.   The income tax rate was reduced gradually from 27.5% in 2008 to 20% in 2014, and will be further reduce to 18.5% as from 2015. Also, tax thresholds were introduced in 2008 to further reduce corporate tax burden. These thresholds were subsequently modified over the 2008-14 period.[141] As from 2014, the corporate income tax has three rates: 5% for incomes up to B$100,000; 10% for incomes above B$100,000 and up to B$250,000; and 20% for incomes above B$250,000. Companies newly incorporated are exempt from income tax for revenue up to B$100,000 during the first three years of assessment.[142]

Tax credits may be claimed for investment in capital goods and human resources (new staff, training, pension plan) . However, they must not exceed 50% of total taxes payable by the enterprise. For expenditure in new machineries and plants incurred between 2012 and 2017, a tax credit of up to 15% of the expenditure may be claimed. This tax credit may be carried forward for a maximum of two years.[143]

In addition, initial and annual allowances for expenditure in industrial buildings were doubled as well as initial allowance for expenditure in machineries and plants.[144] Annual allowance for expenditure in machineries and plants continue to be calculated at a rate comprised between 3% and 25% on the reducing value of assets. However, effective 2009, enterprises may opt for a 33.33% annual allowance for a period of three years. In addition, 100% capital allowance may be claimed for expenditure incurred in machineries and plants not exceeding B$2,000[145] and computers and other office automation equipment.[146] Enterprises are authorized to carry forward capital allowances so long as they carry on the same industrial park.[147]

Further deductions were also introduced on contribution to staff pension plan, and salaries paid to staff on maternity leave.

In addition, a 1% tax on income raised from approved exports was introduced in 2012. Industries and products declared as approved for export are pursuant to section 8A of the Income Tax

(Amendments) Order 2012.[150] Export enterprises may opt to pay the tax on exports in lieu of the standard income tax rate.[151] According to the authorities, so far no enterprise has opted to pay the tax on exports in lieu of the income tax rate.

Business losses may be set off and unabsorbed losses carried forward for a maximum period of six years.[152]

Changes to the Income Tax Act (Chapter 35) do not apply to companies engaged in petroleum activities which are governed by the Income Tax (Petroleum) Act (Chapter 119).[153] Since 2008, there has been no change to the tax regime applied to companies engaged in petroleum activities.

Enterprises manufacturing pioneer products and investing into new assets to increase production volume, may be exempt from income tax under the Investment Incentives Order 2001 (S 48/01) (section 2.4.1.1 and Table 2.2).

Tax credits may be granted under Brunei's double taxation agreements (section 2.4.1).[154] The Income Tax Act (Chapter 35) provides also for avoidance of reciprocal tax relief on income arising from Commonwealth partners; provision ceases if a double taxation treaty is in force.[155]

OTHER FINANCIAL SUPPORT

3.80.   In 1996, Brunei notified the WTO that it did not maintain any subsidy programme.[156]

In 2010, the Department of Agriculture and Agrifood (DOAA) launched the Agriculture and Agrifood Incentive Scheme (SIPA), a subsidy scheme aimed at enhancing productivity and output in the agriculture and agri-food sectors (section 4.1.1.2).[157]

Some varieties of rice[158] and refined white sugar, which are imported and distributed by the State (section 3.3.3), continue to be subsidized to keep affordable retail prices and protect consumers from increases in world commodity prices (section 4.1 and Table 4.3). In addition, price support for subsidized rice and sugar applies also in the form of price monitoring (section 3.3.2.3).

3.83.   Prices of housing, petroleum products (section 4.2.1), utilities (section 4.2.2), as well as education, healthcare, and telecom services (section 4.4.3) continue to be subsidized in Brunei. In 2010, unpaid consumers' bills amounted to B$486 million: B$163 million for electricity, B$67 million for water, B$66 million for telecom, and B$20 million for housing.

Brunei is taking measures to reduce subsidies and increase financial prudence, including through the introduction of a progressive electricity tariff structure in 2012 (section 4.2.2).[159]

Support to SMEs

In 2012, 98% of the businesses established in Brunei were micro, small, and medium sized enterprises (MSMEs)[160] which employed about 92% of total workforce in the private sector. In 2010, MSMEs were concentrated in wholesale and retail trade, construction, mining and quarrying, and manufacturing. Participation of MSMEs in oil and LNG production and sawmilling and timber processing, was limited. MSMEs contribution to GDP amounted to 22% in 2008.[161]

Financial assistance for MSMEs is provided by the Brunei Economic Development Board (BEDB) and the Ministry of Industry and Primary Resources (MIPR). Five grant and loan schemes have been developed to help MSMEs grow, consolidate, and internationalize (Table 3.11) . Under MIPR schemes, 909 applications have been received from 1999 until July 2014; total financial assistance amounted to B$177.49 million (Table 3.11) . Under the 10th National Development Plan 2012-17, B$100 million have been allocated to MSMEs support.[162]

During the review period, BEDB set up three main grant schemes for micro entrepreneurs (Table 3.11): (i) the Village Enterprise Grant Scheme was developed to promote sales of village products in support of the "One Village, One Product" initiative launched by the Ministry of Home Affairs; (ii) the Youth Entrepreneurship Development Programme which has helped 118 micro entrepreneurs start their business[163]; and (iii) the Enterprise Technical Assistance Scheme (ETAS) that covers cost relating to enhancing competitiveness such as improving corporate governance, hiring professional and to overcome common market entry barriers. The BEDB also introduced the Promising Local Enterprise Development Scheme (PLEDS) and the PLEDS Investment Fund to assist local enterprises to expand. Investment per local enterprise is up to B$5 million.

In 2008, the MIPR Micro-Credit Financing Scheme (MFS) and Enterprise Facilitation Scheme (EFS) were significantly revised. The amount of loans was increased to B$50,000 (up from B$30,000) for MFS loans and to B$5 million (up from B$1.5 million) for EFS loans (Table 3.11) . Loan tenures and grace periods were also extended.[164] Both schemes are financed by the Government through the SME Development Fund as of 11 April 2012. The Fund is administered by MIPR; disbursements are jointly managed by Bank Islam Brunei Darussalam (BIBD) and Baiduri Bank Berhad (BBB) .[165]

Most MFS clients are involved in: contract/tender (24%); food services and restaurants (20%); boutique and tailoring (12%); and retail trade (10%) . EFS is aimed at assisting SMEs develop export capacity. Loans are primarily given to those operating in agriculture (28%), fishery (26%), manufacturing (29%), tourism (9%), and, effective from 2008, ICT (3%), construction (4%), and services (1%) . There is no minimum local equity participation required to MSMEs under MFS and EFS, with the exception of joint ventures (30%) .[166]

RESEARCH AND DEVELOPMENT

3.90.   Under the 10th National Development Plan 2012-17, Brunei has allocated 1% of GDP (B$200 million) to R&D to help achieve economic diversification.[167] In 2012, the Brunei Research Incentive Scheme (BRISc) was launched by the BEDB to support R&D. Bruneian-owned and foreign companies engaged in energy, environment, health, food security, and ICT, are eligible under the scheme. BRISc is a cost-sharing grant with a maximum allocation of B$5 million per project. BRISc offers three levels of financing: 80% of the cost of the project is financed by BEDB for projects developed by Bruneian-owned enterprises; 70% for projects developed by foreign enterprises in collaboration with IHLs or governmental agencies; and 50% for projects developed by foreign enterprises. Projects must not exceed three years.[168].

The Income Tax Act (Chapter 35) allows enterprises to deduct R&D costs against taxable income.[169] In addition, tax incentives are granted to enterprises investing in new technology under the Investment Incentives Order 2001 (S 48/01) (section 2.4.1.1 and Table 2.2) .

Supporting Start-Ups and Innovation

During the review period, Brunei created three grant schemes to support start-ups and innovation: (i) in 2010, the Authority of Info-Communications Technology Industry (AITI) set up a grant, for up to B$250,000 and 50% locally-owned enterprises, to enhance ICT product development, improvement, certification, and packaging/marketing[170]; (ii) Local Enterprise Application and Product (LEAP) grant covers up to B$150,000 per project of local SMEs and students and staff from institutes of higher

- 64 -

learning (IHLs) for the development of innovative products and applications with commercial and export potential in a broad range of clusters (e.g. ICT, robotics, engineering, nano technology, biotech, agriculture and aquaculture, and green technology)[171]; and (iii) Start-Up Brunei aims to encourage the start-up of innovative businesses and to attract world-class, high potential start-ups to set up in Brunei. Start-up Brunei is eligible for both local and foreign companies, providing an incentive of up to B$50,000 per company. Foreign companies are also eligible for an additional B$30,000 relocation incentive.[172]

Brunei also has other three schemes to help start-ups and innovation: (i) the Creative Arts Facilities (CRAFT) provides an ecosystem for the development of digital multimedia through provision of shared infrastructure and capacity development programs[173]; (ii) the iCentre is the first ICT incubator aiming to be the centre for nurturing and developing successful entrepreneurs in the industry[174]; and (iii) Entrepreneurship at Campus (E@C), an initiative launched in 2013 by BEDB and Universiti Brunei Darussalam with the support of iCentre E@C, aims to encourage the start-up of innovative businesses amongst students through incubation, mentorship, talks by local and international speakers and other entrepreneurial development activities.

In 2009, BEDB invested B$5 million in Accel-X Pte Ltd., a Singapore-based venture capital fund that helps early stage and innovative technology companies in ICT, interactive digital media, and engineering by providing access to financial support, extensive overseas networks, and mentorships. The Fund allocates a maximum of B$1.5 million per company; higher allocation is possible subject to approval.[175]Innovative ICT enterprises may also apply to the Future Fund which allocates from B$50,000 to B$150,000 to projects.[176]

CREDIT SUPPORT

According to the authorities, Brunei does not have preferential credit facilities to enterprises.

COMPETITION POLICY, CONSUMER PROTECTION, AND PRICE CONTROLS

Brunei does not yet have comprehensive competition legislation. However, in line with commitments under the ASEAN Economic Community to establish a competitive economic region through strong competition regimes, Brunei has been drafting comprehensive competition legislation since 2011. Consultations have been held with local stakeholders as well as regional and international experts on competition policy and law to ensure that the new piece of legislation takes into account Brunei's economic and legal context and is in line with international best practices.

At present, competition issues are addressed on a sector-by-sector basis and tackled by its respective regulator. Competition regulations exist in telecommunications, financial services, and energy, although in limited forms. For example, in telecoms, licensees' behaviour is regulated by AITI under the Telecommunications Order, and licensees are guided by their licence conditions, including a prohibition against anti-competitive behaviour. AITI is currently working towards establishing a competition code of practice that covers telecommunication and broadcasting (section 4.4.3).[177]

CONSUMER PROTECTION

The Consumer Protection (Fair Trading) Order 2011 (S 64/11) entered into force on 1 January 2012. Prior to 2012, Brunei had no specific legal provisions on consumer protection which was covered in several pieces of legislation.[178]

The Consumer Protection (Fair Trading) Order 2011 (S 64/11) allows consumers to take unfair sales practices to civil courts. The Small Claims Tribunals are competent to hear complaints between

For additional analytical, business and investment opportunities information,
please contact Global Investment & Business Center, USA
at (703) 370-8082. Fax: (703) 370-8083. E-mail: ibpusa3@gmail.com
Global Business and Investment Info Databank - www.ibpus.com

consumers and suppliers arising from transactions not exceeding B$10,000. Since 2012, there have been six consumer complaints that were recommended by the Department of Economic Planning and Development (JPKE) to be brought forward to the Small Claims Tribunals as these complaints could not be resolved by JPKE through consultation and mediation. The decision to bring a case into the Small Claims Tribunal is entirely up to the consumer. In addition, when there are reasonable grounds to believe a supplier has engaged in an unfair practice, the legislation provides for JPKE to invite the supplier enter into a voluntary compliance agreement under which he volunteers to compensate the consumer. In any case, consumers' complaints must be filed with JPKE which will decide if they fall under the law. According to the authorities, JPKE usually recommends an aggrieved consumer to bring the case to the Small Claims Tribunals before going to the High Court.

Under the Consumer Protection (Fair Trading) (Cancellation of Contracts) Regulations 2011 (S 65/11), contracts may be cancelled within five days by consumers.

PRICE CONTROLS

Brunei continues to set retail prices for basic commodities and selected goods to keep affordable prices for consumers. Price controls apply to imports and domestically-produced goods. The Price Controller, under JPKE, is responsible for fixing maximum and minimum retail prices, and may also prohibit or restrict trade in price-controlled goods.[179]

3.102.   The number of goods subject to price control increased substantially during the review period. In the previous Review in 2008, retail prices of cigarettes, infant milk powder, motor vehicles, rice, and sugar were reported to be capped. Currently, there are 19 categories of goods for which maximum retail prices are set (Table 3.12); for example, retail prices for rice ranges from B$0.76/kg to B$1.25/kg, and sugar is sold at B$1.25/kg.[180] In December 2012, Brunei also introduced a minimum retail price for cigarettes.[181] Hoarding of price-controlled goods is prohibited, with the exception of cars.[182] The Price Controller sets prices for all products except for subsidized goods: the price for sugar and rice is set by the Supply and State Stores Department (SSSD), while the price for gasoline is set by the Energy Department.[183] Prices are reviewed when deemed necessary.

Price-controlled goods, 2014

Maximum price

1. Asphalt	11. Gasoline (Premium 97, Super 92 and Regular 85)
2. Automotive gas oil (diesel)	12. Passenger motor vehicles
3. Powdered infant milk	13. Plain flour
4. Bitumen	14. Rice
5. Bottled LPG	15. Ready-mix concrete
6. Bricks (clay and concrete)	16. Reinforcement bar
7. Cement	17. Sand
8. Cooking oil (canola, corn , palm, vegetable, sunflower, and soya bean)	18. Stone (aggregate ¾)
9. Dual purpose kerosene	19. Sugar (white, refined, granulated, cane sugar, fine grain)
10. Milk (condensed and evaporated)	

Minimum price

1. Cigarettes and tobacco	

Source: Price Control (Maximum Prices and Charges) Order 2012 (S 91/12) and Price Control (Minimum Prices and Charges) Order 2012 (S 92/12) .

3.3.3   State trading, state-owned enterprises, and privatization

Brunei has not filed notifications on state trading enterprises with the WTO. According to the authorities, Brunei does not have any state-trading enterprise.

Subsidized rice and sugar are imported and distributed through the Supply and State Stores Department (SSSD), under the Ministry of Finance (MOF), to ensure adequate domestic supply.[184] Rice is mainly imported from Thailand, in particular through the Brusiam Food Alliance Co., a joint-venture between MOF and a Thai rice miller.[185] SSSD does not sell rice and sugar directly to consumers but to registered local vendors. SSSD imports and distributes four varieties of rice (Thai Hom Mali, Vietnamese fragrant, Thai white, and Thai glutinous) and white refined sugar. Local vendors that wish to import other varieties of rice and types of sugar must obtained an import permit from SSSD and an approval permit from Customs (section 3.1.5.2) .[186]

Since Brunei's previous TPR, the public sector has continued to exert a direct influence on the economy, mainly through state-owned enterprises (SOEs) . Most of these still operate under monopoly or hold exclusive rights in many sectors, including oil and gas (section 4.2.1.2), manufacturing (section 4.3), banking (section 4.4.2.2), telecom (section 4.4.3), and air transport (section 4.4.4.1) . In particular, the State participates in the oil and gas sector mainly through Petroleum Brunei and British Shell Petroleum, in various manufacturing industries through Semaun Holdings, and in telecommunications via TelBru and Progresif Cellular Sdn Bhd

Main state-owned enterprises, 2014

Sector	SOE	State share (%)
Air transport	Royal Brunei Airlines	Majority
Banking	Baiduri Bank Bank Islam Brunei Darussalam	Majority Majority
Manufacturing	Semaun Holdings	50
Oil and gas (downstream)	Brunei LNG Brunei Methanol Company	50 25
Oil and gas (marketing)	Brunei Shell Marketing	50
Oil and gas (midstream)	Brunei Gas Carriers Brunei Shell Tankers	80 50
Oil and gas (upstream)	Brunei National Petroleum (Petroleum BRUNEI) Brunei Shell Petroleum	100 50
Technical support services to governmental agencies	Royal Brunei Technical Services	100
Telecom (fixed-line operator)	Telbru	100
Telecom (mobile operator)	Progresif Cellular Sdn Bhd	100
Trade in agricultural products	Brusiam Food Alliance Company	..
Halal food and non-food products	Brunei Halal	100

.. Not available.

In line with its National Vision 2035, Brunei seeks further participation of foreign investors to help achieve economic diversification. It has embarked in a Privatization Master Plan which is in the process to be completed.

GOVERNMENT PROCUREMENT

Brunei is not a party to the WTO Agreement on Government Procurement.

Government procurement is regulated by the 1983 Financial Regulations 327-340; Ministry of Finance (MOF) Circular No. 3/2004 (6 October 2004); MOF Circular No. 2/2009 (25 July 2009); and MOF Circular No. 1/2014 (20 March 2014) . MOF Circular No. 2/2009 was issued to standardize the tender fee charged to suppliers and review of the performance bond/Banker's Guarantee charged to awarded suppliers. MOF Circular No. 1/2014 was an update to the performance bond/Banker's Guarantee rates charged to awarded suppliers.

Procurement procedures seek to maintain equity, integrity, and efficiency in the tendering process and ensure purchases are at the best value for money, including price, quality, delivery timelines, supplier's reliability, and after-sale service. Procurement of goods, services, and works is carried out by ministries and departments.

Procurement methods are determined according to specific thresholds. Purchases of up to B$2,000 may be acquired off the shelf or directly from known suppliers. For procurement above B$2,000 and not exceeding B$50,000, ministries/departments must invite at least three qualified suppliers to submit written quotations. Tenderers/vendors who want to participate in quotation must at least have the same nature of business and/or registered with the relevant agency with the type of quotation being issued.

Procurement of goods, services, and works exceeding B$50,000 is made through open tenders. Tenders comprised between B$50,001 and B$500,000 are considered by the Mini Tender Board (MTB) in each ministry and tenders above B$500,000 by the State Tender Board (STB) in the Ministry of Finance. If no contract is awarded under an open tender, a selective tender may be used upon approval by STB/MTB. Only contractors identified as capable of supplying goods, services or works may participate in the selective tender. Open tenders may also be waived upon STB/MTB approval in case supply of goods, services, and works is urgently needed or call for tenders is not feasible.

Only some tenders require suppliers to register with the relevant ministry/departments. The registration aims to ensure that companies participating in certain areas (e.g. construction, supply of medical products and ICT projects) are qualified in terms of their financial capabilities, employees, manpower and equipment. Although a local partner is not mandatory, foreign enterprises are recommended to form a joint-venture with local partners to improve their chances of being awarded a contract as local partners may better liaise with the authorities and ease the registration process.

Tenders and quotations are announced at least two weeks prior to the closing date. They are published in Malay and/or English in the weekly Government's newspaper *Pelita Brunei*[189], and may also be accessed on most of the governmental websites. Tenders may also be advertised in local and/or international newspapers.

Electronic submission of tender documents is not yet accepted; only hard and soft copies in CD-ROM are allowed. Proposals must be in English and prices in Brunei dollars. Tenders are open, recorded, and forwarded by STB or MTB to ministries/departments for evaluation based on, *inter alia*, budget, technical, financial, and commercial criteria. Recommendations made by the ministries/departments are subsequently considered by STB or MTB and endorsed by the Sultan (in his capacity of Minister of Finance) or the relevant minister. Brunei does not yet have a review body on government procurement, but suppliers' complaints on the decisions taken by STB or MTB may file with the relevant ministries/departments. The evaluation, recommendation, approval, and implementation process must not exceed three months from the closing date of a tender.[190]

When procurement is supplied through a quotation, the relevant ministry/department evaluates the offers and makes recommendation to the Quotation Committee for approval. Quotation Committees are formed at the relevant ministry/department. Suppliers may file complaints on decisions taken by a Quotation Committee with the relevant ministries/departments.

In addition, statutory bodies, i.e. BEDB or AITI, conduct their own procurement procedure. In July 2010, the Centre of Science and Technology Research and Development (Ministry of Defence) was established to administer military procurement.[191]

INTELLECTUAL PROPERTY RIGHTS

The main change to Brunei's IPR regime during the review period was the entry into force of a new patent legislation (section 3.3.5.2) and the restructuration and transfer of industrial property administration from the Attorney General's Chambers (AGC) to the Brunei Economic Development Board (BEDB) . The Patent Registry Office (PRO), created in 2012 under BEDB, took gradually over the registration process from AGC.[192] PRO was converted into the Brunei Intellectual Property Office (BruIPO) on 1 June 2013.[193]

Brunei acceded to the following IPR treaties during the review period (date of accession in parentheses): Paris Convention for the Protection of Industrial Property (17 February 2012); Budapest Treaty on the International Recognition of the Deposit of Microorganisms for the Purposes of Patent Procedure (24 July 2012); and Hague Agreement Concerning the International Registration of Industrial Designs (24 December 2013) . Accession to the Madrid Protocol for the protection of trademarks is foreseen; and accession to the WIPO Copyright Treaty and WIPO Performances and Phonograms Treaty is under consideration.[194] Brunei's increased participation in international IP treaties is pursuant to ASEAN commitments for simplified and harmonized IP protection and registration in the ASEAN Economic Community.[195] In 2009, the ASEAN Patent Examination Cooperation (ASPEC) was established. It allows IP offices of ASEAN member States share search and examination reports.[196]

Patents

The Patents Order 2011 (S 57/11), supported by the Patents Rules 2012 (S 19/12)[197] , entered into force on 1 January 2012. It established a national and independent patent system in Brunei and repealed the Inventions Act (Chapter 72) and the Emergency (Patents) Order 1999 (S 42/99) . Under the Inventions Act (Chapter 72), patent protection was granted through re-registration of patents granted in Malaysia, Singapore, and the United Kingdom (including through the European Patent Office) . Applications had to be filed within three years from the date the original patent was granted. Protection in Brunei was granted as long as the patent remained valid in the country of origin.[198] After the Patents Order 2011 (S 57/11) had entered into force, re-registration was still possible during a transition period.[199]

To claim protection under the Patents Order 2011 (S 57/11), patentable invention must be new[200] , involve an inventive step, and have an industrial applicability. Surgical, therapeutic, and diagnostic methods are excluded from patentability.[201]

For additional analytical, business and investment opportunities information,
please contact Global Investment & Business Center, USA
at (703) 370-8082. Fax: (703) 370-8083. E-mail: ibpusa3@gmail.com
Global Business and Investment Info Databank - www.ibpus.com

The patenting process may take up to 4 years (Chart 3.3) . Foreign applicants are recommended to file applications through an authorized patent agent with a local address in Brunei. Applicants may claim priority for applications filed earlier in signatory countries of the Paris Convention or in WTO Members.[203] Since Brunei's accession to the Patent Cooperation Treaty (PCT), they may also file applications using the PCT route.

Brunei's patent system has three characteristics: (a) a first-to-file system, i.e. the first applicant to file an application has priority over others for the same invention; (b) a formality-based system, i.e. BruIPO does not conduct search and examination; and (c) a self-assessment system, i.e. applicants may request the certificate of grant although the examination report shows the invention does not fully meet the patentability criteria. Request for search and examination are processed by BruIPO and based on the approach chosen by the applicant: (a) "local approach", i.e. BruIPO outsources local search and examination to examiners[204]; (b) "foreign approach", i.e. BruIPO relies on search and examination reports issued by prescribed foreign patent offices[205] for a corresponding application; and (c) "mixed approach", BruIPO relies on search reports issued by prescribed foreign patent offices for a corresponding application and requests the conduct of an examination.[206] BruIPO processed 19 requests for search and examination over 2012-13[207]; 95% was conducted under the mixed approach and 5% was under the local approach.

Upon grant, the term of protection is 20 years from the date of filing (or priority date if claimed) .[208] Patent term may be extended in certain instances, in particular for pharmaceutical products that could not be exploited due to the process of obtaining marketing approval.[209] Protection for re-registration granted during the transition period, is 20 years from the date of filing of the original patent.[210]

To maintain a patent in force, the owner must pay an annual renewal fee from the fifth year of the grant until expiration.[211] Rights over a patent are lost if the patent is not renewed. However, restoration of lapsed patents due to unpaid fees may be possible.[212] Effective 1 January 2012, all re-registration patents are liable to pay the annual renewal fee upon evidence that the foreign patent has not been revoked is provided.[213]

Local applicants intending to file a patent abroad must be authorized by BruIPO.[214]

.   The use of patents may be authorized under non-exclusive compulsory licences in return for payment of a fee to the patent owner.[215] Compulsory licences may be granted by the High Court if a market for the patented invention is not being supplied or is not being supplied in reasonable terms in Brunei.

While there are no specific provisions contained in the Patents Order 2011, according to the authorities parallel imports are allowed.

Brunei has no specific legal provisions to protect undisclosed information. However, provisions exist under the common law. Civil actions may be brought against unauthorized disclosure and unfair commercial use of undisclosed information.[216]

In line with its National Vision 2035, which focuses on R&D and innovation as an engine for economic development and diversification (section 1.3), Brunei is encouraging patent registration by locals. This seems to have discouraged patent registration by foreigners

Trademarks, industrial designs and industrial layouts

There was no change to the legislation on trademarks, industrial designs, and industrial layouts of integrated circuits (layout designs) during the review period (Table 3.15) .

Overview of trademarks, industrial designs, and layout designs

	Trade marks	Industrial designs[a]	Layout designs
	Trade Marks Act (Chapter 98, Revised Edition 2000) Trade Marks Rules 2000 (S 27/00)	Emergency (Industrial Designs) Order 1999 (S 7/00) Industrial Designs Rules (S 23/00)	Emergency (Layout Designs) Order 1999 (S 8/00)
Criteria	Be a sign or symbol visually perceptible, capable of graphic representation, and capable of distinguishing goods/services of one trader from another	Be new Have industrial applicability	Be original
Procedure	File application with BruIPO Formal & substantive examination (BruIPO) 2 months to oppose an application Priority claim[b]	File application with BruIPO Formal examination only (BruIPO); no substantive examination conducted Priority claim[b]	Protection is automatic
Duration	10 years from the date of registration (or priority date if claimed), renewable for 10 years	5 years from filing date of application (or priority date if claimed), renewable for 10 years	10 years from the date of commercial exploitation if commercially exploited within 5 years of creation; 15 years in all other cases

The Trade Marks Act (Chapter 98) protects trade, service, collective, and certification marks. If a mark is not used within five years of registration, third parties may request registration to be cancelled.[217] Brunei applies the international trade mark classes outlined in the Nice Agreement 7th Edition of the International Classification of Goods and Services; it has not yet adopted the latest classification. The authorities indicated that foreigners represented 95% of total registrations (3,257) over the 2008-13 period; they must have a local address for the purpose of registration.[218]

The Act also provides for the registration of geographical indications as collective or certification marks.[219] However, the owner of such collective or certification mark cannot prohibit the honest (industrial and commercial) use of geographical indications.[220] Brunei is exploring the possibility of introducing a more comprehensive geographical indication system.

3.133.   An industrial design is eligible for registration if it has been applied by industrial process to more than 50 articles (Table 3.15) .[221] According to the authorities, 111 applications for industrial designs were registered over the 2008-13 period; foreigners accounted for 92% of total registration. The low level of registrations by locals is explained by a lack of information on industrial design protection.[222] Since 2013, applicants have been able to file international applications for industrial designs.

Brunei is finalizing its plant variety protection legislation and preparing for accession to the International Union for the Protection of New Varieties of Plants (UPOV) . It was granted observer status in UPOV in 2012.[223] The Patent Order 2011 provides for a system of plant protection.

Copyright and related rights

An overview of the main legal provisions governing the protection of copyright and related rights is in Table 3.16. The copyright legislation was amended in 2013 to enhance enforcement provisions (section 3.3.5.5) . Copyright legislation is reviewed by the Attorney General's Chambers (AGC) .

Overview of copyright and related rights

Legislation	Emergency (Copyright) Order 1999 (S 14/00), as amended by S 92/13[a]
WIPO (in force)	Berne Convention (30.08.2006)
Registration	Protection is automatic
Duration of copyright	• Literary[b], dramatic, musical, and artistic works: author's life + 50 years • Computer-generated work: 50 years from the date the work was made • Sound recordings and films: 50 years from the date the work was made; or if it was released earlier, 50 years from the date of release • Broadcasts and cable programmes: 50 years from the date they were broadcast or transmitted • Typographical arrangement of published edition: 25 years from the year it was first published
Related rights	Performers' rights and persons with recording rights in relation to a performance: 50 years from the year the first performance took place

ENFORCEMENT

During the review period, Brunei made concerted efforts to curb copyright piracy, in particular with respect to the legal framework. The copyright legislation was amended in 2013 to enhance enforcement provisions.[224] Fines and prison sentences were substantially increased from B$5,000 to B$20,000 and from two years to five years, respectively, the Royal Brunei Police Force (RBPF) is now allowed to enter premises, stop and search vehicles without warrants, and access computerized data.[225] These efforts led to Brunei's removal from the USTR Special 301 Watch List in 2013.[226]

Successive anti-piracy campaigns led to police raids in the retail market and confiscation of pirated music, movies, and software entertainment. For the first time, a local manufacturer of pirated copyright was sentenced to prison.[227] Local and foreign artists may now exercise their rights through the new Brunei Authors and Composers Association (BeAT) established in 2011 to collect royalties. Since 2013, the Customs Law Enforcement Division is present at the border to enhance control and monitoring on the importation and exportation of prohibited, restricted and controlled goods, including IPRs.[228]

In March 2014, BruIPO launched a campaign to raise IPR protection awareness among the public. However, copyright piracy remains a problem with some shops selling pirated works, including counterfeit works originating in neighbouring countries. Illegal downloading from the internet is reportedly also growing fast in Brunei.[230]

The agencies responsible for IPR enforcement are the RBPF and the Royal Customs and Excise Department. Brunei's IPR legislation provides for civil remedies and criminal sanctions against IPR infringement. Prosecution of offences is initiated by the Criminal Justice Division of the Attorney General's Chambers upon complaints filed by the right holders.[231] The Intermediate Court and the High Court are competent to hear civil proceedings and the Magistrate's Court, the Intermediate Court, and the High Court to hear criminal proceedings.[232]

On suspicion of counterfeit and pirated imports, trademark and copyright owners may give written notice to Customs requesting imports to be seized at the border. The written notice must detail the infringing works or goods and the expected shipment into Brunei. Imports are seized for a maximum of ten working days; suspected counterfeit works or goods are treated as prohibited imports. During the detention period, the owner determines whether imports are counterfeit and decides on legal proceedings. Suspected counterfeit works or goods remain within Customs premises pending the court's decision. If legal proceedings do not commence within the ten-day period, imports are released. In addition, if Customs is aware of imports of suspected counterfeit works or goods, it may advise the right holder (if known) to file a notice.[233]

TRADE POLICIES BY SECTOR

AGRICULTURE

MAIN FEATURES AND RECENT DEVELOPMENTS

Agriculture's contribution to Brunei's economy remains marginal; along with fisheries and forestry, it accounts for about 1% of GDP. Area suitable for agriculture in Brunei is limited due to the large proportion of land covered by rainforest (section 4.1.3) . Some 7,193 ha are used for agricultural purposes, 61.6% for crops and 38.4% for livestock. The sector employed 13,887 persons in 2013, with crops as the largest employer.[234] Brunei imports the bulk of its food requirements, except for some livestock products, as domestic production is not sufficient to meet local demand. The share of food imports in total merchandise imports went from 12.3% in 2008 to 13.3% in 2013 (Table A1.1) .

Brunei's agricultural production increased from B$225.4 million in 2008 to B$291.7 million in 2013 (Table 4.1) . Livestock contributed 53.8% to total agricultural output in 2013, compared with 58.4% in 2008. Crops production (including flowers, fruits, rice, and vegetables) accounted for 16.6% of total gross output value in 2013 (down from 18.3% in 2008) .

The agri-food processing industry increased its participation in agricultural production from 23.3% in 2008 to 29.6% in 2013, supported by growing domestic demand for halal food and the authorities' efforts to market the "Brunei Halal brand" at regional and international level.[235] The involvement of local SMEs in the agri-food industry is significant, with 376 entrepreneurs engaged and 1,740 persons employed in 2013.[236] Agri-food is one of the industries identified by Brunei that may rise value-added in the economy, have potential for exports, and create jobs (section 1.3) .

No FDI in agriculture was registered during 2008-13. Foreign investment in primary sectors is capped at 70% (section 2.3.3.1) .

AGRICULTURAL POLICY

The Department of Agriculture and Agrifood (DOAA), under the Ministry of Industry and Primary Resources (MIPR), is responsible for agricultural development and food production. Brunei's key agricultural policy objective are ensuring food security and achieving self-sufficiency by increasing local production of crops (notably rice), livestock and agri-food. DOAA aims to promote a market-driven sustainable and competitive agribusiness focusing, *inter alia*, on halal and food products with more value-added, high quality and safety.

Brunei has reached nearly full self-sufficiency in some livestock products, notably broiler chicken and egg production (Table 4.2) . This has been possible largely because of the involvement of the private sector. Some six large-scale companies account for 65% and 90%, respectively, of total production of broiler chicken and eggs. Despite a recent increase in local production of beef and goat meat (Table 4.1), Brunei is still a major importer of these products.

Brunei's self-sufficiency in vegetables decreased from 65.6% in 2008 to 59.3% in 2013 (Table 4.2) . However, the local leafy vegetable production has allowed 90% self-sufficiency in recent years. The outbreak of pests and diseases in 2013 reduced the domestic production of fruits and rice which significantly affected self-sufficiency as compared to 2012.

In 2009, the "National Rice Production Towards Self-Sufficiency in Brunei Darussalam Programme" was launched. Local rice production almost doubled during the review period

. Brunei faces various constraints in rice production areas, such as unavailability of suitable land, inadequate irrigation and drainage infrastructures, insufficient supply of water due to lower water capacity in the main dam, limited usage of high yielding varieties, and lack of expertise in certain fields.

Steps are being taken by DOAA to increase rice yield, expand areas under rice cultivation, while an irrigation project that involves about 1,000 ha of rice production area in the Brunei Muara district is to be completed in 2015.[237] In addition, DOAA recently launched a new high technology rice mill that will increase production, provide flatbed dryers to farmers, and built proper rice storages and packaging.[238] Moreover, the National Rice Processing Centre Master Plan is being developed in order to achieve the 60% self-sufficiency target set by 2035.

The involvement of private companies is expected to further boost rice production in Brunei through a more efficient use of resources, and better farm management. Private companies are being encouraged to support smallholders as service providers in terms of farm mechanization and transportation (e.g. in land preparation, transplanting or harvesting) .

At the regional level, ASEAN has also taken initiatives to improve food security. The ASEAN Plus Three[239] Emergency Rice Reserve Agreement was signed in 2011 to ensure sufficient stocks of rice in anticipation of unforeseen circumstances. Brunei contributes 3,000 tonnes to the stock.[240]

Agri-food has been identified as one of Brunei's strategic industries to promote value-added, exports, and jobs in the economy (section 2.2) .

MFN and preferential tariffs on agriculture (WTO definition) are zero (Tables 3.2 and 3.3) . Specific import duties apply to 8 coffee lines and 8 tea lines.[241] The bound average tariff for agriculture is 23.1% which allows scope for an increase of the applied rates of agricultural products within their bindings (section 3.1.4.2) .

Some agricultural products, e.g. eggs, salt, and sugar, are subject to import and/or export restrictions (sections 3.1.5 and 3.2.3) . In addition, imports of beef and poultry are subject to Halal requirements and may be imported only from approved abattoirs (section 3.1.8) .

For some agricultural products (e.g. cooking oil, plain flour, milk, rice, and sugar) maximum retail prices are set by the Price Controller (section 3.3.2.3) .

At the time of Brunei's previous Review, the authorities indicated that technical capacity was being developed to calculate the aggregate measures of support (AMS) .[242] However, Brunei has yet to make AMS notifications to the WTO.

4.17. Rice and sugar are imported mainly by the Supply and State Stores Department (SSSD), under the Ministry of Finance, and sold to SSSD registered suppliers. However, SSSD does not have exclusive rights as registered suppliers may import rice and sugar other than those imported by SSSD, subject to an import permit from SSSD and an approval permit from Customs . Most rice is however imported by SSSD which has signed contracts with suppliers from Thailand, Viet Nam and other neighbouring countries to diversify domestic supply hence ensuring stocks to satisfy local consumption.

Brunei maintains a system of subsidy for rice and sugar to protect consumers from increases in commodity prices. The DOAA, through the Agriculture and Agrifood Incentive Scheme (SIPA), provides farmers and agri-food producers with inputs (e.g. padi seeds, fertilizers, chemical poisons) and other materials such as food packaging and machineries at a 50% subsidized price.[244] To apply to SIPA, applicants must fill in the incentive register form with DOAA. In addition, one of SIPA component is the Paddy Guarantee Price Purchasing Scheme. Local rice producers registered with DOAA may be eligible for the Purchasing Scheme; to qualify, they are required to grow only local rice varieties recommended by DOAA.[245] Under the scheme, DOAA buys rice to local producers at a price of B$16 per 10 kg. Retail price for consumers is set at B$12 per 10 kg.[246] Rice and sugar imported by SSSD are also subsidized (Table 4.3) .

Prices of rice and sugar imported by SSSD (B$/10 kg)

	Wholesale price	Wholesale price to registered SSSD suppliers	Retail price
Thai Hom Mali rice	57.50	11.50	12.50
Vietnamese fragrant rice	57.50	11.50	12.50
Thai white rice	38.50	7.70	8.50
Thai glutinous rice	35.50	7.10	7.60
Refined white sugar	57.20	11.44	12.50

FISHERIES

The Department of Fisheries (DoF), under the MIPR, is responsible for managing and administering fishery resources and fishing activities in Brunei's exclusive economic zone. Fisheries are governed by the Fisheries Order 2009 (S 25/09)[247] , which came into force in 2009 and repealed the Fisheries Act (Chapter 61) .[248] Subsidiary legislation enacted under the Fisheries Act has remained in force, including the Fisheries Regulations.[249]

Under the Fisheries Order 2009, licences are issued to local fishing boats and commercial fishing vessels authorized to fish in Brunei's waters under a joint-venture arrangement. There are three types of fishing licences: individual small-scale licences issued by DoF and small-scale fishing licences and commercial fishing licences approved by MIPR and issued by DoF.[250] Licences for foreign fishing boats must be applied for by a local agent; a security deposit may be required to cover potential fines or claims resulting from the activities carried out by the foreign fishing boat.[251] In 2013, there were 2,520 fishing boats, including 45 commercial boats.[252] To date, no foreign fishing vessels have been registered. The registration of fishing boats and commercial fishing vessels is made by the Marine Department (see below) .[253]

Misuse of fishing licences and small-scale fishermen without licences are reported to be among the most common problems in Brunei's waters. To address these issues, DoF has strengthened the surveillance programme and enhanced awareness of the importance of fishing licences among fishermen.[254] Moreover, Brunei's "Action Plan To Prevent, Deter and Eliminate Illegal, Unreported and Unregulated (IUU) Fishing" was launched in 2011. Its main objectives are in line with those of the Regional Action Plan to Combat IUU Fishing: (i) to enhance and strengthen the overall level of fisheries management in Brunei's waters; (ii) to sustain fisheries resources and the marine environment; and (iii) to optimise the benefit of adopting responsible fishing practices. IUU fishing is estimated to cost Brunei over B$19 million annually.

During the review period, registration for fishing boats was introduced. The Merchant Shipping (Registration of Fishing Vessels and Pleasure Craft) Regulations 2011 (S 52/11) came into force in April 2012 and repealed the Merchant Shipping (Harbour and Pleasure Craft) Regulations 1986. The registration process was introduced to manage fishing boats as part of Brunei's efforts towards safety of vessels and security in Brunei's waters, including combating IUU fishing. The 2011 Regulations made fishing boat registration with the Marine Department mandatory prior to applying for a fishing licence. In addition, fishing gears must be licensed by DoF before registration of fishing boats is processed.[255] Full implementation of the registration process may take time as capacity of the fishing community increases.

Brunei has no shipyard capable of building fishing boats exceeding 24 meters. These are imported subject to an import permit valid for a three-month period. The fishing boat must be brought into Brunei before registration may start.[256]

Fisheries' limits are divided into four zones indicated by a demarcation line based on depth and distance parallel from the shoreline: from 0 to 3 nautical miles (nm) seaward for Zone 1; 3.1-20 nm for Zone 2; 20.1-45 nm for Zone 3; and 45.1 nm to 200 nm for Zone 4. A moratorium on small-scale fishing in Zones 1 was implemented in January 2008 to ease the fishing pressure due to overfishing, and to protect the nursery and breeding grounds of fishes as well as the coral reef areas. Commercial fishing, such as trawling, purse seining and long lining are banned within Zone 1.

In 2014, Marine Protected Areas (MPAs) were established near Brunei's coastlines limiting or possibly banning fishing activities in such areas to ensure biodiversity conservation and protection of Brunei's marine life, including coral reefs and associated ecosystems, and the replenishment of depleted fish stocks. Brunei also aims to support sustainable shallow shelf demersal fisheries through protection of spawning of commercial species and export of larvae of those species. Brunei's reefs already show early warning signs of reef degradation, such as depressed populations of large predatory fish such as sharks.

On 8 June 2013, Brunei imposed a ban on the catch and landing of all shark species from its waters, and their sales in the domestic market. Brunei's ban on the importation and trade of shark products has been in place since August 2012 on food security and environmental considerations.

Fish processing establishments and fish culture farms must also be licensed.[257] Only licensed fishing boats may berth in Brunei's fish landing complexes (Muara Fish Landing Complex and Kuala Belait Fisheries Centre) . In addition, vehicles entering the complexes must be authorized.

Capture fisheries led by commercial fisheries accounts for nearly 80% of Brunei's total fishery production over the review period (Table 4.4) . Brunei seeks to develop capture fisheries, in particular in Zones 3 and 4 where exploitation levels are untapped. Basic infrastructures for landing the fish, cold storage, fish-sorting and downstream processing areas are some of the facilities provided to promote good fish handling and food safety.

Brunei's aquaculture production is relatively small and dominated by cultured shrimps (Table 4.4) .[259] Nonetheless, Brunei aims to make aquaculture the main component of its fisheries industry by 2023 with an estimated value of B$200 million. To attract more local and foreign investment in aquaculture, Brunei is providing sites with basic infrastructure (e.g. access roads, electricity, sea water supply and potable water, telephone lines) to reduce investors' costs.

Brunei is taking steps to produce high quality shrimps for exports through high technology and integrated farming. Recently, Brunei started exporting Specific Pathogen Free (SPF) shrimp to China and Malaysia. In addition, it has converted into an aquaculture R&D centre and has been successful in commercializing a disease-free black tiger prawn.[260] Fish processing production mainly is sold on the domestic market.[261] DoF has also established the Aquatic Animal Health Service Centre, a state of the art laboratory for disease surveillance, and will introduce Brunei Good Aquaculture Practice (Brunei GAP) by 2015 to maximize aquaculture production and ensure that cultured products comply with international standards.[262]

Production from the fish processing industry went from 823 tonnes in 2008 to 3,326 tonnes in 2013 (Table 4.4), due to a significant increase in frozen shrimp and fish, as well as new products such as Surimi which is now exported by large-scale firms.

Fisheries activities are eligible to receive loans and other support, including tax exemptions (section 3.2.4.2), the Export Refinancing Scheme (section 3.2.5), and the SME Development Fund administered by MIPR Brunei's MFN tariff on fish and fishery products is zero (Table 3.3) .

FORESTRY

Rainforest covers almost 75% of Brunei's land area of 527,000 ha.[263] However, annual logging production is limited (Table 4.5) as large forest areas are protected from commercial development under Brunei's domestic policy and involvement in the tripartite Heart of Borneo initiative. In addition, Brunei maintains a reduced cut policy which limits annual timber logging production to 100,000 m^3 from Reserved Forests (see below) .[264] There are 24 sawmills licensed by the Department of Forestry which operate under the quota of logs.

The Department of Forestry, under the MIPR, is the main authority in charge of managing, conserving and protecting Brunei's forests and forest resources. It aims to support Brunei's diversification strategy through the development of the forestry sector by providing investment opportunities to the private sector on the basis of sustainable forest management. The implementation of Brunei's Selective Felling System aims to ensure the sustainable growth and production of the local timber industry on the basis of biological diversity conservation, and soil and water conservation.[265]

In line with the National Forestry Policy 1989[266], the Department of Forestry classifies the National Forest Estate (Reserved Forests) into: Protection Forests, Production Forests, Recreational Forest, Conservation Forests, and National Park. To date, the National Forest Estate cover 41% of Brunei's total land area; 138,000 ha are reserved for production of timber to supply domestic demand. Brunei is committed to dedicate 55% of its total land area to reserved forest.[267] In addition, the authorities have implemented a plantation programme to maintain sustainable stocks for timber supply.[268]

To increase the contribution of forestry to economic diversification, the Department of Forestry focuses on encouraging (i) imports of raw material for the development of downstream processing industries; and (ii) exports of value-added timber products.[269] The first value-added timber products were exported in 2010.[270] In addition, economic contribution of forest resources may be enhanced through nature tourism which has developed strongly and is one of Brunei's top tourism products.

During the review period, there were no changes to the Forest Act (Chapter 46)[271] and the Forest Rules (Chapter 46 Rules 1)[272] which regulate forest industry. Logging in Reserved Forests requires a license from the Department of Forestry. Royalties are levied on forest products.

Brunei's average MFN tariff on wood and articles of wood is 3.5% (ranging up to 10%), while that of pulp of wood, paper and paperboard is zero (Table 3.3) .

To ensure domestic supply and for environmental reasons, Brunei continues to restrict imports and exports of timber and products thereof (sections 3.1.5.2 and 3.2.3) .

ENERGY SECTOR

OIL AND GAS - RECENT DEVELOPMENTS

The hydrocarbons industry continues to dominate Brunei's economy in terms of contribution to GDP, government revenues and merchandise exports (section 1.3) . However, production in the oil and gas sector shrunk at an annual average rate of -1.8% during 2008-13. Production of crude oil peaked at about 210,000 barrels a day (b/d) in 2006 and declined to 135,200 b/d in 2013 (Table 4.6) .[273] According to the authorities, this reduction is temporary and the result of maintenance work at the oil refinery and offshore platforms.

Brunei has long-term plans to boost investment and production in the energy sector. The Energy White Paper released in 2014 lays out several key goals, including a target of attracting B$70-80 billion in FDI by 2035.[274] Moreover, the cumulative investment is expected to boost employment in the sector, to an estimated 30,000 people by 2017 and 50,000 in 2035, up from 20,000 in 2010.[275]

Brunei's wealth is based on its hydrocarbon reserves. According to some private estimates it has around 1.1 billion barrels and a reserves-to-production ratio of about 18.2 years.[276] Exploration and development programmes are being carried out by oil companies to improve extraction from mature fields and open new fields both onshore and offshore (section 4.2.1.2) . While the initial results of these programmes have been mixed, the Energy White Paper estimates that 3.5 billion barrels of new reserves will be added by 2035. As a result, the government aims to boost production levels from the current 372,000 barrels of oil equivalent per day (boepd), roughly 40% oil and 60% gas, to 430,000 boepd by 2017 and 650,000 boepd by 2035.[277]

During the review period, oil prices fluctuated from as low as US$64.4 per barrel in 2009 to US$117.6 per barrel in 2012 in consonance with world demand.[278] In 2013, Brunei exported 92% of its total crude oil production (about 135,000 b/d); most of which went to Rep. of Korea (18%), Japan (16%), Australia (15%) and other countries in the region (Table 4.7) . The remaining crude oil output (8%) is refined for domestic use. Despite Brunei's status as a net exporter of oil, it imports about 40% of the refined petroleum products it consumes (e.g. gasoline, gasoil, Jet A1 fuel, and kerosene), as it has limited domestic refining capacity.

Brunei produced an average of 1,200 MMscf of natural gas per day in 2008-13 (Table 4.6), and it is one of the world's largest producers of liquefied natural gas (LNG) . The price for LNG increased from US$12.9 per MMBtu in 2008 to US$16.9 MMBtu in 2013.[279] In 2013, the bulk of Brunei's exports of natural gas went to Japan (66% of the total)[280], Rep. of Korea (15%), and Malaysia (6.5%) . Natural gas is also used domestically for petroleum operators' own-use, power generation, liquefied petroleum gas (LPG) used domestically, and as a reserve for industrial purposes. Approximately 86% of Brunei's natural gas is exported as LNG.

POLICY DEVELOPMENTS

Under the Petroleum Mining Act (Chapter 44), investors, including foreign investors, may apply for petroleum mining agreements in respect of state land, whether onshore or offshore; the applications are considered by the Sultan in Council.

Under the Income Tax (Petroleum) Act (Chapter 119), Brunei levies a corporate tax on petroleum and gas operations at a rate of 55%. Royalties and petroleum income tax are payable on concessions, and production sharing agreements (PSAs) .

The State controls key enterprises in the oil and gas industry (section 3.3.3), notably Petroleum BRUNEI the national oil company[281], and Brunei Shell Petroleum (BSP) a joint-venture owned in equal shares by the Government and the Royal Dutch Shell Group.[282] Petroleum BRUNEI is responsible for managing assets in designated areas, and has the right to take a participating interest in certain blocks.

For additional analytical, business and investment opportunities information,
please contact Global Investment & Business Center, USA
at (703) 370-8082. Fax: (703) 370-8083. E-mail: ibpusa3@gmail.com
Global Business and Investment Info Databank - www.ibpus.com

The Energy Department, under the Prime Minister's Office[283], is responsible for developing and implementing the Government's energy policies, including the oil and gas sector. The Energy Department also manages the BSP assets and Block A, while PetroleumBRUNEI manages other upstream assets assigned to it. Other responsibilities of the Energy Department include: exploiting Brunei's oil and gas reserves; promoting the development of downstream industries; fixing crude oil prices; and ensuring compliance with internationally acceptable technical, accounting, health and safety standards.

Despite efforts to introduce competition in the sector, the largest oil and gas operator and producer remains BSP by virtue of its control of Brunei's major oil and natural gas fields. BSP has two petroleum agreements with the Government until the end of 2022.[284] BSP is taking new measures to improve extraction particularly from mature fields.[285] These measures include a more holistic approach to water flooding to alter reservoir dynamics[286], deploying new technology to access difficult oil fields[287], and an enhanced oil recovery pilot project.

While BSP operates a concession, the exploration and development of a number of new onshore and offshore blocks have been offered on production sharing basis.[289] This includes the various blocks assigned to PetroleumBRUNEI such as Blocks CA1, CA2, L, N and Q (Table 4.8).

MAIN PETROLEUM ACTIVITIES

Companies and ownership	Activities	Agreement
A. Upstream activities		
BSP (Brunei Government 50% and Royal Dutch Shell 50%)	Onshore (422 km^2), offshore (5,062 km^2)	Concession
Shell Deepwater Borneo (53.9%) and PetroleumBRUNEI (46.1%)	Block A (804 km^2)	Concession
TOTAL E&P Borneo B.V. (37.5%), Shell Deepwater Brunei (35%) and PetroleumBRUNEI (27.5%)	Block B (392 km^2)	Concession
TOTAL E&P Deep Offshore Borneo B.V. (54%), BHP Billiton (22.5%), HESS (13.5%), Petronas Carigali Overseas (5%), Canam Brunei Oil (5%)	Block CA1 (5,850 km^2)	Production sharing
Petronas Carigali Brunei (45%), Canam Brunei Oil (30%), Shell Deepwater Borneo (12.5%), Diamond Energy Exploration and Production (6.25%), ConocoPhilips (6.25%)	Block CA2 (6,024 km^2)	Production sharing
Kulczyk Oil Brunei Limited (40%), AED South East Asia Limited (50%), QAF Brunei (10%)	Block L (1,123 km^2)	Production sharing
Petronas Carigali Brunei (50%), Shell Deepwater Borneo (50%)	Block N (883 km^2)	Production sharing
Shell Deepwater Borneo (50%), Petronas Carigali Brunei (50%)	Block Q (1,116 km^2)	Production sharing
B. Midstream, downstream and marketing activities		
Brunei LNG (Brunei Government (50%), Shell Overseas Trading (25%), Mitsubishi (25%))	Commercial LNG plant for export	Joint-venture
Brunei Methanol Company (Mitsubishi Gas Chemicals (50%), Itochu Corporation (25%), PetroleumBRUNEI (25%))	Produces methanol for export	Joint-venture

Brunei Shell Tankers (Brunei Government (50%), Shell Overseas Trading (25%), Mitsubishi (25%))	Owns tankers chartered to Brunei LNG to transport LNG	Joint-venture
Brunei Gas Carriers (Brunei Government (80%), Shell (10%), Mitsubishi (10%))	Owns tankers chartered to Brunei LNG to transport LNG	Joint-venture
Brunei Shell Marketing (Brunei Government (50%), Shell Overseas Holding (50%)	Supply and marketing of petroleum products	Joint-venture

Source: Information provided by the authorities.

BSP also operates the only refinery in Brunei with a capacity of 12,000 b/d for its crude distillation unit and 7,000 b/d for its reformer unit, which meets about 60% of the domestic demand for refined petroleum products. China's Zhejiang Hengyi Group is set to invest US$4 billion in a new refinery and petrochemicals complex, with a capacity of 175,000 b/d. This would represent the biggest FDI project in Brunei so far. The tentative date for the start of refinery operations is 2018.[290] The Government aims to make Brunei self-sufficient in refined products, with remaining capacity available for export.

Brunei is keen to encourage investment in downstream activities related to the petroleum and natural gas sector and has set aside 1 trillion cubic feet (tcf) of gas for industrial use. Currently, 0.5 tcf is utilized by Brunei Methanol Company (BMC) that started operations in 2010 and now produces 850,000 tonnes per year. The remaining 0.5 tcf will be allocated for future petrochemical projects.

In order to meet its ambitious oil production target, in recent years Brunei has been signing agreements with emerging oil-producer nations to play an active role in regional oil industries and ensure reserves abroad. For example, Petroleum BRUNEI is looking at investing in Myanmar's oil and gas sector, and in November 2012 signed an MOU with PetroVietnam.[291] Brunei is also to provide Timor-Leste with expertise and support.[292]

Petroleum products for local consumption are marketed solely by Brunei Shell Marketing Company (BSM) although some of its stations are operated by independent operators or franchises. Retail/end-user prices of gasoline, diesel, kerosene, and bottled LPG have been regulated since 1978, under a Price Stabilization Agreement between the Government and BSM, under which the Government subsidizes prices if the price of crude oil rises above a certain level. The cost of petrol delivered to the stations is fixed, as are margins and final prices. Fuel prices range from B$0.36 per litre for regular (Ron 85) to B$0.53 per litre for premium (Ron 97), while diesel is sold at B$0.31 per litre. Since 2011, subsidization costs amount to over B$350 million per year.[293]

Currently, about 24,000 people work in the energy sector. Together, the private limited companies BSP, BLNG, BSM and BST constitute the largest employer in Brunei after the Government with some 5,000 jobs. By 2035, the Government aims to create 50,000 jobs in the oil and gas sector, 80% of which will be held by Bruneians.[294]

Brunei's average MFN tariff on petroleum is 0.5%, ranging up to 2.2% (Table 3.3).

ELECTRICITY

The electric industry in Brunei is governed by the Electricity Act 1973 and Electricity Act (Amendment) Order, 2002. The Department of Electrical Services (DES), under the Prime Minister's Office, is responsible for the generation, transmission, and distribution of electricity. Other than DES, electricity is also generated by an independent power producer (IPP), the Berakas Power Company (BPC).

In total, Brunei has an installed power capacity of 806 MW. In 2013, total production reached 3,900 GWh, while consumption stood at 3,400 GWh. Nonetheless, still some 0.3% of the population living in remote areas does not have access to the national grid and have stand-alone generators. The largest consumer of electricity is the residential sector, followed by the commercial sector, government buildings, and industry.

Brunei has the cheapest electricity rate and the highest energy intensity of all ASEAN countries. The Government spends some B$40 million per year on its electricity subsidy, out of a total annual energy subsidy of about B$1 billion.[295] In addition, the Government consumes itself over 700 GWh of electricity in terms of lightning and power in the public sector, and pays the bill of unpaid utilities charges for the general public (B$230 million in 2011) . To address this, Brunei is taking steps to reduce 45% its energy intensity by 2035 (with 2005 as base year) and improve efficiency.[296] To do so, in 2012 a new electricity tariff for the residential sector was introduced, i.e. a progressive electricity tariff structure (as opposed to the regressive regime which existed since 1969) to reduce the government power subsidy by more than half.

Almost 99% of electricity uses natural gas as the main fuel while the rest is generated by diesel fuel.[297] The Government is, therefore, exploring ways to increase renewables usage and reduce carbon emissions, including a smart grid and solar plants. The Government aims to have at least 10% of power generation from renewable energy by 2035. The Government is developing a "Feed-in-Tariff" policy to accelerate the use of renewable energy.

MANUFACTURING

Non-oil and gas manufacturing accounted for 0.9% of GDP in 2013 (compared with 0.8% in 2008) . The main large-scale industries are cement production, garment making, and production of pre-cast concrete structures. Other industries include building material products; electronic and electrical products, such as cables, switchboard, and assembly appliances; mineral water; canned food; dairy products; silica sands products; and publishing and printing. Brunei is a net importer of cement and steel. Buoyed by large-scale infrastructure projects included in Brunei's Development Plan 2007-12, imports of cement and steel grew by 78% and 62%, respectively, over the period.[298]

Overall, the performance of the manufacturing sector has been weak in the last years mainly due to the relatively high cost of doing business; shortage of skilled and unskilled workers; lack of competitiveness of local products; and limited access to financing for micro, small and medium-sized enterprises (MSMEs), which compose 98% of local companies and employ some 92% of the private sector workforce.[299]

Manufacturing has continued to be encouraged in order to reduce Brunei's dependence on its petroleum resources, and a number of incentives are used to encourage investment in priority sectors identified by the Government. The incentives include financial assistance to local companies; a lower corporate income tax rate of 20% from 2010; industries granted "pioneer status" are eligible for tax relief of up to five years for investments between B$500,000 and B$2.5 million; investments in excess may be granted eight-year tax relief, extendable by three years if they are located in a high-tech industrial park (section 2.4.1.1 and Table 2.2) .[300] In addition, companies can also receive exemption from import duties on machinery, equipment, component parts, accessories, building structures and raw materials (section 3.2.4.2) .

In priority sectors in which private investment is not forthcoming, the Government invests directly, mainly through its company Semaun Holdings (section 3.3.3) .[301] To date, Semaun Holdings has launched nine joint-ventures in areas such as aquaculture, food processing and fine glass crystal manufacturing where economic diversification is sought.[302]

The Brunei Industrial Development Authority (BINA), under the Ministry of Industry and Primary Resources, had traditionally been the principal custodian of manufacturing development policy. Since 2001, however, the Brunei Economic Development Board (BEDB) has risen to the fore by promoting and managing large-scale industrial estates, including industrial parks that cater to downstream petrochemicals plants.[303] By comparison, BINA concentrates on domestic-business focused designs that provide average plots sized between 0.2 ha and 2 ha.

The design and location of these new industrial parks are expected to assist Brunei's long-term diversification plans. Widely dispersed across Brunei, they are also intended to provide more employment opportunities for Bruneians, and support other economic activities, especially SMEs. There are two flagship sites: the industrial site of Pulau Muara Besar (PMB), and the Sungai Liang Industrial Park (SPARK) . PMB is located adjacent to Brunei's main seaport at Muara and is site for the US$4 billion Zhejiang Hengyi Group's integrated refinery and petrochemicals plant. SPARK is home to BMC's US$600 million plant (section 4.2.1.2) .

In addition, six other sites currently under development will cater to the industrial clusters identified in Brunei's Vision 2035: downstream oil and gas industries, health care and health services (including pharmaceuticals and medicine), information and communications technology (ICT), and halal products.[304]These are: (i) Salambigar Industrial Park which is already host to Simpor Pharma, a joint-venture between Viva Pharmaceutical from Canada and one of Brunei's equity fund manager, Aureos-BICB[305]; (ii) the Rimba Digital site which has already attracted US$102 million investment from a joint-venture between the Government of Brunei and CAE, a Canadian global leader in civil aviation and defence company to set up a Multipurpose Training Centre which will cater both local and regional markets; (iii) the Telisai Industrial Park that will accommodate mixed industries; (iv) the Bukit Panggal project will host energy-intensive industries; (v) the Brunei Agrotech Park will have halal and agro-business; and (vi) the Anggerek Desa Technology Park.

Manufacturing companies are eligible to receive financial support through various initiatives: (i) the Industrial, Commercial and Entrepreneurial Development Programme has allocated B$742 million for the implementation of 42 projects[306]; (ii) various grants and loans are given to MSMEs (Table 3.11); and (iii) the Promising Local Enterprise Development Investment Fund has B$15 million to support local companies that wish to expand abroad.[307] In addition, exporters of manufactured goods are granted income tax exemptions (section 3.2.4.2), and receive loans through the Export Refinancing Scheme (ERS) (section 3.2.5) .

Exports of stone and gravel are prohibited, while exports of some other manufacturing products are restricted (section 3.2.3) .

Brunei's average MFN tariff on manufacturing (major division 3 of ISIC, Revision 2) is 1.9%, ranging up to 30% on some chemical products (Table 3.3) .

SERVICE SECTOR

During the period under review, services grew in general faster than the rest of the economy (section 1.1) . As a result, the share of private services (excluding construction and utilities) in real GDP went from 25% in 2008 to 29% in 2013. The leading services subsectors were: business services (6% of GDP in 2013), wholesale and retail trade (5.8%), transport and communications (5.5%), and finance(4.3%) .

Under the GATS, Brunei made specific commitments in 4 of the 12 sectors listed in the Services Sectoral Classification List: business services (professional, computer, and rental or leasing services without operators); communication services (telecommunication); financial services (insurance, and banking and other financial services); and transport services (air transport) .[308] Further commitments were made in telecommunications services under the Fourth Protocol. In its Article II (MFN) exemptions, future liberalization with regard to foreign equity participation is subject to discretionary changes and dependent on Brunei's development requirements. Brunei also has a preference for recruiting labour from traditional sources of supply to ensure social cohesion in the country. Sector-specific MFN exemptions are also proposed to be maintained for legal services, radio and television services, financial services, reinsurance and retrocession, and banking and other financial services. Brunei submitted an initial conditional offer on services in the framework of the DDA.[309]

Brunei also has services commitments under the ASEAN Framework Agreement on Trade in Services (AFAS) . The AFAS aims to enhance cooperation and substantially eliminate restrictions to trade in services among member states, with a view to realizing a free-trade area in services. Individual commitments contain horizontal and sector-specific commitments and MFN exemptions.

During the review period, Brunei remained active in negotiating and implementing regional trade agreements (RTAs), all of which include services provisions, with the exception of the ASEAN-Japan Comprehensive Economic Partnership (AJCEP) for which provisions on services and investment are under negotiation. A positive-list approach was followed in all RTAs where there is much diversity in Brunei's services commitments (Table A2.2) . In most cases, commitments under Brunei's RTAs go beyond its GATS schedule/offer.

FINANCIAL SERVICES

As of June 2014, Brunei had seven commercial banks, one restricted bank, and 61 non-banking financial institutions comprising: one Islamic Trust Fund (Perbadanan Tabung Amanah Islam Brunei (TAIB)[310]; nine insurance companies; four *takaful* (Islamic) operators; three finance companies[311]; the Employees Trust Fund (ETF)[312], 23 money changers, 21 remittance companies, and one pawnbroker.

Since its establishment in 2011, the Autoriti Monetari Brunei Darussalam (AMBD) is responsible for the supervision and regulation of the financial system (section 1.1) .[313] According to the IMF, AMBD has introduced various initiatives to help maintain financial stability and improve asset quality, notably through the establishment of the Credit Bureau.[314] Since September 2012, the Credit Bureau, under the Regulatory Department of AMBD, provides financial institutions with Credit Reports to help them determine their customers' credit-worthiness.[315] The Credit Bureau also assists the AMBD in making its policy decisions. In September 2014, the Credit Bureau introduced the Self-Inquiry service to the public, which allows individuals or commercial entities to access their own credit reports. The service aims to improve transparency, credit awareness, and incentivise individuals/commercial entities to build and maintain a good credit reputation towards a healthy credit culture.

In March 2013, in order to facilitate credit access, ensure adequate returns to depositors and support long-term diversification plans, the AMBD introduced interest rate regulations on some products provided by financial institutions to their customers. The AMBD has also imposed tighter consumer lending regulations (section 4.4.2.2), which, according to the authorities, has had a positive effect on financial intermediation since overall credit in Brunei went from B$5.2 billion in December 2012 to B$5.5 billion in June 2014. On aggregate basis, banks' profitability (profit before tax) also increased 60.6% from December 2012 to December 2013.

The Brunei Darussalam's Deposit Protection Corporation (BDPC), under the Ministry of Finance, is responsible for the implementation of the asset maintenance regulation and for the National Deposit Insurance Scheme.

Brunei aims to become a regional financial centre for Islamic financial services: Islamic banking, *Takaful* (Islamic insurance) and Islamic capital market products. The National Syariah Financial Supervisory Board was established in 2006 to enhance the Syariah governance and supervision as well as stimulating the growth of the sector.[316] The Board is responsible for making sure that all Islamic products are in accordance with Syariah Law before they are allowed to be distributed.[317]

Brunei does not have its own stock exchange and the capital market still is in an infant stage. A new Securities Market Order came into force on 25 June 2013 (Table A2.1); its regulations have been drafted and are expected to come into force in 2015. The new legislation covers both Islamic and conventional investment activities, and replaced the Securities Order 2001 and Mutual Funds Order 2011, with the aim of facilitating the growth and development of the capital market, and enhancing investor protection.[318]

Brunei is not a signatory to the Fifth Protocol to the GATS (on financial services) .

BANKING

Brunei's banking system is characterized by a dual system consisting of one Islamic bank and six conventional banks, and an Islamic Trust Fund set up under its own statute. Out of the seven banks, two are international[319] , three regional and two domestic. In addition, three offshore banks operate, and the three licensed finance companies are wholly owned subsidiaries of three licensed banks in Brunei. As of June 2014, local banks held about 60% of the banking assets, while 35% was held by the two international banks.

The largest Islamic financial institution in Brunei is Bank Islam Brunei Darussalam (BIBD) . It captures a significant proportion of government business and is the main bank for government payroll. As of June 2014, BIBD had about one-third of both total banking assets and deposits. BIBD has also been active in the *sukuk* (Islamic bond) market, co-leading a US$1 billion issuance for the Government of Indonesia.

The main change in terms of Brunei's banking legislation since its last Review is the adoption of the Islamic Banking Order 2008 which harmonized Islamic and conventional banking regulations. The legal framework for banking is also composed of: Banking Order 2006; International Banking Order 2000; Finance Companies Act (Chapter 89); Hire Purchase Order 2006; Pawnbrokers Order 2002; and Money-Changing and Remittance Businesses Act (Chapter 174); and Moneylenders Act (Chapter 62) . Annual licences fees charged by the AMBD range from B$2,000 for money changes to B$50,000 for headquarters of a licensed bank.[321]

According to the IMF, Brunei's commercial banks are well capitalized, profitable and highly liquid (Table 4.9) .[322] In terms of capital requirements, all banks are currently mandated to have a minimum regulatory capital to risk weighted assets ratio of 10%, and top-quality capital ("Tier 1) to risk weighted assets ratio of 5%, which are above the Basel I and Basel II requirements.[323] Basel III tightens the definition of capital; raises the minimum capital requirement to 4.5% (up from 2% in Basel II) and of "Tier 1" to 6% (up from 4% in Basel II) of risk-weighted assets, after deductions; introduce a maximum Leverage Ratio; and usher in liquidity requirements for banks to withstand liquidity stress over periods of one month (Liquidity Coverage Ratio) and one year (Net Stable Funding Ratio) . According to the authorities, all banks in Brunei fully comply with Basel III.[324]

Since the introduction of the asset maintenance ratio in 2011 as part of the bank's obligations under the Deposit Protection Scheme (DPS)[325] , a shift in banking assets from offshore to onshore has occurred which in principle allows for more funds to be better channelled to domestic sectors. With the introduction of consumer credit regulations the bank's exposure to the personal loan portfolio has decreased from 64% of total credit in the banking system in 2005 to 30% as of June 2014.[326] In turn, this has enabled banks to allocate more funds to productive activities and SMEs.

With Brunei's banking sector looking for new opportunities for revenue growth and the government keen to position Brunei as a prominent regional financial centre, treasury services could provide new opportunities. However, there are no regional treasury centres in Brunei and its regulatory framework and incentive structure would need to change to attract such business. Moreover, Brunei needs to become more competitive and reduce its relatively high banking fees and transaction costs.[327]

INSURANCE

A significant consolidation in the insurance market has taken place in Brunei over the last few years. Indeed, the number of companies went down from 21 in 2006 to 13 as of September 2014, partly due to the increase in the minimum capital requirement from B$1 million to B$8 million for both general and life insurance.[328] Brunei's insurance market is relatively small given the size of the population, the demand for life insurance is limited because Brunei has a welfare system that offers full health care coverage and a generous pension scheme from the age of 60, and most insurance firms do not have the capital to underwrite large-scale projects associated with the lucrative oil and gas industry.

Nine insurance firms in Brunei are conventional, of which 4 are domestic *takaful* and the rest foreign.[329] Like in banking, Brunei's *takaful* companies have been increasing their participation in the market and now account for 50% of gross premiums (31% in 2008), a fifth of all assets and a third of total claims. The largest player in the conventional insurance market is National Insurance with almost 40% market share.[330]

The prospect of establishing a local reinsurance company with substantial paid-up capital is being discussed. Nowadays most of the money earned by domestically operating reinsurers of local insurance schemes goes abroad with the insurers themselves.[331]

In 2013, gross premiums for all general insurance companies totalled B$182.5 million (up from B$115.8 million in 2008) . In general business, *takaful* operators were heavily concentrated in motor insurance, and dominated the market with 40% of total general premiums. In life business, conventional insurers remain the biggest market players as products offered are more extensive compared with *takaful*.

Insurance legislation is composed of: Insurance Order 2006; International Insurance and Takaful Order 2002; Motor Vehicle Insurance (Third Party Risks) Act, Chapter 90; and Takaful Order 2008.

The Insurance/*Takaful* and Capital Market Supervision Division, under AMBD, undertakes the registration, licensing and supervision of insurance and *takaful* companies, their intermediaries, capital market intermediaries, securities and mutual funds (conventional and Islamic) . The main elements of supervision include a security deposit with the Government of B$1 million for insurers underwriting motor insurance, and for licensed life and/or general insurers under the Insurance Order 2006; minimum paid-up capital requirements of B$8 million and for foreign branches the equivalent in surplus of assets over liabilities; a solvency margin for general insurers of 20% of net premium income (NPI) of the previous year; and guidelines for the appointment of foreign employees and motor insurance agents. Application fees range from B$250 for captive insurance to B$1,500 for life and general insurance (composite), while annual fees go from B$1,500 to B$12,000 depending on the type of license.

The Brunei Insurance and Takaful Association (BITA), a representative body for both conventional and Islamic insurers was established in November 2013. General insurers, both conventional and *takaful*, have agreed in principle to a cap on commission to agents ranging from 15% to 25% across the various lines of business.[332]

Brunei made GATS commitments for direct insurance (life and non-life), reinsurance and retrocession, insurance and intermediation (broking and agency services) and auxiliary services (consultancy, actuarial risk assessment, risk management, and maritime loss adjusting) . In general, Brunei's schedule reflects current requirements and restrictions, including commercial presence only through companies registered in Brunei for direct insurance; and purchase of compulsory insurance for motor third-party liability and workmen's compensation only from insurance companies established in Brunei.

TELECOMMUNICATIONS

Brunei aims to increase the contribution of the information and communication technology (ICT) sector to the economy from 1.6% of GDP in 2010 to 6% by 2015. Brunei is making key investments in submarine cables and fibre-to-the-home infrastructure upon which its ICT transformation will be based (see below) . There has also been significant investment in a rural telecoms network, allowing rural and remote areas access to telephone and the Internet.

While fixed-telephone subscribers decreased to 57 per 100 inhabitants in 2013[333], the mobile network has continued to grow over the last few years and mobile penetration had reached 115% by 2013 (up from 106% at end 2008) (Table 4.10) . Internet users increased from 46% to over 60% during the same period. By 2013, there were some 23,800 broadband subscriptions (compared with 16,900 in 2008) . Overall, Brunei is ranked 58th out of 157 countries in the latest ITU's Development Index.[334]

The Ministry of Communications sets national policies for the development of the telecoms sector. The Authority for Info-communications Technology Industry (AITI), an independent statutory body under the Minister of Communications, is the telecoms regulator and ICT industry development promoter. Brunei started the restructuring of the sector in 2001 with the adoption of the following legal framework: the Telecommunication Successor Company Order 2001, the Telecommunications Order 2001, and the AITI Order 2001. These Orders replaced the Telecommunications Act of 1952.[335]

The Telecommunications Order 2001 confers upon AITI the exclusive privilege to operate and provide telecommunication systems and services in Brunei and allows AITI to issue licences to operators and to manage the radio communications spectrum. AITI's licensing regime is technologically neutral, with no distinction drawn on the basis of the technology used. It has a two-tier licensing structure: the InTi (Infrastructure Provider for the Telecommunication Industry) licence is required by licensees who own infrastructure, and the SeTi (Service Provider for the Telecommunication Industry) licence is required by those who provide retail services through wholesale arrangements with InTi licensees. There is no specific regulation to govern prices and tariffs, but AITI has the power to give regulatory directions to licensees in the public interest and to ensure fair and efficient market conduct.[336]

Telekom Brunei (TelBru), a state-owned company registered under Brunei's Companies Act, continues to be the only operator in the fixed-line market.[337] TelBru also provides basic telephony and a range of value-added services such as leased-line services, dial-up internet, ADSL broadband, VoIP, ATM lines and pre-paid calling cards.

Competition in Brunei's mobile telephony market was introduced in 2005. Nonetheless, there are only two mobile operators: Progressif Cellular Sdn Bhd (PCSB)[338], and the DST Communications Sdn Bhd (DSTCom) since 1995.[339] At the end of 2013, B-mobile and DSTCom had about 15% and 85%, respectively, of total mobile subscribers. In November 2013, DST introduced 4G long term evolution (LTE) network which provides faster, and more spectrally-efficient technologies for mobile broadband.

TelBru, PCSB, and companies in the DST group are locally-owned and controlled and have no significant foreign participation. AITI's licensing framework implements policies which require that licensees are locally majority-owned or controlled.

Overall, Brunei is ranked 27th out of 161 countries in the latest ITU's ICT Price Basket. This study finds that measured as a percentage of GNI per capita, fixed-telephone and mobile prices are relatively low in Brunei (ranking 16th and 21st in the world, respectively), but fixed broadband is relatively expensive (52nd).[340]

In 2008, the responsibility for the Broadcasting Act (Chapter 180) was transferred from the Prime Minister's Office to the Ministry of Communications. AITI is undertaking a complete review of the telecoms regulatory framework to have a single converged regulator for telecoms and broadcasting under AITI by 2015.[341]

As part of the convergence exercise, AITI is developing a Telecommunications and Broadcasting Competition Code which will be Brunei's first-sector specific competition code and will mandate, *inter alia*, interconnection between fixed network suppliers and other service providers, local loop unbundling, infrastructure-sharing, and specific obligations to prevent anti-competitive behaviour, in particular affecting licensees with significant market power. The Competition Code, expected to be implemented in 2015, aims to promote efficiency and competitiveness in telecoms and broadcasting, ensure ease of market entry, and provide certainty to telecoms and broadcasting market players.

A new Tariff Regulation Code of Practice will be introduced to regulate retail and wholesale tariffs for telecoms and broadcasting infrastructure and services. The Code will implement *ex ante* tariff regulation methodologies to ensure that affordable prices are offered in Brunei, encourage competition, and ensuring transparency and certainty in the market. It will also streamline the existing filing and tariff control systems.

The introduction of the Competition and Tariff Regulation Codes aims to support the emergence of a competitive retail service provider industry which will complement Brunei's three phase fibre-to-the-home network by 2017. The Government, through TelBru and with the support of AITI, is developing nationwide fibre-to-the-home infrastructure. Phase one is being implemented by TelBru aiming to reach 30% of households. Phases two and three will follow so as to reach, respectively, 80% and 100% of households.

Brunei is partner in the US$400 million South-East Asia–Japan Cable (SJC), which will connect 8,900 km between Brunei; Japan; Hong-Kong, China; the Philippines; and Singapore with an option to extend to Thailand and Viet Nam.[342]

AITI is undertaking some initiatives to provide a platform for recognition and funding for the local ICT industry, such as AITI Accredited Business (AAB) Status, ICT Accredited Business (ICTAB), AITI Grant Scheme, and the AITI Market Creation Programme. AAB and ICTAB is a centralized directory of ICT companies in Brunei, indicating financial and business track record. In 2010, AITI introduced both the Grant Scheme to give partial financial assistance to develop "Brunei-Made" solutions for businesses (section 3.3.1.5), and the AITI Market Creation Programme to assist local ICT SMEs to obtain a ready market for their Brunei-Made ICT products and services.

TRANSPORT

Air transport

The Department of Civil Aviation (DCA) in the Ministry of Communications is responsible for ensuring safe and secure air transport services. The regulatory regime for air transport is contained in the Civil Aviation Order 2006 (S 63/06) and subsidiary legislation, including the Civil Aviation Regulations 2006 (S 69/06), the Airport Fees and Charges Regulations, the Air Transport and Commercial Flying (Licensing) Regulations, and the Air Traffic Control Regulations.[343] There were no changes to the regulatory framework during the review period.

There is one airport in Brunei. Brunei International Airport (BIA) is owned by the State and managed by DCA. To cope with substantial increase in passenger traffic (Table 4.11), BIA passenger terminal is being modernized and expanded to improve facilities and double annual capacity from 1.5 million to 3 million passengers. The project awarded to a Malaysian-Bruneian joint-venture, is supervised by the Brunei Economic Development Board (BEDB) and DCA; completion is expected by end-2014. No upgrade of BIA freight terminal, which has capacity of 50,000 tonnes a year, is foreseen.[344]

Air carriers must obtain an air operator's certificate and an operating licence issued by DCA.

During the review period, two airlines, the Philippine's Cebu Pacific and the Malaysian MASWings, launched flights to Brunei. To date, there are six regional airlines using BIA.[346] The national flag carrier, Royal Brunei Airlines (RB) operates to 14 destinations (as of 17 October 2014), mainly within the region.[347] In 2011, its decision to cut long-haul routes and concentrate on the regional market led to a sharp drop in passengers in transit at BIA most of RB passengers on long-haul flights were passengers in transit as the airline sought to convert Brunei into a hub between Europe and Oceania.[348] Air freight is provided by RB and Syabas Airmark Aviation Sdn Bhd.

Air fares and freight rates must be filed with and approved by DCA at least 25 days prior to implementation.

Airport-related charges include landing, parking, and housing fees[351]; and a passenger service fee. Landing fees are based on the aircraft's maximum weight at take-off[353]; they do not differ from peak and off-peak hours. Fixed charges are set for parking (B\$0.40/10 m^2) and housing (B\$0.80/10 m^2); the first three hours of parking are free of charge. The passenger service tax rate is B\$12 for all passengers embarking at BIA, except those travelling to the Brunei-Indonesia-Malaysia-Philippines East Asia Growth Area (BIMP-EAGA) cities (B\$5) . To encourage increased connectivity and flight frequency, incentives on landing and parking fees were introduced in early 2013 and may be granted to air carriers (Table 4.12) .

Incentives on landing and parking fees

	Recipient
First 6 months: no fees	Airlines operating to/from BIA providing new services to/from new destinations
Next 6 months: 50% discount	New airlines operating to BIA from new destinations
Next 1 year: 25% discount	Freight carriers operating to/from BIA
First 6 months: 50% discount	Airlines increasing flight frequency
Next 6 months: 25% discount	
25% discount	Passenger charter services from new destinations

Source: Department of Civil Aviation online information. Viewed at: http://www.civil-aviation.gov.bn/.

Ground services (fuel supply, flight planning) are provided by RB and private company Glamco Aviation Sdn Bhd.[354] In addition, Brunei International Air Cargo Centre (BIACC) handles all freight transiting through BIA.[355] Wholly-owned RB subsidiary Royal Brunei Catering provides catering services to all aircrafts.[356]

Brunei has liberalized international air transport through bilateral, regional, and plurilateral agreements. To date, it has signed 36 bilateral air agreements (Table A4.1) . During the review period, a number of bilateral air services agreements were updated including with Japan, Kuwait (State of), United Kingdom, and Saudi Arabia (Kingdom of) . Open sky arrangements are provided in five agreements.[357]

Since 2009, three regional open sky agreements[358] liberalized traffic rights (passenger and freight) with the view to establishing the ASEAN Single Aviation Market.[359] ASEAN air carriers are granted full traffic rights under the 3rd, 4th, and 5th freedoms between cities with international airports within the region. In addition, ASEAN engaged in negotiating open sky agreements with dialogue partners. An agreement with China entered into force in 2011. Other partners (EU, India, Japan, and Republic of Korea) have expressed interest in negotiating similar agreements.

Brunei is party to the Multilateral Agreement on the Liberalisation of International Air Transportation (MALIAT) Agreement.[360] It grants full traffic rights for passengers under 3rd, 4th, and 5th freedoms to all parties and under 7th and 8th freedoms to Chile, New Zealand, and Singapore; and (ii) full traffic rights for freight under the 7th freedom to all parties.

Brunei made commitments for rental of aircraft with crew under the GATS.

Maritime transport

Maritime transport is governed by the Merchant Shipping Order 2002 (S 27/02)[363] and subsidiary legislation.[364] There were no substantial changes to the regulatory framework during the review period.

The Marine Department in the Ministry of Communications is responsible for, *inter alia*, vessel registration (including fishing boats (section 4.1.2) and vessel licensing. Registration with the Marine Department is mandatory for locally-owned vessels and self-propelled foreign-owned vessels exceeding 1,600 tonnes. In addition, those vessels not exceeding 100 tonnes must also be licensed by the Department; licences are valid for one year.[365] Licensing applies to both locally- and foreign-owned vessels. However, foreign-owned vessels under this category are only allowed to be used as pleasure boats. Brunei's merchant fleet comprises 1 cargo ships and 8 tankers; no bulk carriers or container ships are registered.[366]

Shipping services are provided by 49 foreign companies and represented by 14 shipping agents. In 2010, the authorities considered the creation of a national shipping company with the view to addressing ASEAN connectivity issues and lowering freight fees. Foreign shipping companies are reported to charge high cargo fees as vessels leaving Brunei are not fully loaded due to the small volume of domestic production.[367] To date, no further actions have been taken to create a national shipping company.

The Ports Department, under the Ministry of Communications, is responsible for port development, except navigational assistance to vessels entering Muara port which is provided by the Marine Department.[368] The authorities have commissioned a study to corporatize and subsequently privatize the Ports Department.[369] Port activities are regulated by the Port Act (Chapter 144) .[370] There was no change to the legal provisions on ports during the review period.

There are three ports owned, managed, and operated by the Ports Department: (i) Muara is Brunei's deep-water port through which 90% of the merchandise trade, except oil and gas, is channelled; (ii) Kuala Belait port facilitates the movement of cargo comprising materials for offshore oil and gas activities via supply vessels; and (iii) Bangar operates a domestic route for cargo transported by barges.[371] The Ports Department also operates the Passenger and Car Ferry Terminals in Serasa to connect passengers to Labuan (Malaysia), as well as the Cruise Ship Centre which provides facilities for passengers/tourists calling via Cruise Vessels. In addition, there are private terminals located in Seria and Lumut where crude oil and LNG are loaded for shipment.

Muara has two terminals for conventional cargo and containers that provide 24/7 service. Muara container terminal (MCT) is operated and maintained under a concession contract which was taken over by New Muara Container Terminal Services[372] in 2009. During 2008-13, the volume of container throughput and cargo handled by Muara port increased (Table 4.13) . However, MCT continued to operate well below its annual capacity (220,000 to 300,000 TEUs) .[373] To help increase traffic and mitigate port fees, which are among the highest in the region, incentives were introduced, including extended free storage period, lower terminal handling charges, and reduced port tariffs.[374]

During the review period, the Ports Department completed two additional inland container depots to reduce congestion and facilitate movement of cross-border cargos. The extension of the container wharf is expected to start in 2015 and be completed by end of 2016.[375] In addition, the Ports Department and the Tourism Brunei Board work jointly to convert Muara into a port of call for cruise liners in order to promote tourism development. Over the 2007-13 period, 168 cruise vessels (150,901 passengers) docked at Muara.[376]

Brunei made no commitments under the GATS on maritime transport.

TOURISM

Tourism has been identified as a contributor to economic development and diversification . During the review period, there was an increase in the number of tourist arrivals. However, there is room for further improvement as tourism's share in the economy remains relatively small at about 2% of GDP.

Brunei's tourism offer is based on nature and Islamic culture and heritage. Brunei's rainforest (75% of total land) is amongst the top 10 in the world. Islamic tourism is developed in cooperation with Tourism Malaysia through joint-packages.[378] Brunei has potential to develop cruise tourism and is taking steps to attract cruise liners (section 4.4.4.2) .

Travel agent services are regulated under the Travel Agents Act (Amendment) Order 2012 and the Travel Agents Act (Amendment) Regulation 2012. Travel agents must be licensed by the Tourism Development Department. Licences are issued for a one-year period and renewed for a one year or three year period.

Investors may apply to obtain loans at a preferential rate under the Enterprise Facilitation Scheme (section 3.3.1.3) . In addition, they may claim income tax exemption for investment made in the tourism industry, other than hotels, for a period of 11 years (section 2.4.1.1) . Since 1999, there have been 25 applications for EFS and three applications for MFS.

Brunei has made no GATS commitments in tourism services. It is a member of the UN World Tourism Organization. As part of the ASEAN Tourism Strategic Plan 2011-15, a Mutual Recognition

Arrangement for Tourism Professionals was signed in 2009 to allow free movement of tourism professionals within ASEAN.[379] The MRA covers 32 job titles, ranging from housekeeping, front office, food and beverages services, and food production for hotel division, travel agencies and tour operators for travel division.

INVESTMETN AND BUSINESS CLIMATE

Brunei is a small energy-rich Sultanate on the northern coast of Borneo in Southeast Asia. Brunei boasts a well-educated, largely English-speaking population, excellent infrastructure, and a government intent on attracting foreign investment and projects. In parallel with Brunei's efforts to attract foreign investment and create an open and transparent investment regime, the country has improved its protections for Intellectual Property Rights (IPR).

Despite repeated calls for diversification, Brunei's economy remains dependent on the income derived from sales of oil and gas, contributing about 60 percent to the country's GDP. Substantial revenue from overseas investment supplements income from domestic hydrocarbon production. These two revenue streams provide a comfortable quality of life for Brunei's population. Citizens are not required to pay taxes, have access to free education through the university level, free medical care, and frequently, subsidized housing and car fuel.

Brunei has a stable political climate and is generally sheltered from natural disasters. Brunei's central location in Southeast Asia, with good telecommunications, numerous airline connections, business tax credits in specified sectors, and no income, sales, or export taxes, offers a welcoming climate for potential investors. Sectors offering U.S. business opportunities in Brunei include aerospace and defense, agribusiness, construction, petrochemicals, energy and mining, environmental technologies, food processing and packaging, franchising, health technologies, information and communication, Islamic finance, and services. In 2014 Brunei released an Energy White Paper outlining its vision of leveraging its oil wealth to diversify its economy, create local employment, increase foreign direct investment (FDI), and sharply increase the use of renewable energy by 2035. Thus far, the government has shown it is committed to the priorities outlined in the Energy White Paper.

In 2014, Brunei began supplementing its existing common law-based penal system with a penal code based on Islamic law, which carries Sharia punishments. The Sharia Penal Code is applicable across the board. The first phase became effective in May 2014 and remains in place today. It expands restrictions regarding alcohol consumption, eating in public during the fasting hours in the month of Ramadan, and indecent behavior. Two subsequent phases, the timing of which is not yet clear, are expected to introduce severe punishments such as stoning to death for certain sex-related offenses and the amputating of limbs. Brunei officials say the most severe punishments will rarely, if ever, be implemented given the very high standard of proof required under the Sharia Penal Code. While the law does not specifically address business-related matters, potential investors should be aware that there is controversy surrounding the Sharia Penal Code issue. Thus far there have been no recorded instances of U.S. citizens, or U.S. investments, being targeted by the Sharia law.

Table 1

Measure	Year	Index/Rank	Website Address
TI Corruption Perceptions Index	2016	41 of 175	http://www.transparency.org/research/cpi/overview
World Bank's Doing Business Report "Ease of Doing Business"	2016	84 of 190	doingbusiness.org/rankings
Global Innovation Index*	2016	N/A	https://www.globalinnovationindex.org/analysis-indicator

| U.S. FDI in partner country ($M USD, stock positions) | 2015 | $ 7.0 M | http://www.bea.gov/ international/factsheet/ |
| World Bank GNI per capita | 2015 | $ 38,010 | http://data.worldbank.org/ indicator/NY.GNP.PCAP.CD |

*Brunei did not participate in the 2016 Global Innovation Index.

1. OPENNESS TO, AND RESTRICTIONS UPON, FOREIGN INVESTMENT

Policies Towards Foreign Direct Investment

Brunei has an open economy favorable to foreign trade and FDI as the government continues its economic diversification efforts to limit its long reliance on oil and gas exports.

FDI is important to Brunei as it plays a key role in the country's economic and technological development. Brunei encourages FDI in the domestic economy through various investment incentives offered by the Energy and Industry Department, Prime Minister's Office, and through activities conducted by the Ministry of Foreign and Trade and the Brunei Economic Development Board.

The 2016 World Bank Ease of Doing Business report indicated that Brunei's ease of doing business ranking improved 21 spots to 84 out of 189 economies. The significant gain due largely to improvements in the "starting a business" indicator, which saw Brunei's ranking improve to the 74th spot from last year's 79th due to the elimination of miscellaneous licensing requirements and streamlining the business registration processes, mostly of which can be done online. Other indicators that have improved include paying taxes (6th in 2016, from 30th in 2015), obtaining construction permits (21st in 2016, from 53rd in 2015), and accessing credit (79th in 2016, from 89th in 2015). Improving Brunei's Ease of Doing Business ranking has become a key focus for the government, and the Prime Minister's Office has setup a special task force, referred to as "PENGGERAK to centralize government efforts to improve this ranking.

Brunei amended its laws to make it easier and quicker for entrepreneurs and investors to establish businesses. The Business License Act (Amendment) of 2016 exempts several business activities (eateries, boarding and lodging houses or other places of public resort; street vendors and stalls; motor vehicle dealers; petrol stations including places for storing petrol and inflammable material; timber store and furniture factories; and retail shops and workshops) from needing to obtain a business license. The Miscellaneous License Act (Amendment) of 2015 reduces the wait times for new business registrants to start operations, with low-risk businesses like eateries and shops able to start operations immediately.

Limits on Foreign Control and Right to Private Ownership and Establishment

There is no restriction on total foreign ownership of companies incorporated in Brunei. The Companies Act requires locally incorporated companies to have at least one of the two directors—or if more than two directors, at least two of them—to be ordinarily resident in Brunei, but exemptions may be obtained in some circumstances. The rate of corporate income tax is the same whether the company is locally or foreign owned and managed.

All businesses in Brunei must be registered with the Registry of Companies and Business Names at the Ministry of Finance. Foreign investors can fully own incorporated companies, foreign company branches, or representative offices, but not sole proprietorships and partnerships. FDI from multinational corporations may not require a local partner in setting up a subsidiary in Brunei if at least one company director is a Brunei citizen or permanent resident.

More information on incorporation of companies can be found here on the Ministry of Finance website.

Other Investment Policy Reviews

The World Trade Organization (WTO) Secretariat prepared a Trade Policy Review of Brunei in December 2014. The review can be found online at the WTO website.

Business Facilitation

As part of Brunei's effort to attract foreign investment, several facilitating agents were established including: the Brunei Economic Development Board (BEDB), FDI Action and Support Center (FAST), and Darussalam Enterprise (DARe). These organizations work together to smoothen the process of obtaining permits, approvals and licenses. Facilitating services are now consolidated into one government website.

BEDB, the frontline agency that promotes and facilitates foreign investment into the country, works with FAST under the Prime Minister's Office to evaluate investment proposals, liaise with government agencies and obtain project approval from the government's Foreign Direct Investment and Downstream Industry Committee. DARe will then support international investments once they are in full operation.

Outward Investment

A major share of outward investment is made by the government through its sovereign wealth funds, which are managed by the Brunei Investment Agency (BIA) under the Ministry of Finance. No data is available on the total investment amount due to a strict policy of secrecy. It is believed that the majority of sovereign wealth funds are invested in foreign portfolio investments and real estate. State-owned Brunei National Petroleum Company has also evolved into an outward foreign investor, winning tenders to explore and develop onshore blocks in Myanmar. Despite the limited availability of public information regarding the amount, the funds are generally viewed positively and managed well by BIA.

2. BILATERAL INVESTMENT AGREEMENTS AND TAXATION TREATIES

Brunei is a member of the Association of Southeast Asian Nations (ASEAN), as association of ten Southeast Asian nations, which has Free Trade Agreements (FTA) with Australia, New Zealand, China, India, and South Korea, and a Comprehensive Economic Partnership Agreement with Japan.

Brunei currently has Bilateral Investment Treaties with Bahrain, China, Germany, India, the Republic of Korea, Kuwait, Oman, and Ukraine. Brunei does not currently have a Bilateral Investment Treaty with the U.S. Information on Brunei's Bilateral Investment Treaties can be found on the Ministry of Finance website.

Brunei served as the ASEAN Coordinator in negotiations for the ASEAN-Australia-New Zealand Free Trade Agreement (AANZFTA), which was signed February 2009 in Thailand and entered into force January 2010. Brunei is also negotiating party to the Regional Comprehensive Economic Partnership (RCEP), and was a founding member of the Trans-Pacific Partnership (TPP) trade agreement.

Brunei does not have a Bilateral Taxation Treaty with the United States. Information on Brunei's taxation treaties can be found on the Ministry of Finance website.

For additional analytical, business and investment opportunities information,
please contact Global Investment & Business Center, USA
at (703) 370-8082. Fax: (703) 370-8083. E-mail: ibpusa3@gmail.com
Global Business and Investment Info Databank - www.ibpus.com

3. LEGAL REGIME

Transparency of the Regulatory System

Brunei's regulatory system is generally seen as lacking in transparency. There is little to no transparency in lawmaking processes, nor is there any available information on whether impact assessments are made prior to proposing regulations. Each ministry is responsible for coordinating with the Attorney General's Chambers to draft proposed legislation. Legislation does not received broad review and few outside of the originating ministry are able to provide their input. The Sultan has final authority to approve proposed legislation. Laws and regulations that are in effect are readily available and accessible from the Attorney General's Chambers.

International Regulatory Considerations

Brunei is an active member of ASEAN, through which if has concluded FTAs with Australia & New Zealand, China, India, Japan and South Korea. Brunei became a WTO member in 1995 and a signatory to the General Agreement on Tariffs and Trade (GATT) in 1993.

Legal System and Judicial Independence

Brunei's constitution does not specifically provide for judicial independence, but in practice the court system operates without government interference. Brunei's legal system includes parallel systems; one based on Common Law and the other based on Islamic law. In 2016, Brunei began to recognize the importance of protecting investors' rights and contracts enforcement, and established a Commercial Court. In 2014, Brunei implemented Phase one of three of the Sharia Penal Code (SPC), which expanded existing restrictions on minor offenses—such as eating during Ramadan—that are punishable by fines.

The second phase of the SPC, which would include amputating the hands of thieves, is not scheduled to come into effect until one year after the publication of a Sharia Courts Criminal Procedure Code (CPC). The CPC has yet to be published. Phase three of the SPC – which includes punishments, in certain situations, such as stoning to death for rape, adultery, or sodomy, and execution for apostasy, contempt of the Prophet Muhammad, or insult of the Quran – is scheduled to be implemented two years after the publication of the CPC. The punishments included in phases two and three include different standards of proof than the common law-based penal code, such as requiring four pious men to witness personally an act of fornication to support a sentence of stoning.

Laws and Regulations on Foreign Direct Investment

The basic legislation on investment includes the Investment Incentive Order 2001 and Income Tax (As Amended) Order 2001Investment Order 2001 supports economic development in strategically important industrial and economic enterprises and through the Energy and Industry Department of the Prime Minister's Office EIDPMO, offers investment incentives through a favorable tax regime. Although Brunei does not have a stock exchange, government plans to establish a securities market are reportedly under way.

Foreign ownership of companies is not restricted, although under the Companies Act, at least one of two directors of a locally incorporated company must be a resident of Brunei, unless granted an exemption from the appropriate authorities.

Business Registration

All businesses in Brunei must be registered with the Registry of Companies and Business Names at the Ministry of Finance. Except for sole proprietorships and partnerships, foreign investors can fully own incorporated companies, foreign company branches, or representative offices. Foreign direct investments by multi-national corporations may not require local partnership in setting up a subsidiary of their parent company in Brunei. However, at least one company director must be a Brunei citizen or permanent resident of Brunei. Brunei's "one-stop-shop" website for investments and business start-ups can be found here.

Competition and Anti-Trust Laws

Brunei does not have any competition legislation pertaining to the regulation of competition issues. In May 2012, Brunei formally started drafting the Brunei Competition Order, which seeks to enact prohibitions against anti-competitive agreements, abuse of dominance, and anti-competitive mergers. As of March 2017, there is no information on when the law might be approved and implemented.

Expropriation and Compensation

There is no history of expropriation of foreign owned property in Brunei. There have been cases of domestically owned private property being expropriated for infrastructure development. Compensation was provided in such cases, and claimants were provided with due process regarding their disputes.

Dispute Settlement

ICSID Convention and New York Convention

Brunei is a member state to the convention on the International Center for Settlement of Investment Disputes (ICSID Convention) and a signatory to the Recognition and Enforcement of Foreign Arbitral Awards (1958 New York Convention).

Investor-State Dispute Settlement

In 2016, Brunei's Supreme Court announced the establishment of a commercial court to deal with business-related cases. More information about Brunei's judiciary system is available at through their website.

International Commercial Arbitration and Foreign Courts

In May 2016, Brunei's Attorney General's Chambers has announced the establishment of the Brunei Darussalam Arbitration Center (BDAC). BDAC delivers services and administration for arbitration and mediation to fulfil the needs of domestic and international users in relation to commercial disputes, as a resolution alternative to court proceedings.

The International Arbitration Order (IAO) which regulates international and domestic arbitrations came into effect in February 2010. More information about Brunei's Attorney General's Chambers is available online.

Bankruptcy Regulations

In 2012, amendments to Brunei's Bankruptcy Act increased the minimum threshold for declaring bankruptcy from BND 500 to BND 10,000 (USD $357 to USD $7,133) and enabled the trustee to direct the Controller of Immigration to impound and retain the debtor's passport, certificate of identity, or travel document to prevent him from leaving the country. The amendment also requires the debtor to deliver all property under his possession to the trustee. Information about Brunei's bankruptcy laws is available on the judiciary's website.

4. INDUSTRIAL POLICIES

Investment Incentives

Companies involved in the exportation of agriculture, forestry, and fishery products can apply for tax relief on export profits. For non-pioneer enterprises, the tax relief period is eight years and up to 11 years for pioneer enterprises.

The corporate income tax rate in Brunei has been reduced from 30 percent (2007 and earlier) to the current rate of 18.5 percent (2015 onwards).

Sole proprietorships and partnerships are not subject to tax. Individuals do not pay any capital gains tax and profits arising from the sale of capital assets are not taxable. Brunei has double-taxation agreements with the United Kingdom, Indonesia, China, Singapore, Vietnam, Bahrain, Oman, Japan, Pakistan, Malaysia, Hong Kong, Laos, Kuwait, Tajikistan, Qatar, and United Arab Emirates. Under the Income Tax (Petroleum) Act, a company is subject to taxes of up to 55 percent for any petroleum operation pursuant to production sharing agreements.

Foreign Trade Zones/Free Ports/Trade Facilitation

Muara Port is Brunei's main seaport with an established Free Trade Zone called the Muara Export Zone (MEZ), which was established to promote and develop Brunei as a trade hub of the region. The establishment of the MEZ was an initial step towards developing other Free Trade Zones in the country. In Brunei's 2017 Legislative Council session, the government announced that a 96 hectare area near Muara Port will be designated to be a Free Trade Zone.

Performance and Data Localization Requirements

The Brunei government seeks to increase the number of Bruneians working in the private sector. Brunei's 2014 Energy White Paper calls for the number of people employed in the energy sector to increase from 20,000 in 2010 to 50,000 in 2035, and for the number of locals employed in the sector to increase from 10,000 to 40,000 during the same period. To advance this goal, all companies competing for a tender in the oil and gas industry are required to have at least half of their employees be Bruneian.

Expatriate employment is controlled by a labor quota system administered by the Labor Department and the issuance of employment passes by the Immigration Department. Brunei allows new companies to apply for special approval to expedite the recruitment of expatriate workers in select positions. According to the Ministry of Home Affairs, the special approval is only available to new companies for up to six months, and covers businesses such as restaurants and shops. The special approval cuts the waiting time for a quota to seven days instead of twenty one.

Currently, Brunei has not announced any specific legislation pertaining to data storage and data localization requirements. In early 2016, the Prime Minister's Office (PMO) announced plans to develop a National Cyber Defense Framework which is expected to be completed by the end of 2017.

5. PROTECTION OF PROPERTY RIGHTS

Real Property

Mortgages are recognized and enforced in Brunei; however, only Bruneians can own land property in Brunei. Foreigners and permanent residents can only hold properties under long-term leases. Most banks are reluctant to grant housing loans to foreigners and permanent residents. According to the International Monetary Fund (IMF) Brunei country report, Brunei did not attract any Foreign Direct Investment for real estate, rentals, and business activity in 2011 (latest data available). Brunei's Department of Economic Planning and Development do not publish FDI data for real estate. The country is currently ranked 135 out of 190 economies for Registering Property in the World Bank's Doing Business Report, this is because every transfer of ownership in Brunei Darussalam requires the approval of "His Majesty in Council" which is a council of officials representing the Sultan. This process can be lengthy and at times opaque.

Amendments to the Land Code are being considered to ban past practices of proxy land sales to foreigners and permanent residents using power of attorney (PA) and trust deeds (TD). PAs and TDs are no longer recognized as mechanisms in land transactions involving non-citizens. The proposed laws will also be retroactive, converting all existing property owned through PAs and TDs into 60-year leases. The government may grant temporary occupation permits over state land to applicants, for licenses to occupy land for agricultural, commercial, housing or industrial purposes. These licenses are not registered, and are granted for renewable annual terms.

Intellectual Property

Brunei's intellectual property rights (IPR) protection and enforcement regime is still in development but is increasingly strong and effective. The country was removed from the U.S. Trade Representative's Special 301 report in 2013, and has stayed off in recognition of its improving IPR protections, increasing enforcement, and efforts to educate the public about the importance of IPR.

Brunei's Copyright (Amendment) Order 2013 was finalized and adopted in December 2013, a development long requested by the U.S. government. The amendment enhanced enforcement provisions for copyright infringement by increasing the penalties for IP offences; adding new offenses; strengthening the enforcement powers of the Royal Brunei Police Force and the Ministry of Finance Customs and Excise Department; and allowing for sanctioned private prosecution. The amendments are designed to deter copyright infringements with fines of BND 10,000 (USD $7,400) to BND 20,000 (USD $14,800) per infringing copy, imprisonment for a term up to five years, or both. The new penalty is up to four times more severe than the previously existing penalty. Enforcement agencies are authorized to enter premises and arrest without warrant, to stop, search, and board vehicles and also to access computerized and digitized data. The amendments further allow for admissibility of evidence obtained covertly and protect the identity of informants. Statistics on seizures of counterfeit goods are unavailable.

Brunei transferred its Registry of Trademarks from the Attorney General's Chambers (AGC) to the Brunei Intellectual Property Office in 2013. The transfer expanded the country's Patents Registry Office's (PRO) ability to accept applications for trademarks registration, in addition to patents and industrial designs.

In September 2013, Brunei acceded to the Geneva (1999) Act of the Hague Agreement Concerning the International Registration of Industrial Designs to protect IP from industrial designs, making it the second ASEAN Member country, following Singapore, to accede. The accession emphasized Brunei's commitment under the ASEAN Intellectual Property Rights Action Plan 2011 – 2015. Brunei also plans and has publicly committed to acceding to other World Intellectual Property Organization's (WIPO) treaties including the Madrid Protocol for the International Registration of Marks, the WIPO Performances and Phonograms Treaty

For additional analytical, business and investment opportunities information,
please contact Global Investment & Business Center, USA
at (703) 370-8082. Fax: (703) 370-8083. E-mail: ibpusa3@gmail.com
Global Business and Investment Info Databank - www.ibpus.com

(WPPT), and the UPOV Convention 1991 for the protection of New Varieties of Plants (PV). In February 2016, Brunei signed the Trans-Pacific Partnership which includes new commitments to IPR.

For additional information about treaty obligations and points of contact at local IP offices, please see WIPO's country profiles at: http://www.wipo.int/directory/en/

Resources for Rights Holders

Contact at U.S. Mission:

Fausto DeGuzman
Political/Economic/Consular Officer
+673 238-4616 ext. 2172
DeguzmanF@state.gov

6. FINANCIAL SECTOR

Capital Markets and Portfolio Investment

In 2013, Brunei signed a Memorandum of Understanding (MOU) with the Securities

Commission Malaysia (SCM) to boost cooperation in the capital markets. The MOU was designed to strengthen collaboration in the development of fair and efficient capital markets in the two countries. It also provided a framework to facilitate greater cross-border capital market activities and cooperation in the areas of regulation as well as capacity building and human capital development, particularly in the area of Islamic capital markets. In 2015, Autoriti Monetari Brunei Darussalam (AMBD)–Brunei's central bank–announced plans to launch a capital market in Brunei by 2017, if the preconditions required for launching a security exchange are met. The plans to open a domestic exchange are welcomed by the finance industry players though it may be difficult to identify the companies interested to be listed.

Money and Banking System

Brunei has a small banking sector which includes both conventional and Islamic banking. The Monetary Authority of Brunei Darussalam (AMBD) is the sole central authority for the banking sector, in addition to being the country's central bank. Banks in the country have high levels of liquidity, good capital adequacy ratios and well-managed levels of non-performing loans. A handful of foreign banks have established operations in the country such as Standard Chartered and Bank of China (Hong Kong). In late 2016, HSBC announced that it will be down-sizing its operations in Brunei. All banks are under the supervision of AMBD, which has also established a credit bureau that centralizes information on an applicant's credit worthiness.

The Brunei dollar (BND) is pegged to the Singapore dollar , and is accepted currency in the country.

Foreign Exchange and Remittances

Foreign Exchange

In June 2013, the Financial Action Task Force (FATF) announced that Brunei is no longer subject to FATF's monitoring process under its global Anti-Money Laundering/Countering the Financing of Terrorism (AML/CFT) compliance process. Brunei will work with the Asia-Pacific Group (APG) as it continues to address the full range of AML/CFT issues identified in its Mutual Evaluation Report. The report cited Brunei's significant progress in improving its AML/CFT regime and noted that Brunei had established the legal and regulatory framework to meet its commitments in its Action Plan regarding the strategic deficiencies that the FATF identified in June 2011.

Remittance Policies

Remittance services are provided by local financial institutions including banks such as Bank Islam Brunei Darussalam (BIBD) and Standard Chartered Bank. AMBD, Brunei's central bank, regulates and supervises these financial institutions that provide remittance services.

Sovereign Wealth Funds

The Brunei Investment Agency (BIA) manages Brunei's General Reserve Fund and their external assets. Established in 1983, BIA's assets are estimated to be USD 170 billion. BIA's activities are not publicly disclosed and are ranked the lowest in transparency ratings by the Sovereign Wealth Fund Institute.

7. STATE-OWNED ENTERPRISES

Brunei's state-owned enterprises (SOEs) lead key sectors of the economy including oil and gas, telecommunications, transport, and energy generation and distribution. These enterprises also receive preferential treatment when tendering for lucrative government contracts. The government does not publish a list of SOEs, but prominent SOEs include:

Under the Telecommunications Order 2001, the Authority for Info-communications Technology Industry (AiTi) regulates the licensing of the telecommunications industry. The establishment, installation, maintenance, provision or operation of unlicensed telecommunication systems or services within Brunei is a punishable offense, resulting in imprisonment, and large fines. AiTi has not opened up the telecommunications industry to foreign participation. The telecommunications industry is dominated by government-linked companies Telekom Brunei (TelBru), Data Stream Technologies (DST) Communications, and Progresif Cellular. Telbru is the sole provider of fixed line telephone and internet services. DST, founded in 1995, and Progresif, which took over from failed telecom company B-Mobile in 2014 and is owned by a government investment fund, provides mobile phone and internet services.

Royal Brunei Technical Services (RBTS), established in 1988 as a government owned corporation, is responsible for managing the acquisition of a wide range of systems and equipment and maintaining those acquired systems and equipment.

Brunei National Petroleum Sendirian Berhad (PB) is the national oil company owned by the Brunei government. The company was granted all the mineral rights in eight prime onshore and offshore petroleum blocks, totaling 20,552 sq. km. Currently, the company manages contractors, including Shell, Total, and Petronas, which are exploring the onshore and deep water offshore blocks.

Privatization Program

Brunei's Ministry of Communication has made corporatization and privatization part of its Strategic Plans for 2008-2017, which calls for the Ministry to shift its role from a service provider to a regulatory body with policy-setting responsibilities. In that role, the Ministry will develop specific policies through corporatization and privatization; establish a regulatory framework and business facilitation. Currently, the Ministry is studying initiatives to privatize a number of state-owned agencies: the Maritime and Port Authority of Brunei Darussalam, the Postal Services Department, and Brunei International Airport management. These services are not yet completely privatized and there is no timeline for privatization, as the Ministry is still in the process of considering the initiative. Guidelines regarding the role of foreign investors and the bidding process are not yet available. The strategy can be found on the Ministry of Communication's website.

8. RESPONSIBLE BUSINESS CONDUCT

Responsible business conduct is a relatively new concept in Brunei, and there are no specific government programs encouraging foreign and local enterprises to follow generally accepted corporate social responsibility (CSR) principles. However, there is broad awareness of CSR among producers and consumers, and individual private and public sector organizations have formalized CSR programs and policies. There are no reporting requirements and no independent NGOs in Brunei that promote or monitor CSR.

OECD Guidelines for Multinational Enterprises

Brunei does not adhere to the OECD guidelines for multinational enterprises. OECD's guidelines for multinational enterprises can be found on the OECD website.

9. CORRUPTION

Since 1982, Brunei has enforced the Emergency (Prevention of Corruption) Act. In 1984, the Act was renamed the Prevention of Corruption Act (Chapter 131). The Anti-Corruption Bureau (ACB) was established in 1982 for the purpose of enforcing the Act. The Prevention of Corruption Act provides specific powers to the ACB for the purpose of investigating accusations of corruption. The Act authorizes ACB to investigate certain offences under other written laws, provided such offences were disclosed during the course of ACB investigation.

The ACB strives to ensure a corruption-free public service. Corrupt practices are punishable under the Prevention of Corruption Act. The Act also applies to Brunei citizens abroad. There is the perception that corruption is more prevalent in the private sector than in the public sector. This has prompted the ACB to focus on the private sector, as the private sector plays a critical role in Brunei's economic diversification. Brunei is a member of the International Association of Anti-Corruption Authorities.

In 2016, Brunei was ranked the 41st of 176 countries worldwide in Transparency International's corruption perception index. No scores were recorded for 2014 and 2015, but the ranking is an improvement from its 2013 ranking.

U.S. companies do not generally identify corruption as an obstacle to conducting business in Brunei.

The level and extent of corruption in Brunei is relatively low. For example in June 2016, a police officer was found guilty of accepting a USD 30 bribe in exchange for not taking action over a driver's alleged traffic offenses of not wearing a seatbelt and using a mobile phone while driving.

Apart from the Anti-Corruption Bureau, there are no international, regional, local or nongovernmental organizations operating in Brunei that monitor corruption.

Brunei has signed and ratified the UN Anticorruption Convention.

Resources to Report Corruption

Government Point of Contact:

Name: Dato Paduka Haji Mohammad Juanda bin Haji Abdul Rashid
Title: Director
Organization: Anti-Corruption Bureau Brunei Darussalam
Address: Old Airport Berakas, BB 3510 Brunei Darussalam
Tel: +673 238-3575
Fax: +673 238-3193
Email: info.bmr@acb.gov.bn

10. POLITICAL AND SECURITY ENVIRONMENT

Brunei is an absolute monarch and has no recent history of political violence. Sultan Hassanal Bolkiah is an experienced and popular monarch who rules the country as Prime Minister while also retaining the titles of Minister of Finance, Minister of Defense, and Minister of Foreign Affairs and Trade. The country experienced an uprising in 1962, when it was a British protectorate, which ended through the intervention of British troops. The country has been ruled peacefully under emergency law ever since. Brunei has managed to avoid demands for political reform by making use of its hydrocarbon revenues to provide its citizens with generous welfares and subsidies.

11. LABOR POLICIES AND PRACTICES

Brunei relies heavily on foreign labor in lower-skill and lower-paying positions, with approximately 6.9 percent of the labor force coming in from abroad to fulfill specific contracts. The largest percentage of those work in construction, followed by wholesale and retail trade, and then professional, technical, administrative and support services. Most unskilled laborers in Brunei are immigrants from Bangladesh, India, Indonesia, Malaysia, and the Philippines, and enter the country on renewable two-year contracts.

The skilled labor pool includes both foreign laborers on short-term visas and Bruneian citizens and permanent residents, who often are well-educated but who generally prefer to work for the government due to generous benefits such as bonuses, education allowances, interest-free loans, and housing allowances. The 2014, the latest year for which there are available statistics, Labor Force Survey stated that approximately 43.5 percent of the total Brunei citizen workforce is employed in the public sector. In 2016, the Department of Labor under the Ministry of Home Affairs, introduced the improved Foreign Workers License process that with stricter policies in an effort to create more employment opportunities for Brunei citizens.

While Brunei law permits the formation of trade union federations, it forbids affiliation with international labor organizations unless there is consent from the Minister of Home Affairs and the Department of Labor. Under the Trade Unions Act of 1961, unions must be registered with the government. The government prohibits strikes, and the law makes no explicit provision for the right to collective bargaining. The law prohibits employers from discriminating against workers in connection with union activities, but it does not provide for reinstatement for dismissal related to union activity.

All workers, including civil servants other than those serving in the military and those working as prison guards or police officers, may form and join trade unions of their choice without previous authorization or excessive requirements. The only active union in the country, which is composed of Brunei Shell Petroleum workers, appears to have minimal activity in recent years. There are no other active unions or worker organizations.

Various domestic laws prohibit the employment of children under age 16. Parental consent and approval by the Labor Commission are required for those under age 18. Female workers under age 18 may not work at night or on offshore oil platforms. The Department of Labor, which is part of the Ministry of Home Affairs, effectively enforced laws related to the employment of children. There were no reports of violations of child labor laws.

The law does not set a minimum wage, but most employed citizens recieve good salaries. The public sector pay scale covers all workers in government jobs. Wages for employed foreign residents are wide ranging. Some foreign embassies set minimum wage requirements for their nationals working in the country.

Government data from 2014, the latest data available, indicated approximately 86,500 foreigners lived in the country temporarily. Foreign workers receive a mandatory brief on labor rights from the Department of Labor when they sign their contract. The government also protects the rights of foreign workers through inspections of facilities and a telephone hotline for worker complaints. Immigration law allows prison sentences and caning for workers who overstay their work permits, for workers who fall into irregular status due to their employers' negligence.

12. OPIC AND OTHER INVESTMENT INSURANCE PROGRAMS

Overseas Private Investment Corporation (OPIC) programs are not available in Brunei given the country's affluence.

13. FOREIGN DIRECT INVESTMENT AND FOREIGN PORTFOLIO INVESTMENT STATISTICS

Table 2: Key Macroeconomic Data, U.S. FDI in Host Country/Economy

	Host Country Statistical Source		USG or International Statistical Source		USG or International Source of Data: BEA; IMF; Eurostat; UNCTAD, Other
Economic Data	Year	Amount	Year	Amount	
Host Country Gross Domestic Product (GDP) ($M USD)	2016	$11.25 Billion	2015	$12.93 Billion	http://data.worldbank.org/ country/brunei-darussalam
Foreign Direct Investment	Host Country Statistical source		USG or International Statistical Source		USG or International Source of Data: BEA; IMF; Eurostat; UNCTAD, Other
U.S. FDI in partner country ($M USD, stock positions)	2015	$6.92 million	2015	$7.0 million	BEA data available at http://bea.gov/international/direct_investment_ multinational_companies_ comprehensive_data.htm
Host country's FDI in the United States ($M USD, stock positions)	2015	N/A	2015	$9.0 million	BEA data available at http://bea.gov/international/direct_investment_ multinational_companies_ comprehensive_data.htm
Total inbound stock of FDI as % host GDP	2015	$170 million	N/A	N/A	N/A

Brunei's GDP data obtained from Brunei Darussalam Statistical Yearbook 2015. Data is not available for US-Brunei's stock FDI positions.

IMPORTANT LAWS AND REGULATIONS RELATED TO BUSINESS, TRADE AND INVESTMENT ACTIVITIES

IMPORTANT LAWS AFFECTING BUSINESS AND INVESTMENTS

INVESTMENT INCENTIVES ORDER

In exercise of the power conferred by subsection (3) of section 83 of the Constitution of Brunei Darussalam, His Majesty the Sultan and Yang Di-Pertuan hereby makes the following Order —

PART I PRELIMINARY
Citation, commencement and long title.

1. (1) This Order may be cited as the Investment Incentives Order, 2001 and shall commence on 1st. June, 2001.

(2) The long title of this Order is "An Order to make new provision for encouraging the establishment and development in Brunei Darussalam of industrial and other economic enterprises, for economic expansion and for incidental and related purposes".

Order to be construed as one with the Income Tax Act (Chapter 35).

2. This Order shall, unless otherwise expressly provided for in this Order, be construed as one with the Income Tax Act.

Interpretation.

3. In this Order, unless the context otherwise requires —

"approved foreign loan" means a loan which is certified under section 75 to be an approved foreign loan;

"approved product" means a product declared under section 30 to be an approved product;

"Collector" means the Collector of Income Tax appointed under the Income Tax Act (Chapter 35);

"company" means any company incorporated or registered in accordance with the provisions of any written law relating to companies;

"expanding enterprise" means any company which has been approved by the Minister and to which an expansion certificate has been issued under section 31;

"expansion certificate" means an expansion certificate issued under section 31;

"expansion day", in relation to an expanding enterprise, means the date specified in its expansion certificate under subsection (4) or (5) of section 31; "export enterprise" means any company which has been approved by the Minister and

to which an export certificate has been issued under section 40;

"export enterprise certificate" means an export enterprise certificate issued under section 40; "export produce" means a produce of agriculture, forestry and fisheries approved

under section 39 as export produce; "export product" means a product approved under section 39 as export product; "export year" means the year specified in the export enterprise certificate under

subsection (2) of section 40 or section 41; "foreign loan certificate" means a foreign loan certificate issued under section 75; "high-tech park" means an area declared by the Minister to be a high-tech park; "manufacture", in relation to a product, includes any process or method used in

making or developing the product;

"Minister" means the Minister charged with the responsibility for industrial development; "new trade or business" means the trade or business of a pioneer enterprise deemed

under section 8 to have been set up and commenced on the day following the end of its

tax relief period; "officer of customs" and "senior officer of customs" have the same meanings as in the Customs Act (Chapter 36);

"old trade or business" means the trade or business of a pioneer enterprise carried on by it during its tax relief period in accordance with section 8, and which either ceases within or is deemed, under that section, to cease at the end of that period;

"pioneer certificate" means a pioneer certificate issued under section 5;

"pioneer enterprise" means any company which has been approved by the Minister and to which a pioneer certificate has been issued under section 5; "pioneer industry" means an industry declared under section 4 to be a pioneer

industry; "pioneer product" means a product declared under section 4 to be a pioneer product;

"production date", in relation to a pioneer enterprise, means the date specified in its pioneer certificate under subsection (3) or (4) of section 5;

"productive equipment" means machinery or plant which would normally qualify for deduction under sections 16, 17 and 18 of the Income Tax Act (Chapter 35);

"repealed Act" means the Investment Incentives Act (Chapter 97) repealed by this Order;

"tax" means income tax imposed by the Income Tax Act (Chapter 35);

PART II PIONEER INDUSTRIES

For additional analytical, business and investment opportunities information, please contact Global Investment & Business Center, USA at (703) 370-8082. Fax: (703) 370-8083. E-mail: ibpusa3@gmail.com Global Business and Investment Info Databank - www.ibpus.com

Power and procedure for declaring an industry and a product a pioneer industry and a pioneer product.

4. (1) Subject to subsection (2), the Minister may, if he considers it expedient in the public interest to do so, by order declare an industry, which is not being carried on in Brunei Darussalam on a scale adequate to the economic needs of Brunei Darussalam and for which in his opinion there are favourable prospects for development, to be a pioneer industry and any specific product of that industry to be a pioneer product.

(2) The Minister may revoke any order made under this section but any such revocation shall not affect the operation of any pioneer certificate issued to any pioneer enterprise before the revocation.

Application for and issue and amendment of pioneer certificate.

5. (1) Any company which is desirous of producing a pioneer product may make an application in writing to the Minister to be approved as a pioneer enterprise in such form and with such particulars as may be prescribed.

(2) Where the Minister is satisfied that it is expedient in the public interest to do so and, in particular, having regard to the production or anticipated production of the pioneer product from all sources of production in Brunei Darussalam, he may approve that company a pioneer enterprise and issue a pioneer certificate to the company, subject to such terms and conditions as he thinks fit.

(3) Every pioneer certificate issued under this section shall specify —

(a)

the date on or before which it is expected that the pioneer enterprise will commence to produce in marketable quantities the product specified in the certificate; and

(b)

the rate of production of that product which it is expected will be attained on or before that date,

and that date shall be deemed to be the production day of the pioneer enterprise for the purposes of this Order.

(4) The Minister may, in his discretion, upon the application of any pioneer enterprise, amend its pioneer certificate by substituting for the production day specified therein such earlier or later date as he thinks fit and thereupon the provisions of this Order shall have effect as if the date so substituted were the production day in relation to that pioneer enterprise.

Tax relief period of pioneer enterprise.

6. (1) The tax relief period of a pioneer enterprise shall commence on its production day and shall continue for a period of —

(a)

5 years, where its fixed capital expenditure is not less than $500,000 but is less than $2.5 million;

(b)

8 years, where its fixed capital expenditure is more than $2.5 million;

(c)

11 years, where it is located in a high tech park.

(2)

Where the tax relief period of a pioneer enterprise is 5 years and the Minister is satisfied that it has incurred by the end of the year following the end of that period fixed capital of not less than $2.5 million, the Minister may extend its tax relief period to 8 years from the production day.

(3)

In this section, "fixed capital expenditure" in relation to a pioneer enterprise, means capital expenditure incurred by the pioneer enterprise on its factory building (excluding land) or on plant, machinery or other apparatus used in Brunei Darussalam in connection with and for the purposes of the pioneer enterprise.

Further extension of tax relief period.

7. (1) The Minister may, subject to such terms and conditions as he may impose, extend the tax relief period of a pioneer enterprise (other than a pioneer enterprise that is located in a high-tech park) for such further period or periods as he may determine except that the tax relief period of the pioneer enterprise shall not in aggregate exceed 11 years.

(2) The Minister may, subject to such terms and conditions as he may impose, extend the tax relief period of a pioneer enterprise that is located in a high-tech park for such further period or periods not exceeding 5 years at any one time as he may determine except that the tax relief period of the pioneer enterprise shall not in aggregate exceed 20 years.

Provisions governing old and new trade or business.

8. For the purposes of the Income Tax Act (Chapter 35) and this Order —

(a)

the old trade or business of a pioneer enterprise shall be deemed to have permanently ceased at the end of its tax relief period;

(b)

the pioneer enterprise shall be deemed to have set up and commenced a new trade or business on the day immediately following the end of its tax relief period;

(c)

the pioneer enterprise shall make up accounts of its old trade or business for a period not exceeding one year, commencing on its production day, for successive periods of one year thereafter and for the period not exceeding one year ending at the date when its tax relief period ends; and

(d)

in making up the first accounts of its new trade or business the pioneer enterprise shall take as the opening figures for those accounts the closing figures in respect of its assets and liabilities as shown in its last accounts in respect of its tax relief period, and its next accounts of its new trade or business shall be made up by reference to the closing figures in such first accounts an any subsequent accounts shall be similarly made up by reference to the closing figures of the preceding accounts of its new trade or business.

Restrictions on trading before end of tax relief period.

9. (1) During its tax relief period, a pioneer enterprise shall not carry on any trade or business other than the trade or business relating to the relevant pioneer product, unless the Minister has given his permission in writing therefor.

(2)

Where the carrying on of a separate trade or business has been permitted under subsection (1), separate accounts shall be maintained in respect of that trade or business and in respect of the same accounting period.

(3)

Where the carrying on of such separate trade results in a loss in any accounting period, the loss shall be brought into the computation of the income of the pioneer enterprise for that period unless the Collector, having regard to all the circumstances of the case, is satisfied that the loss was not incurred for the purpose of obtaining a tax advantage.

(4)

Where the carrying on of such separate trade results in a profit in any accounting period, and the profit, computed in accordance with the provisions of the Income Tax Act as modified by this section, amounts to less than 5% on the full sum receivable from the sale of goods or the provision of services, the statutory income from that source shall be deemed to be 5% (or such lower rate as the Minister may specify in any particular case) of the full sum so receivable and the income of the pioneer enterprise shall be abated accordingly.

(5)

Where in the opinion of the Collector the carrying on of such separate trade is subordinate and incidental to the carrying on of the trade or business relating to the relevant pioneer product, the income or loss arising from such activities shall be deemed to form part of the income or loss of the pioneer enterprise.

(6)

In this section, "relevant pioneer product" means the pioneer product specified in its pioneer certificate.

Power to give directions.

10. For the purposes of the Income Tax Act and this Order, the Collector may direct that —

(a)

any sums payable to a pioneer enterprise in any accounting period which, but for the provisions of this Order, might reasonably and properly have been expected to be payable, in the normal course of business, after the end of that period shall be treated —

(i)

as not having been payable in that period but as having been payable on such date, after that period as the Collector thinks fit; and

(ii)

where that date is after the end of the tax relief period of the pioneer enterprise, as having been so payable, on that date, as a sum payable in respect of its new trade or business;

(b)

any expense incurred by a pioneer enterprise within one year after the end of its tax relief period which, but for the provisions of this Order, might reasonable and properly have been expected to be incurred, in the normal course of business, during its tax relief period shall be treated as not having been incurred within that year but as having been incurred —

(i)

for the purposes of its old trade or business; and

(ii)

on such date, during its tax relief period, as the Collector thinks fit.

Ascertainment of income in respect of old trade or business.

11. (1) The income of a pioneer enterprise in respect of its old trade or business shall be ascertained in accordance with the provisions of the Income Tax Act after making such adjustments as may be necessary in consequence of any direction given under section 10.

(2)

In determining the income of a pioneer enterprise referred to in subsection (1), the allowances provided for in sections 13, 14, 15, 16, 17 and 18 of the Income Tax Act shall be taken into account.

(3)

Where the tax relief period of a pioneer enterprise referred to in subsection (1) expires during the basis period for any year of assessment, for the purpose of determining the income in respect of its old trade or business and its new trade or business for that year of assessment, there shall be deducted allowances provided for in sections 13, 14, 15, 16, 17 and 18 of the Income Tax Act; and for the purpose of computing such allowances —

(a)

the allowances for that year of assessment shall be computed as if the old trade or business of the pioneer enterprise had not been deemed to have permanently ceased at the end of the tax relief period; and

(b)

the allowances computed in accordance with paragraph (a) shall be apportioned between the old trade or business and the new trade or business of the pioneer enterprise in such manner as appears to the Collector to be reasonable in the circumstances.

(4)

Where in any year of assessment full effect cannot, by reason of an insufficiency of profits for that year of assessment, be given to the allowances mentioned in subsection (2), then the balance of the allowances shall be added to, and be deemed to form part of, the corresponding allowances, if any, for the next succeeding year of assessment, and, if no such corresponding allowances fall to be made for that year, shall be deemed to constitute the corresponding allowances for that year, and so on for subsequent years of assessment.

Application of Part X of Income Tax Act (Chapter 35).

12. Part X of the Income Tax Act (relating to returns of income) shall apply in all respects as if the income of a pioneer enterprise in respect of its old trade or business were chargeable to tax.

Collector to issue statement of income.

13. For each year of assessment, the Collector shall issue to the pioneer enterprise a statement showing the amount of income for that year of assessment, and Parts XI and XII of the Income Tax Act (relating to objections and appeals) and any regulations made thereunder shall apply with the necessary modifications, as if that statement were a notice of assessment given under those provisions.

Exemption from income tax.

14. (1) Subject to subsection (6) of section 15, where any statement issued under section 13 has become final and conclusive, the amount of the income shown by the statement shall not form part of the statutory income of the pioneer enterprise for any year of assessment and shall be exempt from tax.

(2) The Collector may, in his discretion and before such a statement has become final and conclusive, declare that a specified part of the amount of such income is not in dispute and such an undisputed amount of income is exempt from tax, pending such a statement becoming final and conclusive.

Certain dividends exempted from income tax.

15. (1) As soon as any amount of income of a pioneer enterprise has been exempt under section 14, that amount shall be credited to an account to be kept by the pioneer enterprise for the purposes of this section.

(2)

Where that account is in credit at the date on which any dividends are paid by the pioneer enterprise out of income which has been exempted, an amount equal to those dividends or to that credit, whichever is the less, shall be debited to the account.

(3)

So much of the amount of any dividends so debited to that account as are received by a shareholder of the pioneer enterprise shall, if the Collector is satisfied with the entries in the account, be exempt from tax in the hands of the shareholder.

(4)

Notwithstanding subsection (3), where a dividend is paid on any share of a preferential nature, it shall not be so exempt in the hands of the shareholder.

(5)

Any dividends debited to that account shall be treated as having been distributed to the shareholders of the pioneer enterprise or any particular class of those shareholders in the same proportions as the shareholders were entitled to payment to payment of the dividends giving rise to the debit.

(6)

The pioneer enterprise shall deliver to the Collector a copy of that account, made up to a date specified by him, whenever called upon to do so by notice in writing sent by him to its registered office, until such time as he is satisfied that there is no further need for maintaining the account.

(7)

Notwithstanding section 14 and subsections (1) to (6), where it appears to the Collector that —

(a)

any amount of exempted income of a pioneer enterprise; or

(b)

any dividend exempted in the hands of any shareholder, including any dividend paid by a holding company to which subsection (10) applies,

ought not to have been exempted by reason of any direction made under section 10 or the revocation under section 114 of a pioneer certificate issued to the pioneer enterprise, the Collector may subject to section 62 of the Income Tax Act —

(i)

make such assessment or additional assessment upon the pioneer enterprise or any such shareholder as may appear to be necessary in order to counteract any profit obtained from any such amount; or

(ii)

direct the pioneer enterprise to debit its account, kept in accordance with subsection (1), with such amount as the circumstances require.

(8)

Parts XI and XII of the Income Tax Act (relating to objections and appeals) and any regulations made thereunder shall apply, with the necessary modifications, to any direction given under subsection (7) as if it were a notice of assessment given under those provisions.

(9)

Section 36 of the Income Tax Act shall not apply in respect of any dividend or part thereof which is debited to the account required to be kept for the purposes of this section.

(10)

Where an amount has been received by way of dividend from a pioneer enterprise by a shareholder and the amount is exempt from tax under this section, if that shareholder is a company (referred to in this section as the holding company) which holds, throughout its tax relief period, the beneficial interest in all the issued shares of the pioneer enterprise (or in not less than such proportion of those shares as the Minister may require at the time when the pioneer certificate is issued to that pioneer enterprise) any dividends paid by the holding company to its shareholders, to the extent that the Collector is satisfied that those dividends are paid out of that amount, shall be exempt from tax in the hands of those shareholders; and section 36 of the Income Tax Act shall not apply in respect of any dividend or part thereof so exempt.

(11)

Any holding company may, with the approval of the Minister and subject to such terms and conditions as he may impose, pay such exempt dividends to its shareholders even if it has not held the requisite shareholding in the pioneer enterprise for the whole of the tax relief period.

Carry forward of loss and allowance.

16. (1) Where a pioneer enterprise has, during its tax relief period, incurred a loss for any year, that loss shall be deducted as provided for in subsection (2) of section 30 of the Income Tax Act but only against the income of the pioneer enterprise as ascertained under section 11, except that the balance of any such loss which remains unabsorbed at the end of its tax relief period is available to the new trade or business in accordance with that Act.

(2) Notwithstanding paragraph *(a)* of section 8, the balance of any allowance as provided for in section 11 which remains unabsorbed at the end of the tax relief period of the pioneer enterprise is available to the new trade or business in accordance with the Income Tax Act.

PART III PIONEER SERVICE COMPANIES

Interpretation of this Part.

17. For the purposes of this Part, unless the context otherwise requires —

"commencement day", in relation to a pioneer service company, means the date specified under subsection (3) or (4) of section 18 in the certificate issued to that company under that section;

"pioneer service company" means a company which has been issued with a certificate under section 18;

"qualifying activity" means any of the following —

(a)

any engineering or technical services including laboratory, consultancy and research and development activities;

(b)

computer-based information and other computer related services;

(c)

the development or production of any industrial design;

(d)

(e) services and activities which relate to the provision of leisure and recreation;

(f) publishing services;

(g) services which relate to the provision of education;

(h) medical services;

(i) services and activities which relate to agricultural technology;

(j) services and activities which relate to the provision of warehousing facilities;

(k) services which relate to the organisation or management of exhibitions and conferences;

(l) financial services;

(m) business consultancy, management and professional services;

(n) venture capital fund activity;

(o) operation or management of any mass rapid transit system;

(p) services provided by an auction house;

(q) maintaining and operating a private museum; and

such other services or activities as the Minister may prescribe.
Application for and issue and amendment of certificate for pioneer service company.

18. (1) Where a company is engaged in any qualifying activity, the company may apply in the prescribed form to the Minister for approval as a pioneer service company.

(2) The Minister may, if he considers it expedient in the public interest to do so, approve the application and issue the company with a certificate subject to such terms and conditions as he thinks fit.

(3) Every certificate issued under this section shall specify a date as the commencement day from which the company shall be entitled to tax relief under this Part.

(4) The Minister may in his discretion, upon the application of the company, amend its certificate by substituting for the commencement day specified therein such earlier or later date as he thinks fit and thereupon the provisions of this Part shall have effect as if the date so substituted were the commencement day in relation to that certificate.
Tax relief period of pioneer service company.

19. The tax relief period of a pioneer service company, in relation to any qualifying activity specified in any certificate issued to that company under section 18, shall commence on the commencement day and shall continue for a period of 8 years or such longer period, not exceeding 11 years, as the Minister may determine.

Application of sections 8 to 16 to pioneer service company.

20. Sections 8 to 16 shall apply to a pioneer service company under this Part and for the purposes of such application —

(a)

any reference to a pioneer enterprise shall be read as a reference to a pioneer service company;

(b)

any reference to a pioneer product shall be read as a reference to a qualifying activity;

(c)

any reference to the production day of a pioneer enterprise shall be read as a reference to the commencement day of a pioneer service company;

(d)

any reference to a pioneer certificate shall be read as a reference to a certificate issued under section 18.

PART IV POST-PIONEER COMPANIES

Interpretation of this Part.

21. For the purposes of this Part, unless the context otherwise requires —

"commencement day", in relation to a post-pioneer company, means the date specified under subsection (3) of section 22 in the certificate issued to that company under that section; "pioneer company" means a company certified by a pioneer certificate to be a pioneer company under the repealed Act;

"post-pioneer company" means a company which has been issued with a certificate under subsection (2) of section 22;

"qualifying activity", in relation to a post-pioneer company, means its trade or business in respect of which tax relief had been granted under Part II, III or VII and any other trade or business approved by the Minister.

Application for and issue of certificate to post-pioneer company.

22. (1) Any company which is —

(a)

a pioneer company on or after 1st. May, 1975;

(b)

a pioneer enterprise or a pioneer service company;

(c)

an export enterprise which had been a pioneer enterprise immediately before its tax relief period as an export enterprise,

may apply in the prescribed form to the Minister for approval as a post-pioneer company.

(2)

For additional analytical, business and investment opportunities information,
please contact Global Investment & Business Center, USA
at (703) 370-8082. Fax: (703) 370-8083. E-mail: ibpusa3@gmail.com
Global Business and Investment Info Databank - www.ibpus.com

The Minister may, if he considers it expedient in the public interest to do so, approve the application and issue the company with a certificate subject to such terms and conditions as he may impose.

(3)

(a)
Every certificate issued to a post-pioneer company under this section shall specify —

(b)
a date as the commencement day from which the company shall be entitled to tax relief under this Part;

(c)
its qualifying activities; and

(4)
the concessionary rate of tax to be levied for the purposes of this Part.

(5)
The Minister may, in his discretion, upon an application of a post-pioneer company, amend its certificate by substituting for the commencement day specified therein such other date as he thinks fit and thereupon the provisions of this Part shall have effect as if that date were the commencement day in relation to that certificate.

Notwithstanding section 35 of the Income Tax Act, tax at such concessionary rate, not being less than 10% as the Minister may specify, shall be levied and paid for each year of assessment upon the income derived by a post-pioneer company during its tax relief period from its qualifying activities.

Tax relief period of post-pioneer company.

23. (1) The tax relief period of a post-pioneer company shall commence on its commencement day and shall continue for a period not exceeding 6 years as the Minister may determine.

(2) The Minister may, subject to such terms and conditions as he may impose, extend the tax relief period of a post-pioneer company for such further period or periods as he may determine except that the tax relief period of the company shall not in the aggregate exceed 11 years.

Ascertainment of income in respect of other trade or business.

24. (1) Where during its tax relief period a post-pioneer company carries on any trade or business other than its qualifying activities, separate accounts shall be maintained in respect of that other trade or business and in respect of the same accounting period and the income from that other trade or business shall be computed and assessed in accordance with the Income Tax Act with such adjustments as the Collector thinks reasonable and proper.

(2) Where in the opinion of the Collector the carrying on of such other trade or business is subordinate or incidental to the carrying on of the qualifying activities of the post-pioneer company, the income or losses arising from such other trade or business shall be deemed to form part of the income or loss of the post-pioneer company in respect of its qualifying activities.

Deduction of losses.

25. The Minister may, in relation to post-pioneer companies, by regulations provide for —

(a)
the manner in which expenses, capital allowances and donations allowable under the Income Tax Act are to be deducted; and

(b)

For additional analytical, business and investment opportunities information, please contact Global Investment & Business Center, USA at (703) 370-8082. Fax: (703) 370-8083. E-mail: ibpusa3@gmail.com Global Business and Investment Info Databank - www.ibpus.com

the deduction of capital allowances and of losses otherwise than in accordance with sections 20 and subsection (2) of section 30 of the Income Tax Act.
Certain dividends exempted from income tax.

26. (1) As soon as any amount of income of a post-pioneer company has been subject to tax at the concessionary rate under section 22, the net amount of the income after deduction of the tax shall be credited to a special account (referred to in this section as the account) to be kept by the post-pioneer company for the purposes of this section.

(2)

Where the account is in credit at the date on which any dividends are paid by the post-pioneer company out of the net amount of the income credited to that account, an amount equal to those dividends or to that credit, whichever is the less, shall be debited to the account.

(3)

So much of the amount of any dividends so debited to the account as are received by a shareholder of the post-pioneer company shall, if the Collector is satisfied with the entries in the account, be exempt from tax in the hands of the shareholder.

(4)

Notwithstanding subsection (3), where a dividend is paid on any share of a preferential nature, it shall not be so exempt in the hands of the shareholder.

(5)

Section 36 of the Income Tax Act shall not apply in respect of any dividends or part thereof which are debited to the account.

(6)

Where an amount of dividends debited to the account has been received by a shareholder, and that shareholder is a company (referred to in this section as the holding company) which holds, throughout its tax relief period, the beneficial interest in all the issued shares of the post-pioneer company (or in not less that such proportion of those shares as the Minister may require at the time when the post-pioneer certificate is issued to the post-pioneer company) any dividends paid by the holding company to its shareholders, to the extent that the Collector is satisfied that those dividends are paid out of such amount, shall be exempt from tax in the hands of those shareholders; and section 36 of the Income Tax Act shall not apply to any such dividends or part thereof so exempt.

(7)

Any holding company may, with the approval of the Minister and subject to such terms and conditions as he may impose, pay such exempt dividends to its shareholders even if it has not held the requisite shareholding in the post-pioneer company for the whole of the tax relief period.

(8)

The post-pioneer company shall deliver to the Collector a copy of the account made up to any date specified by him whenever called upon to do so by notice in writing sent by him to its registered office, until such time as he is satisfied that there is no further need for maintaining the account.

(9) Notwithstanding subsections (1) to (7), where it appears to the Collector that —

(a)

any income of a post-pioneer company which has been subject to tax at the concessionary rate under section 22; or

(b)

any dividend, including a dividend paid by a holding company under subsection (6), which has been exempted from tax in the hands of any shareholder, ought not to have been so taxed or exempted for any year of assessment, the Collector may subject to section 62 of the Income Tax Act —

(i)

make such assessment or additional assessment upon the company or any such shareholder as may be necessary in order to make good any loss of tax; or

(ii)

direct the company to debit the account with such amount as the circumstances require.
Power to give directions.

27. For the purposes of the Income Tax Act and this Order, the Collector may direct that —

(a)

any sums payable to a post-pioneer company in the tax relief period which might reasonably and properly have been expected to be payable, in the normal course of business, after the end of that period shall be treated as not having been payable in that period but as having been payable on such date, after that period, as the Collector thinks fit; and

(b)

any expense incurred by a post-pioneer company within one year after the end of its tax relief period which might reasonably and properly have been expected to be incurred, in the normal course of business, during its tax relief period shall be treated as not having been incurred within that year but as having been incurred for the purposes of its qualifying activities and on such date, during its tax relief period, as the Collector thinks fit.
Ascertainment of income in respect of qualifying activities.

28. (1) The qualifying income of a post-pioneer company shall, subject to subsection (2) and section 29, be ascertained in accordance with the provisions of the Income Tax Act after making such adjustments as may be necessary in consequence of any direction given under section 27.

(2) In determining the qualifying income of the post-pioneer company for the basis period for any year of assessment —

(a)

the allowance provided for in sections 13, 14, 15, 16, 17 and 18 of the Income Tax Act shall be taken into account;

(b)

the allowances referred to in paragraph (a) for that year of assessment shall firstly be deducted against the qualifying income, and any unabsorbed
allowances shall be deducted against the other income of the company subject to tax at the rate of tax under section 35 of the Income Tax Act in accordance with section 29;

(c)

the balance, if any, of the allowances after the deduction in paragraph (b) shall be available for deduction for any subsequent year of assessment in accordance with section 20 of the Income Tax Act and shall be made in the manner provided in paragraph (b);

(d)

any loss incurred for that basis period shall be deducted in accordance with section 29 against the other income of the company subject to tax at the rate of tax under section 35 of the Income Tax Act; and

(e)

the balance, if any, of the losses after the deduction in paragraph (d) shall be available for deduction for any subsequent year of assessment in accordance with section 30 of the Income Tax Act firstly against the qualifying income, and any balance of the losses shall be deducted against the other income of the company subject to tax at the rate of tax under section 35 of the Income Tax Act in accordance with section 29.

Adjustment of capital allowances and losses.

29. (1) Where, for any year of assessment, there are any unabsorbed allowances or losses in respect of the qualifying income of a post pioneer company, and there is any chargeable normal income of the company, those unabsorbed allowances and losses shall be deducted against the chargeable normal income in accordance with the following provisions —

(a)
    in the case where those unabsorbed allowances or losses do not exceed that chargeable normal income multiplied by the adjustment factor, that chargeable normal income shall be reduced by an amount arrived at by dividing those unabsorbed allowances or losses by the adjustment factor, and those unabsorbed allowances or losses shall be nil; and

(b)
    in any other case, those unabsorbed allowances or losses shall be reduced by an amount arrived at by multiplying that chargeable normal income by the adjustment factor, and those unabsorbed allowances or losses so reduced shall be added to, and be deemed to form part of, the corresponding allowances or losses in respect of the qualifying income, for the next succeeding year of assessment in accordance with section 20 or 30 (as the case may be) of the Income Tax Act, and that chargeable normal income shall be nil.

(2)
    Where, for any year of assessment, there are any unabsorbed allowances or losses in respect of the normal income of a post-pioneer company, and there is any chargeable qualifying income of the company, those unabsorbed allowances or losses shall be deducted against that qualifying income in accordance with the following provisions —

(a)
    in the case where those unabsorbed allowances or losses do not exceed that chargeable qualifying income multiplied by the adjustment factor, that chargeable qualifying income shall be reduced by an amount arrived at by dividing those unabsorbed allowances or losses by the adjustment factor, and those unabsorbed allowances or losses shall be nil; and

(b)
    in any other case, those unabsorbed allowances or losses shall be reduced by an amount arrived at by multiplying that chargeable qualifying income by the adjustment factor, and those unabsorbed allowances or losses so reduced shall be added to, and be deemed to form part of, the corresponding allowances or losses in respect of the normal income, for the next succeeding year of assessment in accordance with section 20 or 30 (as the case may be) of the Income Tax Act, and that chargeable qualifying income shall be nil.

(3)
    Where a post pioneer company ceases to derive any qualifying income in the basis period for any year of assessment but derives normal income in that basis period, subsection (1) shall apply, with the necessary modifications, to any unabsorbed allowances or losses in respect of the qualifying income of the company for any year of assessment subsequent to that year of assessment.

(4)
    Where a post pioneer company ceases to derive any normal income in the basis period for any year of assessment but derives qualifying income in that basis period, subsection (2) shall apply, with the necessary modifications, to any unabsorbed allowances or losses in respect of the normal income of the company for any year of assessment subsequent to that year of assessment.

(5)
    Nothing in subsections (1) to (4) shall be construed as affecting the application of section 20 or 30 of the Income Tax Act unless otherwise provided in this section.

(6) In this section —

"adjustment factor", in relation to any year of assessment, means the factor ascertained in accordance with the formula

A , B

where A is the rate of tax under section 35 of the Income Tax Act for that year of assessment; and

B is the concessionary rate of tax for that year of assessment at which the qualifying income is subject to tax;

"allowances" means the allowances under section 13, 14, 16, 16A, 17, 18 or 20 including unabsorbed allowances which arose in any year of assessment prior to the year of assessment 2002;

"chargeable normal income" means normal income after deducting expenses, donations, allowances or losses allowable under the Income Tax Act against the normal income;

"chargeable qualifying income" means the qualifying income after deducting expenses, donations, allowances or losses allowable under the Income Tax Act against the qualifying income;

"losses" means losses which are deductible under section 30 of the Income Tax Act including unabsorbed losses incurred in respect of any year of assessment prior to the year of assessment 2002;

"normal income" means income subject to tax at the rate of tax under section 35 of the Income Tax Act;

"unabsorbed allowances or losses in respect of the qualifying income" means the balance of such allowances or losses after deducting expenses, donations, allowances or losses allowable under the Income Tax Act against the qualifying income;

"unabsorbed allowances or losses in respect of the normal income" means the balance of such allowances or losses after deducting expenses, donations, allowances or losses allowable under the Income Tax Act against the qualifying income;

"qualifying income" means the income of a post-pioneer company in respect of its qualifying activities.

PART V EXPANSION OF ESTABLISHED ENTERPRISES

Power and procedure for declaring an industry and a product an approved industry and an approved product.

30. (1) Subject to subsection (2), where the Minister is satisfied that the increased manufacture of the product of any industry would be of economic benefit to Brunei Darussalam, he may, if he considers it expedient in the public interest to do so, by order, declare that industry to be an approved industry and the product thereof to be an approved product for the purposes of this Part.

(2) The Minister may revoke any order made under this section but any such revocation shall not affect the operation of any expansion certificate issued to any expanding enterprise before the revocation.

For additional analytical, business and investment opportunities information,
please contact Global Investment & Business Center, USA
at (703) 370-8082. Fax: (703) 370-8083. E-mail: ibpusa3@gmail.com
Global Business and Investment Info Databank - www.ibpus.com

Issue of expansion certificate and amendment thereof.

31. (1) Any company intending to incur new capital expenditure for the purpose of the manufacture or increased manufacture of an approved product may —

(a)

where the expenditure exceeds $1 million; or

(b)

where the expenditure is less than $1 million but exceeds $500,000, and will result in an increase of not less than 30% in value at the original cost of all the productive equipment of the company,

make an application in writing to the Minister to be approved as an expanding enterprise, in such form and with such particulars as may be prescribed.

(2)

Where the Minister is satisfied that it is expedient in the public interest to do so, he may approve that company as an expanding enterprise and issue an expansion certificate to the company, subject to such terms and conditions as he thinks fit.

(3)

In this Part, "new capital expenditure" means expenditure incurred by a company in the purchase of productive equipment which is intended to increase its production or profitability.

(4)

Any expenditure incurred in the purchase of productive equipment which is not new shall be deemed not to be new capital expenditure unless it is proved to the satisfaction of the Minister that —

(a)

the purchase of the productive equipment is economically justifiable; and

(b)

the purchase price represents a fair open market value of the productive equipment.

(5)

Every expansion certificate issued under this section shall specify the date on or before which the productive equipment shall be put into operation and that date shall be deemed to be the expansion day for the purpose of this Part.

(6)

The Minister may, in his discretion, upon the application of any expanding enterprise, amend its expansion certificate by substituting for the expansion day specified therein such earlier or later date as he thinks fit and thereupon the provisions of this Part shall have effect as if the date so substituted were the expansion day in relation to that expanding enterprise.

Tax relief period of expanding enterprise.

32. (1) The tax relief period of an expanding enterprise shall commence on its expansion day or if the expansion day falls within the tax relief period specified in any certificate previously issued to the enterprise under Part II or VII for the same or similar product, commence on the day immediately following the expiry of that tax relief period and shall —

(a)

where such expanding enterprise has incurred new capital expenditure not exceeding $1 million, continue for a period of 3 years; and

(b)

where such expanding enterprise has incurred new capital expenditure exceeding $1 million, continue for a period of 5 years.

(2) The Minister may, where he is satisfied that it is expedient in the public interest to do so and subject to such terms and conditions as he may impose, extend the tax relief period of an expanding enterprise for such further period or periods, not exceeding 3 years at any one time, as he may determine, except that the tax relief period of the expanding enterprise shall not in the aggregate exceed 15 years.

Application of section 10 to expanding enterprise.

33. Section 10 shall apply, with the necessary modifications, to an expanding enterprise as it applies to a pioneer enterprise.

Tax relief.

34. (1) Subject to the provisions of this Order, an expanding enterprise is entitled, during its tax relief period, to relief in the manner provided by this section.

(2)

The income of the expanding enterprise in respect of its trade or business to which its expansion certificate relates (referred to in this Part as the expansion income) shall be ascertained, for any accounting period during its tax relief period, in accordance with the provisions of the Income Tax Act and any regulations made under this Order.

(3)

In determining the income of the expanding enterprise, the allowances provided for in sections 13, 14, 15, 16, 17 and 18 of the Income Tax Act shall be taken into account.

(4)

Where an expanding enterprise carries on trading activities other than those to which its expansion certificate relates, the expansion income to be ascertained for the purposes of this section shall be determined in such manner as appears to the Collector to be reasonable in the circumstances.

(5)

Where in the opinion of the Collector the carrying on of such trading activities is subordinate or incidental to the carrying on of the trade or business to which its expansion certificate relates, the income or loss arising from such activities shall be deemed to form part of the expansion income of the expanding enterprise.

(6)

The expansion income so ascertained shall be compared with the average corresponding income (referred to in this section as the pre-relief income) of the expanding enterprise as determined in subsection (8) and relief shall be given to the following extent —

(a)

where the pre-relief income equals or exceeds the expansion income, no relief shall be given;

(b)

where the expansion income exceeds the pre-relief income, the amount of the excess shall not form part of the statutory income of the expanding enterprise for any year of assessment and shall be exempt from tax.

(7)   .

The amount of exempt income shall not, unless the Minister in his discretion otherwise decides, exceed the sum which bears the same proportion to the expansion income as the new capital expenditure on productive equipment bears to the total of such new capital expenditure and the value at original cost of the productive equipment owned or used by the expanding enterprise prior to its expansion.

(8)

For the purposes of subsection (6), the average corresponding income of an expanding enterprise, in relation to a certificate issued under section 31, shall be determined by taking one-third of the total of the corresponding income of the expanding enterprise for the 3 years immediately preceding the expansion day specified in that certificate.

(9)

Where an expanding enterprise has carried on the trade or business to which its certificate relates for less than 3 years immediately prior to its expansion day or where the expanding enterprise has no corresponding income for any of those 3 years, the Minister may specify such amount to be its average corresponding income as he thinks fit.

(10)

Where an expanding enterprise has been approved as a pioneer enterprise or as an export enterprise or as both, the total amount of income exempted under this section and Part II or VII shall not exceed 100% of the expansion income.
Exemption from income tax of dividends from expanding enterprise.

35. (1) As soon as any amount of expansion income has become exempt under section 34, that amount shall be credited to an account to be kept by the expanding enterprise for the purposes of this section.

(2)

Where that account is in credit at the date on which any dividends are paid by the expanding enterprise out of income which has been exempted, an amount equal to those dividends or to that credit, whichever is the less, shall be debited to the account.

(3)

So much of the amount of any dividends so debited to that account as are received by a shareholder of the expanding enterprise shall, if the Collector is satisfied with the entries in the account, be exempt from tax in the hands of the shareholder.

(4)

Notwithstanding subsection (3), where a dividend is paid on any share of a preferential nature, it shall not be so exempt in the hands of the shareholder.

(5)

Any dividends debited to that account shall be treated as having been distributed to the shareholders of the expanding enterprise or any particular class of those shareholders in the same proportions as the shareholders were entitled to payment of the dividends giving rise to the debit.

(6)

The expanding enterprise shall deliver to the Collector a copy of that account, made up to a date specified by him, whenever called upon to do so by notice in writing sent by him to its registered office, until such time as he is satisfied that there is no further need for maintaining the account.

(7)

Notwithstanding section 34 and subsections (1) to (6) where it appears to the Collector that —

(a)

any amount of exempted income of an expanding enterprise; or

(b)

any dividend exempted in the hands of any shareholder, including any dividend paid by a holding company to which subsection (10) applies,

ought not to have been exempted by reason of a direction under section 10 (as applied to this Part by section 33) or the revocation under section 114 of an expansion certificate issued to the expanding enterprise, the Collector may, subject to section 62 of the Income Tax Act —

(i)

(ii)

make such assessment or additional assessment upon the expanding enterprise or any such shareholder as may appear to be necessary in order to counteract any profit obtained from any such amount; or

direct the expanding enterprise to debit its account, kept in accordance with subsection (1), with such amount as the circumstances require.

(8)

Parts XI and XII of the Income Tax Act (relating to objections and appeals) and any regulations made thereunder shall apply, with the necessary modifications, to any direction given under subsection (7) as if it were a notice of assessment given under those provisions.

(9)

Section 36 of the Income Tax Act shall not apply in respect of any dividend or part thereof which is debited to the account required to be kept for the purposes of this section.

(10)

Where an amount has been received by way of dividend from an expanding enterprise by a shareholder and the amount is exempt from tax under this section, if that shareholder is a company (referred to in this section as the holding company) which holds, at the time any dividend is declared, the beneficial interest in all the issued shares of the expanding enterprise (or in not less than such proportion of those shares as the Minister may approve), any dividends paid by the holding company to its shareholders, to the extent that the Collector is satisfied that those dividends are paid out of that amount, shall be exempt from tax in the hands of those shareholders; and section 36 of the Income Tax Act shall not apply in respect of any dividend or part thereof so exempt.

PART VI EXPANDING SERVICE COMPANIES

Application for and issue and amendment of certificate for expanding service company.

36. (1) Where a company engaged in any qualifying activity as defined in section 17 intends to substantially increase the volume of that activity, it may make an application in writing to the Minister to be approved as an expanding service company.

(2)

Where the Minister is satisfied that it is expedient in the public interest to do so, he may approve that company as an expanding service company and issue a certificate to the company, subject to such terms and conditions as he thinks fit.

(3)

Every certificate issued under this section shall specify a date (not earlier than 1st. January, 2001) on or before which the expansion of the qualifying activity shall commence and that date shall be deemed to be the expansion day for the purpose of this Part.

Tax relief period of expanding service company.

37. (1) The tax relief period of an expanding service company shall —

(a)

commence on its expansion day; or

(b)

if the expansion day falls within the tax relief period specified in any certificate previously issued to the company for the same or similar qualifying activity under Part III, commence on the day immediately following the expiry of that tax relief period,

and shall continue for such period, not exceeding 11 years, as the Minister may, in his discretion, determine.

(2) The Minister may, where he is satisfied that it is expedient in the public interest to do so and subject to such terms and conditions as he may impose, extend the tax relief period of an expanding enterprise for such further period or periods, not exceeding 5 years at any one time, as he may determine, except that the tax relief period of the expanding enterprise shall not in the aggregate exceed 20 years.

Application of certain sections to expanding service company.

38. Subsection (6) of section 31 and sections 33 to 35 shall apply to an expanding service company under this Part and for the purposes of such application —

(a)
   any reference to an expanding enterprise shall be read as a reference to an expanding service company;

(b)
   any reference to an expansion certificate shall be read as a reference to a certificate issued under subsection (2) of section 36;

(c)
   subsection (7) of section 34 shall not have effect.

PART VII PRODUCTION FOR EXPORT

Power to approve a product or produce as an export product or export produce.

39. The Minister may, if he considers it expedient in the public interest to do so, approve any product manufactured in Brunei Darussalam or any produce of agriculture, forestry or fisheries as an export product or export produce for the purposes of this Part.

Application for the issue of export enterprise certificate.

40. (1) The Minister may, on the application in the prescribed form of any company which is manufacturing or proposes to manufacture any export product or is engaged or proposes to engage in agriculture, forestry and fishery activities, either wholly or partly for export, approve the company as an export enterprise and issue to the company an export enterprise certificate subject to such terms and conditions as he thinks fit.

(2) Every export enterprise certificate issued under this section shall specify the accounting period in which it is expected that the export sales of the export product or export produce —

(a)
   will be not less than 20% of the value of its total sales; and

(b)
   will not be less than $20,000,

and that accounting period shall be deemed to be the export year of the export enterprise for the purposes of this Part.

(3) For the purposes of this Part —

"export sales" means export sales (f.o.b.) whether made directly by the export enterprise or through an agent or independent contractor;

"f.o.b." means free on board.

Amendment of export enterprise certificate.

41. The Minister may, in his discretion, upon the application of the export enterprise, amend its export enterprise certificate by substituting for the export year specified therein such other earlier or later accounting period as he thinks fit and thereupon the provisions of this Part shall have effect as if the accounting period so substituted were the export year in relation to that export enterprise.

Tax relief period.

42. (1) The tax relief period of an export enterprise shall —

(a)

not being a pioneer enterprise, commence from its export year and shall continue for a period of 8 years inclusive of the export year; or

(b)

being a pioneer enterprise, commence on the first day of its export year or, if the export year falls within the period of its old trade or business, on the date of the commencement of its new trade or business, and shall continue for a period of 6 years and shall not in the aggregate exceed 11 years.

(2) Notwithstanding subsection (1), where an export enterprise has incurred or is intending to incur a fixed capital expenditure of —

(a)

not less than $50 million; or

(b)

not less than $500,000 but less than $50 million and —

(i)

more than 40% of the paid-up capital of the export enterprise is held by citizens and persons to whom a Resident Permit has been granted under regulations made under the Immigration Act (Chapter 17); and

(ii)

in the opinion of the Minister the export enterprise will promote or enhance the economic or technological development of Brunei Darussalam,

its tax relief period —

(A)

where the export enterprise is not a pioneer enterprise, shall commence from its export year and continue for a period of 15 years inclusive of the export year; or

(B)

where the export enterprise is a pioneer enterprise, shall commence from its export year or, if the export year falls within the period of its old trade or business, from the date of the commencement of its new trade or business, and continue for such period as together with its tax relief period as a pioneer enterprise will extend in the aggregate to 15 years.

(3)

The Minister may, where he is satisfied that it is expedient in the public interest to do so and subject to such terms and conditions as he may impose, extend the tax relief period of any export enterprise for such further period as he thinks fit.

(4)

In subsection (2), "fixed capital expenditure" means capital expenditure which has been or is intended to be incurred by the export enterprise, in connection with its export product, on its factory building (excluding land) in Brunei Darussalam, and on any new plant or new machinery used in Brunei Darussalam and, subject to the approval of the Minister, on any secondhand plant or secondhand machinery used in Brunei Darussalam.

Power to give directions.

43. Section 10 shall apply, with the necessary modifications, to an export enterprise as it applies to a pioneer enterprise.

Application of Part X of Income Tax Act.

44. (1) Part X of the Income Tax Act (relating to returns of income) shall apply in all respects as if the whole of the income of an export enterprise in respect of its export profits were chargeable to tax.

(2) The annual return of income shall be accompanied by a separate export statement showing the quantity and value at f.o.b. prices of its export product or export produce exported during the accounting period in respect of which the return is furnished, together with such further evidence as, in the opinion of the Collector, is necessary to verify the accuracy of the export statement.

Cognizance of export.

45. For the purposes of tax relief to an export enterprise, the Collector may take cognizance of the export of any export product or export produce when the export has been made in accordance with the provisions of the Customs Act (Chapter 36) or any regulations made thereunder, as the case may be, but if the Collector is satisfied that in the course of the export of the product or produce a breach of the provisions of this Order or any regulations made thereunder has been committed, he may refuse to take cognizance of the export of the product or produce and refuse a claim for tax relief in respect of the export.

Export to be in accordance with regulations and conditions.

46. No export product or export produce shall be exported by an export enterprise except in accordance with such regulations as are prescribed and under such conditions as may be approved by the Controller of Customs.

Computation of export profits.

47. (1) The income of an export enterprise in respect of its trade or business to which its export enterprise certificate relates shall be ascertained (after making any necessary adjustments in consequence of a direction under section 10, as applied to this Part by section 43) for any accounting period during its tax relief period in accordance with the provisions of the Income Tax Act, before taking into account the allowances provided for in sections 13, 14, 15, 16, 17 and 18 of that Act.

(2) The total export profits of an export enterprise shall be deemed to be that part of the income so ascertained which bears the same proportion to that income as the total value of the export sales (f.o.b.) of its export product or export produce whether made, directly or indirectly, by sale to an independent exporter (referred to in this Part as the export sales) bears to the total value of the sums receivable in respect of —

(a)

its domestic sales of manufactured products or produce at ex-factory prices;

(b)

its export sales (f.o.b.) of its export product and export produce;

(c)

its export sales (f.o.b.) of other products; and

(d)

all other sales and provisions of service,

(referred to in this Part as the total sales).

(3)

Where a company exports any products or produce to which its export enterprise certificate relates, the amount of its export profit arising from the export of those products or produce which will qualify for the relief provided by section 49 is the excess of that profit over a fixed sum to be determined in the following manner —

(a)

in the case of a company which has previously exported those products or produce, the average annual export profit of the company shall be ascertained in the manner provided by subsection (5); and

(b)

in the case of a company which has not prior to its application under section 38 exported those products or produce for 3 years immediately preceding its application, the fixed sum shall be such an amount as the Minister may determine having regard to the total sales of the company and the percentage of the total sales of other major export enterprises exporting like articles.

(4)

Where such a company is a pioneer enterprise, subsection (3) shall apply notwithstanding that the company was deemed to commence a new trade or business at the end of its tax relief period as a pioneer enterprise.

(5) For the purposes of this section —

(a)

"average annual export profit" means a sum equal to one-third of the total export profits of the company from the export of those products or produce ascertained in the manner provided by subsection (2) during the 3 years immediately preceding the date of its application under section 40; and

(b)

where a company has adopted an accounting period ending on a date other than 31st. December, the Collector may make such adjustment on a time

basis as appears to him to be reasonable in ascertaining the total export profits of that period.

Conditions for relief.

48. (1) The tax relief provided under this Part applies to an export enterprise during its tax relief period subject to the following conditions —

(a)

in respect of the first year of assessment, for which the export year forms the basis period, the export sales shall amount, in proportion, to not less than 20% of the total sales and, in value, to not less than $20,000 during that accounting period;

(b)

in respect of subsequent years of assessment, subject to the export sales having satisfied that minimum proportion and value in the export year or where a direction has been made by the Minister under subsection (2) in respect of that year, the export sales shall amount in value to not less than $20,000 during the relevant accounting period; and

(c)

where the minimum requirements as to proportion and value have not been satisfied in the export year, and no direction has been made by the Minister under subsection (2), the relief provided by this Part shall apply for the first time only in respect of a year of assessment where during the relevant accounting period the minimum requirements as to proportion and value have both been satisfied or where a direction to this effect has been made by the Minister under subsection (2), and thereafter shall continue to be available where during the relevant accounting period the minimum requirement as to value has been satisfied.

(2) Notwithstanding subsection (1), where, in its export year, the export sales of an export enterprise amount in value to $20,000 or more, but in proportion, to less than 20% of the total sales, and the Minister is satisfied, on the representations of the enterprise that the failure to realise that proportion of the total sales was due to causes beyond the control of the enterprise, or having regard to the quantum of its output and sales other than export sales, it is reasonable and expedient in the public interest to do so, the Minister may direct that the relief provided under this Part shall apply in respect of the year of assessment corresponding to its export year or in respect of any subsequent year of assessment during its tax relief period.

Tax relief on export profits.

49. (1) Where an amount of the export profit of an export enterprise qualifies under sections 47 and 48 for the relief provided by this section (referred to in this section as the qualifying export profit), there shall be deducted from that amount such part of the allowances provided for in sections 13, 14, 15, 16, 17 and 18 of the Income Tax Act as may be attributable to the qualifying export profit; and the part of the allowances so attributable to the qualifying export profit shall be deemed to be such amount which bears the same proportion to the total allowances deductible by the export enterprise under sections 13, 14, 15, 16, 17 and 18 of the Income Tax Act as the amount of the qualifying export profit bears to the income of the export enterprise ascertained under subsection (1) of section 47.

(2)

For each year of assessment the Collector shall issue to the export enterprise a statement for that year of assessment showing the balance of the qualifying export profit after deduction of the allowances under subsection (1) and the provisions of Parts XI and XII of the Income Tax Act (relating to objections and appeals) and any regulations made thereunder shall apply, with the necessary modifications, as if such a statement were a notice of assessment given under those provisions.

(3)

Subject to subsection (7) of section 50, where any statement issued under subsection (2) has become final and conclusive, an amount equal to 100% of the balance of such qualifying export profit shall not form part of the statutory income of the export enterprise for that year of assessment and shall be exempt from tax.

Certain dividends exempted from income tax.

50. (1) As soon as any amount of export income has become exempt under section 49, that amount shall be credited to an account to be kept by the export enterprise for the purposes of this section.

(2)

Where that account is in credit at the date on which any dividends are paid by the export enterprise out of income which has been exempted, an amount equal to those dividends or to that credit, whichever is the less, shall be debited to the account.

(3)

So much of the amount of any dividends so debited to that account as are received by a shareholder of the export enterprise shall, if the Collector is satisfied with the entries in the account, be exempt from tax in the hands of the shareholder.

(4)

Notwithstanding subsection (3), where a dividend is paid on any share of a preferential nature, it shall not be so exempt in the hands of the shareholder.

(5)

Any dividends debited to that account shall be treated as having been distributed to the shareholders of the export enterprise or any particular class of the shareholders in the same proportions as the shareholders were entitled to payment of the dividends giving rise to the debit.

(6)

The export enterprise shall deliver to the Collector a copy of that account, made up to a date specified by him, whenever called upon to do so by notice in writing sent by him to its registered office, until such time as he is satisfied that there is no further need for maintaining the account.

(7)

Notwithstanding section 49 and subsections (1) to (6) where it appears to the Collector that —

(a)

any amount of exempted income of an export enterprise; or

(b)

any dividend exempted in the hands of any shareholder, including any dividend paid by a holding company to which subsection (10) applies,

ought not to have been exempted by reason of a direction under section 10, as applied to this Part by section 43, having been made with respect to the export enterprise, after any income of that enterprise has been exempted under the provisions of this Order or the revocation under section 114 of a certificate issued to the export enterprise, the Collector may, subject to section 62 of the Income Tax Act —

(i)

make such assessment or additional assessment upon the export enterprise or any such shareholders as may appear to be necessary in order to counteract any profit obtained from any such amount which ought not to have been exempted; or

(ii)

direct the export enterprise to debit its account, kept in accordance with subsection (1), with such amount as the circumstances require.

(8)

Parts XI and XII of the Income Tax Act (relating to objections and appeals) and any regulations made thereunder shall apply, with the necessary modifications, to any direction given under subsection (7) as if it were a notice of assessment given under those provisions.

(9)

Section 36 of the Income Tax Act shall not apply in respect of any dividend or part thereof which is debited to the account required to be kept for the purposes of this section.

(10)

Where an amount has been received by way of dividend from an export enterprise by a shareholder and the amount is exempt from tax under subsections (1) to (9), if that shareholder is a company (referred to in this section as the holding company) which holds, at the time any dividend is declared, the beneficial interest in all the issued shares of the export enterprise (or in not less than such proportion of those shares as the Minister may approve), any dividends paid by the holding company to its shareholders, to the extent that the Collector is satisfied that those dividends are paid out of that amount, shall be exempt from tax in the hands of those shareholders; and section 36 of the Income Tax Act shall not apply in respect of any dividend or part thereof so exempt.

Power of entry into premises and taking of samples.

51. Any officer, authorised by the Collector or any senior officer of customs or any officer of customs authorised by a senior officer of customs for the purpose, shall at all times have access to any premises of an export enterprise or of an independent exporter of any export product or export produce or any place where any export product or export produce is stored, for the purpose of checking the production, storage and packing of the export product or export produce and all records and accounts thereof, and for such other purpose as may be deemed necessary, and may take samples of any goods therefrom.

No relanding of export product or export produce.

52. No export product or export produce shall, unless the Controller of Customs otherwise authorises, be relanded at any time in Brunei Darussalam after they have been exported.

Powers of search, seizure and arrest by officers of customs.

53. Notwithstanding any written law to the contrary, if there is reasonable cause to believe that an offence has been or is being committed under section 46 or 52 of this Order or any regulations made thereunder in relation to any export product or export produce, sections 90 and 91 and Part XII of the Customs Act (Chapter 36) (relating to search, seizure and arrest) shall apply, insofar as they are applicable, as if the export product or export produce were goods that were dutiable and uncustomed goods or goods liable to forfeiture under the Customs Act, and as if the offence had been or were being committed under that Act.

Offence under other laws deemed to be an offence under this Order.

54. Where an export product or export produce is the subject-matter of an offence committed under the Customs Act (Chapter 36), or any regulations made thereunder, and the Collector is satisfied that, if the offence had not been detected, the export enterprise concerned in the commission of such an offence would have been able to claim relief from tax to which it was not entitled, then such an offence shall be deemed to be an offence under this Order whether a claim for tax relief has been made or not and may be dealt with accordingly but so that no person shall be punished more than once for the same offence.

PART VIII EXPORT OF SERVICES

Interpretation of this Part.

55. For the purposes of this Part, unless the context otherwise requires —

"commencement day", in relation to an export service company or export service firm, means the date specified under subsection (3) of section 56 in the certificate issued to that company or firm under that section;

"export service company" means a company which has been issued with a certificate under subsection (2) of section 56;

For additional analytical, business and investment opportunities information,
please contact Global Investment & Business Center, USA
at (703) 370-8082. Fax: (703) 370-8083. E-mail: ibpusa3@gmail.com
Global Business and Investment Info Databank - www.ibpus.com

"qualifying services" means any of the following services undertaken with respect to overseas projects for persons who are neither residents of nor permanent establishments in Brunei Darussalam —

(a)

technical services including construction, distribution, design and engineering services;

(b)

consultancy, management, supervisory or advisory services relating to any technical matter or to any trade or business;

(c)

fabrication of machinery and equipment and procurement of materials, components an equipment;

(d)

data processing, programming, computer software development, telecommunications and other computer services;

(e)

professional services including accounting, legal, medical and architectural services;

(f)

educational and training services; and

(g)

any other services as the Minister may prescribe.

Application for and issue of certificate to export service company.

56. (1) Where a company is engaged in any qualifying service, the company may apply in the prescribed form to the Minister for approval as an export service company.

(2)

The Minister may if he considers it expedient in the public interest to do so, approve the application and issue the company with a certificate, subject to such terms and conditions as he may impose.

(3)

Every certificate issued to an export service company under this section shall specify —

(a)

a date as the commencement day from which the company shall be entitled to tax relief under this Part;

(b)

its qualifying services; and

(c)

its base amount of income for the purpose of subsection (2) of section 59.

(4)

The Minister may, in his discretion, upon the application of an export service company, amend its certificate by substituting for the commencement day specified therein such earlier or later date as he thinks fit and thereupon the provisions of this Part shall have effect as if the date so substituted were the commencement day in relation to that certificate.

Tax relief period of export service company.

57. (1) The tax relief period of an export service company shall commence on its commencement day and shall continue for such period, not exceeding 11 years, as the Minister may, in his discretion, determine.

(2) The Minister may, where he is satisfied that it is expedient in the public interest to do so and subject to such terms and conditions as he may impose, extend the tax relief period of any export service company or firm for such further periods, not exceeding 3 years at any one time, as he may

determine, except that the tax relief period of the export service company shall not in the aggregate exceed 20 years.

Application of certain sections to export service company.

58. (1) Section 10 shall apply, with the necessary modifications, to an export service company as it applies to a pioneer enterprise.

(2)
Section 50 shall apply, with the necessary modifications, to an export service company as it applies to an export enterprise.

(3)
Sections 68 and 69 shall apply, with the necessary modifications, to an export service company as they apply to an international trading company and for the purposes of such application, the reference in subsection (2) of section 68 to the export sales of qualifying manufactured goods, Brunei Darussalam domestic produce and qualifying commodities shall be read as a reference to the provision of qualifying services.

Ascertainment of income of export service company.

59. (1) The income of an export service company in respect of its qualifying services shall be ascertained (after making such adjustments as may be necessary in consequence of a direction under section 10 as made applicable by section 58) for any accounting period during its tax relief period in accordance with the Income Tax Act, and, in particular, the following provisions shall apply —

(a)
income from sources other than the qualifying services shall be excluded and separately assessed;

(b)
there shall be deducted in arriving at the income derived from the qualifying services —

(i)
all direct costs and expenses incurred in respect of the qualifying services;

(ii)
all indirect expenses which are reasonably and properly attributable to the qualifying services;

(c)
the allowances provided for in sections 13 to 18 of the Income Tax Act attributable to income derived from the qualifying services during the tax relief period shall be taken into account; and

(d)
for the purposes of subparagraph (ii) of paragraph (b) and paragraph (c), the amounts attributable to the qualifying services shall be determined on such basis as the Collector thinks reasonable and proper.

(2) The amount of income ascertained under subsection (1) which will qualify for the relief under section 60 shall be the excess of the amount of the income ascertained under subsection (1) over a base amount of income to be determined by the Minister.

Controller to issue statement of income.

60. (1) For each year of assessment, the Collector shall issue to an export service company or firm a statement for that year of assessment showing the amount of income ascertained under subsection (2) of section 59 which will qualify for the relief provided by this section, and Parts XI and XII of the Income Tax Act (relating to objections and appeals) and any regulations made thereunder shall apply, with the necessary modifications, as if that statement were a notice of assessment given under those provisions.

(2) Subject to subsection (7) of section 50, where any statement issued under subsection (1) has become final and conclusive, 100% of the amount of the qualifying income referred to in subsection (1) shall not form part of the statutory income of the export service company or firm for the year of assessment to which the income relates and shall be exempt from tax.

Certification by auditor.

61. The Controller may require an auditor to certify the income derived by an export service company from its qualifying services and any direct costs and expenses incurred therefor.

Deduction of allowances and losses.

62. The Minister may by regulations provide, in relation to an export service company, for the deduction of —

(a)

any unabsorbed allowances provided for under sections 13 to 18 of the Income Tax Act attributable to income derived from qualifying services by it during its tax relief period otherwise than in accordance with section 20 of that Act; and

(b)

losses incurred by it during its tax relief period otherwise than in accordance with subsection (2) of section 30 of the Income Tax Act.

PART IX

INTERNATIONAL TRADE INCENTIVES

Interpretation of this Part.

63. For the purposes of this Part, unless the context otherwise requires — "commencement day", in relation to an international trading company, means the date specified in the certificate issued to the company as the date from which that company shall be entitled to tax relief under this Part;

"export sales" means export sales free on board but shall exclude the cost of samples, gifts, test-market materials, trade exhibits and other promotional materials;

"international trading company" means a company which has been issued with a certificate under section 64;

"qualifying commodities" means any commodity in respect of which one or more certificates of origin or other documents have been issued by the Minister for the purpose of the export of such commodity;

"qualifying manufactured goods" means Brunei Darussalam manufactured goods in respect of which one or more certificates of origin or other documents indicating that the goods are manufactured in Brunei Darussalam have been issued by the Minister for the purpose of the export of such goods;

For additional analytical, business and investment opportunities information,
please contact Global Investment & Business Center, USA
at (703) 370-8082. Fax: (703) 370-8083. E-mail: ibpusa3@gmail.com
Global Business and Investment Info Databank - www.ibpus.com

"relevant export sales" means the export sales of an international trading company in respect of qualifying manufactured goods and Brunei Darussalam domestic produce or in respect of qualifying commodities, as the case may be;

"Brunei Darussalam domestic produce" means prawns, fish (including aquarium fish), chicken, ornamental plants and orchids produced in Brunei Darussalam and such other domestic produce as may be approved by the Minister.

International trading company.

64. (1) Where a company is engaged in —

(a)
    international trade in qualifying manufactured goods or Brunei Darussalam domestic produce and the export sales of those goods or produce separately or in combination exceed or are expected to exceed $3 million per annum; or

(b)
    entrepot trade in any qualifying commodities and the export sales of those qualifying commodities exceed or are expected to exceed $5 million per annum,

the company may apply in the prescribed form to the Minister for approval as an international trading company.

(2)
    The Minister may, if he considers it expedient in the public interest to do so, approve the application and issue the company with a certificate subject to such terms and conditions as he thinks fit.

(3)
    The Minister may issue separate certificates to an international trading company for the purposes of paragraphs *(a)* and *(b)* of subsection (1).

(4)
    Every certificate issued under this section shall specify a date as the commencement day from which the company shall be entitled to tax relief under this Part.

(5)
    The Minister may, in his discretion upon the application of an international trading company, amend its certificate by substituting for the commencement day specified therein such earlier or later date as he thinks fit and thereupon the provisions of this Part shall have effect as if the date so substituted were the commencement day in relation to that certificate.

(6)
    A company shall furnish to the Minister at the time of application to be an international trading company a statement of all its associated companies and export agents and the activities they are engaged in and such other particulars as may be required; and where there is any change in the particulars, the company shall notify the Minister as soon as possible of the change.

Tax relief period of international trading company.

65. The tax relief period of an international trading company, in relation to any certificate issued to that company, shall commence on the commencement day and shall continue for a period of 8 years.

Power to give directions

66. For the purposes of the Income Tax Act and this Order, the Collector may direct that —

(a)

any sums payable to an international trading company in any accounting period which, but for the provisions of this Order might reasonably and properly have been expected to be payable, in the normal course of business, after the end of that period shall be treated as not having been payable in that period but as having been payable on such date, after that period, as the Collector thinks fit and, where that date is after the end of the tax relief period of the international trading company, as having been so payable on that date as a sum payable in respect of its post tax relief trade or business; and

(b)

any expenses incurred by an international trading company within one year after the end of its tax relief period which, but for the provisions of this Order might reasonably and properly have been expected to be incurred, in the normal course of business, during its tax relief period shall be treated as not having been incurred within that year but as having been incurred on such date, during its tax relief period, as the Collector thinks fit.
Application of Part X of Income Tax Act.

67. (1) Part X of the Income Tax Act (relating to returns of income) shall apply in all respects as if the whole of the income of an international trading company were chargeable to tax.

(2) The annual return of income shall be accompanied by such evidence as, in the opinion of the Collector, is necessary to verify the income derived from the export sales of qualifying manufactured goods, Brunei Darussalam domestic produce and qualifying commodities.

Ascertainment of income in respect of other trade or business.

68. Where during its tax relief period an international trading company carries on any trade or business which is distinct from the trade or business which includes its relevant export sales, separate accounts shall be maintained in respect of that distinct trade or business and in respect of the same accounting period, and the income from that distinct trade or business shall be computed and assessed in accordance with the provisions of the Income Tax Act with such adjustments as the Collector thinks reasonable and proper.

Computation of export income and exemption from tax.

69. (1) The total income of an international trading company, in respect of its trade or business which includes its relevant export sales, shall be ascertained (after making such adjustments as may be necessary in consequence of any direction given under section 66), for any accounting period during its tax relief period in accordance with the provisions of the Income Tax Act, and, in particular, the following provisions shall apply —

(a)

income from any commissions and other non-trading sources shall be excluded and separately assessed;

(b)

the allowances provided for in sections 13, 14, 15, 16, 17, and 18 (where applicable) of the Income Tax Act shall be taken into account, and where in any year of assessment full effect cannot, by reason of an insufficiency of profits for that year of assessment, be given to those allowances, section 20 of the Income Tax Act shall apply;

(c)

the amount of any unabsorbed allowances in respect of any year of assessment immediately preceding the tax relief period which would otherwise be available under section 20 of the Income Tax Act shall be taken into account;

(d)

section 30 of the Income Tax Act shall apply in respect of any loss incurred prior to or during its tax relief period;

(e)

any unabsorbed allowances granted under sections 13, 14, 16 and 17 of the Income Tax Act and losses incurred in respect of any distinct trade or business shall be brought into the computation;

(f)

any unabsorbed allowances granted under sections 13, 14, 16 and 17 of the Income Tax Act and losses incurred in respect of the trade or business referred to in this subsection shall, during the tax relief period, only be deducted against the income derived from that trade or business;

(g)

subject to sections 20 and 30 of the Income Tax Act, any allowances and losses which remain unabsorbed at the end of the tax relief period shall be available for deduction in its post tax relief period.

(2)

The amount of the export income of an international trading company which will qualify for the relief for any year of assessment shall be deemed to be such amount which bears to the total income ascertained under subsection (1) the same proportion as the excess of the total value of the relevant export sales over the relevant base export value bears to the total amount of the sums received or receivable in respect of its total sales; and subject to section 70, one-half of the amount of the export income which qualifies for the relief as ascertained in this subsection shall not form part of the chargeable income of the international trading company for that year of assessment and shall be exempt from tax.

(3) The relevant base export value referred to in subsection (2) shall be —

(a)

for the basis period for the first year of assessment within the tax relief period of an international trading company, a sum equal to one-third of the total value of the relevant export sales during the 3 years immediately preceding the date of its application to be an international trading company; and

(b)

for the basis period for any subsequent year of assessment within the tax relief period, a sum equal to one-third of the total value of the relevant export sales during the 3 qualifying years immediately preceding that basis period.

(4)

For the purposes of paragraph (b) of subsection (3), a "qualifying year" is a year in which the export sales —

(a)

in respect of qualifying manufactured goods or Brunei Darussalam domestic produce exceed $3 million; and

(b)

in respect of qualifying commodities exceed $5 million.

(5) Where an international trading company —

(a)

was engaged in the trading of qualifying manufactured goods, Brunei Darussalam domestic produce or qualifying commodities for less than 3 years immediately preceding its application under this Part;

(b)

during its tax relief period has acquired any sales in respect of qualifying manufactured goods, Brunei Darussalam domestic produce or qualifying commodities from any person or has acquired the beneficial interest, directly or indirectly, of any company engaged in similar trade or business; or

(c)

has less than 3 qualifying years for the purpose of determining its relevant base export value under paragraph *(b)* of subsection (3), the Minister may specify such other relevant base export value for one or more basis periods as he thinks fit having regard to the circumstances of the case.

Conditions for relief.

70. The tax relief provided under section 69 shall, for a year of assessment, apply only if an international trading company has complied with the conditions stipulated under this Part and such other conditions as may be specified in its certificate.

Certain dividends exempted from income tax.

71. (1) As soon as any amount of chargeable income of an international trading company has become exempt under section 69, that amount shall be credited to a tax exempt account to be kept by the company for the purposes of this Part.

(2)

Where a tax exempt account is in credit at the date on which any dividends are paid by a company, out of income which has been so exempted, an amount equal to those dividends or to that credit, whichever is the less, shall be debited to the account.

(3)

So much of the amount of any dividends so debited to the tax exempt account as is received by a shareholder of the company shall, if the Collector is satisfied with the entries in the account, be exempt from tax in the hands of the shareholder.

(4)

Notwithstanding subsection (3), where a dividend is paid on any share of a preferential nature, it shall not be exempt from tax in the hands of the shareholder.

(5)

Any dividends debited to the tax exempt account shall be treated as having been distributed to the shareholders of the company or any particular class of those shareholders in the same proportions as the shareholders were entitled to payment of the dividends giving rise to the debit.

(6)

The company shall deliver to the Collector a copy of the tax exempt account, made up to a date specified by him, whenever called upon to do so by notice in writing sent by him to its registered office, until such time as he is satisfied that there is no further need for maintaining the account.

(7)

Where an amount has been received by way of dividend from a company by a shareholder and the amount is exempt from tax under this Part, if that shareholder is a company, any dividends paid by that company to its shareholders, to the extent that the

Collector is satisfied that those dividends are paid out of that amount, shall be exempt from tax in the hands of those shareholders.

Recovery of tax exempted.

72. Notwithstanding any other provisions of this Part, where it appears to the Collector that —

(a)

any amount of exempted income of an international trading company; or

(b)

any dividend exempted in the hands of any shareholder,

ought not to have been exempted by reason of a direction made under section 66 or the revocation under section 114 of the certificate issued under section 64 to the company, the Collector may subject to section 62 of the Income Tax Act —

(i)

make such assessment or additional assessment upon the company or any such shareholder as may appear to be necessary in order to recover such tax as may have been exempted under this Part; or

(ii)

direct the company to debit its tax exempt account with such amount as the circumstance require.

Application of Parts XI and XII of Income Tax Act.

73. (1) Parts XI and XII of the Income Tax Act (relating to objection and appeals) and any regulations made thereunder shall apply, with the necessary modifications, to any direction given under section 72 as if it were a notice of assessment given under those provisions.

(2) Section 36 of the Income Tax Act shall not apply in respect of any dividend or part thereof which is exempted from tax under this Part.

Application of certain sections to international trading company.

74. Sections 45, 51, 52, 53 and 54 shall apply, with the necessary modifications, to an international trading company as they apply to an export enterprise and the reference to export product or export produce in those sections shall be read as a reference to qualifying manufactured goods, Brunei Darussalam domestic produce or qualifying commodities.

PART X FOREIGN LOANS FOR PRODUCTIVE EQUIPMENT

Application for and issue of approved foreign loan certificate.

75. (1) Where a company engaged in any industry is desirous of raising a loan of not less than $200,000 from a non-resident person (referred to in this Part as a foreign lender) by means of a financial agreement whereby credit facilities are granted for the purchase of productive equipment for the purposes of its trade or business, the company may apply to the Minister for a certificate certifying that foreign loan to be an approved foreign loan.

(2)

The Minister may, where he thinks it expedient to do so, consider an application for a foreign loan certificate in respect of a foreign loan of less than $200,000.

(3)

The application shall be in such form and with such particulars as may be prescribed, and shall be accompanied by a copy of the financial agreement.

(4)

Where the Minister is satisfied as to the *bona fides* of such an application and that it is expedient in the public interest to do so, he may issue a certificate certifying the loan specified in the application as an approved foreign loan.

(5)

Every certificate issued under subsection (4) shall be in such form and contain such particulars as may be prescribed, and shall be subject to such terms and conditions as the Minister thinks fit.

Restriction on disposal of specified productive equipment.

76. Any productive equipment purchased and financed from an approved foreign loan shall not be sold, transferred, or otherwise disposed of without the prior written permission of the Minister, unless the loan has been repaid in full.

Exemption of approved foreign loan interest from tax.

77. (1) Notwithstanding section 37 of the Income Tax Act, the Minister may, subject to subsection (2), if he is satisfied that it is expedient in the public interest to do so, by an endorsement to that effect on the approved foreign loan certificate, exempt from tax any interest on an approved foreign loan payable to a foreign lender.

(2)

> **Where a company has contravened section 76 or any conditions imposed by the Minister under subsection (4) of section 75, the amount which, but for subsection (1), would have been deductible by the company from the interest paid by it to the foreign lender under section 37 of the Income Tax Act shall be deemed to have been deducted from that interest and shall be a debt due from the company to the Government and be recoverable in the manner provided by section 76 of the Income Tax Act.**

(3) No action shall be taken by the Collector to recover any debt under subsection (2)

> without the prior sanction of the Minister.
>
> Exemption of additional interest on approved foreign loan from tax.

78. (1) Subject to subsection (3), section 77 shall apply to any additional interest payable on an approved foreign loan by reason of any arrangement whereby the period within which the loan must be repaid in full has been extended.

(2)

> The rate of interest payable in respect of any such extended period shall not, without the prior sanction of the Minister, be higher than the rate of interest specified in the certificate relating to the approved foreign loan.

(3)

> Any company making any such arrangement shall give notice thereof in writing to the Minister within 30 days from the date on which the arrangement is made.

PART XI INVESTMENT ALLOWANCES

Interpretation of this Part.

79. (1) For the purposes of this Part, unless the context otherwise requires —

"approved project" means a project approved by the Minister under subsection

(2)

> of section 80;

"construction operations" means —

(a)

> construction, alteration, repair, extension or demolition of buildings and structures;

(b)

> construction, alteration, repair, extension or demolition of any works forming, or to form, part of any land; or

(c)

any operations which form an integral part of, or are preparatory to, or are for renderings complete the operations described in paragraph *(a)* or *(b)* including site clearance, earth-moving excavation, laying of foundations, site restoration , landscaping and the provision of drains and of roadways and other access works;

"fixed capital expenditure" means capital expenditure to be incurred on an approved project by a company on factory building (excluding land) in Brunei Darussalam, on the acquisition of any know-how or patent rights, and on any new productive equipment (and, subject to the approval of the Minister, on any secondhand productive equipment) to be used in Brunei Darussalam, and the reference to factory building in this definition shall, in relation to a project under paragraph *(b)*, *(c)*, *(d)*, *(f)* or *(g)* of subsection (1) of section 80, include a building or structure specially designed and used for carrying out that project;

"investment day", in relation to a company, means the date specified in its certificate as the date from which the company shall qualify for the investment allowance;

"research and development" has the same meaning as in the Income Tax Act (Chapter 35).

(2) For the purposes of this Part, fixed capital expenditure shall not be deemed to be incurred by a company unless —

(a)

in the case of any factory building or productive equipment to be constructed or installed on site, the expenditure is attributable to payment against work done in the construction of the building or the construction or installation of the productive equipment;

(b)

in the case of any productive equipment, other than that to be constructed or installed on site, the company has received delivery of the equipment in Brunei Darussalam.
Capital expenditure investment allowance.

80. (1) Where a company proposes to carry out a project —

(a)

for the manufacture or increased manufacture of any product;

(b)

for the provision of specialised engineering or technical services;

(c)

for research and development;

(d)

for construction operation;

(e)

for the recycling of domestic and industrial waste;

(f)

in relation to any qualifying activity as defined in section 17;

(g)

for the promotion of the tourist industry (other than a hotel) in Brunei Darussalam,

the company may apply in the prescribed form to the Minister for the approval of an investment allowance in respect of the fixed capital expenditure for the project.

(2)

Where the Minister considers it expedient, having regard to the economic, technical and other merits of the project, he may approve the project and issue the company with a certificate which shall qualify the company for an investment allowance (as stipulated in the certificate) in respect of the fixed capital expenditure for the approved project subject to such terms and conditions as he thinks fit.

(3)

Every certificate issued under this section shall specify a date as the investment day from which the company shall be entitled to investment allowance under this Part.

(4)

The Minister may, in his discretion upon the application of a company amend its certificate by substituting for the investment day specified therein such earlier or later date as he thinks fit and thereupon the provisions of this Part shall have effect as if the date so substituted were the investment day in relation to that certificate.

Investment allowance.

81. (1) The investment allowance granted under section 80 shall be a specified percentage not exceeding 100% of the amount (which may be subject to a specified maximum) of fixed capital expenditure incurred on each item specified by the Minister under subsection (2) on an approved project if the fixed capital expenditure is incurred —

(a)

within such period (referred to in this Order as the qualifying period), not exceeding 5 years, commencing from the investment day as the Minister may determine; and

(b)

in the case of a project under paragraph (g) of subsection (1) of section 80, within such period (hereinafter referred to as the qualifying period), not exceeding 11 years, commencing from the investment day as the Minister may determine.

(2) The Minister —

(a)

shall specify the items of the fixed capital expenditure for the purposes of subsection (1); and

(b)

may specify the maximum amount of the investment allowance granted for the approved project.

(3) Where any question arises as to whether a particular item qualifies as one of the items under paragraph (a) of subsection (2), it shall be determined by the Minister whose decision shall be final.

(4) In subsection (1), "specified" means specified by the Minister.

Crediting of investment allowance.

82. (1) Where in the basis period for a year of assessment a company has incurred fixed capital expenditure, the company shall be given for that year of assessment an investment allowance in respect of such amount of the fixed capital expenditure as qualifies for the investment allowance under the terms and conditions of its certificate and in accordance with section 81.

(2) Where any investment allowance is given to a company for an approved project, the investment allowance shall be kept in an account to be called "investment allowance account" which shall be kept by the company for the purposes of this Part.

Prohibition to sell, lease out or dispose of assets.

83. (1) During its qualifying period or within 2 years after the end of its qualifying period, a company shall not, without the written approval of the Minister, sell, lease out or otherwise dispose of any assets in respect of which an investment allowance has been given.

(2)
Where during its qualifying period or within 2 years after the end of its qualifying period, a company has sold, leased out or otherwise disposed any asset in respect of which an investment allowance has been given, an amount equal to the aggregate of the investment allowance given in respect of that asset shall be recovered.

(3)
Where that account is insufficient to give full effect to the recovery, an assessment or additional assessment in respect of the amount unrecovered shall be made upon the company or any shareholder of the company and the tax exempt account, kept in accordance with section 71 (as made applicable by section 85), shall be debited accordingly.

(4)
Notwithstanding subsections (2) and (3), the Minister may waive wholly or partly the recovery of the investment allowance.

Exemption from income tax.

84. (1) Where for any year of assessment the investment allowance account of a company is in credit and the company has for that year of assessment any chargeable income —

(a)
an amount of the chargeable income, not exceeding the credit in the investment allowance account, shall be exempt from tax and the investment allowance account shall be debited with such amount; and

(b)
any remaining balance in the investment allowance account shall be carried forward to be used by the company in the first subsequent year of assessment when the company has chargeable income, and so on for subsequent year of assessment until the credit in the investment allowance account has been fully used.

(2) Any amount of chargeable income of a company debited from the investment allowance account shall be exempt from tax.

Certain dividends exempted from income tax.

85. Section 71 shall apply, with the necessary modifications, to a company which has been granted an investment allowance under this Part as it applies to an international trading company and the reference to section 69 in that section shall be read as a reference to section

84.

Recovery of tax exempted.

86. Notwithstanding any other provisions in this Part, where it appears to the Collector that —

(a)
any amount exempted income of a company; or

(b)

any dividend exempted in the hands of any shareholder,

ought not to have been exempted by reason of the revocation under section 114 of the certificate issued under section 80 to the company, the Collector may subject to section 62 of the Income Tax Act —

(i)

make such assessment or additional assessment upon the company or any such shareholder as may appear to be necessary in order to recover such tax as may have been exempted under this Part; or

(ii)

direct the company to debit its tax exempt account with such amount as the circumstances require.

Application of Parts XI and XII of Income Tax Act.

87. (1) Parts XI and XII of the Income Tax Act (relating to objections and appeals) and any regulations made thereunder shall apply, with the necessary modifications, to any direction given under section 86 as if it were a notice of assessment given under those provisions.

(2) Section 36 of the Income Tax Act shall not apply in respect of any dividend or part thereof which is exempted from tax under this Part.

PART XII WAREHOUSING AND SERVICING INCENTIVES

Interpretation of this Part.

88. For the purposes of this Part, unless the context otherwise requires — "commencement day", in relation to a warehousing company or a servicing company, means the date specified in its certificate as the date from which that company shall be entitled to tax relief under this Part;

"earnings" means —

(a)

in relation to a warehousing company, the consideration received or receivable from the sales of goods (including the provisions of services connected with or related to such sales) or the commissions received or receivable therefrom; and

(b)

in relation to a service company, the consideration received or receivable from the provision of services;

"eligible goods or services", in relation to a warehousing company or a servicing company, means the eligible goods or services specified in the certificate issued to that company under subsection (3) of section 89;

"export earnings" means —

(a)

in relation to a warehousing company, the consideration received or receivable from export sales free on board of eligible goods (including the provision of services connected with or related to such sales) or the commissions received or receivable therefrom; and

(b)

in relation to a servicing company, the consideration received or receivable from the provision of eligible services to persons outside Brunei Darussalam who are not resident in Brunei Darussalam.

"fixed capital expenditure" means capital expenditure to be incurred on any building (excluding land) and on any new productive equipment (and, subject to the approval of the Minister, on any secondhand productive equipment) to be used in Brunei Darussalam;

"servicing company" means a company which has been approved as a servicing company under section 89;

"warehousing company" means a company which has been approved as a warehousing company under section 89.

Approved warehousing company or servicing company.

89. (1) Any company intending to incur fixed capital expenditure of not less than $2 million for —

(a)

the establishment or improvement of warehousing facilities wholly or mainly for the storage and distribution of manufacture goods to be sold and

exported by the company, with or without processing or the provision of related services; or

(b)

the purpose of providing technical or engineering services (or such other services as the Minister may, by notification in the *Gazette*, specify) wholly or mainly to persons not resident in Brunei Darussalam,

may apply in the prescribed form to the Minister for approval as a warehousing company or a servicing company.

(2)

Where the Minister considers it expedient in the public interest to do so, he may approve the application and issue a certificate to the company subject to such terms and conditions as he thinks fit.

(3) Every certificate issued under this section shall specify —

(a)

a date as the commencement day from which the company shall be entitled to tax relief under this Part; and

(b)

the eligible goods or services for the purpose of tax relief under this Part.

(4)

The Minister may, in his discretion, upon the application of a warehousing company or a servicing company, amend its certificate by substituting for the commencement day specified therein such earlier or later date as he thinks fit and thereupon the provisions of this Part shall have effect as if the date so substituted were the commencement day in relation to that certificate.

Tax relief period of warehousing company or servicing company.

90. (1) The tax relief period of a warehousing company or a servicing company shall commence on its commencement day and shall continue for such period, not exceeding 11 years, as the Minister may, in his discretion, determine.

(2) The Minister may, where he is satisfied that it is expedient in the public interest to do so and subject to such terms and conditions as he may impose, extend the tax relief period of any warehousing company or servicing company for such further period or periods, not exceeding 3 years at any one time, as he may determine, except that the tax relief period of the warehousing company or servicing company shall not in the aggregate exceed 20 years.

Prohibition of acquisition without approval.

91. (1) During its tax relief period, a warehousing company shall not acquire any sales and a servicing company shall not acquire any services from any other person in connection with its trade or business without the written approval of the Minister.

(2) Where the Minister permits a warehousing company or a servicing company to acquire such sales or services, he may vary the base export earnings as determined under subsection (3) of section 94 and impose such terms and conditions as he thinks fit.

Application of certain sections to warehousing company or servicing company.

92. (1) Sections 66 and 68 shall apply, with the necessary modifications, to a warehousing company or a servicing company as they apply to an international trading company, and the reference in section 68 to relevant export sales shall be read as a reference to export of eligible goods or provision of eligible services.

(2) Sections 45, 46, 51, 52, 53 and 54 shall apply, with the necessary modifications, to a warehousing company as they apply to an export enterprise and the reference to export product or export produce in those sections shall be read as a reference to eligible goods.

Application of Part X of Income Tax Act.

93. (1) Part X of the Income Tax Act (relating to returns of income) shall apply in all respects as if the whole of the income of a warehousing company or a servicing company were chargeable to tax.

(2) The annual return of income shall be accompanied by such evidence as, in the opinion of the Collector, is necessary to verify the income derived by a warehousing company or a servicing company.

Computation of export earnings and exemption from tax.

94. (1) The total income of a warehousing company or a servicing company in respect of its trade or business which includes its export of eligible goods or provision of eligible services shall be ascertained (after making such adjustments as may be necessary in consequence of any direction given under section 66 as made applicable by section 92), for any accounting period during its tax relief period in accordance with the provisions of the Income Tax Act, and, in particular, the following provisions shall apply —

(a)
income from other non-trading sources shall be excluded and separately assessed;

(b)
the allowances provided for in sections 13, 14, 15, 16, 17 and 18 (where applicable) of the Income Tax Act shall be taken into account notwithstanding that no claim for those allowances has been made, and where in any year of assessment full effect cannot, by

reason of an insufficiency of profits for that year of assessment, be given to those allowances, section 20 of the Income Tax Act shall apply;

(c)

the amount of any unabsorbed allowances in respect of any year of assessment immediately preceding the tax relief period which would
otherwise be available under section 20 of the Income Tax Act shall be taken into account;

(d)

section 30 of the Income Tax Act shall apply in respect of any loss incurred prior to or during its tax relief period;

(e)

any unabsorbed allowances granted under sections 13, 14, 16, 17 and 18 of the Income Tax Act and losses incurred in respect of any distinct trade or business shall be brought into the computation;

(f)

any unabsorbed allowances granted under sections 13, 14, 16, 17 and 18 of the Income Tax Act and losses incurred in respect of the trade or business referred to in this subsection shall, during the tax relief period, only be deducted against the income derived from that trade or business; and

(g)

subject to sections 20 and 30 of the Income Tax Act, any allowances and losses which remain unabsorbed at the end of the tax relief period shall be available for deduction in its post tax relief period.

(2)

The amount of the export income of a warehousing company or a servicing company which will qualify for the relief for any year of assessment shall be deemed to be such amount which bears to the total income ascertained under subsection (1) the same proportion as the excess of the total amount of the export earnings of that company over its base export earnings bears to the total amount of its earnings; and one-half of the amount of the export income which qualifies for the relief as ascertained in this subsection shall not form part of the chargeable income of the company for the year of assessment and shall be exempt from tax.

(3)

The base export earnings referred to in subsection (2) shall be where a warehousing company or a servicing company has been carrying on its trade or business —

(a)

for 3 or more years immediately preceding the date of its application under this Part, an amount equal to one-third of the export earnings for the 3 years immediately preceding the date of its application under this Part; and

(b)

for less than 3 years immediately preceding the date of its application under this Part, such amount as the Minister may specify having regard to the export earnings of other warehousing companies or servicing companies, as the case may be.

Certain dividends exempted from income tax.

95. Section 71 shall apply, with the necessary modifications, to a warehousing company or a servicing company as it applies to an international trading company and the reference to section 69 in subsection (1) of section 71 shall be read as a reference to section 94.

Recovery of tax exempted.

96. Notwithstanding any other provisions of this Part, where it appears to the Collector that —

(a)

any amount of exempted income of a warehousing company or a servicing company; or

(b)

any dividend exempted in the hand of any shareholder,

ought not to have been exempted by reason of a direction made under section 66 (as made applicable by section 92) or the revocation under section 114 of the certificate issued under section 89 to the warehousing company or the servicing company, the Collector may subject to section 62 of the Income Tax Act —

(i)

make such assessment or additional assessment upon the company or any such shareholder as may appear to be necessary in order to recover such tax as may have been exempted under this Part; or

(ii)

direct the company to debit its tax exempt account with such amount as the circumstances may require.

Application of Parts XI and XII of Income Tax Act.

97. (1) Parts XI and XII of the Income Tax Act (relating to objections and appeals) and any regulations made thereunder shall apply, with the necessary modifications, to any direction given under section 96 as if it were a notice of assessment given under those provisions.

(2) Section 36 of the Income Tax Act shall not apply in respect of any dividend or part thereof which is exempted from tax under this Part.

PART XIII INVESTMENTS IN NEW TECHNOLOGY COMPANIES

Interpretation of this Part.

98. For the purposes of this Part, unless the context otherwise requires —

"eligible holding company", in relation to a technology company, means a company incorporated in Brunei Darussalam —

(a)

which is resident in Brunei Darussalam;

(b)

which holds shares in the technology company; and

(c)

in respect of which not less than 30% of the paid-up capital is beneficially owned by citizens or persons to whom a Resident Permit has been granted under regulations made under the Immigration Act (Chapter 17) throughout the whole of the qualifying period of the technology company, unless the Minister otherwise decides;

"qualifying period", in relation to a technology company, means a period of 3 years from the day it commences, for the purposes of the Income Tax Act (Chapter 35), to carry on its relevant trade or business;

"relevant trade or business", in relation to a technology company, means the trade or business to which the certificate, issued to the company under subsection (2) of section 99, relates;

"technology company" means a company approved as a technology company under subsection (2) of section 99.

Application for and issue of certificate to technology company.

99. (1) Any company incorporated in Brunei Darussalam which is desirous of using in Brunei Darussalam a new technology in relation to a product, process or service may make an application in the prescribed form to the Minister to be approved as a technology company.

(2)

Where the Minister is satisfied that the technology, if introduced in Brunei Darussalam, would promote or enhance the economic or technological development in Brunei Darussalam, he may approve the company as a technology company and issue a certificate to that company subject to such conditions as he thinks fit.

(3)

Every certificate issued under this section shall specify a percentage, not exceeding 30%, of such amount of the paid-up capital of the technology company as is held by any eligible holding company for the purpose of determining the deduction under section

100.

Deductions allowable to eligible holding company.

100. (1) Where a technology company has incurred an overall loss in respect of its relevant trade or business at the end of its qualifying period, it may, within 6 years from that date, by notice in writing to the Collector elect for the overall loss (less any amount which has been deducted up to the date of the notice) and the amount of any unabsorbed capital allowances (less any amount which has been deducted up to the date of the notice) to be made available to an eligible holding company as a deduction against the statutory income of the eligible holding company.

(2)

The deduction to be made available to an eligible holding company under subsection (1) shall be an amount to be ascertained by multiplying the overall loss (less any amount which has been deducted up to the date of the notice) or the unabsorbed capital allowances (less any amount which has been deducted up to the date of the notice), as the case may be, by the percentage of the paid-up capital of the technology company held by that eligible holding company throughout the whole of the qualifying period of the technology company.

(3)

The deduction shall not in the aggregate exceed such percentage as may be specified in the certificate issued to the technology company under section 99 of the paid-up capital of the technology company held by the eligible holding company (excluding any shares acquired from other shareholders of the technology company) as at the end of such qualifying period.

(4)

Notwithstanding subsections (2) and (3), where the percentage of the paid-up capital of the technology company held by an eligible holding company is increased at any time during the qualifying period of the technology company, the Minister may, upon the application by the eligible holding company, if he considers it just and reasonable to do so, increase the amount of the deduction available under subsection (2) up to 50% of the paid-up capital of the technology company held by the eligible holding company as at the end of such qualifying period.

(5)

Where any deduction is made available to an eligible holding company in accordance with this section, any overall loss or unabsorbed capital allowances to the extent of the deductions so made available shall cease to be deductible by the technology company under section 20 or 30 of the Income Tax Act (Chapter 35), and those sections shall apply to the eligible holding company in respect of the deduction made available as if the eligible holding company was carrying on the trade or business in respect of which the overall loss or the unabsorbed capital allowances were made.

(6)

The overall loss or unabsorbed capital allowances made available to an eligible holding company under this section shall first be deducted against the statutory income of the eligible holding company for the year of assessment immediately following the year in which the notice given under subsection (1).

(7) In this section —

"overall loss", in relation to a technology company, means the amount by which the total of the losses exceed the total of the statutory income arising from its relevant trade or business for the whole of its qualifying period ascertained in accordance with the provisions of the Income Tax Act and subject to such regulations as may be prescribed under this Order;

"unabsorbed capital allowances", in relation to a technology company, means the balance of any allowance provided for in sections 13, 14, 15, 16, 17 and 18 of the Income Tax Act which remain unabsorbed at the end of the qualifying period of the company in respect of capital expenditure incurred for the purpose of its relevant trade or business before the end of the qualifying period.

(8) For the purposes of the Income Tax Act and this Part, the Collector may direct that —

(a)

any sums payable to a technology company before or after its qualifying period which, but for the provisions of this Part, might reasonably and properly have been expected to be payable to the technology company, in the normal course of business, during its qualifying period shall be treated as having been payable on such date within the qualifying period, as the Collector thinks fit; and

(b)

any expense incurred by a technology company during its qualifying period which, but for the provisions of this Part, might reasonably and properly have been expected to be incurred, in the normal course of business, before or after the qualifying period shall be treated as not having been incurred within the qualifying period but as having been incurred on such date before or after that qualifying period, as the Collector thinks fit.
Prohibition of other trade or business.

101. (1) During its qualifying period, a technology company shall not, without the written approval of the Minister, carry on any trade or business other than its relevant trade or business.

(2) Where the carrying on of a separate trade or business has been approved under subsection (1), separate accounts shall be maintained in respect of that trade or business.

Recovery of tax.

102. Notwithstanding anything in this Part, where it appears to the Collector that any deduction under section 100 ought not to have been given to an eligible holding company by reason of any direction under subsection (8) of section 100 or the revocation under section 114 of a certificate issued to a technology company, the Collector may, subject to section 62 of the Income Tax Act, make such assessment or additional assessment upon the eligible holding company or any of its shareholders as may be necessary in order to recover any tax which should have been payable by the eligible holding company.

PART XIV OVERSEAS INVESTMENT AND VENTURE CAPITAL INCENTIVES

Interpretation of this Part.

103. For the purposes of this Part, unless the context otherwise requires —

"eligible holding company", in relation to a venture company, a technology investment company or an overseas investment company, means a company incorporated in Brunei Darussalam —

(a)
      which is resident in Brunei Darussalam;

(b)
      which has invested not less than 60% of its shareholders' fund in Brunei Darussalam;

(c)
      which holds not less than 30% of the shares in the venture company, the technology investment company or the overseas investment company; and

(d)
      in respect of which not less than 30% of the paid-up capital is beneficially owned by citizens or person to whom a Resident Permit has been granted under regulations made under the Immigration Act (Chapter 17) throughout the period during which it holds shares in the venture company, the technology investment company or the overseas investment company, unless the Minister otherwise decides;

"overseas investment company" means a company approved as an overseas investment company under subsection (4) of section 105;

"technology investment company" means a company approved as a technology investment company under subsection (2) of section 105;

"venture company" means a company approved as a venture company under subsection (2) of section 104;

"shareholders' fund" means the aggregate amount of a company's paid up capital (in respect of preference shares and ordinary shares and not including any amount in respect of bonus shares to the extent they were issued out of capital reserves created by revaluation of fixed assets), reserves (other than any capital reserve which was created by revaluation of fixed assets and provisions for depreciation, renewals or replacements and diminution in value of assets), balance of share premium account (not including any amount credited therein at the instance of issuing bonus shares at premium out of capital reserve created by revaluation of fixed assets), and balance of profit and loss appropriation account.

Application for and issue of certificate to venture company.

104. (1) Any company incorporated in Brunei Darussalam which is desirous of developing or using in Brunei Darussalam a new technology in relation to a product, process or service may make an application in the prescribed form to the Minister to be approved as a venture company.

(2) Where the Minister is satisfied that the technology, if introduced in Brunei Darussalam, would promote or enhance the economic or technological development of Brunei Darussalam, he may approve the company as a venture company and issue a certificate to the company subject to such terms and conditions as he may impose.

For additional analytical, business and investment opportunities information,
please contact Global Investment & Business Center, USA
at (703) 370-8082. Fax: (703) 370-8083. E-mail: ibpusa3@gmail.com
Global Business and Investment Info Databank - www.ibpus.com

Application for and issue of certificate to technology investment company or overseas investment company.

105. (1) Any company, incorporated and resident in Brunei Darussalam, desirous of investing in an overseas company which is developing or using a new technology in relation to a product, process or service may make an application in the prescribed form to the Minister to be approved as a technology investment company.

(2)

Where the Minister is satisfied in respect of any application under subsection (1) that the technology, if introduced in Brunei Darussalam would promote or enhance the economic or technological development of Brunei Darussalam, he may approve the company as a technology investment company and issue a certificate to the company subject to such terms and conditions as he may impose.

(3)

Any company, incorporated and resident in Brunei Darussalam, desirous of investing in an overseas company for the purpose of acquiring for use in Brunei Darussalam any technology from the overseas company or for the purpose of gaining access to any overseas market for its eligible holding company or any subsidiary thereof, may make an application in the prescribed form to the Minister to be approved as an overseas investment company.

(4)

Where the Minister is satisfied in respect of any application under subsection (3) that the technology acquired, if introduced in Brunei Darussalam or the access which would be gained to any overseas market, would promote or enhance the technological or economic development of Brunei Darussalam, he may approve the company as an overseas investment company and issue a certificate to the company subject to such terms and conditions as he may impose.

Deduction of losses allowable to eligible holding company.

106. (1) Where any eligible holding company has incurred any loss arising from —

(a)

the sale of shares held by it in a venture company; or

(b)

the liquidation of a venture company,

the loss shall be allowed as a deduction against the statutory income of the company in accordance with subsection 2 of section 30 of the Income Tax Act as if the loss were incurred from a trade or business carried on by it.

(2) Where any eligible holding company has incurred any loss arising from —

(a)

the sale of shares held by it in a technology investment company or an overseas investment company; or

(b)

the liquidation of a technology investment company or an overseas investment company,

the loss shall be allowed as a deduction against its statutory income in accordance with subsection (2) of section 30 of the Income Tax Act as if the loss were incurred from a trade or business carried on by it.

For additional analytical, business and investment opportunities information, please contact Global Investment & Business Center, USA at (703) 370-8082. Fax: (703) 370-8083. E-mail: ibpusa3@gmail.com Global Business and Investment Info Databank - www.ibpus.com

(3)

Notwithstanding subsections (1) and (2), no deduction shall be allowed in respect of any loss referred to in those subsection if —

(a)

the shares in respect of which the loss was incurred were held by an eligible holding company in a venture company, or by an eligible holding company in a technology investment company or in an overseas investment company, for a period of less than 3 years from the date of issue of the shares, unless the loss was incurred as a result of the liquidation of the venture company, technology investment company or overseas investment company; or

(b)

the sale of shares or liquidation occurred after 8 years from the date of approval under this Part of the venture company, technology investment company or overseas investment company.

(4)

For the purposes of subsections (1) and (2), the loss shall be the excess of the purchase price of the shares —

(a)

over the proceeds from the sale; and where the open market value at the date of the sale (or the value of net asset backing as determined by the Collector in the case of a company not quoted on any stock exchange) of the shares is greater than the sale proceeds, that value shall be deemed to be the proceeds from the sale; or

(b)

over the proceeds from the liquidation,

as the case may be.

Prohibition of other trade or business.

107. (1) A venture company shall not, without the written approval of the Minister, carry on any trade or business other than the trade or business to which its certificate relates.

(2) A technology investment company and an overseas investment company shall not carry on any trade or business.

Recovery of tax.

108. Notwithstanding anything in this Part, where it appears to the Collector that any deduction under section 106 ought not to have been given to an eligible holding company by reason of the revocation under section 114 of a certificate issued to a venture company, a technology investment company or an overseas investment company, the Collector may, subject to section 62 of the Income Tax Act, make such assessment or additional assessment upon the eligible holding company (or any of its shareholders) as may be necessary in order to recover any tax which should have been payable by the eligible holding company (or any of its shareholders).

PART XV RELIEF FROM IMPORT DUTIES
Exemption from import duties.

109. (1) Notwithstanding the provision of section 11 of the Customs Act (Chapter 36) or any written laws or regulations in force, the Minister may, subject to such terms and conditions as he thinks fit, exempt a pioneer enterprise or an export enterprise from the payment of the whole or any part of any customs duty which may be payable on any machinery, equipment, component parts and accessories including prefabricated factory or building structures to be installed as necessary part of parts of the factory:

Provided that similar machinery, equipment, component parts, accessories or building structures of approximately equal price and equal quality are not being produced or available within Brunei Darussalam.

Restriction on disposal.

110. No machinery, equipment, component parts and accessories imported under section 109 shall be sold, transferred, mortgaged or otherwise disposed of or used for other purposes than those specified or allowed by the Minister without the written approval of the Minister.

Duty to be paid if disposed.

111. (1) Any machinery, equipment, component parts and accessories imported under section 109 which are sold, transferred, mortgaged or otherwise disposed of under section 110 shall be subject to payment of customs duty imposed under the Customs Act (Chapter 36).

(2) For the purpose of determining the duty imposed under subsection (1), all machinery, equipment, component parts and accessories shall be assessed and valued by the Controller of Customs and duties shall be payable on the assessed value.

Exemption from import duties on raw material.

112. Notwithstanding the provision of section 11 of the Customs Act or any written laws or regulations in force, a pioneer enterprise and an export enterprise shall be exempt from the payment of import duties on raw materials imported for use in the pioneer enterprise to be used in the production of a pioneer product specified in the pioneer certificate:

Provided that such raw materials are not available or produced within Brunei Darussalam.

PART XVI MISCELLANEOUS PROVISIONS

Prohibition of publication of application and certificate.

113. (1) The contents of any application made by, or of any certificate issued to, any company under any of the provisions of this Order shall not, except at the instance of the company, be published.

(2) The Minister may cause to be published by notification in the *Gazette* the name of any company to which any such certificate has been issued or whose certificate has been revoked, and the industry and product or produce to which the certificate relates.

Revocation of certificate.

114. (1) Where the Minister is satisfied that any company to which a certificate has been issued under the provisions of this Order has contravened or has failed to comply with any of the provisions of this Order or any regulations made thereunder, or of any terms or conditions imposed on the certificate, he may, by notice in writing, require the company within 30 days from the date of service of the notice to show cause why the certificate should not be revoked; and if the Minister is satisfied that, having regard to all the circumstances of the case it is expedient to do so, he may revoke the certificate.

(2) Where a certificate is revoked under subsection (1), the Minister shall specify the date, which may be the date of the certificate, from which its revocation shall be operative and the provisions of this Order shall cease to have effect in relation to the certificate from that date.

Provisions of Income Tax Act (Chapter 35) not affected.

115. Except as otherwise provided, nothing in this Order shall exempt any company to which a certificate has been issued under the provisions of this Order from making any return to the Collector or from complying with the provisions of the Income Tax Act in any respect so as to establish the liability to tax, if any, of the company.

Offences and penalties.

116. (1) Any person who contravenes or fails to comply with section 46 or 52 or any regulations made under this Order shall be guilty of an offence and shall be liable on conviction to a fine not exceeding $10,000, to imprisonment for a term not exceeding 2 years or both.

(2) Any person who —

(a)
obstructs or hinders any senior officer of customs or officer of customs acting in the discharge of his duty under this Order or any regulations made thereunder; or

(b)
fails to produce to a senior officer of customs or officer of customs any invoices, bills of lading, certificates of origin or of analysis or any other documents relating to the export of any export product or export produce which the officer may require, shall be guilty of an offence and shall be liable on conviction to a fine not exceeding $5,000, to imprisonment for a term not exceeding 12 months or both.

(3)
Any person required by a senior officer of customs or officer of customs to give information on any subject into which it is the officer's duty to inquire and which it is in the person's power to give, who refuses to give such information or furnishes as true information that which he knows or has reason to believe is false shall be guilty of an offence and shall be liable on conviction to a fine not exceeding $5,000, or imprisonment for a term not exceeding 12 months or both.

(4)
When any such information is proved to be untrue or incorrect, in whole or in part, it is no defence to allege that the information, or any part thereof, was furnished inadvertently, without criminal intent or fraudulent intent, or was misinterpreted or not fully interpreted by an interpreter provided by the informant.

(5)
Nothing in subsection (3) shall oblige a person to furnish any information which would have a tendency to expose him to a criminal charge or to a penalty or forfeiture.

Attempts or abetments.

117. Any person who attempts to commit any offence punishable under section 46, 52 or 116 or any regulations made under this Order or abets the commission of any such offence shall be liable to the punishment provided for that offence.

Conduct of prosecution.

118. Any prosecution in respect of an offence under section 46, 52 or 116 or any regulations made under this Order may be conducted by an officer authorised by the Controller of Customs.

Composition of offences.

119. (1) Any officer authorised by the Collector or any senior officer of customs may compound any offence which is prescribed to be a compoundable offence by accepting from the person reasonably suspected of having committed the offence a sum not exceeding $1,000.

(2) On payment of that sum, the person reasonably suspected of having committed an offence, if in custody, shall be discharged, any property seized shall be released and no further proceedings shall be taken against that person or property.

Offences by companies and by employees and agents.

120. (1) Where an offence under section 46, 52 or 116 or any regulations made under this Order has been committed by a company, any person who at the time of the commission of the offence was a director, secretary or other similar officer of the company, or was purporting to act in such capacity shall be deemed to be guilty of that offence unless he proves that the offence was committed without his consent or connivance and that he exercised all such diligence to prevent the commission of the offence as he ought to have exercised, having regard to the nature of his functions in that capacity and to all the circumstances.

(2) Where any person would be liable under section 46, 52 or 116 to any punishment, penalty or forfeiture for any act, omission, neglect or default, he shall be liable to the same punishment, penalty or forfeiture for every such act, omission, neglect or default of any employee or agent, or of the employee of an agent, provided that the act, omission, neglect or default was committed by the employee in the course of his employment or by the agent when acting on behalf of that person or by the employee of the agent when acting in the course of his employment in such circumstance that had the act, omission, neglect or default been committed by the agent his principal would have been liable under this section.

Action of officers no offence.

121. Nothing done by an officer of the Government in the course of his duties shall be deemed to be offence under this Order.

Regulations.

122. (1) The Minister, with the approval of His Majesty the Sultan and Yang Di-Pertuan, may make such regulations as may be necessary or expedient for the purpose of carrying out the provisions of this Order.

(2)

Without prejudice to the generality of subsection (1), the Minister may make regulations for or with respect to all or any of the following matters —

(a)

any matters required by this Order to be prescribed;

(b)

the procedure relating to applications for and the issue of certificates under this Order;

(c)

the terms and conditions to be imposed on any certificate issued under this Order; and

(d)

the furnishing of such information, including progress and sales reports and statements of accounts, as may be required for the purposes of this Order.

(3)

The Minister may in writing authorise any person or authority to prescribe such forms as are required to be or may be prescribed under this Order.

Repeal of Chapter 97, saving and transitional.

123. (1) The Investment Incentives Act is repealed.

(2) Anything done under the Investment Incentives Act (repealed by this Order) shall, upon the commencement of this Order, continue to be of full force and effect until other provisions has been made therefor under this Order.

Made this 28th. day of Safar, 1422 Hijriah corresponding to the 22nd. day of May, 2001 at Our Istana Nurul Iman, Bandar Seri Begawan, Brunei Darussalam.

BRUNEI INVESTMENT AGENCY (CHAPTER 137)

An Act to establish a body corporate to be called the Brunei Investment Agency the principal objects of which shall be the holding and management of the General Reserve Fund of the Government and all external assets of the Government, to provide the Government with money management services and to carry out such other objects as His Majesty the Sultan and Yang Di-Pertuan may specify.

Commencement: 1st July 1983

PART I PRELIMINARY

Citation.
1. This Act may be cited as the Brunei Investment Agency Act.
Interpretation.
2. In this Act, unless the context otherwise requires —
"Agency" means the Brunei Investment Agency establishedunder section 3 of this Act;
"bank" means a bank licensed under the Banking Act (Chapter 95); or the Islamic Banking Act (Chapter 168);

[S 43/92]

"board" means the board of directors of the Agency;
"director" means a director appointed under subsection (2) ofsection 5 of this Act and the chairman of the board and the deputy chairman;
"General Reserve Fund of the Government and all external assets of theGovernment" means the moneys as defined in Article 7(3) of theConstitution (Financial Procedure) Order (Const. III);

[S 20/85]

"managing director" means a director appointed undersubsection (1) of section 7 of this Act;
"Minister of Finance" in respect of the period prior to 1st January 1984 means the Menteri Besar and in respect of the period after 1st January 1984 where the context permits includes the Deputy Minister of Finance.

PART II ESTABLISHMENT AND ADMINISTRATION OF THE AGENCY

Establishment of the Agency.
3. (1) There shall be established an Agency to be called the "Brunei Investment Agency" which shall be a body corporate and shall have perpetual succession and may sue and be sued in its own name.

(2) The Agency shall have a common seal and such seal may, from time totime, be broken, changed, altered and made anew as to the Agency seems fit, and,until a seal is provided under this section, a stamp bearing the inscription"The Brunei Investment Agency" may be used as the common seal.

(3) All deeds, documents and other instruments requiring the seal of theAgency shall be sealed with the common seal of the Agency by the authority ofthe Agency in the presence of the managing director and of some other personduly authorised by the Agency to act in that behalf and shall be signed by themanaging director and by such duly authorised person, and such signing shall besufficient evidence that the common seal of the Agency has been duly andproperly affixed and that the said seal is the lawful common seal of theAgency.

(4) The Agency may by resolution or otherwise appoint an officer of theAgency or any other agent either generally or in a particular case to execute orsign on behalf of the Agency any agreement or other instrument not under seal inrelation to any matter coming within the powers of the Agency.

Principal objects.

4. The principal objects of the Agency shall be —

(a) to hold and manage in Brunei Darussalam and overseas the GeneralReserve Fund of the Government and all external assets of the Government;

(b) to provide the Government with money management servicesin respect of such sums as the Government may from time to time remit and inrespect of interest, dividend and any other payments or corporate actionsarising from the investment of such sums;

(ba) to take all steps and incur any expenditure that may be required in order to recover or protect assets and property that are or may be, or are or may be derived (directly or indirectly and in whole or in part) from, the property of the Government or the Agency and to hold, manage and deal with the same on such terms as the Agency (acting in its own name or by the use of subsidiaries or agents) in its absolute discretion shall see fit;

[S 22/99]

(c) to carry out such other objects as His Majesty the Sultan and YangDi-Pertuan may by Order published in the Government *Gazette* specify.

Board of directors.

5. (1) There shall be a board of directors of the Agency which shallbe responsible for the policy and general administration of the affairsand business of the Agency.

(2) The board shall consist of a Chairman and such number of otherdirectors as His Majesty may appoint.

(3) The board may with the approval of His Majesty invite any person as itthinks fit to attend a meeting of the board for the purpose of giving advice tothe board on any matter.

Appointment of directors.

6. (1) The directors so appointed —

(a) shall not act as delegates on the board from any commercial,financial, agricultural, industrial or other interests with which they may beconnected;

(b) shall hold office for a term not exceeding 3 years and shall beeligible for reappointment;

(c) may be paid by the Agency out of the funds of the Agency such remuneration and allowances as may be determined by His Majesty.

(2) The provisions of paragraph *(b)* of subsection (1) of thissection does not apply to a director who is appointed managing director undersection 7 of this Act.

Appointment of managing director.

7. (1) His Majesty shall appoint one of the directors appointedunder section 5 of this Act to be the managing director.

[S 7/87]

(2) The managing director shall be engaged on such terms andconditions of service as His Majesty may decide.

(3) The managing director shall be entrusted with the day-to-dayadministration of the Agency, and may, subject to this Act, make decisions andexercise all powers and do all acts which may be exercised or done by theAgency.

(4) The managing director shall be answerable to the board for his acts anddecisions.

For additional analytical, business and investment opportunities information,
please contact Global Investment & Business Center, USA
at (703) 370-8082. Fax: (703) 370-8083. E-mail: ibpusa3@gmail.com
Global Business and Investment Info Databank - www.ibpus.com

(5) In the event of the absence or inability to act of the managingdirector, His Majesty may appoint a director to discharge his duties during theperiod of such absence or inability.

Disqualification of directors.

8. His Majesty may terminate the appointment of any director appointedunder subsection (1) of section 5 of this Act if he —

(a) resigns his office;

(b) becomes of unsound mind or incapable of carrying out hisduties;

(c) becomes bankrupt or suspends payment to or compounds with hiscreditors;

(d) is convicted of an offence involving dishonesty or fraud ormoral turpitude;

(e) is guilty of serious misconduct in relation to his duties;

(f) is absent, without leave, from 3 consecutive meetings of theboard; or

(g) fails to comply with his obligations under section 11 of this Act.

Vacancies in the office of director.

9. If any director dies or resigns or otherwise vacates his officebefore the expiry of the term for which he has been appointed another person maybe appointed by His Majesty for the unexpired period of the term of office ofthe director in whose place he is appointed.

Meeting and decisions of the board.

10. (1) The Chairman of the board shall summon meetings as often asmay be required but not less frequently than once in 3 months.

[S 7/87]

(2) At every meeting of the board a quorum shall consist of 3directors, and decisions shall be adopted by a simple majority of the votes ofthe directors present and voting except that in the case of an equality of votesthe Chairman shall have a casting vote.

Director's interest in contract to be made known.

11. (1) A director who is directly or indirectly interested in acontract or investment made or disposed of, or proposed to be made or disposedof, by the Agency shall disclose the nature of his interest at the first meetingof the board at which he is present after the relevant facts have come to his knowledge.

(2) A disclosure under subsection (1) of this section shall berecorded in the minutes of the board and, after the disclosure, the director—

(a) shall not take part in any deliberation or decision of the boardwith respect to that contract; and

(b) shall be disregarded for the purpose of constituting aquorum of the board for any such deliberation or decision.

(3) No act or proceeding of the board shall be questioned by any person whois not a member of the board on the ground that a director has contravened theprovisions of this section.

Preservation of secrecy.

12. (1) Except for the purpose of the performance of his duties orthe exercise of his functions or when lawfully required to do so by any court orunder the provisions of any written law, no director, officer or employee of theAgency shall disclose to any person any information relating to the affairs of the Agency or any person which he has acquired in the performance ofhis duties or the exercise of his functions.

(2) Any person who contravenes the provisions of subsection (1) of thissection shall be guilty of an offence under this Act and shall be liable onconviction to imprisonment for 3 years and to a fine of $5,000.

Remuneration not to be related to profits.

13. No salary, fee, wage or other remuneration shall be computed byreference to the results of any money management services undertaken by or onbehalf of the Agency pursuant to this Act.

Public servants.

14. (1) The directors, including the managing director, and theofficers and employees of the Agency of every description shall be deemed to bepublic servants within the meaning of the Penal Code (Chapter 22).

(2) The officers and employees of the Agency shall be deemed to hold office in the Public Service for the purposes of the Pensions Act (Chapter 38) and shall be eligible for the allowances, pensions and gratuities provided thereunder.

PART III PROVISIONS RELATING TO STAFF, TRANSFER OF FUNCTIONS, EMPLOYEES AND ASSETSETC.

List of posts and appointment of employees.

15. (1) The Agency may from time to time approve a list of posts (excluding the directors) which it thinks necessary for the purposes of this Act and may add to or amend this list.

(2) Subject to the provisions of this section —

(a) appointments and promotions to all posts shall be made by theAgency; and

(b) the termination of appointment, dismissal and disciplinarycontrol of the employees of the Agency shall be vested in the Agency.

(3) In the discharge of its functions under subsection (2) of this sectionthe Agency shall, if directed by His Majesty, in any particular case orgenerally, consult with the Public Service Commission before exercising any ofits powers under subsection (2).

(4) Notwithstanding the provisions of this section, the Agency may appointpersons temporarily for a period not exceeding one year to posts in the list ofposts for the time being in force.

(5) The Agency may, with the approval of His Majesty, make rules, notinconsistent with the provisions of this Act or of any other written law, for the appointment, promotion, disciplinary control and terms andconditions of service of all persons employed by the Agency.

(6) Without prejudice to the generality of subsection (5) of thissection, the Agency shall prescribe the rates of remuneration payable to personsemployed by the Agency and no person so employed shall be paid otherwise than inaccordance with such rates.

Transfer of assets and liabilities to the Agency.

16. (1) Upon the coming into operation of this Act such movable property, assets, rights, interests and privileges as constitute any part of the General Reserve Fund, together with any debts, liabilities or obligations connected therewith or appertaining thereto shall be deemed to have been transferred to and vested in the Agency without the requirement of any further action.

(2) The Minister of Finance shall have power to do all acts or things thathe considers necessary or expedient to give effect to the provisions ofsubsection (1) of this section.

(3) If the question arises as to whether —

(a) any of the functions, duties and powers; or

(b) any movable property, assets, rights, interests, privileges,debts, liabilities and obligations,

have been transferred to or vested in the Agency under subsection (1) of thissection, a certificate executed by the Minister of Finance shall be conclusiveevidence of such transfer or vesting.

PART IV POWERS, DUTIES AND FUNCTIONS OF THE AGENCY

Powers, duties and functions of the Agency.

17. (1) The Agency may, for the purpose of carrying out theprovisions of this Act, exercise and discharge the following powers, duties and functions, that is to say, it may —

(a) open and operate securities and cash clearing accounts and placedeposits on such terms as it may decide;

(b) purchase, acquire by exchange or other means, hold, sell orotherwise dispose of various types of investment assets as shall be specificallyauthorised by this Act or by His Majesty on the recommendations of theBoard;

(c) borrow money, establish credits and give guarantees in anycurrency inside and outside Brunei Darussalam on such terms and conditions as itmay deem fit;

(d) open and operate accounts with central banks outside Brunei Darussalam;

(e) purchase, acquire or develop, inside or outsideBrunei Darussalam facilities for accounting for and reporting on the assets andliabilities of the General Reserve Fund and any other assets or liabilitiesvested in the Agency;

(f) enter into contracts with third parties inside or outside Brunei Darussalam for the purpose set forth in section 20 of this Act;

(g) underwrite loans and securities in which it may invest;

For additional analytical, business and investment opportunities information, please contact Global Investment & Business Center, USA at (703) 370-8082. Fax: (703) 370-8083. E-mail: ibpusa3@gmail.com Global Business and Investment Info Databank - www.ibpus.com

(h) undertake the issue and management of loans publiclyissued by the Government or by any public authority;

(i) pay the expenses of the Agency, including specifically anypayments contemplated by sections 6(1) *(c)* , 7(2), 15(6) and 20 *(b)* of this Act out of the assets transferred to and vested in the Agency pursuantto section 16(1) of this Act; and

(j) do generally all such things as may be commonly done by investmentmanagers and are not inconsistent with the exercise of its powers or thedischarge of its duties under this Act.

(2) After the coming into operation of this Act, there shall be vested inthe Agency such other functions, duties and powers as His Majesty may, from timeto time, by notification in the Government *Gazette* , specify.

Investment of funds.

18. Investments which the Agency may hold, as provided inparagraph *(b)* of subsection (1) of section 17 of this Act shall include—

(a) gold coin or bullion and other precious metals;

(b) real property and interests therein;

(c) notes, coin, bank balances and money at call in such country orcountries as may be approved by the board;

(d) Treasury bills of such government or governments as may beapproved by the board;

(e) securities of, or guaranteed by, such government orgovernments or international financial institutions as may beapproved by the board;

(f) such other classes of investments assets as may beauthorised by the board from time to time and set forth in a written investmentguideline to the Agency; and

(g) such other specific investments not otherwise authorisedhereunder as may be authorised by His Majesty on therecommendation of the board.

Agency as a financial agent of the Government and manager of its externalassets.

19. (1) The Agency shall act as a financial agent of theGovernment.

(2) Whenever the Agency receives and disburses Government moneys itshall keep account thereof.

(3) The Agency may act generally as representative for theGovernment on such terms and conditions as may be agreed between the Agency andthe Government, where the Agency can do so appropriately and consistently withthe provisions of this Act and with its duties and functions.

Representatives.

20. In the exercise of its powers and the performance of its functionsunder this Act the Agency may —

(a) establish offices and representatives at such places outside Brunei Darussalam as it thinks fit;

(b) arrange or contract with and authorise a person or persons,which may be individuals or corporate entities, to act as agent orrepresentative of the Agency outside Brunei Darussalam, including the performance of investment management, legal, auditing and measurement ofinvestment performance activities on behalf of the Agency, and in conjunctionwith the performance of such activities such agents or representatives may bepaid fees for services rendered and may be reinbursed by the Agency forout-of-pocket expenses.

PART V MISCELLANEOUS

Agency's financial year.

21. The financial year of the Agency shall begin on the 1st day of January and end on the 31st day of December of each year except that for the year 1983 the financial year shall begin on the date of the establishment of the Agency and shall end on the 31st day of December 1983.

Audit.

22. The accounts of the Agency shall be audited by the Auditor Generalor by such independent auditors as His Majesty may appoint.

Preparation and publication of annual account and annual report.

[S 24/98]

23. The Agency shall within 6 months from the close of its financialyear submit to His Majesty the Sultan and Yang Di-Pertuan of Brunei Darussalamin Council —
(a) a copy of the annual accounts; and
(b) a report by the Board on the working of the Agencythroughout the year.

Power to appoint attorney.
24. The Agency may, by instrument under its common seal, appoint aperson (whether in Brunei Darussalam or in a place outside Brunei Darussalam) to be its attorney, and the person so appointed may,subject to the instrument, do any act or execute any power or function which heis authorised by the instrument to do or execute.

Validity of act and transactions of Agency.
25. The validity of an act or transaction of the Agency shall not becalled in question in any court on the ground that any provision of this Act hasnot been complied with.

Guarantee by Government.
26. The Government shall be responsible for the payment of all moneysdue by the Agency but nothing in this section authorises a creditor or otherperson claiming against the Agency to sue the Government in respect of hisclaim.

Fiat of Attorney General.
27. No prosecution in respect of any offence under this Act shall beinstituted without the consent in writing of the Attorney General.

Jurisdiction.
28. Notwithstanding the provisions of any other written law, a Courtof a Magistrate has jurisdiction to try all offences under this Act and toimpose the full penalty prescribed therefor.

[S 7/87]

Power of Agency to make regulations.
29. The Agency may, with the approval of His Majesty, make regulationsfor the better carrying out of the objects and purposes of this Act.

Preliminary acts and expenses.
30. Notwithstanding the provisions of section 1 of this Act theMinister of Finance may at any time before the date of the coming into operationof Part II of this Act do all such acts and incur all such expenses as he mayconsider necessary in connection with the establishment of the Agency; and uponthat date all such acts and expenses shall be deemed to have been done andincurred by the board.

PART VI TRANSITIONAL

Transitional provisions.
31. Any legal proceeding or cause of action pending or existing immediately before the commencement of this Act by or against the Government in respect of any functions or assets which under and by virtue of this Act are transferred to, or vested in, the Agency, may be continued and enforced by or against the Agency as it might have been by or against the Government, as the case may be, had this Act not come into operation.

IMPORTANT EXPORT-IMPORT REGULATIONS

Examination is carried out after the declaration of goods has been accepted and duties have been collected.

Goods for examination must be produced by the importer or the importer's agent at prescribed places during the normal working hours. If an importer or the importer's agent request his/her goods to examined outsite the normal working hours, he/she has to pay overtime fees to Customs.

- Examination is carried out in the presence of the importer or the importer's agent. He/she will be responsible for opening, weighting, sorting and marking of goods and all other necessary operations as directed by the Customs Officer.
- Examination is carried out to the satisfaction of the Customs Officer. He/she may, as his/her duty requires, take samples of any goods or cause such goods to be detained.

LICENCE OR PERMIT

Licence or Permit is a verification or approval given/issued by the relevant Government Department/Agency responsible for the commodities before importation or exportation.

Application of licence/permit

Written application or completed form (subject to the requirement of the Department/Agency) must be submitted to the Government/Agency responsible for such prohibited and controlled commodities.

Additional requirement

There are some prohibited or controlled commodities that require A.P (Approval Permit) issued by the RCED other than the license/permit issued by the relevant Government Agency before being imported or exported.

Types of commodities and issuing Government Department/Agency

Types of Commodities	Government/Agency	Hotlines/email
Religious Publications/ Prints, Films, CD, LD VCD, DVD, Cassette, Recital of Al-Quran, Hadith, Religious books, Talisman commodities (such as textiles/clothing /etc.), bearing dubious Chop/photo	Royal Brunei Police Force	-+673-2459500 -info@police.gov.bn
	Islamic Dakwah Center	-+673-2382525 -info@pusat-dakwah.gov.bn
	Internal Security Department	-+673-2223225 -info@internal-security.gov.bn
Halal, Fresh, Cold And Frozen Meat	Halal Import Permit Issuing Board	-+673-2382525 -info@religious-affairs.gov.bn

	Health Services Department	-+673-2381640 -info@moh.gov.bn
	Agriculture Department	-+673-2380144 -info@agriculture.gov.bn
	Royal Customs and Excise department	-+673-2382333 -info@customs.gov.bn
Firearms, Explosives, Fire Crackers, Dangerous Weapons, Scrap Metal	Royal Brunei Police Force	-+673-2459500 -info@agriculture.gov.bn
Plants, Crops, Live Animals, Vegetables, Fruits, Eggs	Agriculture Department	-+673-2380144 -info@police.gov.bn
Fishes, Prawns, Shells, Water Organisms and Fishing equipments etc	Fisheries Department	-+673-2382068 -info@fisheries.gov.bn
Poison, chemicals and radioactive materials. Medicines, Herbal, Health Foods, Soft Drinks and Snacks. Department)	Ministry of Health (Refer to the Food Quality Control Section. Health Services (Refer to Medical Enforcement Section, Pharmaceutical Services Department	-+673-2381640 -info@moh.gov.bn
Radio Transmitter and Receiver and Communications Equipment such as Telephone, Fax Machines, Walkie- Talkie, etc.	Info-Communication Technology Industry (AiTi)	-+673-2333780 -aiti@brunet.bn

For additional analytical, business and investment opportunities information,
please contact Global Investment & Business Center, USA
at (703) 370-8082. Fax: (703) 370-8083. E-mail: ibpusa3@gmail.com
Global Business and Investment Info Databank - www.ibpus.com

Used Vehicles such as Cars, Motorcycles, Mini Buses, Pickups, Trucks, Trailers and non-motor vehicles such as Bicycles	Land Transport Department	-+673-2451979 -info@land-transport.gov.bn
	Royal Customs and Excise Department	-+673-2382333 -info@customs.gov.bn
Timber and products thereof	Forestry Department	-+673-2381013 -info@forestry.gov.bn
Badges, Banners, Souvenirs comprising of Government Flags and emblems, Royals Regalias, Government flags and crests	Adat Istiadat Department	-+673-2244545 -info@adat-istiadat.gov.bn
Historical Antiques made or found in Brunei	Museums Department	-+673-2244545 -info@museums.gov.bn
Mineral water and Building Construction Materials such as cements	Ministry of Industry and Primary Resources	-+673-2382822 -info@mipr.gov.bn
Rice, Sugar and Salt	Information Technology and State Store Department	-+673-2382822 -info@itss.gov.bn
Broadcasting Equipments such as Parabola, Decorder, etc.	Prime Minister's Office	-+673-2242780 -info@jpm.gov.bn

CUSTOM IMPORT DUTY (CUSTOM TAXES)

According to Section 9 Part B of Customs Import Duties Order 1973, passengers aged 17 and above arriving to this country are allowed to bring in their personal effect not exceeding the given concession as follows:-

Personally used goods (not new)

- Perfume - 60 milliliters
- Scented Water - 250 grams
- Cigarettes - 200 sticks or Tobacco - 250 grams
- Alcoholic beverages
  For non-muslim passengers over 17 years of age may be allowed to bring in not more than:-
  - 2 bottles of liquor (approximately 2 liters)
  - 12 cans of beer @ 330ml

- The importer may only import alcoholic liquor not less than 48 hours since the last importation.

- The alcoholic liquor shall be for importer's personal used and not to be given, transferred or sold to another person.

- The alcoholic liquor shall be stored and consumed at the place of residence of importer.

- The owner should declare liquor to Customs Officers in charge.

- Liquor form can be obtained from any Customs Control Posts or Customs Branches of Passenger Ships.

IMPORT AND EXPORT PROCEDURES OF GOODS UNDER CEPT SCHEME. DOCUMENT PROCEDURE

Type of declaration

- For import - Customs Import Declaration.
- For export - Customs Export Declaration.

Processing and approval
Traders are required to submit their application to the Customs at the point of importation or exportation.

Requirement for issuing CEPT form
- Manufactures must first apply to the Ministry of Foreign Affairs and Trade (MoFAT).
- Application must be complied with rules of origin of the CEPT Scheme.
- With the approved CEPT Form D, the manufacturers or exporters may apply for the Customs Export Declarations.

Customs Export Declarations

The CEPT Form D comprises of 4 copies. The original and triplicate are given to the importer for submission to the Customs authority at the importing country. The duplicate copy is retained by MoFAT and the quadruplicate is retained by the manufacturer or exporter.

Import Procedure

The importer shall produce the cargoes together with Customs Import Declaration, CEPT Form D, invoice, packing list, bill of landing/airway bill and other relevent supporting document to the Customs at the entry point for verification and examination.

- Dutiable goods imported to Brunei Darussalam are subject to Customs Import Duties Order 2007. ASEAN Common Effective Preferential Tariff (CEPT) could be given to importer based on qualification given by Ministry of Foreign Affairs and Trade (MoFAT). Most import duties are imposed based on Ad Valorem rate and only some taxes are based on specific rate. Ad Valorem is the percentage, for example, 20% of the price of good, while specific rate is calculated by the amount of weight or quantity such as $60 per kg or $220 per tonne. Determination of classification of imported goods whether dutiable or not are based on Customs Import Duties Order 2007. Since 1973 Brunei did not impose duties on exported goods. It is intended to promote local enterpreneurship.

CUSTOMS IMPORT DUTY GUIDE

Every person arriving in Negara Brunei Darussalam shall declare all dutiable goods in his possession, either on his person OR in any baggages OR in any vehicles to the proper officer of customs for examination.
If failed to do so, such goods shall be deemed to be uncustomed goods and imprisonment OR fine can be imposed.

Dutiable Goods

All goods subject to payment of customs duty and on such duty has not yet been paid.
According to paragraph 3(3) of customs import duties order 2007 where the total amount of import duty:

- Is less than $1 no import duty shall be charged.
- Exceed $1 and includes a fraction of $ 1, the fraction shall be treated as a complete dollar.

Importer of Dutiable Goods shall:
- Declare his/her goods.
- Produce documents such as invoice, bill and etc.
- Produce customs dutiable import declaration form no 5/C-16. (If necessary)

List of some Dutiable Goods and rate of Customs Import Duty

DUTIABLE GOODS	RATE OF CUSTOMS IMPORT DUTY
Coffee (not roasted)	11 cents/ 1 kg
Coffee (roasted)	22 cents/ 1 kg
Tea	22 cents/ 1 kg
Instant coffee/tea (Extract, essences and concentrates)/ coffee mate	5%
Grease	11 cents/ 1 kg
Lubricants	44 cents/ 1 kg
Carpet and other textile floor covering	5%
Mat and matting	10%
Wood and articles of wood	20%
Footware, slippers and the like	5%
Headgear and parts thereof	10%
Cosmetic, perfumes, toilet waters, soap, hair shampoo and other washing preparations	5%
Other preparations for use on the hair	30%
Electrical goods	5% OR 20%
Auto parts	20%
Articles of apparel and clothing accessories, of leather OR of composition leather	10%
Jewellery including imitation jewellery	5%
Clocks and watches and parts thereof	5%
Musical instruments	10%

EXPORT-IMPORT PROCEDURES

Goods To Be Imported & Export

All goods may be imported or exported except for restricted, prohibited and controlled goods under Section 31 of the Customs order, 2006.

Customs Declaration

Every imported & exported goods should be declared to the RCED by a declaration form except for the following goods:
- Passenger hand baggage's or personal effect on arrival.
- Goods arriving by post except for dutiable goods.

Declaration should give full and true account of the number of packages, cases description of goods, value, weight, measure or quantity and country of origin of the goods.

Customs Declaration Form must be submitted in triplicate and attached together with the following supporting documents :
- Invoice or purchase bill.
- Freight and Insurance Payment Slips.
- Delivery Order or Air Waybill.
- Packing List.

Other than the above documents, importer should also provide other documents related to the

imported goods required by Customs coinciding with the declaration of goods such as:
- Certificate of Origin.
- Certificate of Analysis.
- A.P (Approval Permit) of the RCED.
- Import license issued by the relevant Government Department/Agencies.
- Verification Certificate of a recognized foreign agency.
- Other relevant documents.
- Personal qualified to declare.

The owners:

- The owners or importers or exporters are qualified to declare the imported/exported goods to RCED.

Representatives:

- The owner may authorize the agents or forwarders as their representatives in declaration.

Conditions of qualification of importer and exporter:

- Trader or Agent ID registrations;
- Every company or agents/forwarder must be registered with the RCED.
- Individual registration is not compulsory however customers (traders) are advised to make use of the services of Customs agents (forwarders).

Registration of Company:

- Application form available at the Customer Services Unit of RCED Headquaters, Jalan Menteri Besar.
- The application will be entered into the computer system of RCED, i.e Computer Control and Information System (CCIS).

Documents for Registration:

- A copy of the company's registration certificate.

- A copy of smart identity card.

CHAPTER 196 ELECTRONIC TRANSACTIONS ACT

AN ACT TO MAKE PROVISION FOR THE SECURITY AND USE OF ELECTRONIC TRANSACTIONS AND FOR CONNECTED PURPOSES

Commencement (except Part X): 1st May 2001 [S 40/01]

PART I PRELIMINARY

CITATION.

1. (1) This Act may be cited as the Electronic Transactions Act.

(2) The Minister may, with the approval of His Majesty the Sultan and Yang Di-Pertuan, by notification in the *Gazette*, appoint different dates for the commencement of different provisions of this Act and for different purposes of the same provision.

INTERPRETATION.

2. In this Act, unless the context otherwise requires —

"asymmetric cryptosystem" means a system capable of generating a secure key pair, consisting of a private key for creating a digital signature, and a public key to verify the digital signature;

"certification authority" means a person who or an organisation that issues a certificate;

"certification practice statement" means a statement issued by a certification authority to specify the practices that the certification authority employs in issuing certificates;

"Controller" means the Controller of Certification Authorities appointed under section 41(1) and includes a Deputy or an Assistant Controller of Certification Authorities appointed under section 41(2);

"correspond", in relation to private or public keys, means to belong to the same key pair;

"data message" means information generated, sent, received or stored by electronic, optical or similar means, including, but not limited to, electronic data interchange (EDI), electronic mail, telegram, telex or telecopy;

"digital signature" means an electronic signature consisting of a transformation of an electronic record using an asymmetric cryptosystem and a hash function such that a person having the initial untransformed electronic record and the signer's public key can accurately determine —

(a)
    whether the transformation was created using the private key that corresponds to the signer's public key; and
(b)
    whether the initial electronic record has been altered since the transformation was made;

"electronic record" means a record generated, communicated, received or stored by electronic, magnetic, optical or other means in an information system or for transmission from one information system to another;

"electronic signature" means any letters, characters, numbers or other symbols in digital form attached to or logically associated with an electronic record, and executed or adopted with the intention of authenticating or approving the electronic record;

"hash function" means an algorithm mapping or translating one sequence of bits into another, generally smaller, set (the hash result) such that —

(a)
    a record yields the same hash result every time the algorithm is executed using the same record as input;
(b)

it is computationally infeasible that a record can be derived or reconstituted from the hash result produced by the algorithm; and

(c)

it is computationally infeasible that 2 records can be found that produce the same hash result using the algorithm;

"information" includes data, text, images, sound, codes, computer programs, software and databases;

"information system" means a system for generating, sending, receiving, storing or otherwise processing data messages;

"key pair", in an asymmetric cryptosystem, means a private key and its mathematically related public key, having the property that the public key can verify a digital signature that the private key creates;

"licensed certification authority" means a certification authority licensed by the Controller pursuant to regulations made under section 42;

"Minister" means the Minister of Finance;

"operational period of a certificate" begins on the date and time the certificate is issued by a certification authority (or on any later date and time stated in the certificate), and ends on the date and time it expires as stated in the certificate or when it is earlier revoked or suspended;

"private key" means the key of a key pair used to create a digital signature;

"public key" means the key of a key pair used to verify a digital signature;

"record" means information that is inscribed, stored or otherwise fixed on a tangible medium or that is stored in an electronic or other medium and is retrievable in perceivable form;

"repository" means a system for storing and retrieving certificates or other information relevant to certificates;

"revoke a certificate" means to permanently end the operational period of a certificate from a specified time;

"rule of law" includes a written law;

"security procedure" means a procedure for the purpose of —

(a)

verifying that an electronic record is that of a specific person; or

B.L.R.O. 4/2008

(b)

detecting error or alteration in the communication, content or storage of an electronic record since a specific point in time,

which may require the use of algorithms or codes, identifying words or numbers, encryption, answerback or acknowledgement procedures, or similar security devices;

"signed" or "signature" includes any symbol executed or adopted, or any methodology or procedure employed or adopted, by a person with the intention of authenticating a record, including electronic or digital methods;

"subscriber" means a person who is the subject named or identified in a certificate issued to him and who holds a private key that corresponds to a public key listed in that certificate;

"suspend a certificate" means to temporarily suspend the operational period of a certificate from a specified time;

"transaction" includes a transaction of a non-commercial nature;

"trustworthy system" means computer hardware, software and procedures that —

(a) are reasonably secure from intrusion and misuse;

(b)
   provide a reasonable level of availability, reliability and correct operation;
(c)
   are reasonably suited to performing their intended functions; and

(d) adhere to generally accepted security procedures;

"valid certificate" means a certificate that a certification authority has issued and which the subscriber listed in it has accepted;

"verify a digital signature", in relation to a given digital signature, record and public key, means to determine accurately —

(a)
   that the digital signature was created using the private key corresponding to the public key listed in the certificate; and
(b)
   the record has not been altered since its digital signature was created.

PURPOSES AND CONSTRUCTION.

3. (1) This Act shall be construed consistently with what is commercially reasonable under the circumstances and to give effect to the following purposes —

(a)
   to facilitate electronic communications by means of reliable electronic records;
(b)
   to facilitate electronic commerce, eliminate barriers to electronic commerce resulting from uncertainties over writing and signature requirements, and to promote the development of the legal and business infrastructure necessary to implement secure electronic commerce;
(c)
   to facilitate electronic filing of documents with government agencies and statutory corporations, and to promote efficient delivery of government services by means of reliable electronic records;
(d)

to minimise the incidence of forged electronic records, intentional and unintentional alteration of records, and fraud in electronic commerce and other electronic transactions;

(e)

to help to establish uniformity of rules, regulations and standards regarding the authentication and integrity of electronic records; and

(f)

to promote public confidence in the integrity and reliability of electronic records and electronic commerce, and to foster the development of electronic commerce through the use of electronic signatures to lend authenticity and integrity to correspondence in any electronic medium.

(2)

In the interpretation of this Act, regard is to be had to its international origin and the need to promote uniformity in its application and the observance of good faith.

(3)

Questions concerning matters governed by this Act which are not expressly settled in it are to be settled in conformity with the general principles on which this Act is based.

APPLICATION.

4. (1) Parts II or IV shall not apply to any rule of law requiring writing or signatures in any of the following matters —

(a)

the creation of any legal instrument or document under any written law relating to Islamic law;

(b)

the creation or execution of a will under any written law relating wills;

(c) negotiable instruments;

(d)

the creation, performance or enforcement of an indenture, declaration of trust or power of attorney with the exception of constructive and resulting trusts;

(e)

any contract for the sale or other disposition of immovable property, or any interest in such property;

(f)

the conveyance of immovable property or the transfer of any interest in such property;

(g) documents of title relating to immovable property.

(2) The Minister may, with the approval of His Majesty the Sultan and Yang Di-Pertuan, by order in the *Gazette* modify the provisions of subsection (1) by adding, deleting or amending any class of transactions or matters mentioned therein.

VARIATION BY AGREEMENT.

5. As between parties involved in generating, sending, receiving, storing or otherwise processing electronic records, any provision of Parts II or IV may be varied by agreement.

PART II ELECTRONIC RECORDS AND SIGNATURES GENERALLY

LEGAL RECOGNITION OF ELECTRONIC RECORDS.

6. For the avoidance of doubt, it is hereby declared that information shall not be denied legal effect, validity or enforceability solely on the ground that it is in the form of an electronic record.

REQUIREMENT FOR WRITING.

7. Where any rule of law requires information to be written in writing to be presented in writing or provides for certain consequences if it is not, an electronic record satisfies that rule of law if the information contained therein is accessible so as to be usable for subsequent reference.

ELECTRONIC SIGNATURES.

8. (1) Where any rule of law requires a signature, or provides for certain consequences if a document is not signed, an electronic signature satisfies that rule of law.

(2) An electronic signature may be proved in any manner, including by showing that a procedure existed by which it is necessary for a party, in order to proceed further with a transaction, to have executed a symbol or security procedure for the purpose of verifying that an electronic record is that of such party.

RETENTION OF ELECTRONIC RECORDS.

9. (1) Where any rule of law requires that certain documents, records or information be retained, that requirement is satisfied by retaining them in the form of electronic records if the following conditions are satisfied —

(a)
  the information contained therein remains accessible so as to be usable for subsequent reference;
(b)
  the electronic record is retained in the format in which it was originally generated, sent or received, or in a format which can be demonstrated to represent accurately the information originally generated, sent or received;

B.L.R.O. 4/2008

(c)
  such information, if any, as enables the identification of the origin and destination of an electronic record and the date and time when it was sent or received, is retained; and
(d)
  the consent of the department or ministry of the Government, organ of State, or the statutory corporation which has supervision over the requirement for the retention of such records has been obtained.
(2)
  An obligation to retain documents, records or information in accordance with subsection (1)*(c)* shall not extend to any information necessarily and automatically generated solely for the purpose of enabling a record to be sent or received.
(3) A person may satisfy the requirement referred to in subsection
(1)
  by using the services of any other person, if the conditions in subsections (1)*(a)* to *(d)* are complied with.
(4)
  Nothing in this section shall —
(a)
  apply to any rule of law which expressly provides for the retention of documents, records or information in the form of electronic records;

(b)

preclude any department or ministry of the Government, organ of State or a statutory corporation from specifying additional requirements for the retention of electronic records that are subject to the jurisdiction of such department, ministry, organ of State or statutory corporation.

PART III LIABILITY OF NETWORK SERVICE PROVIDERS

LIABILITY OF NETWORK SERVICE PROVIDERS.

10. (1) A network service provider shall not be subject to any civil or criminal liability under any rule of law in respect of third-party material in the form of electronic records to which he merely provides access if such liability is founded on —

(a) the making, publication, dissemination or distribution of such materials or any statement made in such material; or
(b) the infringement of any rights subsisting in or in relation to such material.

(2) Nothing in this section shall affect —

(a) any obligation founded on contract;
(b) the obligation of a network service provider as such under a licensing or other regulatory regime established under any written law; or
(c) any obligation imposed under any written law or by a court to remove, block or deny access to any material.

(3)
For the purposes of this section —

"providing access", in relation to third-party material, means the provision of the necessary technical means by which third-party material may be accessed and includes the automatic and temporary storage of the third-party material for the purpose of providing access;

"third-party", in relation to a network service provider, means a person over whom the provider has no effective control.

PART IV ELECTRONIC CONTRACTS

FORMATION AND VALIDITY.

11. (1) For the avoidance of doubt, it is hereby declared that in the context of the formation of contracts, unless otherwise agreed by the parties, an offer and the acceptance of an offer may be expressed by means of electronic records.

(2) Where an electronic record is used in the formation of a contract, that contract shall not be denied validity or enforceability on the sole ground that an electronic record was used for that purpose.

EFFECTIVENESS BETWEEN PARTIES.

12. As between the originator and the addressee of an electronic record, a declaration of intent or other statement shall not be denied legal effect, validity or enforceability solely on the ground that it is in the form of an electronic record.

ATTRIBUTION.

13. (1) An electronic record is that of the originator if it was sent by the originator himself.

(2) As between the originator and the addressee, an electronic record is deemed to be that of the originator if it was sent —

(a) by a person who had the authority to act on behalf of the originator in respect of that electronic record; or

(b) by an information system programmed by or on behalf of the originator to operate automatically.

(3)

As between the originator and the addressee, an addressee is entitled to regard an electronic record as being that of the originator and to act on that assumption if —

(a) in order to ascertain whether the electronic record was that of the originator, the addressee properly applied a procedure previously agreed to by the originator for that purpose; or

(b) the data message as received by the addressee resulted from the actions of a person whose relationship with the originator or with any agent of the originator enabled that person to gain access to a method used by the originator to identify electronic records as its own.

(4) Subsection (3) shall not apply —

(a) from the time when the addressee has both received notice from the originator that the electronic record is not that of the originator and had reasonable time to act accordingly;

(b) in a case within subsection (3)*(b)*, at any time when the addressee knew or ought to have known, had it exercised reasonable care or used any agreed procedure, that the electronic record was not that of the originator; or

(c) if in all the circumstances of the case, it is unconscionable for the addressee to regard the electronic record as that of the originator or to act on that assumption.

(5)

Where an electronic record is that of the originator or is deemed to be that of the originator, or the addressee is entitled to act on that assumption, then, as between the originator and the addressee, the addressee is entitled to regard the electronic record received as being what the originator intended to send, and to act on that assumption.

(6)

The addressee is not so entitled when the addressee knew or should have known, had the addressee exercised reasonable care or used any agreed procedure, that the transmission resulted in any error in the electronic record as received.

(7)

The addressee is entitled to regard each electronic record received as a separate electronic record and to act on that assumption, except to the extent that the addressee duplicates another electronic record and the addressee knew or should have known, had the addressee exercised reasonable care or used any agreed procedure, that the electronic record was a duplicate.

(8)

Nothing in this section shall affect the law of agency or the law on the formation of contracts.

ACKNOWLEDGEMENT OF RECEIPT.

14. (1) Subsections (2), (3) and (4) shall apply where, on or before sending an electronic record, or by means of that electronic record, the originator has requested or has agreed with the addressee that receipt of the electronic record be acknowledged.

(2)

Where the originator has not agreed with the addressee that the acknowledgement be given in a particular form or by a particular method, an acknowledgement may be given by —

(a)

any communication by the addressee, automated or otherwise; or

(b)

any conduct of the addressee, sufficient to indicate to the originator that the electronic record has been received.

(3)

Where the originator has stated that the electronic record is conditional on receipt of the acknowledgement, the electronic record shall be treated as though it had never been sent, until the acknowledgement is received.

(4)

Where the originator has not stated that the electronic record is conditional on receipt of the acknowledgement, and the acknowledgement has not been received by the originator within the time, specified or agreed or, if no time has been specified or agreed within a reasonable time, the originator —

(a)

may give notice to the addressee stating that no acknowledgement has been received and specifying a reasonable time by which the acknowledgement must be received; and

(b)

if the acknowledgement is not received within the time specified in paragraph (a), may, upon notice to the addressee, treat the electronic record as though it has never been sent, or exercise any other rights it may have.

(5)

Where the originator receives the addressee's acknowledgement of receipt, it is presumed, unless evidence to the contrary is adduced, that the related electronic record was received by the addressee, but that presumption does not imply that the content of the electronic record corresponds to the content of the record received.

(6)

Where the received acknowledgement states that the related electronic record meets technical requirements, either agreed upon or set forth in applicable standards, it is presumed, unless evidence to the contrary is adduced, that those requirements have been met.

(7)

Except in so far as it relates to the sending or receipt of the electronic record, this Part is not intended to deal with the legal consequences that may flow either from that electronic record or from the acknowledgement of its receipt.

TIME AND PLACE OF DISPATCH AND RECEIPT.

15. (1) Unless otherwise agreed to between the originator and the addressee, the dispatch of an electronic record occurs when it enters an information system outside the control of the originator or the person who sent the electronic record on behalf of the originator.

(2)

Unless otherwise agreed between the originator and the addressee, the time of receipt of an electronic record is determined as follows —

(a)

if the addressee has designated an information system for the purpose of receiving electronic records, receipt occurs —

(i)

at the time when the electronic record enters the designated information system; or

(ii)

if the electronic record is sent to an information system of the addressee that is not the designated information system, at the time when the electronic record is retrieved by the addressee;

(b)

if the addressee has not designated such an information system, receipt occurs when the electronic record enters an information system of the addressee.

(3)

Subsection (2) shall apply notwithstanding that the place where the information system is located may be different from the place where the electronic record is deemed to be received under subsection (4).

(4)

Unless otherwise agreed between the originator and the addressee, an electronic record is deemed to be dispatched at the place where the originator has its place of business, and is deemed to be received at the place where the addressee has its place of business.

(5)

For the purposes of this section —

(a)

if the originator or the addressee has more than one place of business, the place of business is that which has the closest relationship to the underlying transaction or, where there is no underlying transaction, the principal place of business;

(b)

if the originator or the addressee does not have a place of business, reference is to be made to the usual place of residence; and

(c)

"usual place of residence" in relation to a body corporate, means the place where it is incorporated or otherwise legally constituted.

(6)

This section shall not apply to such circumstances as the Minister may by regulations prescribe.

PART V SECURE ELECTRONIC RECORDS AND SIGNATURES

SECURE ELECTRONIC RECORD.

16. (1) If a prescribed security procedure or a commercially reasonable security procedure agreed to by the parties involved has been properly applied to an electronic record to verify that the electronic record has not been altered since a specified point in time, such record shall be treated as a secure electronic record from such specified point in time to the time of verification.

(2) For the purposes of this section and of section 17, whether a security procedure is commercially reasonable shall be determined having regard to the purposes of the procedure and the commercial circumstances at the time the procedure was used, including —

(a) the nature of the transaction;
(b) the sophistication of the parties;
(c) the volume of similar transactions engaged in by either or all parties;
(d) the availability of alternatives offered to but rejected by any party;
(e) the cost of alternative procedures; and
(f) the procedures in general use for similar types of transactions.

SECURE ELECTRONIC SIGNATURE.

17. If, through the application of a prescribed security procedure or a commercially reasonable security procedure agreed to by the parties involved, it can be verified that all electronic signature was, at the time it was made —

(a) unique to the person using it;
(b) capable of identifying such person;
(c) created in a manner or using a means under the sole control of the person using it; and
(d) linked to the electronic record to which it relates in a manner such that if the record was changed the electronic signature would be invalidated, such signature shall be treated as a secure electronic signature.

PRESUMPTIONS RELATING TO SECURE ELECTRONIC RECORDS AND SIGNATURES.

18. (1) In any proceedings involving a secure electronic record, it shall be presumed, unless evidence to the contrary is adduced, that the secure electronic record has not been altered since the specific point in time to which the secure status relates.

(2)
    In any proceedings involving a secure electronic signature, it shall be presumed, unless evidence to the contrary is adduced, that —
(a) the secure electronic signature is the signature of the person with whom it correlates; and
(b) the secure electronic signature was affixed by that person with the intention of signing or approving the electronic record.

(3) In the absence of a secure electronic record or a secure electronic signature, nothing in this Part shall create any presumption relating to the authenticity and integrity of the electronic record or an electronic signature.

(4) For the purposes of this section —

"secure electronic record" means an electronic record treated as a secure electronic record by virtue of sections 16 or 19;

"secure electronic signature" means an electronic signature treated as a secure electronic signature by virtue of sections 17 or

PART VI EFFECT OF DIGITAL SIGNATURES

SECURE ELECTRONIC RECORD WITH DIGITAL SIGNATURE.

19. The portion of an electronic record that is signed with a digital signature shall be treated as a secure electronic record if the digital signature is a secure electronic signature by virtue of section 20.

SECURE DIGITAL SIGNATURE.

20. When any portion of an electronic record is signed with a digital signature, the digital signature shall be treated as a secure electronic signature with respect to such portion of the record if —

(a)
    the digital signature was created during the operational period of a valid certificate and is verified by reference to the public key listed in such certificate; and

(b)

For additional analytical, business and investment opportunities information,
please contact Global Investment & Business Center, USA
at (703) 370-8082. Fax: (703) 370-8083. E-mail: ibpusa3@gmail.com
Global Business and Investment Info Databank - www.ibpus.com

the certificate is considered trustworthy, in that it is an accurate binding of a public key to a person's identity because —

(i)

the certificate was issued by a licensed certification authority operating in compliance with the regulations made under section 42;

(ii)

the certificate was issued by a certification authority outside Brunei Darussalam recognised for this purpose by the Controller pursuant to requirements made under section 43;

(iii) the certificate was issued by a department or ministry of the Government, an organ of State or a statutory body or corporation approved by the Minister to act as a certification authority on such conditions as he may by regulations impose or specify; or

(iv) the parties have expressly agreed between themselves (sender and recipient) to use digital signatures as a security procedure, and the digital signature was properly verified by reference to the sender's public key.

PRESUMPTIONS REGARDING CERTIFICATES.

21. It shall be presumed, unless evidence to the contrary is adduced, that the information listed in a certificate issued by a licensed certification authority is correct, except for information identified as subscriber information which has not been verified, if the certificate was accepted by the subscriber.

UNRELIABLE DIGITAL SIGNATURES.

22. Unless otherwise provided by any rule of law or by contract, a person relying on a digitally signed electronic record assumes the risk that the digital signature is invalid as a signature or authentication of the signed electronic record, if reliance on the digital signature is not reasonable under the circumstances having regard to the following factors —

(a) facts which the person relying on the digitally signed electronic record knows or has notice of, including all facts listed in the certificate or incorporated in it by reference;
(b) the value or importance of the digitally signed record, if known;
(c) the course of dealing between the person relying on the digitally signed electronic record and the subscriber and any available indicia of reliability or unreliability apart from the digital signature; and
(d)

usage of trade, particularly trade conducted by trustworthy systems or other electronic means.

PART VII GENERAL DUTIES RELATING TO DIGITAL SIGNATURES

RELIANCE ON CERTIFICATES FORSEEABLE.

23. It is foreseeable that persons relying on a digital signature will also rely on a valid certificate containing the public key by which the digital signature can be verified.

PREREQUISITES TO PUBLICATION OF CERTIFICATE.

24. No person shall publish a certificate or otherwise make it available to a person known by that first-mentioned person to be in a position to rely on the certificate or on a digital signature that is verifiable with reference to a public key listed in the certificate, if that first-mentioned person knows that —

For additional analytical, business and investment opportunities information,
please contact Global Investment & Business Center, USA
at (703) 370-8082. Fax: (703) 370-8083. E-mail: ibpusa3@gmail.com
Global Business and Investment Info Databank - www.ibpus.com

(a)
  the certification authority listed in the certificate has not issued it;

(b) the subscriber listed in the certificate has not accepted it; or

(c)
  the certificate has been revoked or suspended, unless such publication is for the purpose of verifying a digital signature created prior to such suspension or revocation.

PUBLICATION FOR FRAUDULENT PURPOSE.

25. Any person who knowingly creates, publishes or otherwise makes available a certificate for any fraudulent or unlawful purpose shall be guilty of an offence and be liable on conviction to a fine not exceeding $20,000, imprisonment for a term not exceeding 2 years or both.

FALSE OR UNAUTHORISED REQUEST.

26. Any person who knowingly misrepresents to a certification authority his identity or authorisation for the purpose of requesting for a certificate or for suspension or revocation of a certificate shall be guilty of an offence and be liable on conviction to a fine not exceeding $10,000, imprisonment for a term not exceeding 6 months or both.

PART VIII DUTIES OF CERTIFICATION AUTHORITIES

TRUSTWORTHY SYSTEM.

27. A certification authority must utilise trustworthy systems in performing its services.

DISCLOSURE.

28. (1) A certification authority shall disclose —

(a) its certificate that contains the public key corresponding to the private key used by that certification authority to digitally sign another certificate (referred to in this section as a certification authority certificate);

(b) any relevant certification practice statement;

(c)
  notice of the revocation or suspension of its certification authority certificate; and

(d) any other fact that materially and adversely affects either the reliability of a certificate that the authority has issued or the authority's ability to perform its services.

(2) In the event of an occurrence that materially and adversely affects a certification authority's trustworthy system or its certification authority certificate, the certification authority shall —

(a) use reasonable efforts to notify any person who is known to be or foreseeably will be affected by that occurrence; or

(b) act in accordance with procedures governing such an occurrence specified in its certification practice statement.

ISSUING OF CERTIFICATE.

29. (1) A certification authority may issue a certificate to a prospective subscriber only after the certification authority —

(a) has received a request for issuance from the prospective subscriber; and

(b) has —

(i) if it has a certification practice statement, complied with all of the practices and procedures set forth in such certification practice statement including procedures regarding identification of the perspective subscriber; or
B.L.R.O. 4/2008
(ii) in the absence of a certification practice statement, complied with the conditions in subsection (2).

(2) In the absence of a certification practice statement, the certification authority shall confirm by itself or through an authorised agent that —

(a) the prospective subscriber is the person to be listed in the certificate to be issued;
(b) if the prospective subscriber is acting through one or more agents, the subscriber authorised the agent to have custody of the subscriber's private key and to request issuance of a certificate listing the corresponding public key;
(c) the information in the certificate to be issued is accurate;
(d) the prospective subscriber rightfully holds the private key corresponding to the public key to be listed in the certificate;
(e) the prospective subscriber holds a private key capable of creating a digital signature; and
(f) the public key to be listed in the certificate can be used to verify a digital signature affixed by the private key held by the prospective subscriber.

REPRESENTATIONS UPON ISSUANCE OF CERTIFICATE.

30. (1) By issuing a certificate, a certification authority represents, to any person who reasonably relies on the certificate or a digital signature verifiable by the public key listed in the certificate, that the certification authority has issued the certificate in accordance with any applicable certification practice statement incorporated by reference in the certificate, or of which the relying person has notice.

(2)
In the absence of such certification practice statement, the certification authority represents that it has confirmed that —
(a) the certification authority has complied with all applicable requirements of this Act in issuing the certificate, and if the certification authority has published the certificate or otherwise made it available to such relying person, that the subscriber listed in the certificate has accepted it;
(b) the subscriber identified in the certificate holds the private key corresponding to the public key listed in the certificate;
(c) the subscriber's public key and private key constitute a functioning key pair;
(d) all information in the certificate is accurate, unless the certification authority has stated in the certificate or incorporated by reference in the certificate a statement that the accuracy of specified information is not confirmed; and
(e) that the certification authority has no knowledge of any material fact which if it had been included in the certificate would adversely affect the reliability of the representations in paragraphs *(a)* to *(d)*.

(3) Where there is an applicable certification practice statement which has been incorporated by reference in the certificate, or of which the relying person has notice, subsection (2) shall apply to the extent that the representations are not inconsistent with the certification practice statement.

SUSPENSION OF CERTIFICATE.

31. Unless the certification authority and the subscriber agree otherwise, the certification authority that issued a certificate shall suspend the certificate as soon as possible after receiving a request by a person whom the certification authority believes to be —

(a) the subscriber named in the certificate;

(b) a person duly authorised to act for that subscriber; or

(c) a person acting on behalf of that subscriber, who is unavailable.

REVOCATION OF CERTIFICATE.

32. A certification authority shall revoke a certificate that is issued after —

(a) receiving a request for revocation by the subscriber named in the certificate; and, confirming that the person requesting revocation is the subscriber or is an agent of the subscriber with authority to request the revocation;

(b) receiving a certified copy of the subscriber's death certificate, or upon confirming by other evidence that the subscriber is dead; or

(c) upon presentation of documents effecting a dissolution of the subscriber, or upon confirming by other evidence that the subscriber has been dissolved or has ceased to exist.

REVOCATION WITHOUT SUBSCRIBER'S CONSENT.

33. (1) A certification authority shall revoke a certificate, regardless of whether the subscriber listed in the certificate consents, if the certification authority confirms that —

(a) a material fact represented in the certificate is false;

(b) a requirement for issuance of the certificate was not satisfied;

(c) the certification authority's private key or trustworthy system was compromised in a manner materially affecting the certificate's reliability;

(d) an individual subscriber is dead; or

(e) a subscriber has been dissolved, wound-up or otherwise ceased to exist.

(2) Upon effecting such a revocation, other than under subsections (1)*(a)* or *(e)*, the certification authority shall immediately notify the subscriber named in the revoked certificate.

NOTICE OF SUSPENSION.

34. (1) Immediately upon suspension of a certificate by a certification authority, the certification authority shall publish a signed notice of the suspension in the repository specified in the certificate for publication of notice of suspension.

(2) Where one or more repositories are specified, the certification authority shall publish signed notices of the suspension in all such repositories.

NOTICE OF REVOCATION.

35. (1) Immediately upon revocation of a certificate by a certification authority, the certification authority shall publish a signed notice of the revocation in the repository specified in the certificate for publication of notice of revocation.

For additional analytical, business and investment opportunities information, please contact Global Investment & Business Center, USA at (703) 370-8082. Fax: (703) 370-8083. E-mail: ibpusa3@gmail.com Global Business and Investment Info Databank - www.ibpus.com

(2) Where one or more repositories are specified, the certification authority shall publish signed notices of the revocation in all such repositories.

PART IX DUTIES OF SUBSCRIBERS

GENERATING KEY PAIR.

36. (1) If the subscriber generates the key pair whose public key is to be listed in a certificate issued by a certification authority and accepted by the subscriber, the subscriber shall generate that key pair using a trustworthy system.

(2) This section shall not apply to a subscriber who generates the key pair using a system approved by the certification authority.

OBTAINING CERTIFICATE.

37. All material representations made by the subscriber to a certification authority for purposes of obtaining a certificate, including all information known to the subscriber and represented in the certificate, shall be accurate and complete to the best of the subscriber's knowledge and belief, regardless of whether such representation are confirmed by the certification authority.

ACCEPTANCE OF CERTIFICATE.

38. (1) A subscriber shall be deemed to have accepted a certificate if he —

(a) publishes or authorises the publication of a certificate —

(i) to one or more persons; or
(ii) in a repository; or

(b) otherwise demonstrates approval of a certificate while knowing or having notice of its contents.

(2) By accepting a certificate issued by himself or a certification authority, the subscriber listed in the certificate certifies to all who reasonably rely on the information contained in the certificate that —

(a) the subscriber rightfully holds the private key corresponding to the public key listed in the certificate;
(b) all representations made by the subscriber to the certification authority and material to the information listed in the certificate are true; and
(c) all information in the certificate that is within the knowledge of the subscriber is true.

CONTROL OF PRIVATE KEY.

39. (1) By accepting a certificate issued by a certification authority, the subscriber identified in the certificate assumes a duty to exercise reasonable care to retain control of the private key corresponding to the public key listed in such certificate and prevent its disclosure to a person not authorised to create the subscriber's digital signature.

(2) Such duty shall continue during the operational period of the certificate and during any period of suspension of the certificate.

For additional analytical, business and investment opportunities information,
please contact Global Investment & Business Center, USA
at (703) 370-8082. Fax: (703) 370-8083. E-mail: ibpusa3@gmail.com
Global Business and Investment Info Databank - www.ibpus.com

INITIATING SUSPENSION OR REVOCATION.

40. A subscriber who has accepted a certificate shall as soon as possible request the issuing certification authority to suspend or revoke the certificate if the private key corresponding to the public key listed in the certificate has been compromised.

PART X REGULATION OF CERTIFICATION AUTHORITIES

APPOINTMENT OF CONTROLLER AND OTHER OFFICERS.

41. (1) The Minister shall be the Controller of Certification Authorities for the purposes of this Act.

(2) The Minister may appoint such number of Deputy and Assistant Controllers of Certification Authorities and officers as he considers necessary to exercise and perform all or any of the powers and duties of the Controller under this Act or any regulations made thereunder.

(3) The Controller, the Deputy and Assistant Controllers and officers appointed under subsection (2) shall exercise, discharge and perform the powers, duties and functions conferred on the Controller under this Act or any regulations made thereunder, subject to such directions as may be issued by the Minister.

(4) The Controller shall maintain a publicly accessible database containing a certification authority disclosure record for each licensed certification authority which shall contain all the particulars required under the regulations made under this Act.

(5) In the application of the provisions of this Act to certificates issued by the Controller and digital signatures verified by reference to those certificates, the Controller shall be deemed to be a licensed certification authority.

REGULATION OF CERTIFICATION AUTHORITIES.

42. (1) The Minister may, with the approval of His Majesty the Sultan and Yang Di-Pertuan, make regulations for the regulation and licensing of certification authorities and to define when a digital signature qualifies as a secure electronic signature.

(2) Without prejudice to the generality of subsection (1), the Minister may make regulations for or with respect to —

(a) applications for licences or renewal of licences of certification authorities and their authorised representatives and matters incidental thereto;

(b) the activities of certification authorities including the manner, method and place of soliciting business, the conduct of such solicitation and the prohibition of such solicitation from members of the public by certification authorities which are not licensed;

(c) the standards to be maintained by certification authorities;

(d) prescribing the appropriate standards with respect to the qualifications, experience and training of applicants for any licence or their employees;

(e) prescribing the conditions for the conduct of business by a certification authority;

(f)

providing for the content and distribution of written, printed or visual material and advertisements that may be distributed or used by a person in respect of a digital certificate or key;

(g)

prescribing the form and content of a digital certificate or key;

(h)

prescribing the particulars to be recorded in, or in respect of, accounts kept by certification authorities;

(i)

providing for the appointment and remuneration of an auditor appointed under the regulations and for the costs of an audit carried out under the regulations;

(j)

providing for the establishment and regulation of any electronic system by a certification authority, whether by itself or in conjunction with other certification authorities, and for the imposition and variation of such requirements, conditions or restrictions as the Controller may think fit;

(k)

the manner in which a holder of a licence conducts its dealings with its customers, conflicts of interest involving the holder of a licence and its customers, and the duties of a holder of a licence to its customers with respect to digital certificates;

(l)

prescribing any forms for the purposes of the regulations; and

(m)

prescribing fees to be paid in respect of any matter or thing required for the purposes of this Act and the regulations.

(3) Regulations made under this section may provide that a contravention of a specified provisions shall be an offence and may provide for penalties for a fine not exceeding $50,000, imprisonment for a term not exceeding one year or both.

RECOGNITION OF FOREIGN CERTIFICATION AUTHORITIES.

43. The Minister may, by order published in the *Gazette,* recognise certification authorities outside Brunei Darussalam that satisfy the prescribed requirements for any of the following purposes —

(a) the recommended reliance limit, if any, specified in a certificate issued by the certification authority;

(b) the presumption referred to in sections 20*(b)*(ii) and 21.

RECOMMENDED RELIANCE LIMIT.

44. (1) A licensed certification authority shall, in issuing a certificate to a subscriber, specify a recommended reliance limit in the certificate.

(2) The licensed certification authority may specify different limits in different certificates as it considers fit.

LIABILITY LIMITS FOR LICENSED CERTIFICATION AUTHORITIES.

45. Unless a licensed certification authority waives the application of this section, a licensed certification authority —

(a)

shall not be liable for any loss caused by reliance on a false or forged digital signature of a subscriber if, with respect to the false or forged digital signature, the licensed certification authority complied with the requirements of this Act;

(b)

shall not be liable in excess of the amount specified in the certificate as its recommended reliance limit for either —

(i) a loss caused by reliance on a misrepresentation in the certificate of any fact that the licensed certification authority is required to confirm; or

ii) failure to comply with sections 29 and 30 in issuing the certificate.

REGULATION OF REPOSITORIES.

46. The Minister may, with the approval of His Majesty the Sultan and Yang Di-Pertuan, make regulations for the purpose of ensuring the quality of repositories and the services they provide, including provisions for the standards, licensing or accreditation of repositories.

PART XI GOVERNMENT USE OF ELECTRONIC RECORDS AND SIGNATURES

ACCEPTANCE OF ELECTRONIC FILING AND ISSUE OF DOCUMENTS.

47. (1) Any department or ministry of the Government, organ of State or statutory body that, pursuant to any written law —

(a) accepts the filing of documents, or requires that documents be created or retained;

(b)
issues any permit, licence or approval; or
(c) provides for the method and manner of payment,

may, notwithstanding anything to the contrary in such written law —

(i) accept the filing of such documents, or the creation or retention of such documents in the form of electronic records;
(ii) issue such permit, licence or approval in the form of electronic records; or

(iii) make such payment in electronic form.

(2) In any case where a department or ministry of the Government, organ of State or statutory body decides to perform any of the functions in subsections (1)(i), (ii) or (iii), it may specify —
(a) the manner and format in which such electronic records shall be filed, created, retained or issued;
(b) where such electronic records have to be signed, the type of electronic signature required including, if applicable, a requirement that the sender use a digital signature or other secure electronic signature;
(c) the manner and format in which such signature shall be affixed to the electronic record, and the identity of or criteria that shall be met by any certification authority used by the person filing the document;
(d) control processes and procedures as appropriate to ensure adequate integrity, security and confidentiality of electronic records or payments; and

(e) any other required attributes for electronic records or payments that are currently specified for corresponding paper documents.

(3)

Nothing in this Act shall by itself compel any department or ministry of the Government, organ of State or statutory body to accept or issue any document in the form of electronic records.

PART XII GENERAL

OBLIGATION OF CONFIDENTIALITY.

48. (1) Except for the purposes of this Act or for any prosecution for an offence under any written law or pursuant to any order of court, no person who has, pursuant to any powers conferred under this Part, obtained access to any electronic record, book, register, correspondence, information, document or other material shall disclose such electronic record, book, register, correspondence, information, document or other material to any other person.

(2) Any person who contravenes subsection (1) shall be guilty of an offence and be liable on conviction to a fine not exceeding $10,000, imprisonment for a term not exceeding one year or both.

OFFENCES BY BODIES CORPORATE.

49. Where an offence under this Act or any regulations made thereunder committed by a body corporate is proved to have committed with the consent or connivance of, or to be attributable to any act or default on the part of, any director, manager, secretary or other similar officer of that body corporate, or of any person purporting to act in any such capacity, he, as well as the body corporate, shall also be guilty of that offence and be liable to be proceeded against and punished accordingly.

AUTHORISED OFFICERS OR EMPLOYEES.

50. (1) The Controller may in writing authorise any officer or employee to exercise any of the powers of the Controller under this Part.

(2)

Any such officer or employee shall be deemed to be a public servant for the purposes of the Penal Code (Chapter 22).

(3)

In exercising any of the powers of enforcement under this Act, an authorised officer or employee shall on demand produce to the person against whom he is acting the authority issued to him by the Controller.

CONTROLLER MAY GIVE DIRECTIONS FOR COMPLIANCE.

51. (1) The Controller may by notice in writing direct a certification authority or any officer or employee thereof to take such measures or stop carrying on such activities as are specified in the notice if they are necessary to ensure compliance with the provisions of this Act or any regulations made thereunder.

(2) Any person who fails to comply with any direction specified in a notice issued under subsection (1) shall be guilty of an offence and be liable on conviction to a fine not exceeding $50,000, imprisonment for a term not exceeding one year or both.

POWER TO INVESTIGATE.

52. (1) The Controller or an authorised officer or employee may investigate the activities of a certification authority in relation to its compliance with this Act and any regulations made thereunder.

(2) For the purposes of subsection (1), the Controller may in writing issue an order to a certification authority to further its investigation or to secure compliance with this Act or any regulations made thereunder.

ACCESS TO COMPUTERS AND DATA.

53. (1) The Controller or an authorised officer or employee shall —

(a) be entitled at any time to —
(i) have access to and inspect and check the operation of any computer system and any associated apparatus or material which he has reasonable cause to suspect is or has been in use in connection with any offence under this Act;
(ii) use or caused to be used any such computer system to search any data contained in or available to such computer system; or
(b) be entitled to require —
(i) the person by whom or on whose behalf the Controller or authorised officer has reasonable cause to suspect the computer is or has been so used; or
(ii) any person having charge of, or otherwise concerned with the operation of, the computer, apparatus or material, to provide him with such reasonable technical and other assistance as he may require for the purposes of paragraph *(a)*.

(2) Any person who obstructs the lawful exercise of the powers under subsection (1)*(a)* or who fails to comply with a request under subsection (1)*(b)* is guilty of an offence and liable on conviction to a fine not exceeding $20,000, imprisonment for a term not exceeding one year or both.

OBSTRUCTION OF AUTHORISED OFFICER OR EMPLOYEE.

54. Any person who obstructs, impedes, assaults or interferes with the Controller or any authorised officer or employee in the performance of his functions under this Act shall be guilty of an offence.

PRODUCTION OF DOCUMENTS, DATA ETC.

55. The Controller or an authorised officer or employee shall, for the purposes of the execution of this Act, have power to do all or any of the following —

(a) require the production of records, accounts, data and documents kept by a licensed certification authority and to inspect, examine and copy any of them;
(b) require the production of any identification document from any person in relation to any offence under this Act or any regulations made thereunder;
(c) make such inquiry as may be necessary to ascertain whether the provisions of this Act or any regulations made thereunder have been complied with.

GENERAL PENALTIES.

56. Any person guilty of an offence under this Act or any regulations made thereunder for which no penalty is expressly provided shall be liable on conviction to a fine not exceeding $20,000, imprisonment for a term not exceeding 6 months or both.

SANCTION OF PUBLIC PROSECUTOR.

57. No prosecution in respect of any offence under this Act or any regulations made thereunder shall be instituted except by or with the sanction of the Public Prosecutor.

JURISDICTION OF COURTS.

58. A Court of a Magistrate shall have jurisdiction to hear and determine all offences under this Act and any regulations made thereunder and, notwithstanding anything to the contrary in any other written law, shall have power to impose the full penalty or punishment in respect of any such offence.

COMPOSITION OF OFFENCES.

59. (1) The Controller may, in his discretion, compound any offence under this Act or any regulations made thereunder which is prescribed as being an offence which may be compounded by collecting from any person reasonably suspected of having committed that offence a sum not exceeding $5,000.

(2) The Minister may, with the approval of His Majesty the Sultan and Yang Di-Pertuan, make regulations prescribing the offences which may be compounded under this Act.

POWER TO EXEMPT.

60. Notwithstanding anything contained in this Act or in any other written law, the Minister may exempt, subject to such terms and conditions as he thinks fit, any person or classes of person from all or any of the provisions of this Act or any regulations made thereunder.

REGULATIONS.

61. (1) The Minister may, with the approval of His Majesty the Sultan and Yang Di-Pertuan, make regulations to prescribe anything which is required to be prescribed under this Act and generally for the carrying out of the provisions of this Act.

(2) Any regulations made under this Act may make different provision for different cases or classes of case and for different purposes of the same provision.

STRATEGIC BUSINESS AND LEGAL INFORMATION

Brunei Darussalam is still very much dependent on revenues from crude oil and natural gas to finance its development programs. Aside from this, Brunei Darussalam also receives income from rents, royalties, corporate tax and dividends. Due to the non-renewable nature of oil and gas, economic diversification has been in Brunei Darussalam's national development agenda. In the current Seventh national Development Plan, 1996-2000, the government has allocated more than $7.2 billion for the implementation of various projects and programs.

Brunei Darussalam is the third largest oil producer in Southeast Asia and it produced 163,000 barrels per day. It is also the fourth largest producer of liquefied natural gas in the world.

Brunei Darussalam is the third largest oil producer in Southeast Asia and it produced 163,000 barrels per day. It is also the fourth largest producer of liquefied natural gas in the world.
National Development Plan 1996 – 2000

Brunei welcomes foreign investment. Foreign investors are invited to actively participate in the current economic diversification programme of the country. The programme hinges on the development of the private sector. The Ministry of Industry and Primary Resources was formed in 1989 with the responsibility of promoting and facilitating industrial development in Brunei Darussalam. Brunei Darussalam offers all investors security, stability, continuity, confidence and competitiveness.

Competitive investment incentives are ready and available for investors throughout the business cycle of start up, growth, maturity and expansion. The Investment Incentive Act which was enacted in 1975 provides tax advantages at start up and ongoing incentives throughout growth and expansion that are comparable if not better than those offered by other countries in the region.

The Investment Incentives Act makes provision for encouraging the establishment and development of industrial and other economic enterprises, for economic expansion and incidental purposes.

Investment incentive benefits vary from one program to other. Amongst the benefits are:

- Exemption from income tax;
- Exemption from taxes on imported duties on machinery, equipment, component parts, accessories or building structures;
- Exemption from taxes on imported raw material not available or produced in Brunei Darussalam intended for the production of the pioneer products;
- Carry forward of losses and allowances.

This Act provides tax relief for a company which is granted pioneer status.

- Companies awarded pioneer status are exempted from corporate tax, tax import of raw materials and capital goods for a period ranging from 2 to 5 years, depending on fixed capital expenditure with possible extension at the discretion of the relevant authorities.
- Enterprises which are given expansion certificates are given tax relief for a period between 3 to 5 years.
- Approved foreign loans can be exempted from paying the 20% withholding tax for interest paid to non-resident lenders.

Brunei Darussalam is flexible towards foreign equity requirements. 100% foreign equity can be considered for export-oriented industries with the exception of industries based on local resources, industries related to national food security and car dealership whereby some level of local participation is required.

Industrial activities are classified into four categories:

- Industries related to national food security
- Industries for local market
- Industries based on local resources
- Industries for export market

Industrial policies including manpower, ownership, government support and facilities remain open and flexible for all categories of industrial activities. Brunei Darussalam maintains a realistic approach where a variety of arrangements are feasible. Policies relating to ownership allow for full foreign ownership, majority foreign ownership and minority foreign ownership, as per the type of industry and situation.

Only activities relating to national food security and those based on local resources require some level of local participation. Industries for the local market not related to national food security and industries for total export can be totally foreign owned. Overall, in Brunei Darussalam, any industrial enterprise will be considered.

The Investment Incentives Order 2001 expanded the tax holidays avaiable to investors. Examples include:

- Corporate tax relief of up to 5 years for companies that invest B$500,000 to B$2.5 million in approved ventures
- 8-years tax relief for investing more than B$2.5 million
- An 11-year tax break if the venture is located in a high-tech industrial park.

INVESTMENT AND BUSINESS CLIMATE

Brunei Darussalam has enormous business potential that is yet to be exploited. The country has the advantage of peace and political stability, which is favourable for business activities.

Foreign investments are always welcome in Brunei and foreign investors are invited to actively engage in the current economic diversification programme.

The Ministry of Industry and Primary Resources, which was established in 1989, is the main government agency that promotes and facilitates investment, business and trade activities in the country.

Competitive investment incentives are ready and available for investors throughout the business cycle of start up, growth, maturity and expansion.

The Investment Incentive Act enacted in 1975 provides tax advantages at start up and ongoing incentives throughout growth and expansion that are comparable if not better than those offered by other countries in the region.

WHY INVEST IN BRUNEI DARUSSALAM?

¨ Brunei Darussalam is a stable and prosperous country that offers not only excellent infrastructure but also a strategic location within the Asean group of countries.

¨ No personal income tax is imposed in Brunei. Businesses are also not imposed sales tax, payroll, manufacturing and export tax. Approved foreign investors can enjoy a company tax holiday of up to eight years.

¨ The regulations relating to foreign participation in equity are flexible. In many instances there can be 100% foreign ownership.

¨ Approval for foreign workers, ranging from labourers to managers, can be secured.
¨ The cost of utilities is among the lowest in the region.
¨ The local market, while relatively small, is lucrative and most overseas investors will encounter little or no competition.

¨ The living conditions in Brunei Darussalam are among the best and most secure in the region
¨ On top of all, His Majesty's Government genuinely welcomes foreign investment in almost any enterprise and will ensure that you receive speedy, efficient and practical assistance on all your inquiries.

SUPPORTIVE ENVIRONMENT

Brunei Darussalam offers vast land and a variety of facilities throughout all four districts in the country. The majority of the 12 industrial sites presently developed are ready and available for occupation. Large expanses for agroforestry and aquaculture are also available. Rental terms and tenancy agreements are competitive and the sites offer a range of facilities, infrastructure and resources. Brunei Darussalam gives priority to ensuring the stability of the natural environment. As such, all sites are free from pollution and are ecologically well balanced. The government's philosophy is sustainable development. Therefore, all polluting industries are banned and one of the continuing criteria for engaging any industry's participation is the impact on the environment.

INFRASTRUCTURE

The country's infrastructure is well developed and ready to cater for the needs of the new and vigorous economic activities under the current economic diversification programme. The country's two main ports, at Muara and Kuala Belait, offer direct shipping to Hong Kong, Singapore and several other Asian destinations. Muara, the deep-water port situated 29 kilometres from the capital was opened in 1973 and has since been considerably developed. It has 12,542 sq. metres of transit sheds. Container yards have been increased in size and a container freight station handles unstuffing operations. Meanwhile, Pulau Muara Besar is being developed as a centre for dockyard, ship salvaging and for other related industries. The recently expanded Brunei International Airport in Bandar Seri Begawan can now handle 1.5 million passengers and 50,000 tonnes of cargo a year. The 2,000 kilometre road network serving the entire country is being expanded and modernised. A main highway runs the entire length of the country's coastline. It conveniently links Muara, the port of entry at one end, to Belait, the oil producing district at the western end of the state.

ECONOMY

The economy of the country is dominated by the oil and gas and liquefied natural gas industries and Government expenditure patterns. The country's exports consist of three major commodities namely crude oil, petroleum products and liquefied natural gas. Exports are destined mainly for Japan, the United States and Asean countries. The second most important industry is the construction industry. This is directly the result of increased investment by the Government in development and infrastructure projects within the five-year National Development Plans. Brunei Darussalam has entered a new phase of development in its drive towards economic diversification from dependence on the oil and liquefied natural gas-based economy. Official statistics showed that exports during the 1996 to 2000 period increased from B$3,682.1 million in 1996 to B$6,733.5 million in 2000, while imports declined from B$3,513.6 million to B$1,907.8 million. This trend has increased the balance of trade from B$168.9 million in 1996 to B$3289.0 million in 2000. In the current 8th National Development Plan, which is the last phase of Brunei's 20-year National Development Programme, the government is allocating a total of B$1.1 billion for commerce and industry. The Brunei International Financial Centre (BIFC) set up in 2000, is another effort undertaken by the government to diversify the country's economy. Brunei Darussalam has the potential to become an international financial centre and has the capability to provide similar facilities as those available in other successful financial centres. Brunei has political stability, modern infrastructure and up-to-date international communications system. Seven bills have been passed to govern the establishment and supervision of BIFC. These include the International Business Companies Order 2000, International Limited Partnership Order 2000, International Banking order 2000, International Trust Order 2000, Registered Agents and Trust Licensing order 2000, Money Laundering Order 2000 and Criminal Conduct (Recovery of Proceed) Order 2000. The BIFC also plans to establish international Islamic banks in Brunei whose legal framework has been provided under the International Banking Order 2000. The establishment of the international Islamic banks is in line with the national aspirations of encouraging the development of Islamic finance and also of making the Sultanate as a regional and international Islamic financial centre.

INDUSTRIES

Industrial activities are classified into four categories:

1. Industries related to national food security
2. Industries for local market
3. Industries based on local resources
4. Industries for export market

FLEXIBLE POLICIES

Industrial policies including manpower, ownership, government support and facilities remain open and flexible for all categories of industrial activities. Brunei Darussalam maintains a realistic approach where a variety of arrangements are feasible. Policies relating to ownership allow for full foreign ownership, majority foreign ownership and minority foreign ownership, as per type of industry and situation. Only activities relating to national food security and industries for total export can be totally foreign owned. Overall, in Brunei Darussalam, any industrial enterprise will be considered.

FINANCE, BANK AND INSURANCE

Brunei Darussalam has no central bank, but the Ministry of Finance through the Treasury, the Currency Board and the Brunei Investment Agency exercises most of the functions of a central bank. Brunei Darussalam has not established a single monetary authority. All works related to finance are being carried out by three institutions.

· The Brunei Currency Board (BCB) is responsible for the circulation and management of currencies in the country.

· The Financial Institution Division (FID) is tasked with the issuing of licenses and regulations to financial institutions including the enforcement of minimum cash balance in accordance to specified rates for the interest of investors

· The Banks Association of Brunei determines the daily interest rates. However, there is also an indication that a single monetary authority may be established in the future to undertake these functions.

In 2000, it was recorded that there were 85 financial institutions including banks, financial companies, security companies, conventional insurance companies, Takaful companies, remittance companies and moneychangers. The existing nine commercial banks have established many branches from 29 in 1995 to 61 in 2000. The number of finance companies has also increased from three in 1996 to five in 2000. Security companies remain at two and the number of conventional insurance companies decreased from 22 in 1996 to 19 in 2000. This is the result of the merging of the branch and parent companies. The number of Takaful companies have risen from two in 1996 to three in 2000. In 1996 and 1997 there were 20 moneychangers operating in the country. The number increased to 33 in 1998 but has reduced to 24 in 2000. Remittance companies have also experienced the same trend as they increased from 16 in 1996 to 30 in 1998 but have reduced to 23 in 2000. The Brunei dollar is pegged to the Singapore dollar. The Ministry of Finance believes that the Monetary Authority of Singapore exercises sufficient caution and such a link will not have detrimental effects on the economies of either country.

CURRENCY

Currency matters are under the jurisdiction of the Brunei Currency Board (BCB) which manages and distributes currency notes and coins in the country with the main mission of ensuring the integrity of the currency issued to safeguard public interest. In September 2000, the money supply comprising currency in circulation and demand deposits amounted to B$2,295 million compared to B$3,366 million, B$2,430 million, B$2,493 million and B$2,727 million in 1996, 1997, 1998 and 1999 respectively.

FOREIGN EXCHANGE

There is no restriction in foreign exchange. Banks permit non-resident accounts to be maintained and there is no restriction on borrowing by non-residents.

TAXATION

Brunei Darussalam has no personal income tax. Sole proprietorship and partnership businesses are not subject to income tax. Only companies are subject to income tax and it is one of the lowest in the region. Moreover tax advantages at start-up and ongoing incentives throughout growth and expansion offer investors profitable conditions that are comparable if not better than those offered by other countries in the region.

COMPANY TAXATION

Companies are subject to tax on the following types of income: -
¨ Gains of profits from any trade, business or vocation,
¨ Dividends received from companies not previously assessed for tax in Brunei Darussalam
¨ Interest and discounts
¨ Rent, royalties, premiums and any other profits arising from properties.

There is no capital gains tax. However, where the Collector of Income Tax can establish that the gains form part of the normal trading activities, they become taxable as revenue gains.

a. Scope of Income Tax
A resident company in Brunei Darussalam is liable to income tax on its income derived from or accrued in Brunei Darussalam or received from overseas. A non-resident company is only taxed on its income arising in Brunei Darussalam.

b. Concept of Residence

A company, whether incorporated locally or overseas, is considered as resident in Brunei Darussalam for tax purposes if the control and management of its business is exercised in Brunei Darussalam. The control and management of a company is normally regarded as resident in Brunei Darussalam if, among other things, its directors' meetings are held in Brunei Darussalam. The profits of a company are subject to tax at the rate of 30%. Tax concession may be available. The profit or loss of a company as per its account is adjusted for income tax purposes to take into account certain allowable expenses, certain expenses prohibited from deduction, wear and tear allowances and any losses brought forward from previous years, in order to arrive at taxable profits.

TREATMENT OF DIVIDENDS

Dividends accruing in, derived from, or received in Brunei Darussalam by a corporation are included in taxable income, apart from dividends received from a corporation taxable in Brunei Darussalam which are excluded.No tax is deducted at source on dividends paid by a Brunei Darussalam corporation. Dividends received in Brunei Darussalam from United Kingdom or Commonwealth countries are grossed up in the tax computation and credit is claimed against the Brunei Darussalam tax liability for tax suffered either under the double tax treaty with the United Kingdom or the provision Commonwealth tax relief.

Any other dividends are included net in the tax computation and no foreign tax is available. Brunei Darussalam does not impose any withholding tax on dividends.

ALLOWABLE DEDUCTIONS

All expenses wholly or exclusively incurred in the production of taxable income are allowable as deduction for tax purposes.
These deductions include:
¨ Interest on borrowed money used in acquiring income
¨ Rent on land and buildings used in the trade or business
¨ Costs of repair of premises, plant and machinery
¨ Bad debts and specific doubtful debts, with any subsequent recovery being treated as income when received, and
¨ Employer's contribution to approved pensions or provident funds

DISALLOWABLE DEDUCTIONS

Expenses not allowed as deductions for tax purposes include:
¨ Expenses not wholly or exclusively incurred in acquiring income
¨ Domestic private expenses
¨ Any capital withdrawal or any sum used as capital
¨ Any capital used in improvement apart from replanting of plantation
¨ Any sum recoverable under an insurance or indemnity contract
¨ Rent or repair expenses not incurred in the earning of income
¨ Any income tax paid in Brunei Darussalam or in other countries and
¨ Payments to any unapproved pension or provident funds

Donations are not allowable but claimable if they are made to approved institutions.

ALLOWANCES FOR CAPITAL EXPENDITURE

Depreciation is not an allowable expense and is replaced by capital allowances for qualifying expenditure. The taxpayer is entitled to claim wear and tear allowances calculated as follows:

a. Industrial Buildings

An initial allowance of 10% is given in the year of expenditure, and an annual allowance of 2% of the qualifying expenditure is provided on a straight-line basis until the total expenditure is written off.

b. Machinery and Plant

An initial allowance of 20% of the cost is given in the year of expenditure together with annual allowances calculated on the reducing value of the assets. The rates prescribed by the Collector of Income Tax range from 3% to 25%, depending on the nature of the assets. Balancing allowances or charges are made on disposal of the industrial building machinery or plant. These adjustments cover the shortfall or excess of the tax written down value as compared to the sale proceeds. Any balancing charge is limited to tax allowances previously granted, and any surplus is considered a capital gain and therefore does not become part of chargeable income. Unabsorbed capital allowances can be carried forward indefinitely but must be set off against income from the same trade.

LOSS CARRYOVERS

Losses incurred by a company can be carried forward for six years for setoff against future income and can be carried back one year. There is no requirement regarding continuity of ownership of the company and also the loss set-off is not restricted to the same trade.

FOREIGN TAX RELIEF

A double taxation agreement exists with the United Kingdom and provides proportionate relief from Brunei Darussalam income tax upon any part of the income which has been or is liable to be charged with United Kingdom income tax.

Tax credits are only available for resident companies. Unilateral relief may be obtained on income arising from Commonwealth countries that provide reciprocal relief. However, the maximum relief cannot exceed half the Brunei Darussalam rate. This relief applies to both resident and non-resident companies.

STAMP DUTY

Stamp duties are levied on a variety of documents. Certain types of documents attract an ad valorem duty, whereas with other documents the duty varies with the nature of the documents.

PETROLEUM TAXES

Special legislation exists in respect of income tax from petroleum operations, which is taxable under the Income Tax (Petroleum) Act 1963 as amended.

WITHHOLDING TAXES

Interest paid to non-resident companies under a charge, debenture or in the respect of a loan, is subject to withholding tax of 20%. There are no other withholding taxes.

ESTATE DUTY

Estate duty is levied on an estate of over $2 million at 3% flat rate for a person who has died on or after 15th December 1988.

IMPORT DUTY

In general, basic foodstuffs and goods for industrial use are exempted from import duties. Electrical equipment and appliances, timber products, photographic materials and equipment, furniture, motor vehicles and spare parts are levied minimum duties, while cosmetics and perfumes are subject to 30% duty. Cigarettes are dutiable items, but the rates are low compared with neighbouring countries.

BUSINESSES AND COMPANIES

Registration and Guidelines
In Brunei Darussalam a business may be set up under any of the following forms:
¨ Sole proprietorship
¨ Partnership
¨ Company (Private or Public Company)
¨ Branch of foreign company

All businesses must be registered with the Registrar of Companies and Business Names. The proposed name of business or companies must first of all be approved by the Registrar of Companies and Business Names. For each name proposed, a fee of $5.00 is imposed.

Sole Proprietorship
¨ Upon arrival, a business name certificate is issued and a fee of $30.00 is imposed
¨ At the moment, it is not subject to corporate tax
¨ Foreigners are not eligible to register

Partnership
¨ May consist of individuals, local companies and/or branches of foreign companies
¨ The maximum permitted number of partners is 20
¨ Upon approval, a business name certificate is issued and a fee of $30.00 is imposed
¨ Application by foreign individuals are subject to prior clearance by the Immigration Department, Economic Planning and Development Unit and the Labour Department before they are registered
¨ At the moment, it is not subject to corporate tax

Private Company
¨ May be limited by shares, guarantee or both by shares and guarantee or unlimited
¨ Must have at least two and not more than 50 shareholders
¨ Shareholders need not be Brunei citizens or residents.
¨ Restrict the right of members to transfer shares and prohibit any invitations to the public to subscribe for shares and debentures
¨ A subsidiary company may hold shares in its parent company
¨ Memorandum and Articles of Association must be filed with the Registrar of Companies and Business Names with other incorporation documents in the prescribed form
¨ Upon arrival, a Certificate of Incorporation will be issued and a fee of $25 is imposed
¨ The registration fees are based on a graduated scale on the authorised share capital of the company
¨ No minimum share capital is required
¨ Private Companies are required to do the following:
1. Appoint auditors who are registered in Brunei Darussalam
2. Prepare a profit and loss account and balance sheet, accompanied by the Director's Report annually
3. Submit accounting data annually to the Economic Development and Planning Department of the Ministry of Finance
4. File annual returns, containing information on directors and shareholders
5. Keep the following records:
a. Minute Book of Members' Meetings
b. Minute Book of Director's Meetings
c. Minute Book of Manager's Meetings
d. Register of Members
e. Register of Directors and Managers
f. Register of Charges
¨ Subject to corporate tax of 30% of the gross yearly profit

For additional analytical, business and investment opportunities information,
please contact Global Investment & Business Center, USA
at (703) 370-8082. Fax: (703) 370-8083. E-mail: ibpusa3@gmail.com
Global Business and Investment Info Databank - www.ibpus.com

PUBLIC COMPANY
¨ May be limited or unlimited
¨ May issue freely transferable shares to the public
¨ Must have at least seven shareholders
¨ Shareholders need not be Brunei citizens or residents
¨ Subsidiary company may hold shares in its parent companies
¨ Half the directors in the company must be either Brunei Citizens or ordinary residents in Brunei Darussalam.
¨ Memorandum and Articles of Association must be registered with other incorporation documents in the prescribed forms
¨ Upon approval, Registration of Companies Certificate will be issued and a fee of $25.00 is imposed
¨ The registration fees are based on a graduated scale on the authorised share capital of the company.
¨ No minimum share capital is required
¨ Public Companies are required to do the following:
1. Appoint auditors who are registered in Brunei Darussalam
2. Prepare each year's profit and loss account and balance sheet, accompanied by the Director's Report annually.
3. Submit accounting data annually to the Economic Development and Planning Department of the Ministry of Finance
4. File annual returns, containing information on directors and shareholders
5. Keep the following records:
a. Minute Book of Members' Meetings
b. Minute Book of Director's Meetings
c. Minute Book of Manager's Meetings
d. Register of Members
e. Register of Directors and Managers
f. Register of Charges
¨ Subject to corporate tax of 30% of the gross yearly profit.

BRANCH OF FOREIGN COMPANY
The following documents must be filed with the Registrar of Companies and Business Names.
a. A certified copy of the charter, statutes or Memorandum and Articles of Association or other instruments defining the constitution of the foreign company duly authenticated and, when necessary, with English translation.
b. A list of directors together with their particulars and the names and addresses of one or more persons residing in Brunei Darussalam authorised to accept notices on the company's behalf.

¨ Upon approval, a Certificate of Incorporation will be issued and a fee of $25 is imposed
¨ The registration fees are based on a graduated scale on the authorised share capital of the company.
¨ No minimum share capital is required
¨ Branch of foreign company is required to do the following:
1. Appoint auditors who are registered in Brunei Darussalam
2. Prepare each year's profit and loss account and balance sheet, accompanied by the Director's Report annually.
3. Submit accounting data annually to the Economic Development and Planning Department of the Ministry of Finance
4. File annual returns, containing information on directors and shareholders
5. Keep the following records:
a. Minute Book of Members' Meetings
b. Minute Book of Director's Meetings
c. Minute Book of Manager's Meetings
d. Register of Members

e. Register of Directors and Managers
f. Register of Charges
¨ Subject to corporate tax of 30% of the gross yearly profit.

REGISTRATION OF TRADEMARKS AND PATENTS

Trademarks are registrable provided the requirements laid down in the Trademarks Act (Cap 98) are satisfied. Once registered, they are viable for an initial period of seven years and renewable for a further period of 14 years.

Any person who obtains a grant of a patent in the UK or Malaysia or Singapore may apply to the Ministry of Law within three years of the date of issue of such grant to have the grant registered in Brunei Darussalam under the Invention Act (Cap 72). There is no specific legislation for copyright protection, but UK legislation would apply where necessary.

EMPLOYMENT REGULATIONS

All non-Brunei Darussalam citizens require a work permit which are valid for two years. Application must first be made to the Labour Department for a labour license. On the recommendation of the Labour Department, the Immigration Department will give permission for the workers to enter Brunei Darussalam. The Labour Department requires either a cash deposit or a banker's guarantee to cover the cost of a one-way airfare to the home country of an immigrant worker. An approved labour licence cannot be altered for at least six months after issue. Applications will not be accepted until the formation of a local company or branch of a foreign company has been officially approved and registered.

INDUSTRIAL RELATIONS

The Trade Disputes Act (Cap 129) accords to trade unions the customary immunities and protections in respect of facts done in furtherance of trade disputes. It prescribes procedures for conciliation and subject to the consent of the parties, arbitration in disputes where machinery within the industry concerned does not exist or has failed to achieve settlement. Trade unionism of either the employers or workers is extensively practiced in Brunei Darussalam. As has been already observed, the industrial structure consists almost entirely of small scale enterprises. This state of affairs and nature and cultural characteristics of the population are conductive to accommodation and a 'give and take attitude' rather than a confrontational attitude. Except in the oil industry, the system of collective bargaining has not emerged. Relations between employers and employees are generally good. Existing labour laws have adequate provisions such as for termination of employment, medical care, maternity leave and compensation for disablement. Labour disputes are very rare. The Government has recently implemented the Workers' Provident Fund Enactment to cover workers both in the public and private sectors.

INTERNATIONAL RELATION AND TRADE DEVELOPMENT

In the perspectives of economic co-operation with foreign countries at the bilateral and multilateral levels, Brunei Darussalam seeks relevant agencies that can contribute to development and networking.

The areas of concern are:
¨ To facilitate investment into Brunei Darussalam
¨ To facilitate the development of trade
¨ To enhance human resources development and technology transfer, and
¨ To enhance bilateral, regional and multilateral economic cooperation

In pursuing these areas, mechanism for consultations and cooperation have been established through bilateral, regional and multilateral forum such as Association of Southeast Asian Nations (ASEAN), Asia Pacific Economic Cooperation (APEC), Organisation of Islamic Countries (OIC), European Union (EU), the Commonwealth, United Nation (UN) and the Non-Aligned Movement (NAM).

INVESTMENT PROMOTION

In the area of investment, Brunei Darussalam is currently engaged in a programme to improve its investment climate to create and enhance investment opportunities in Brunei Darussalam, both for local and foreign investors. The programme involves the establishment of bilateral trade investment treaties with foreign Government and Memorandums of Understanding (MoUs) between Brunei Darussalam's private sector and private sectors of other countries.

TRADE DEVELOPMENT

In the area of trade development, Brunei Darussalam is facilitating market opportunities to increase market access in the region as well as globally. Brunei Darussalam practices open multilateral trading system which are being pursued through regional and multilateral trading arrangements such as the ASEAN Free Trade Area (AFTA) and General Agreement of Trade and Tariffs (GATT). This open trade policy is consistent with Brunei Darussalam's efforts in pursuing outward looking economic policies that will assist the country in expanding its industrial and primary resource-based industries.

HUMAN RESOURCE DEVELOPMENT AND TECHNOLOGY TRANSFER

In the area of human resource development and technology transfer, there is a need to improve the technological capabilities of existing local industries, which are mainly small and medium scale enterprises. This is in view of the existing shortage of local manpower and thus the need to import foreign workers. The programmes are targeted towards the development of the mid-band occupational structure in which Brunei Darussalam has the advantage in view of cost factors such as the non-existence of income tax. Within the context of general economic cooperation, Brunei Darussalam will continue to enhance economic linkages with other countries in the region as well as outside the region.

THE INVESTMENT & TRADING ARM OF THE GOVERNMENT

Semaun Holdings Sdn Bhd
Semaun Holdings Sendirian Berhad, incorporated on 8th December 1994, is a private limited company that serves as an investment/trading arm of the Government with the purpose of accelerating industrial development in Brunei Darussalam through direct investment. Semaun Holdings is wholly owned by His Majesty's Government and plays an important role in supporting the economic diversification programmes in the country. The Chairman is the Honourable Minister of Industry and Primary Resources, Pehin Orang Kaya Setia Pahlawan Dato Seri Setia Haji Awang Abdul Rahman bin Dato Setia Haji Mohammad Taib, who is also the Chairman to the Industrial and Trade Development Council, a body entrusted with facilitating the industrialisation programme of Brunei Darussalam. The mission of Semaun Holdings is to spearhead industrial and commercial development through direct investment in key industrial sectors. Its primary objectives are:

¨ To accelerate and commercial development in Brunei Darussalam
¨ To generate industrial and commercial opportunities for active participation of citizens

Investment Philosophy
a. Local investment
First priority shall be given to investment in the country. Investment shall be in areas of strategic importance and NOT in direct competition with local companies
b. Overseas Capital
The Holdings may invest overseas in activities which reinforce the position of its local investment, preferably through strategic partnering with suitable local companies

Authorised Capital
BND 500 million (Five hundred million dollars)

Type of Investment
The Holdings shall invest through its
" Wholly owned operations
" Joint Venture Companies
" Equity Participation

Scope of Operation
The Holdings shall invest in business, trading and commercial enterprises including agriculture, fishery, forestry, industry and mining activities in Brunei Darussalam. Participation in investment related activities outside the country are also considered.
For more information please contact:
Semaun Holdings Sdn Bhd,
Office Unit No. 02, Block D,
Complex Yayasan Sultan Haji Hassanal Bolkiah,
Bandar Seri Begawan 2085,
Brunei Darussalam
Telephone no: (673) 223-2957 Fax : (673) 223-2956

NATIONAL DEVELOPMENT PLAN

The current National Development Plan 1996 - 2000 is the 7th in the series and primarily aims at giving an all-round enhancement to all facets of life of the people, with emphasis to economic diversification through the development of export-oriented non- oil based industries. The Government has allocated a total of $7.2 billion for this purpose, with social services taking the lion's share at $1.98 billion; Public Utilities, $1.58 billion; Transport and Communications, $1.4 billion; Industry and Commerce, $907.66 million; Public Buildings, $623.83 million; Security, $528.1 million; and Miscellaneous, $173.3 million.

COMMUNICATIONS

Airport

The present day Brunei International Airport, located at Berakas about fifteen minutes drive from Bandar Seri Begawan operates 24 hours a day, providing facilities for both regional and international air traffic. It has a 4000-metre runway that can accommodate any type of aircraft currently in service, including the 'Jumbo' 747s. Its passenger and cargo handling facilities can handle 1.5 million passengers and 50,000 tones of cargo a year. Equipped with the latest state-of the-art technology in surveillance and tracking, the airport boasts radar, flight and auxiliary data processing, 2,000-line, high-resolution color raster displays, simulation facilities, voice switching system, voice and data recording and VHF/UHF air-ground transmitters. The national air carrier is Royal Brunei Airlines founded in November 18, 1974.

Another airport, at Anduki near Seria, is used by the Brunei Shell Petroleum Company for its helicopter services.

Ports

The main Port is Muara, which is about 28 kilometers from Bandar Seri Begawan. The port can accommodate ships over 196 meters L.O.A. and take up to 7 or 8 vessels averaging 8,000 Gross

Registered Tonnage {GRT} or a single ship of up to 30,000 {GRT} with a draught of not more than 9.5 meters.

Since 1973, the port has undergone extensive improvements. These include extensions to the wharf bringing the total length to 948 meters including 250 meters dedicated container wharf and 87 meters aggregate wharf. The overall storage space in the form of covered storage is 16,950 square meters, long storage warehouses 16,630 square meters and open storage space 5 hectares. Facilities for the dedicated container wharf covers an area of 92,034 square meters including 8,034 square meters covered areas.

Besides Muara Port, there are two smaller ports located one at Bandar Seri Begawan and one at Kuala Belait. The port at Bandar Seri Begawan is utilized by vessels under 93 meters LOA drawing less than 5 meters draught carrying conventional cargoes for direct deliveries and passenger launches plying between Bandar Seri Begawan, Limbang and Temburong. The wharf also accommodates various small government crafts. The port at Kuala Belait can accommodate vessels with draught of 4 meters which carries mainly general cargo for Kuala Belait and the Brunei Petroleum Shell Company.

Road

The road network in Brunei Darussalam is the primary means of movement for people, goods and services on land. It plays a vital role in the overall growth and development of the State. The network has been designed to integrate housing, commercial and industrial development. The Sultanate has constructed a good road network with various types of road throughout the country that includes highways, link roads, flyovers and round-abouts. A major road, which was completed in 1983, is a 28-kilometre highway linking Muara through Berakas and Jerudong to a point in Tutong, where it connects with the existing Bandar Seri Begawan-Tutong-Seria trunk road thus providing an alternative routes to these places.

An 11-km road between Sungai Teraban and Sungai Tujoh, makes the journey from Brunei Darussalam to Sarawak's Fourth Division such as Miri and other parts of Sarawak much easier.

The State had 2,525 kilometers (km) of roads, of which 2,328 km were covered with asphalt, 187 with pebbles, and 10 km with concrete. Of the total 1,514 km were in Brunei/Muara, 481 km in Belait, 400 km in Tutong and 130 km in Temburong district.

BRUNEY INDUSTRIAL ACHIEVEMENTS

Today, twelve years since its formation, BINA has managed to achieve a considerable measure of success in what it originally set out to do. In putting these achievements in perspective, one has to bear in mine circumstances Brunei has to contend with, the most critical of which is the local market which is approximately about 300,000 people compared to our regional neighbours.

DIVERSIFICATION OF INDUSTRIAL ACTIVITIES

Allocated at BINA's industrial sites in all the four districts, 213 projects have been approved to date which is a combination of new and relocation/expansion projects. The following list is a selection of those approved projects which should give some perspective of BINA's achievement so far.

- Clinker grinding plant (cement manufacture)

- Production of construction materials (e.g. paint aluminium doors & windows, roofing products, PVC pipes, concrete blocks, stainless steel products, etc)
- Bottling of artesian water
- Assembly of electrical appliances
- Electrical equipment (switchboard, control panels & feeder pillars)
- Production of electrical cables & wires
- Manufacturing of garments for export
- Food & beverages (e.g. ice cream, soft drinks, bakery, spices, etc)
- Production of solar panels for export
- Aluminium sulphate & sodium carbonate for use in water treatment
- Food repackaging
- Warehousing
- Manufacture of furniture
- Manufacture of cans
- Canning of tuna

Not just limited to the capability of setting up factories, some manufacturers have actually managed to get accreditation for their products ftorn reputable foreign establishments such as SIRIM & SISIR while others have successfully implemented the internationally recognised management standard ISO 9002.

INVESTMENT

The total investment value of those projects based on approved projects is B$619,608,331 in which foreign investments accounts for approximately one-quarter of the pie (B$126,071,802). Local investments stands at B$493,536,529.

EMPLOYMENT CREATION

Those investments have also helped to create 14,753 new job opportunities for both the skilled and unskilled categories. This positive development goes a long way in helping reduce the Government's burden of unemployment which is often accompanied by social problems.

EXPORT ACTIVITIES

Other developments are the creation of export industries, which at the moment is still limited to garment. Apart from enhancing the credibility of

local companies, exports help to offset imports in the national balance of trade figures and is also the way forward if a company wants to grow

sitinificantly because of the competitive nature and large size of the international market. The local garment industry export value still has a long way to go to offset the nations huge demand for imported products and

services but has taken the right step forward to establish itself especially with trade liberalisation agreements, that Brunei is party to, coming into effect at the beginning of the next century. Below is a table of the industry's export figures:

Year	Value (US$)	Quantity (Dozen)
1989	5,377,741	179,936
1990	9,685,408	261,805
1991	18,942,925	406,764
1992	19,214,188	464,926
1993	24,309,781	569,238
1994	28,809,553	789,605
1995	41,514,308	969,472
1996	46,753,607	1,022,917
1997	57,528,747	1,230,730
Total	252,136,258	5,895,393

IMPORT SUBSTITUTION

It is admittedly difficult for local producers to replace the products that consumers import because the oil and gas industry aside, Brunei is a net importer. But in any case, Brunei has managed to produce certain products locally such as construction materials, processed food, furniture, electrical products, etc which is a good start in replacing simple products which are within the technological and financial capacity of local manufacturers/producers.

VALUE-ADDING

As mentioned earlier, some of the projects approved at BINA's sites are relocations with the aim of expansion. Some examples of these are the car dealership, warehousing, timber, and furniture industry where bigger land area, proper and better physical infrastructure provided at the industrial sites has given the industries the impetus to offer better and more varied products and services.

COOPERATIVE DEVELOPMENT

Formed on Ist August 1974, Cooperative Development Department's function is to enhance community's unity and the social and economic status of the people. With its subsequent merger with Industrial Unit, Ministry of Industry and Primary Resources to become BINA, the primary function continues as it was but with more emphasis to promote and develop cooperatives to be more competitive and dynamic.

Over the twenty-four years of its establishment, 164 cooperatives have been registered with 14,314 members (as of September 1998). Recent data shows that there are only limited lines of business ventures these cooperatives are involved in, such as transportation, fishery, agriculture, consumer, school and multi-purpose with a net profit gained of about $2 millions Brunei (1998). Having gone through these developments, BINA have restructured its cooperative development section and taken few steps and some of these steps are being undertaken towards enhancing awareness and level of cooperative's expertise and professionalism. Future direction and strategies of cooperatives would be formulated following the national level seminar to be held at the end of this year. This would enable BINA in developing a cooperative development plan; analysing the existing Cooperative Act for any changes, deemed necessary; improve existing administrative assistance; encourage interaction and

For additional analytical, business and investment opportunities information, please contact Global Investment & Business Center, USA at (703) 370-8082. Fax: (703) 370-8083. E-mail: ibpusa3@gmail.com Global Business and Investment Info Databank - www.ibpus.com

cooperation's with private sector; and for cooperatives to venture into other potential business sectors for example manufacturing, marketing, insurance, wholesales, etc.

BOOSTING THE ECONOMY THROUGH PRIVATISATION

Brunei Darussalam continued with efforts to diversify its economy from the oil and gas sector through encouraging industrial development and commerce.

Under the Sixth Five-Year Development Plan, the industry and commerce sector is allocated $550.9 million, which makes up 10 percent of the total budget for development.

Of this, $100 million has been specifically budgeted for industrial promotion and development. The government has consistently aimed its policies at maximising the economic utilisation of its national resources, develop new industries and encourage and nurture the development of Bumiputera leaders in industry and commerce.

In its endeavour to boost economic growth, the authorities are also introducing the concept of privatisation. Besides being a stimulus for economic growth, privatisation is also being seen as a way to remove spending while improving efficiency in public services.

Crucial in the successful implementation of the privatisation programmes are the awareness and understanding of the people in the government, the private sector as well as the public.

Through privatisation, the government could optimize spending in providing services to the public, the Minister of Development Pengiran Dato Haji Ismail said. When opening a two-day seminar on privatisation in June.

It is also required in the expansion of the nation's economic base and in promoting the construction and service sectors, he added.

It would be better to implement the project on a small scale initially so that we can understand better the concept of privatisation, the minister said.

Plan to hold more seminars on privatisation
The two-day seminar was attended by more than 200 people from various ministries, departments and private companies.

In fact, more seminars are planned on privatisation aimed at preparing the business sector ready for the new business situation. The seminars would be organised on a smaller scale involving smaller groups of people. This would ensure that such sessions are more effective in achieving understanding and imparting knowledge to participants about privatisation.

The effort by the Ministry of Development in organising the seminar was seen by some participants as a signal that the ministry in particular is gearing up to privatise some of its service.

The Development Ministry is one of the largest in the government and includes the Public Works Department, the Electrical Services Department, Town and Country Planning, the Survey Department, the Housing Development Department and the Land Department.

The government in its Sixth Five-Year Development Plan due to end this year, has allocated more than $5 billion for national development, more than a billion dollars more than it had spent in the Fifth FDP.

Some 50.9 million dollars for the Sixth Plan was allocated to developing 619 projects starting from 1991 to 1995.

29.3 percent or $1614.6 million of the total budget is for social services that include national housing, education, medical and health, religious affairs and public facilities.

ECONOMIC INDICATORS

GDP at current prices (Million B$) : 8.051.0 (1997 estm.)
Average annual inflation rate: 2.7 percent
Unemployment rate: 4.9 percent

Although Brunei Darussalam is no giant when it comes to landmass, it has been blessed with rich natural resources and a strategic location within the region. The majority of the country is covered in tropical rainforests teeming with exotic flora and fauna. Anxious to promote the conservation of its lush surroundings, eco-tourism has gained importance in the country's economic activities.

Human resources are central to the successful transformation of Brunei Darussalam into a diversified industrial economy. As in most developing nations, there is a shortage of skilled workforce in the country. Therefore, greater emphasis is placed upon education. The main areas of interest in human resources development are managerial and industrial skills, with particular emphasis on entrepreneurial skills as well as vocational and technical training.

Brunei Darussalam's main exports consist of three major commodities - crude oil, petroleum products and liquefied natural gas - sold largely to Japan, the United States and ASEAN countries. The Government's move to promote non-oil and gas activities has been largely successful with figures showing 64% of GDP in 1996 compared to only 24.3% in 1991.

AGRICULTURE

Agriculture plays a major role in the security of food supply. To ensure a continuity of supply of food in the country, the Department of Agriculture promotes domestic agricultural activities and at the same time facilitate import of foods to meet national requirements. The Department has established a new framework to encourage greater efficiency in farm production, revitalise rural communities, foster agro-industrial development and encourage sustainable agriculture to conserve the natural resources. The aim is to accelerate food production in the country to promise a meaningful degree of food security.

Over the past few years, special efforts have been made to encourage greater private participation in food production. Incentives and agricultural services have been provided to attract investment. These facilities have stimulated greater private sector involvement in agriculture.

The cooperation from the farming communities has been overwhelming. We are now completely self-sufficient in table eggs (99.6%), produce 76.1 percent of the poultry meat requirement, satisfy 70 percent of the demand for vegetables, meet 7.7 percent (and increasing) of the tropical fruits requirement, and have expanded food processing and packaging activities. The symbiotic relationship between Department of Agriculture and the farmers has sustained growth in food production.

Today, Department of Agriculture through its dedicated staff and within the operational machinery have, and will continue to provide, the supportive services to develop agriculture and increase local food production. The Department is conscious of the need to protect the environment and conserve the country's natural resources and biodiversity for the benefit of future generations. To meet the changing needs of the producers and consumers, the Department has implemented a coordinated approach in administration, regulation, research and extension.

Future challenges and opportunities are enormous. The Department of Agriculture is constantly adjusting and consolidating to increase efficiency in order to meet the needs of the farming communities and consumers. The goals are to strengthen and direct efforts towards a stable relationship between the Department of Agriculture, importers, farmers and consumers in shaping a strong and efficient agricultural sector. Collectively, these efforts will guarantee the country's security of food supply.

The agro-economy makes up just one per cent of GDP and Brunei has to import 80 per cent of its food needs. Efforts are being made to diversify the economy, away from a heavy dependence on oil and gas towards a more independent agricultural sector. While land, finance and irrigation facilities are available, what is needed is manpower resources.

The first of the Government's four major objectives is to enhance domestic production of padi, vegetables, poultry and livestock. Secondly, to develop the agro-industry as a whole, and thirdly, to produce high value-added products using advanced technological farming methods. Last but not least, Brunei aims to conserve and protect the existing bio-diversity.

Since 1994, Brunei egg farms have successfully supplied the 20 eggs a month that each person in Brunei consumes. The figures for rice, a staple for the Asian country's 283,500 people, however show that the country is able to meet just 2 percent of the 27,500-tonne demand a year.

Almost all of its beef are imported. Brunei brings in live cattle, mostly from Australia, where the Sultanate has a 579,000-hectare ranch in Willeroo, and substantially from Malaysia and New Zealand. Frozen and chilled beef are imported from all over the world.

Local production of chicken, a favorite meat as much for its taste as for its reputation as a healthier, lower-cholesterol white meat, has made great strides. About 28 percent of the chicken sold in Brunei markets is local produce. To supplement the 17,400 tones of chicken meat the country consumes annually, a proportion of Brunei hens are grown from imported day-old chicks.

The growing concern for a healthier way of life also tends towards including more vegetables in the Bruneian diet. Brunei has done well to encourage this trend by ensuring that more than half of the vegetables prepared in kitchens here are locally grown, with the other 46 percent imported mostly from Sabah and Sarawak, particularly from Limbang, Miri and Lawas.

In Brunei, you get a good variety of both tropical and temperate climate fruits, though only a small proportion of what you eat here are locally grown. A hefty 93 percent of it is bought from neigboring countries, mostly from Thailand.

Efforts are being made to collect specimens of local fruit trees and to develop small plantations as well as to produce seedlings which will subsequently support the development of large-scale, less

For additional analytical, business and investment opportunities information, please contact Global Investment & Business Center, USA at (703) 370-8082. Fax: (703) 370-8083. E-mail: ibpusa3@gmail.com Global Business and Investment Info Databank - www.ibpus.com

labor-intensive mechanized fruit farms. Areas in the Tutong district have been singled as ideal for planting orchards.

The government is trying to stimulate greater interest in the agriculture industry through the establishment of model farms, providing training, advice and support.

Existing infrastructure and facilities are being upgraded in rural areas. As the high rainfall, temperature and humidity conditions are not conducive to manual labor, localized farming may be encouraged with sophisticated machinery and equipment,

With agriculture playing a major role in the security of food supply, the Department of Agriculture has actively been promoting domestic agricultural activities while facilitating import of various foods to meet national requirements.

Over the past few years, special efforts have been made to encourage greater private sector participation in the production of food. Incentives and agricultural services have been provided to attract investment. These efforts have successfully stimulated an increase in private sector involvement in agriculture.

AGRICULTURE & LIVESTOCK
The cooperation from the farming communities has been overwhelming. The Department is now completely self-sufficient in table eggs (99.6%). They produce 76.1% of the poultry meat requirement, satisfy 70% of the demand for vegetables, meet 7.7% (and increasing) of the tropical fruits requirement, and has expanded food processing and packaging activities. The symbiotic relationship between the Department of Agriculture and farmers has sustained growth in food production.

RICE
Various efforts have been made by the government to encourage rice production during the last decade and the yield per acre has increased due to the introduction of better agricultural methods.

Approximately 290 tonnes or 1% of the nation's rice needs are produced locally from 613 hectares of rice fields scattered around the country.

As a first step towards the attainment of self-sufficiency in rice, the Government launched an experimental large scale mechanised rice planting project at Kampong Wasan in 1978. Covering an area of 400 hectares, the project was a joint undertaking between the Agriculture Department and the Public Works Department.

The responsibility of the Public Works Department was to provide the required infrastructure, clear the land and give other basic provisions. The responsibility of the Agriculture Department was to plant, maintain, harvest and process. The aim was to plant paddy twice a year, from April to September and from October to March.

VEGETABLES
Locally grown vegetables constitute about 6,700 tonnes or just over 65% of the country's needs. With more people taking up vegetable farming, the amount is increasing gradually.

Vegetable production in Brunei Darussalam has progressed well with the entry of commercial operators. Much of the tropical leafy vegetables are now produced locally.

For additional analytical, business and investment opportunities information,
please contact Global Investment & Business Center, USA
at (703) 370-8082. Fax: (703) 370-8083. E-mail: ibpusa3@gmail.com
Global Business and Investment Info Databank - www.ibpus.com

The Department of Agriculture is encouraging the development of high technology protected cultivation to produce quality pesticide-free vegetative crops of high market value to complement the production from conventional farms.

Brunei Darussalam is still dependent on imports to satisfy demand for temperate vegetables, fruit vegetables, roots and tubers. Most of these vegetables can be produced locally.

The local consumption for tropical and temperate vegetables recorded during the year 2001 was 17,131.1 metric tonnes. According to the statistics, 52.1% was produced locally.

FRUITS

Fruit farming is largely performed on a small scale. There is a vast range of locally produced tropical fruits that meet about 11% of the domestic requirement of more than 14,000 tonnes.

In 1975, the Agriculture Department initiated a fruit-farming scheme to encourage fruit cultivation in the country. In an effort to increase the production of local fruits, the Government through the agricultural stations in Batang Mitus, Tanah Jambu and Lumapas, planted seedlings of various fruit trees.

Orchards and backyard gardens produce a wide range of seasonal and non-seasonal tropical fruits. Traditional production systems produce non-seasonal fruits such as bananas, papayas, pineapples, watermelons, and seasonal fruits namely, durian, chempedak, tarap, rambutan, langsat, belunu, asam aur aur, and membangan to meet the domestic demand for fruits.

Many other types of indigenous fruits, some of which are not commonly found in other parts of Southeast Asia, are also supplied by these traditional production systems.

Production is insufficient to meet local demand and large quantities of both tropical and temperate fruits are imported annually. The total consumption for tropical and temperate fruits in the year 2001 was estimated at 23,083.2 metric tonnes. Only 17.9% were produced locally, according to the provided statistics.

LIVESTOCK

The country produces about 1,000 heads of cattle and buffaloes for the market annually, making up about 6% of its own beef consumption. The Government assists local stock farmers with calves, machinery, feed, seedlings, fertilisers and veterinary care.

The country requires 3,000 to 5,000 tonnes of meat annually, with per capita consumption of between nine and 17 kg. To meet this demand, the government imports an average of between 4,000 and 7,000 heads of live cattle from its Willeroo Ranch in Northern Australia.

Another importer of slaughter cattle (of various breeds, including Angus and Brahman Cross) from Australia is PDS Abattoir. PDS Abattoir is a local company that owns an international standard abattoir in Tutong, specialising in the production of chilled and frozen western cuts.

Meanwhile, local fresh milk production contributes about 199 thousand litres annually.

Research has been carried out to ascertain the best possible way to increase buffalo population. Towards this end, the Agriculture Department has launched a research project covering 4,000 hectares in the Batang Mitus area in the Tutong District. So far, over 200 hectares have already been initiated. The farm's main aim will be to assess local and imported stock towards producing highbred buffaloes for commercial purposes.

For additional analytical, business and investment opportunities information, please contact Global Investment & Business Center, USA at (703) 370-8082. Fax: (703) 370-8083. E-mail: ibpusa3@gmail.com Global Business and Investment Info Databank - www.ibpus.com

Local beef, which is mainly from cattle and buffaloes, is capable of supplying 4% (5,206.75 metric tonnes) of the total beef requirement in the year 2001. 92.1% of the total beef requirement comes from the importation of live animals (18,742 heads or an equivalent to 4,796.31 metric tonnes) and frozen and chilled beef amounting to 203.39 metric tonnes.

Meanwhile, a total of 2,449 heads of goats have been slaughtered and this is equivalent to 42.75 metric tonnes of mutton. Out of the total number of slaughtered goats, 8.7 per cent (331 heads or 3.72 metric tonnes) are locally produced while the rest are imported from Australia.

Goats are popularly consumed only by the ethnic groups and races such as Indians, Nepalese, Gurkhas, Malays and occasionally Chinese. The demand for goats tends to be higher during the Islamic festive months of Aidil-Fitri, Aidil-Adha and Ramadhan.

FISHERIES
Fisheries has been identified as one of the sectors that can contribute towards economic diversification.

The Fisheries Industry comprises three sectors: capture industry, aquaculture industry and processing industry. The estimate is that together, they will contribute at least B$200 million per year to the Gross Domestic Product (GDP) by 2003. The capture industry is estimated to contribute at least B$112 million, aquaculture B$71 million and processing at least B$17 million to the GDP.

Along with traditional fishing, marine fish is the principal source of protein for the people of Brunei Darussalam. The per capita fish consumption is one of the highest in the region at around 45 kilogrammes per year.

CAPTURE INDUSTRY
With an estimated population of about 344,500, the total annual consumption of fish is estimated to be around 15,500 metric tonnes. However, with only about 925 full-time fishermen, Brunei Darussalam still has to import about 50% of its fish requirement to supplement the local production.

The industry, however, is developing especially after the declaration of the 200 nautical miles Brunei Fishery Limits. There has also been a change in policy that allows joint ventures.

The Government, wanting to obtain maximum economic gains while ensuring the sustainability of the resources, is only allowing exploitation of up to the "maximum economic yield" (MEY), which is taken to be 20% below the usually used "maximum sustainable yield" (MSY) level. In this regard, the surveyed fishing areas of Brunei Darussalam have about 21,300 metric tonnes of fish at MEY: Demersal resources - 12,500 metric tonnes and Pelagic resources - 8,800 metric tonnes.

In addition, Brunei Darussalam is also found to be in the migration path of tuna resources. Their volume will be surveyed in the near future.

At the same time, there are large resources associated with the numerous offshore oil-rigs, purposely-sunk tyres, man-made concrete reefs and old oil-rigs that act as artificial reefs. With appropriate gear and technology, these resources can be exploited.

AQUACULTURE
The aquaculture industry in Brunei Darussalam, although in its infancy compared to other countries in the region, is developing quite fast. The high demand for aquaculture products and conducive physical conditions such as unpolluted waterways, the absence of typhoons and floods have made aquaculture a very promising industry.

The major activities in the aquaculture industry are the cage culture of marine fish and the pond culture of marine shrimp. Development of technology on seed production and culture of other species that are of high commercial value are one of the priorities of the Department of Fisheries.

It is anticipated that the steady increase of population will increase existing demand. With the current liberalisation of trade, opportunities for export are there, even though as it is, the local demand and market price in itself have already made the fisheries industry attractive.

The Government, through the Fisheries Department, has therefore been actively promoting suitable foreign involvement, either in the form of joint partnership or other forms of strategic alliances, aimed at developing the fisheries sector towards a competitive, efficient and commercially lucrative venture.

FORESTRY

Forests, Brunei's most permanent asset, cover about 81 percent of the total land area of 5,765 sq km. They grow in a diverse mix of mangrove, peat, swamp, heath, dipterocarp and montane. Primary forest makes up 58 percent of the land. The Department of Forestry, in line with the country's policy of continuous conservation, has marked out plans to sustain the forests as well as programs for environmental and industrial forestry.

The former covers the management of protected forests, conservation, recreational and national parks, while the latter involves guidelines for the development and management of forest products as well as their processing and consumption.

Logging is strictly controlled in a bid to nurture a stable environment, unlike countries which have severely depleted their forests. Brunei has escaped this fate in some measure because the availability of revenue from its hydrocarbon deposits allows it to exercise the freedom of refraining from exploiting the land for timber and other commercial uses.

Restricted timber production, destined only for local consumption, has been reduced to around 100,000 cubic meters per annum from the former 200,000 cubic meters limit. Timber extraction for export is strictly prohibited.

Within the framework of the Forest Conservation Policy, efforts to reforest earmarked areas were drawn up and a sum of $26 million was allocated in the sixth Plan. Up to the date of publication, 700 of the 30,000 hectares earmarked over the next 30 years have been cultivated. In time, about 1,000 hectares will be reforested every year.

There are 11 forest reserves managed by the department. Forestry projects include the building of biodiversity conservation centers, establishing facilities and sites for nurseries, fields for forest trees and commercial rattan and bamboo.

In the Ex-Situ Forest Conservation center in Sungai Lumut, efforts focus on enriching the plants in the Andulau Forest Reserve, which has seen almost 50 years of logging.

TRADITIONAL FOREST PRODUCTS

Aside from timber, the forests have also been the source of traditional products. In the early days, latex from jelutong trees was extracted and exported. It was used in the manufacture of chewing gum. Cutch used to be harvested from the bark of bakau trees in the mangroves; this was used primarily for leather tanning. Firewood and charcoal are to this day still derived from the mangroves. And even at the present time, wild animals, rattan, bamboo, leaves, fibers, bark, fruits, and a host of other materials are gathered from the forest. These are utilised for food, medicine, building houses, and related domestic and commercial applications.

For food, the shoots of bamboo (rabong), rattan (ombut), fern (paku and lamiding), and the fruit of petai (Parkia javanica) are widely popular as vegetable. The fruits of terap (Artocarpus odoratissimus), kembayau (Dacryodes spp.), durian (Durio spp.), etc. are also local favourites. Moreover, assorted materials collected from the forests are fashioned into furniture, handicraft, boats, and other traditional goods.

Another major commodity gathered from the forest are medicinal plants and related materials. These are of great importance in the lives of the local people, particularly those in rural areas. Traditional herbal medicine and native healing methods have of late, gained growing interest in global scene. Biotechnology and bioengineering have given rise to entirely new industries based on tropical biodiversity. Thus, in this context, the natural forests of the country play increasingly valuable conservation and socio-economic roles in national development.

COMMERCIAL TIMBER

There are at least 48 timber or species groups in the country which are of known commercial value. These are classified in accordance with conventions adopted by most Southeast Asian countries. Only one softwood species, tolong or bindang (Agathis borneensis), is represented and it occurs in higher elevations as well as on sand terraces in lowland peat swamps. It is a highly regarded decorative and fancy wood, particularly when used as paneling and interior finishing.

The hardwoods, on the other hand, are categorized into three groups, based on wood density and natural strength and durability. The first group consists of the heavy hardwoods, which have air-dry densities of over 880 kg. per cubic meter, and which are inherently durable. Examples are the selangan batu (heavy Shorea species) and resak (Cotylelobium spp.), which are used for key structural purposes. Shingles of belian (Eusideroxylon zwageri) had been traditionally used for house roofing, and it was not uncommon for the wood to last 50 or 60 years.

Second category is composed of the medium heavy hardwoods, with densities of 650-880 kg. per cubic meter, strong but which are not naturally durable. These include the kapur (Dryobalanops spp.), keruing (Dipterocarpus spp.), and kempas (Koompassia malaccensis). For places in h wood deterioration is not a problem these timbers can be used as structural material. Otherwise, their durability may be significantly lengthened preservative treatment.

The light hardwoods constitute the third group. These have densities of less 650 kg. per cubic meter, and are used mainly for general purposes. Among the species in this group are the red meranti (Shorea spp.), nyatoh (Sapotaceae species), ramin (Gonystylus spp.), medang (Lauraceae species), and others.

OIL & GAS

The oil and gas industry remains the fundamental sector in Brunei's economy and it continues to play a dominant role even as the nation strives to diversify into non-oil industrialization.

The government's policy, initiated in 1988, is to conserve this natural resource by reducing production of crude oil to around 150,000 barrels per day (b/d).

For additional analytical, business and investment opportunities information, please contact Global Investment & Business Center, USA at (703) 370-8082. Fax: (703) 370-8083. E-mail: ibpusa3@gmail.com Global Business and Investment Info Databank - www.ibpus.com

At the same time, the search for new reserves and for alternative sources of energy is being intensified.

Brunei Shell Petroleum Sendirian Berhad (BSP) announced a major gas discovery in July 1995 at Selangkir-1 well, which is about 12 kilometers west of the Champion Field.

BSP has seven offshore oil fields, including Champion. The others are Southwest Ampa, Fairley, Fairley-Baram (which is shared with Malaysia), Magpie, Gannet and Iron Duke -BSP's newest field which came on stream in 1992. Two more fields are situated onshore.

The Brunei Government is an equal partner with the Royal Dutch Shell Company. Besides Shell, another active concession holder is Jasra-Elf.

Based in Brunei Darussalam since 1986, the Jasra-Elf Joint Venture has been actively exploring for hydrocarbons offshore and has made some discoveries, in particular in the Maharaja Lela Field (Block B).

Having confirmed technically that there is a significant amount of oil and gas reserves in this field, the Joint Venture is presently concentrating its efforts towards the development and production of these reserves in the most efficient and optimized way.

The country's production of oil reached a peak of 250,000 b/d 1979 but in the Eighties, a ceiling of about 150,000 b/d was introduced. In 1991, production went up to 162,000 b/d, rising to 180,000 b/d in 1992 and falling slightly to 174,000 b/d in 1993.

At the current rate of extraction, it is estimated that the country's oil reserve would run out in about 27 years' time.

Some 40 per cent of the country's reserves are found in the Champion Field, which is situated in 30 meters of water about 70 km north-east of Seria. This field produces more than 50,000 b/d.

The oldest field is Southwest Ampa, 13 kilometers off Kuala Belait. It holds more than half of Brunei's total gas reserves and the gas production accounts for 60 per cent of the country's total output.

The onshore oilfield in Seria, which is the country's first oil well drilled in 1929, still produces around 10,000 b/d used mainly for domestic consumption. On the domestic market, unleaded petrol was introduced in 1992.

The main foreign markets for Brunei's crude oil are Thailand, Singapore, the Philippines, Australia, China, Japan, South Korea, Taiwan and the United States of America.

The contribution of crude oil to the country's Gross Domestic Product has seen a decline from 88 per cent in 1974 to 58 per cent in 1990. In terms of employment, the oil and gas sector's share of the total labor force was only 5 per cent in 1990.

This means it has the highest value-added ratio per worker and labor productivity remains highest among all sectors while its workers are among the highest paid in the country.

Brunei is the world's fourth largest producer of liquefied natural gas (LNG). The current gas production is approximately 27 million cubic meters per day, and 90 per cent of it is exported to Japan, namely the Tokyo Electric, Tokyo Gas and Osaka Gas Companies.

For additional analytical, business and investment opportunities information,
please contact Global Investment & Business Center, USA
at (703) 370-8082. Fax: (703) 370-8083. E-mail: ibpusa3@gmail.com
Global Business and Investment Info Databank - www.ibpus.com

The Japanese companies and Brunei Coldgas of Brunei LNG signed a further 20-year contract in 1993. The new contract is believed to have raised the quantity and price of gas.

The Brunei Liquefied Natural Gas plant in Lumut, one of the largest in the world, was upgraded and expanded at a cost of around B$100 million in 1993.

The LNG from the plant is transported to Japan by a fleet of seven specially-designed 100,000-tonne tankers with a capacity of 73,000 cubic meters of LNG each. The sale of LNG has grown to be as important a revenue earner as oil exports.

The domestic market takes up only 2 per cent of the LNG produced.

At the current rate of production, the proven reserves of natural gas is estimated to last another 40 years.

However, the discoveries of new gas fields and the possibility of more finds will enable Brunei to benefit from the growing demand for LNG in Asia, which is needed primarily for power generation.

Despite the uncertainty that surrounds the global oil market, the hydrocarbon industry looks set to continue to be the beacon of Brunei's economy. The Brunei Petrochemical Industry Master Plan, completed in May 2001, has identified a number of potential petrochemical industries - both upstream and downstream - for development over the next decades.

Brunei has been described as "the next epicenter of deepwater activity in Asia." Deepwater exploration for oil and gas is going on strong in Brunei, with a number of offshore acreages awarded to major prospectors in the industry.
In 1982, Brunei made legal claims to its EEZ, allowing the Sultanate to take measures to tap the wealth potential of its offshore areas. But Brunei has been prospecting offshore for oil since the 1960s. The first offshore discovery was made in 1963, at the South West Ampa Offshore Field.

DEEPWATER DRILLING
Deepwater drilling allows:
1. for the full realisation of the country's potential oil and gas reserves
2. for the tapping of mature fields to their full potential, with the advent of new technologies
3. for the rejuvenation of existing fields and infrastructures
Deepwater prospecting in Brunei takes place in blocks located some 200 kilometres off the country's coastline, but still within its EEZ. Drilling would be conducted into waters between 1.5 to 2.5 kilometres deep.

Brunei is fortunate in that the waters of the South China Sea where the prospecting takes place is rather calm, posing very little or no threat at all to the safety of drilling rigs. Ultra deepwater drilling is, however, relatively new to Brunei. Thus far, only two ultra deepwater blocks - of 10,000 square kilometers each - had been awarded to drilling consortia, consisting of major players in the global oil and gas industry.

TotalFinaElf owns 60% of the consortium that operates in Block J, followed by BHP Billiton with 25% and Amerada Hess with 15%. The Block K group, meanwhile, consists of Shell (50%), Conoco (25%) and Mitsubishi (25%).

For additional analytical, business and investment opportunities information, please contact Global Investment & Business Center, USA at (703) 370-8082. Fax: (703) 370-8083. E-mail: ibpusa3@gmail.com Global Business and Investment Info Databank - www.ibpus.com

An average of 50 producer and injection wells are anticipated for each drilling field, which should result in a massive drilling activity in the next 10 to15 years, involving a very high demand for specialised technology and engineering services.

It is hoped that deepwater-drilling endeavours in Brunei would also result in a transfer of new technology and skills to benefit locals. These activities are also expected to stimulate business activities in support services and create new job opportunities, as well as increase the number of local and international joint venture opportunities.

THE FUTURE OF OIL

Economic and social development in Asia over the next decades will fuel the need for power supply, vis-a-vis oil and gas, to drive generators. Worldwide demand for oil is expected to increase some 60% in the next 25 years, with an "economically buoyant" Asia to lead the rise, said industry experts during the OSEA 2002 oil and gas conference in Singapore in October 2002.

"Energy consumption continues to grow especially in the Asia-Pacific region," an industry captain said. "This growing trend shows a greater increasing demand for gas to be used for power generation and this will continue to fuel the development of offshore oil fields."

Rising demand for oil and gas will drive the sector in the medium and long term, especially in the "increasingly popular" field of deep-sea exploration for natural gas deposits, experts said.

By 2020, Asia will be the largest net importer of oil, "surpassing Europe and North America," said Singapore's Minister of State for Foreign Affairs and Trade, Raymond Lim at the conference. The demand for gas is projected to exceed the demand for oil as well by 2020.

All these bode well for the Brunei hydrocarbons industry, as it endeavours to tap its vast offshore oil and gas potential. The move to explore the deep waters of Brunei presents both risks and opportunities, wrote the Managing Director of TotalFinaElf John Perry in the magazine 'Asia Inc'.

"In their location and required technology, the deep water permits are literally at the frontier of exploration and production activities," he added. "Developing oil and gas fields in 2,000 metres of water is no easy business. It carries significant risk and huge costs, perhaps US$3-4 billion to develop a commercial discovery.

"Yet, the potential is there to succeed."

Success, he said, will take not just the form of a revenue stream for His Majesty's Government, but will also provide a "stable economic base, founded on a global commodity, to enable Brunei's economy to diversify beyond the oil and gas sector."

But the country is not going just upstream with its deepwater ventures. The afore-mentioned Petrochemical Industry Master Plan also has a number of downstream industries that could be developed to complement the new drilling activities in Brunei. For instance, the Plan mentioned methane-based industries like the production of ammonia, urea and methanol from hydrocarbon derivatives; olefins and aromatic derivatives from naphtha crackers, "with the possible integration with a refinery" and energy-intensive activities like aluminium smelting.

DOWNSTREAM ACTIVITIES

Indeed, the Government has set aside two sites for use of such downstream industries. The 1,000sq km Pulau Muara Besar, located just across the Muara deepwater port, will be used for the development of integrated petrochemical projects in the mid-term. In addition, the 230 hectare Sungai Liang site is "readily available for development", complete with existing gas pipelines to the nearby Lumut BLNG plant, as well as the TFE onshore gas processing plant.

The Sungai Liang site is given "priority" for immediate development, especially for stand-alone projects.

The Government agency that oversees the oil and gas industry in Brunei is PetroleumBRUNEI. It was formed in 2001 to:
1. strengthen and to push, and to jointly spearhead the development of the local petroleum industry
2. play a more active role in the exploration and development of the petroleum industry
3. accelerate economic development based on the domestic petroleum industry

Still, "gas is the energy of the future," Perry wrote. The GASEX gathering in May 2002 - a "quality event" which attracted "quality delegates" - was an indication of the high regard Brunei is held in the gas industry.

The Minister of Industry and Primary Resources, Pehin Dato Hj Abd Rahman, in his capacity as chairman of the Brunei Oil and Gas Authority (BOGA), in 2001 said: "The Government of His Majesty continues to place a great importance on the long-term sale of LNG in generating revenue, while at the same time strengthening efforts in diversifying its economy from non-renewable resources.

"Having said that, the government has also ensured that sufficient gas will be made available to fulfil the nation's energy requirements well into the next millennium."

BRUNEI DARUSSALAM INTERNATIONAL FINANCIAL CENTRE

The Sultanate of Brunei Darussalam ('the Abode of Peace") is situated on the north-west coast of the island of Borneo, at 5 degrees North of the equator. The total area of 5,769 square kilometers borders Sarawak in Malaysia, and the South China Sea.

The Sultanate is the geographical hub of Asia and flying time to Hong Kong, Peoples Republic of China, Taiwan, Bangkok, Jakarta, Kuala Lumpur, Manila and Singapore is between 1 ½ and 3 hours. Royal Brunei Airlines, the modern and well-equipped national carrier has daily direct flights to many centers, including Singapore, China, the Gulf, the Middle East, Europe, Perth, Brisbane, and London. Malaysian Airlines, Garuda, Singapore Airlines and Royal Thai Airways operate regular routes. Brunei's Time zone of GMT +8 coincides with Asia and Southeast Asia, with large time-windows to Australasia.

CENTURIES-LONG POLITICAL STABILITY

Brunei Darussalam has an enviable centuries-long history of political stability under its monarchial system of government. This is further strengthened under the able, strong and visionary leadership of His Majesty Sultan Haji Hassanal Bolkiah Mui'zaddien Waddaulah and his late father, Sultan Haji Omar Ali Saifuddien Saadul Khairi Waddien. Brunei Darussalam is member of the major international and regional organizations, notably the United Nations and ASEAN, providing added security to the country.

CONTINUOUS ECONOMIC PROSPERITIES

Political stability and the excellent vision of His Majesty the Sultan and Yang DiPertuan have made it possible for Brunei Darussalam to achieve sustainable economic prosperity and stability which has benefited the whole population. Brunei Darussalam continues to register reasonable growth despite the turmoil of oil price and financial crisis in Asia. Central to this economic achievement is the government's Five-Year National Development Plans, which provide strategic guidelines and direction for the economy. The country continues to pursue an economic diversification policy away from the traditional reliance on the oil and gas sector in order to enjoy rapid growth like that of its partners in the Asia-Pacific region.

INFRASTRUCTURE

The government is totally committed to maintaining a sophisticated telecommunication system. There are two earth satellite stations providing direct telephone, telex and facsimile links to all parts of the world. Several systems currently in operation include digital telephone exchange, fibre-optic cable links with Singapore and Manila, exchanges for access to high-speed computer bases overseas, cellular mobile telephone and paging systems.

Through its National Development Plans, Brunei Darussalam continues to upgrade other communication facilities. Brunei International Airport is currently undergoing major upgrading work to cater substantial increase in both passengers and cargo traffic. There are two seaports that offer direct shipping to numerous destinations. More than 2,000-kilometre of modern and extensive road networks serving the entire country. An excellent and wide range of motor vehicles is provided, whether for purchase or hire. The country enjoys one of the highest ratios of vehicles per head of population in the world. Fuels sell at very economic rates.

EDUCATED POPULATION

The population of Brunei Darussalam is around 350,000 English is widely spoken and is used in business. The University of Brunei Darussalam and other higher educational institutes in the country release hundreds of graduates every year. There is also a significant resource of Bruneians who have taken good tertiary qualifications in various aspects of international business (mostly in the U.K.), and the IFC will offer these professionals rewarding careers in what will be a high class and very busy jurisdiction. The work ethic and commercial standards of the community are refreshing, with an emphasis on the provision of good service at a fair price.

EXPATRIATES AND PROFESSIONALS IN BRUNEI

Brunei Darussalam hosts a large expatriate community involved in the oil and gas and professional services industries. Government's assistance in granting approvals for foreign workers up to and including executive level is experienced and considerable.

HIGH QUALITY HEALTH AND EDUCATION FACILITIES

Both the health and education sectors are established to an extremely high standard at all levels. Indeed the Brunei opportunities and standards n these areas compare more than favorably with the facilities in most Developed Nations.

Expatriate staff always find that excellent in these areas is achieved at very reasonable cost in a manner which takes full advantage of the combination of a healthy lifestyle, quality of teaching staff and facilities which surpass those available "back home". In broader terms, both the environment and the cost of living in Brunei, coupled with zero tax, combine to produce a most attractive lifestyle.

HEALTHY LIFE STYLES

Eco-tourism is growing and great care has been taken with the preservation of extensive rain forest resources. Superb and very convenient facilities enable even the short-term visitor to observe and experience the natural resources of fauna and flora which the country has carefully preserved in a natural state. Similarly, magnificent fishing, diving, sailing, golfing, tennis, riding and other recreational facilities abound.

Alcohol and drug abuse is almost totally absent, and a serene and secure social environment prevails. Brunei maintains tranquil and moderate Islamic traditions, which flow through into its unique capabilities for Islamic financial growth. Fair dealing and avoidance of usury produces a philosophy, which has much in common with English based equitable principles. Religious freedom is guaranteed under the Constitution, and the country's commitment to the rule of law is built on the strong foundations of the inherited systems of English Common Law and the independence of its judiciary.

The climate is tropical and average daytime temperatures range between 26 C and 35 C. Brunei Darussalam has never experienced typhoons, earthquakes or severe flood conditions.

There are hotels to suit all tastes and pockets. Traditional hospitability and quality services reflect the experienced gained by operators in this very busy area of activity. Room occupancy rates are healthy, booking is desirable.

BRUNEI IFC: INTRODUCTION

Brunei has for many years been a significant player in the ASEAN region. Its very strong ties with the United Kingdom, Singapore and regional countries have led to the build-up of considerable commercial activity. The economy has been dominated by the oil and liquefied natural gas industries and Government expenditure patterns. Brunei Darussalam's exports consist of three major commodities, namely: crude oil, petroleum products and liquefied natural gas. Exports are destined mainly for Japan, the United Stated and ASEAN countries. But the country has entered a new phase of development in its drive towards economic diversification and maturity.

Prior to formal establishment of the IFC, Brunei was already a busy commercial centre, as witness the existing active presences in the Banking sector of HSBC, Standard Chartered, Overseas Union Bank, Citibank, Maybank, Baiduri Bank, Tabung Amanah Islam Brunei and Islamic Bank of Brunei Berhad. All the major accounting firms have significant presences, and there are some fifteen law firms.

NATIONAL GOALS

Unlike many IFCs, Brunei has the advantage of already being an affluent society based on the fossil-fuel economy. The country's motives in establishing an IFC regime are therefore more subtle and soci0-economic than simply to generate and income-stream to supplement tourism.

The goals motivating the establishment of the IFC include developing the capacity to –

- Diversify, expand into and grow the value added financial service sector of the economy of Brunei and the Asia Pacific Region (APR).

For additional analytical, business and investment opportunities information,
please contact Global Investment & Business Center, USA
at (703) 370-8082. Fax: (703) 370-8083. E-mail: ibpusa3@gmail.com
Global Business and Investment Info Databank - www.ibpus.com

- Provide a secure, cost-effective, sensibly regulated IFC facility, which will offer a safe harbour for the conduct of significant regional and international business for corporate and private clients.
- Attract overseas professionals to assist in running the IFC to the highest standards.
- Encourage expatriate professionals to become involved in training and development of rewarding opportunities for professionally qualified and trained Bruenians in the International Business Sector.
- Increase returns for the hospitality, transport and amenity industries, including eco-tourism, culminating in an holistic result for the country's economy.
- Position Brunei as an equal partner in the globalisation of financial and commercial activity, and thereby, to generate greater communication with and between other nations.

THE MEANS TO ACHIEVE THESE GOALS

Brunei will deploy its sovereignty, wealth and human resources in a conservative but assertive manner to establish a jurisdictional environment which will be tax-free, and free form over-regulation or "business pollution". Brunei IFC offers a range of international legislation carefully crafted to permit flexible, cost effective capabilities which are right up-to-date. Such capabilities will include the full range of facilities necessary for the efficient conduct of global business. There will be regular liaison with regulatory bodies internationally.

EXCLUSION OF MONEY LAUNDERING A FIRST PRIORITY

As a sovereign nation of high repute (capable, for example of hosting the September 2000 APEC Summit), Brunei is serving notice at the outset that criminal abuses of its financial systems will not be tolerated. The country is taking these steps voluntarily, rather than under pressure. This reflects responsible economic and social attitudes.

The first tranche of legislation enacted for the IFC regime therefore includes Money-Laundering and Proceeds of (serious) Crime measures implemented to international standards. Severe Drug Trafficking legislation has been in place for some time. Moreover, meaningful and enforceable regulation of the Trust, Company Administration, Insurance and Banking industries has been legislated for before these activities commence. At the outset Brunei IFC will in this regard be well prepared.

The initial legislation consists of the anti-crime measures already mentioned and the following:

International Banking Order, 2000 ('IBO')

International Business Companies Order, 2000 (IBCO')

Registered Agents and Trustees Licensing Order, 2000 ('RATLO')

International Trusts Order, 2000 ('ITO')

International Limited Partnerships Order, 2000 ('ILPO')

Insurance, Securities and Mutual fund legislation is expected to be enacted early in the second half of the year 2000.

GENERAL SCHEME – PARALLEL JURISDICTIONS

For additional analytical, business and investment opportunities information,
please contact Global Investment & Business Center, USA
at (703) 370-8082. Fax: (703) 370-8083. E-mail: ibpusa3@gmail.com
Global Business and Investment Info Databank - www.ibpus.com

Accordingly, Brunei will be a "dual jurisdiction", whereby the international legislation offers "offshore" facilities, alongside the usual ranges of "domestic" legislation drawn form the at of England and Wales. The jurisdictional distinction is thus jurisprudential rather than physical.

The judicial system will be common to both domestic and international law. In this regard, Brunei is fortunate in His Majesty's choice of senior and highly respected judges drawn form Commonwealth countries. In a recent judgment, Dato Sir Denys Roberts, KCMG, SPMP, a former Chief Justice of Hong Kong who for some years has held that office in Brunei had occasion to observe. "There has never been any interference by the executive with the judiciary, which has remained staunchly independent..." All members of the (Brunei) Court of Appeal are distinguished Commonwealth Judges. The importance of such a strong and experienced "British/Commonwealth" judiciary in an Asian regional context cannot be overstated. Final civil appeals are to the Privy Council in London.

REGULATORY – THE AUTHORITY

Brunei Darussalam has no central bank and the Ministry of Finance exercises most of those functions. Monetary policy has been determined by linking the Brunei Darussalam's dollar to the Singapore Dollar and there is parity between the two. The Singapore link is seen as a stabilizing influence. Nor are there any exchange controls. Domestic companies are taxed, but there is no personal income tax in Brunei.

The "international" legislation is supervised by "the Authority", a segregated unit of the Ministry of Finance acting through the Financial Institutions Division and the head of supervision (IFC). The Authority comprises a multi-disciplinary unit with appropriate banking, insurance, corporate and trust supervisory skills. It is a one-step Authority in the true sense, with line command passing directly form the Minister of Finance, the Minister responsible for the international legislation.

International Business Companies Order, 2000 (IBCO)

IBCO makes provision for tax-free corporate facilities at highly competitive cost levels. As an affluent State, Brunei is more concerned with attracting a critical mass of good business than with struggling to achieve a fee-based income stream at a high cost to end users. Thus the total Government Fee for company incorporation and year one maintenance is US$500, while renewal fees from year 2 onwards are set at US$400. Again, the private sector is encouraged to match Government's approach charging on a cost-plus basis, and to look beyond establishment to subsequent corporate transactional activity involving Brunei and overseas professionals.

International Business Companies may be:-

- Limited by shares
- Limited by guarantee
- Limited by shares and guarantee
- Of limited duration
- Dedicated Cell companies (akin to the Guernsey/Mauritius and other models more commonly referred to as "Protected" cell companies).
- Created by conversion (akin to continuance), re-domiciled (or discontinued) in Brunei
- Foreign, or overseas companies may register branch operations as Foreign International Companies.

IBCs are incorporated by trust companies subscribing to Memorandum and Articles. A Certificate of Due Diligence must be filed with the constituent documents. This Certificate contains an undertaking by the trust company concerned that the IBC complies with applicable provisions of IBCO and that due diligence in respect of beneficial owners and the source of finding has been conducted, or will be conducted prior to commencement of business. A similar certificate is required at every annual renewal.

IBCO requires the "official" name of an IBC to be in Romanised form. Chinese and Japanese characters or Arabic or Cyrillic script, or other characters, alphabet or script may by arrangement with the Registrar of International Business Companies be adopted in addition. Such alternative names and all documents in a foreign language are required to be presented with a certified translation.

There are simple prospectus provisions relating to invitations to subscribe for share or loan issues. However, an invitation or offer addressed to a restricted circle of persons whereby the invitation is addressed to an identifiable category, group or body of persons to whom it is directly communicated or where such persons are the only persons who may accept the offer and are in possession of sufficient information to be able to make a reasonable evaluation of the invitation or offer are not "invitations to the public". The number of persons to whom the invitation or offer is communicated cannot exceed fifty. Since "person" includes a body corporate, this is seen as liberal.

POWERS OF IBCS

Subject to its Memorandum and Articles, an IBC has, irrespective of corporate benefit, power to perform all acts conducive to its business, and may include in its Memorandum a statement that is objects are to engage in any act not prohibited under the laws of Brunei. In which case such objects are by statute attributed to the company in those terms. Standard Memorandum and Articles for the three classes of limited company are Scheduled and may be adopted in full or as modified. Other than bearer shares, which are prohibited, an IBC may issue the usual wide range of shares and classes of shares, including Dedicated Cell shares, options, warrants or rights to acquire securities of an IBC, including convertible securities.

Powers to purchase, redeem or acquire a company's own shares are contained in IBCO, and provisions facilitating the acquisition and treatment of Treasury shares are made, subject to solvency and creditor-related requirements. Assistance to purchase the shares of an IBC may similarly be provided by it.

Powers to purchase, redeem or acquire a company's own shares are contained in IBCO, and provisions facilitating the acquisition and treatment of Treasury shares are made, subject to solvency and creditor-related requirements. Assistance to purchase the shares of an IBC may similarly be provided by it.

Share capital may be reduced by 75% resolution, subject to solvency and creditor concerns being appropriately addressed. There is a mechanism whereby the Register of International Business Companies may adjudicate on creditor concerns, with power to refer to the Court where necessary.

Directors may be individual or corporate, as may secretaries. A Resident Secretary provided by a Trust Company is mandatory. Audits are optional (except as required under banking, trust company, insurance and dealing licensing provisions).

Filing of charges or a statement of particulars of charge is provided for and where such a filling is not made, the charge may, so far as creating a security against the assets of the company, be void as against a liquidator or creditor. Comprehensive Mergers and Consolidation provisions are prescribed. Including mergers or consolidations will overseas companies. The rights of dissenting members are protected.

Foreign International companies are registered under Part XI, on lodgment through a trust company of the specified constituent documents, certain other information and a certificate of compliance and due diligence. Changes in particulars must be notified in the usual way.

Conversion/continuance occurs where permitted by the former domicile, subject to certain requirements including solvency and registration of (IBCO-compatible) Memorandum and Articles. There is provision for the Court to strike form the Brunei register a company, which continues to exist in another jurisdiction following conversion.

Dedicated Cell Companies ("DCC") are established pursuant to Part XIIA of IBCO, and subject to the prior consent of the Authority, may be initially established or reconstituted as a DCC. A DCC is a single legal person and may establish one or more cells for the purpose of segregating and protecting dedicated assets. The assets are either dedicated assets or general assets, and separate records and protection of dedicated assets by way of segregation and identification must be maintained.

Creditors are restricted in their rights to the cell in respect of which they have made funds available or have a claim.

There is implied in every transaction entered into by a DCC the following terms:-

- That no party may seek to exert any claim against assets attributable to a cell in respect of a liability not attributable to that cell;
- That if any party succeeds to the contrary, he will be liable to the company to repay the value of the benefit;

Further, a person who willfully and without colour of right "attacks" a cell in respect of which he has no rights commits an offence.

A DCC may by a 75% resolution of the company or of the holders of dedicated shares in a cell of a DCC effect of a reduction of capital generally, and without the need for confirmation by the Court)-

(a) where the resolution is passed by the company, in respect of any of the company's cells; or

(b) where the resolution is passed by the holders of dedicated shares, in respect of the cell in which the dedicated shares are held;

Any such reduction of dedicated share capital must comply with the requirements relating to reduction of capital of IBCs generally.

Notice of a proposed resolution authorizing the reduction of dedicated share capital must be given to:-

(a) the DCC (except where the company is itself the applicant);

(b) the receiver liquidator or administrator (if any) of the cell, the Authority, all holders of dedicated shares of the cell, every creditor and such other persons as the Authority may direct.

The name of a DCC must include the expression "Dedicated cell" or "DCC" or a cognate expression approved by the Authority, the memorandum shall state that it is a DCC, and each cell of a DCC shall have its own distinct name or designation.

Disputes as to liability attributable to cells. The Court may make a declaration in respect of the matter in dispute.

A DCC must inform any person with whom it transact that it is a DCC; and identify the cell in respect of which that person is transacting, failing which the directors may incur personal liability. The Court may relieve a director of personal liability if such director satisfies the Court that he ought fairly to be so relieved.

WINDING-UP OF IBCS

Basically, the provisions of Parts V (Winding-up) and VI (Receivers and Managers) of the (domestic) Companies Act (Chapter 39) apply to the winding-up of an IBC as they apply to the winding-up of a domestic company.

Striking off for failure to pay prescribed fees

If an IBC fails to pay a prescribed renewal fee and the failure continues for over two months the Registrar shall initiate striking-off. If an IBC has been struck off the register, the former IBC or a creditor, member or liquidator of it may apply to the Court to have the IBC restored to the register.

Confidentiality

The records of an IBC may only be searched subject to the prior grant of certain consents, except where circumstances, such as criminal activity, are adjudged by the Registrar to have arisen. This applies both to the Registrar's records and those of the IBC held at its registered office.

INTERNATIONAL LIMITED PARTNERSHIPS

An International Limited Partnerships is a partnership which

- Consists of one or more general partners;
- Is formed for any lawful purpose to be carried out;
- Is undertaken in or from within Brunei Darussalam or elsewhere; and
- Is registered in accordance with ILPO;
- Does not carry on business with any person resident in Brunei Darussalam

In an ILP a general partner is personally liable for all the debts and obligations of the ILP but, except in so far as the partnership agreement or ILPO otherwise provides, a limited partner is not so liable. At the time of becoming a limited partner, a limited partner contributes, or undertakes to contribute, a stated amount (or property valued at a stated amount) to the capital of the partnership. Provision for confirmation of value exists.

At least one partner in an ILP shall be either an IBC, a trust corporation or a wholly owned subsidiary thereof or a partnership which is an ILP.

Subject to that, the partners in an ILP shall be resident domiciled, established, incorporated or registered in a country or territory outside Brunei Darussalam.

Every ILP must

- Have a name which includes the words "International Limited Partnership" or the letters "ILP";

- Maintain a registered office in Brunei at the registered office of a trust corporation and
- Keep at this registered office such accounts and records as are sufficient to show and explain the ILPs transactions and to disclose with treasonable accuracy, at any time, the financial position of the ILP at that time.

Except as permitted or required under ILPO, a limited partner shall not take part in the conduct of the business of an ILP, and all letters, contracts, deeds, instruments or documents whatsoever must be entered into by the general partner on behalf of the ILP. If a limited partner, other than a trust corporation acting in such capacity for the purposes of ILPO, takes part in the conduct of the business of the ILP in its dealings with persons who are not partners, then in the event of the insolvency of the ILP, the limited partner many be liable as though he or she were a general partner.

ILPs are registered through a trust corporation by the payment of a year one fee of US$500. The annual renewal fee thereafter is US$400. A statement must be filed by the trust company concerned setting out:

(a) the name of the ILP;

(b) the general nature of the business of the ILP;

(c) the address in Brunei Darussalam of the ILP;

(d) the term, if any, for which the ILP is entered into or, if it is for unlimited duration, the date of its commencement and that the ILP is without limit of time; and

(e) the full name and address of the general partner or, if there is more than one, of each general partner.

A certificate of due diligence and a certificate signed by the trust corporation certifying that the requirements of the Order in respect of registration have been compiled with must also be filed. Until the date indicated on the certificate of registration (issued by the Registrar) of an ILP no limited partner in the ILP to which the certificate relates has limited liability.

The ILP Registrar maintains a record of each ILP and on payment of the prescribed fee any partner, director however described or liquidator of the ILP, the Authority or the trust corporation for the time being of the ILP or any other person with the written permission of such director, partner or liquidator or who can demonstrate to the Authority or the ILP Registrar that he has a cogent reason for doing so.

If at any time any change is made in any of the matters previously specified and filed, an ILP must file, within sixty days of the change, a statement in the prescribed form including, where a new partner is to be admitted an appropriate re-affirmation of the certificate of due diligence, specifying the nature of the change,. A brief annual return is required to be filed each year. Registration of an ILP may be revoked by the ILP Registrar acting on the advice of the Authority on the grounds set out in ILPO. However, where the ILP Registrar intends to revoke the legislation of an ILP he must give notice of his intention to the registered office of the ILP and allow a reasonable opportunity to show cause why the registration of partnership should not be revoked.

THE INTERNATIONAL BANKING ORDER

The International Banking Order ("IBO") governs the provision of international banking services to non-residents. While encompassing the traditional definition of banking by reference to taking of

For additional analytical, business and investment opportunities information,
please contact Global Investment & Business Center, USA
at (703) 370-8082. Fax: (703) 370-8083. E-mail: ibpusa3@gmail.com
Global Business and Investment Info Databank - www.ibpus.com

deposits, the IBO recognizes that this is not the daily concern of a sophisticated International Bank. The IBO expands its horizons in line with the banking industry's modern development and trends.

Four classes of license are provided for:

- A full international license for the purpose of carrying on international banking business generally;
- An international investment banking license for the purpose of carrying on international Islamic banking business, granted in respect of full, investment or restricted activities.
- A restricted international banking license for the purpose of carrying on international banking business subject to the restriction that the licensee may not offer, conduct or provide such business except to or for persons name d or described in an undertaking embodied in the application for the license.

"International banking business" includes the taking of deposits from the (non-resident) public, the granting of credits, the issue of credit cards and money collections and transmissions. /nut the definition is expanded to embrace foreign exchange transactions, the issue of guarantees., trade finance, development finance and sectoral credits, consumer credit, investment banking, Islamic banking business., broking and risk management services whether conducted by conventional practices or using Internet or other electronic technology and includes electronic banking.

"International investment banking business" includes –

- providing consultancy and advisory services relating to corporate and investment matters, industrial strategy and related questions, and advice and services relating to mergers and restructuring and acquisitions, or making and managing investments on behalf of any person;
- providing credit facilities including guarantees and commitments;
- participation in stock, or share issues and the provision of services relating thereto: or
- the arrangement and underwriting of debt and equity issues.

"International Islamic banking business" is banking business whose aims and operations do not involve any element which is not approved by the Islamic Religion. Provision for Shari'ah Law to override a conflicting provision in the IBO is made, subject to good banking practice, and there is a requirement of the appointment of a Shari'ah Council. The restriction to local ownership which applies under the domestic Islamic Banking Act does not apply to the international regime.

The IBO imposes strict standards of confidentiality on both the Authority and the banks and their officers. In line with what are becoming expected international standards, mutual assistance between designated supervisory authorities exercising similar powers to the Authority in other jurisdictions is permitted. This is, subject to continuing confidentiality and guarantees of reciprocal assistance.

In respect of banking supervisory actions, the Authority will require –

- To receive audited annual accounts,
- To conduct on-site inspection
- To be given notice of significant charges in ownership and key personnel (which respectively attract consent procedures for Brunei headquartered banks), and
- To investigate and take action in appropriate cases of criminal or unlawful acts and when the circumstances of the bank justify intervention.

And is empowered to apply to the High Court for such assistance as may be necessary in appropriate cases to avert criminal or solvency / liquidity matters which are beyond the mutually-exercised corrective measures available to the bank and the Authority acting in concert.

Those who conduct activities included in the services also offered by the banks will be exempted from the IBO provisions. But companies which conduct banking activities without any regulatory controls, consents or licenses will not be permitted to do so in Brunei, except by means of full disclosure and Ministerial exemption in exceptional cases, on specified terms.

Brunei expects and looks to attract the presence of good quality institutions whose credentials are based on quality and activity rather than size alone.

International banks will pay no tax, and neither will their staff, customers or products.

Annual Fees:	U.S.$	
Full license	$50,000	
Investment	$35,000	
Islamic (Full, Investment)		$50,000
Restricted	$25,000	

INTERNATIONAL TRUSTS ORDER

The Order applies only to an international trust ("IT") as defined. An It must be in writing, (including declarations and wills), settled by a non-resident of Brunei, declared in its terms to be an international trusts (on creation or migration to Brunei), and at least one trustee must be a licensed under The Registered Agents and Trustees Licensing Order, 2000 (RATLO) or an authorized wholly-owned subsidiary of a licensee. Generally, only non-residents may be beneficiaries when an IT is first established. The retention of certain powers (specified in the ITO) by the settler will not invalidate an IT. Such powers are not, however, deemed to exist in the absence of specific provision in the trust instrument.

There are wide powers of investment, with an ability for trustees to seek "proper advice" as defined. Having done so, a trustee will not be liable for acts taken pursuant to such advice.

There are powers to appoint agents and to delegate. Trustees may charge, and similar provisions appear for enforcers and protectors. Powers of maintenance and advancement are wide, spendthrift and protective trusts are recognized.

Arrangements for appointment or change of trustees follow generally accepted lines. The Court is given wide powers to interpret, assist and amend. Hearings may be held in camera. Trustees may pay funds into Court for determination of matters arising in the course of administering the fund, and there is power to apply to the Court for an opinion, advice or a direction relating to trust assets.

Purpose trusts are provided for, whether charitable or non-charitable. Without prejudice to the generality, a trust for the purpose of holding securities or other assets is by statute deemed a purpose trust. The purposes must be reasonable, practicable, not immoral nor contrary to public policy. The trust instrument must state that the trust is to be an authorized purpose trust at creation or on migration to Brunei. Provision must be made for the disposal of surplus assets (although no perpetuity period applies), and an enforcer is required. On completion or impossibility of achieving purposes, further trusts may be activated.

SPECIAL TRUSTS

In Part IX of ITO a power is said to be held on trust if granted or reserved subject to any duty to exercise the power. A trust or power is subject to Part IX and is described as a special trust, if at the creation of the trust or when it first becomes subject to the law of Brunei Darussalam the settler is non-resident and the trust instrument provides that the trust is to be a special trust. The objects of a special trust or power may be persons or purposes or both, the person may be of any number, and the purposes may be of any number of kind, charitable or non-charitable.

The hallmark of a special trust is that a beneficiary does not as such have standing to enforce the trust or any enforceable right to the trust property. The only persons who have standing to enforce a special trust are such persons as are appointed to be its enforcers –

- By the trust instrument; or
- Under the provisions of the trust instrument; or
- By the Court

An enforcer of a special trust has a duty to act responsibly with a view to enforcing the proper execution of the trust, and to consider at appropriate intervals whether and how to exercise his powers and then to act accordingly. A trustee or another enforcer, or any person expressly authoresses by the trust instrument, has standing to being an action against an enforcer to compel him to perform his duties. An enforcer is entitled to necessary rights of access to documents and records. Generally a special trust is not void for uncertainty, and its terms may give to the trustee or any other person power to resolve any uncertainty as to its objects or mode of execution.

If such an uncertainty cannot be resolved as aforesaid, the Court may act to resolve the uncertainty, and insofar as the objects of the trust are uncertain and the general intent of the trust cannot be found form the admissible evidence as a manner of probability, any declare the trust void. If the execution of a special trust is or becomes in whole or in part – impossible or impracticable; or

(a) unlawful or contrary to publish policy; or

(b) obsolete in that, by reason of changed circumstances it fails to achieve the general intent of the special trust,

the trustee must, unless the trust is reformed pursuant to it own terms, apply to the Court to reform the trust cy-pres.

REGISTERED AGENTS AND TRUSTEES LICENSING ORDER, 2000

Brunei has opted for a regulated trust and corporate regime ab initio. The Registered Agents and Trustees Licensing Order ("RATLO") restricts the provision of "international business services" to companies licensed under that Order.

"International business services" includes international companies management business, international partnerships management business and international trust business.

"International companies management business" includes –

acting as registered agent for the incorporation or registration of IBCs and Foreign International Companies ("IFCs") under the International Business Companies Order, 2000 ("IBCO"), the conversion of overseas companies into IBCs, and the merger, consolidation, continuation, renewal, extension of the duration of, or migration of IBCs.

Providing registered offices, share transfer offices or administration offices of the receipt of post or other articles, IBCs and FICs.

Providing or appointing persons to perform the functions of directors, (mandatory) resident, secretary, nominees, preparing, keeping or fillng books, accounts, registers, records, minutes and returns for IBCs and FICs, and other matters relating to corporate administration, including the establishment of IBCs as Dedicated Cell Companies or Limited Life Companies.

All documents to be filed with the Registrar of International Business Companies (and Limited Partnerships) are filed by trusts companies.

Similarly, trust companies must be involved in all International Limited Partnerships (ILP) and "qualifying" trusts – i.e. International Trusts formed pursuant to the ITO and trusts which are established under the laws of other jurisdictions but administered in Brunei.

Trust companies and banks will also be involved in the forthcoming Mutual Fund Order regime, which will govern both domestic and international schemes.

Trusts licenses will be available by way of application to the Authority to institutions, professional groups and independent trusts groups. A comprehensive licensing, process and approval of senior personnel, is involved and ongoing supervision will include the filing of audited accounts of the trust companies (but not their clients) with the Authority. Notifications and approvals of appointments and changes of Key Personnel apply. Minimum capitalization of B$150,000 either paid-up in full or 50% paid-up with the other 50% guaranteed is required. Insurance requirements (but no bond) apply. The Authority's concern is continuing liquidity and sufficiency of working capital, and a 3 year business plan is required with tall applications for licenses under RATLO.

The application fee for a Trust and registered Agent's license is US$2,500 and an Annual License Fee of US$2,000 is imposed.

Trust licensees will, with the approval of the Authority, be permitted to establish wholly-owned subsidiaries (whose operations trust be fully guaranteed by the licensee). Such a subsidiary may be an IBC (as may the licensee itself) and may for the purpose of the licensee's business act as a trustee, nominee, secretary or director in respect of international business services. The aim is to permit accountable flexibility and segregating in, for example, Collective Investment Scheme, Private Trust Company and Special Purpose Vehicle situations, including the commercial deployment of special and purpose trusts.

Trust companies, (including overseas trust companies establishing a branch in Brunei) as well as the entities they administer, will be totally exempt from all tax in respect of Brunei operations. Again, nor will their officers, customers or products be taxed.

This attractive entry-level package for RATLO licensees is intended to encourage suitable local and overseas applicants to seek licenses and to achieve a critical mass of private and corporate "trust" activities in the broader sense. The relatively low cost of living and of a well-educated support staff

For additional analytical, business and investment opportunities information,
please contact Global Investment & Business Center, USA
at (703) 370-8082. Fax: (703) 370-8083. E-mail: ibpusa3@gmail.com
Global Business and Investment Info Databank - www.ibpus.com

pool adds to the appeal. Low fees, however, should not be taken as an indication that the supervisory regime will be any other than through and strictly enforced. It is hoped that participants will follow Government's lead in keeping the cost of their services reasonable. It is a false argument that high class jurisdictions must charge high fees to maintain their reputation and that high fees will discourage criminals. Good corporate vehicles at reasonable cost is the aim.

BUSINESS AND INVESTMENT CLIMATE

Investors will find that Brunei Darussalam offers a favourable and conducive environment for a profitable investment. Some of the key reasons are:-

* Brunei Darussalam is a stable and prosperous country which offers not only excellent infrastructure but also a strategic location within the ASEAN group of countries;

* Brunei Darussalam has no personal income tax, no sales tax, payroll, manufacturing or export tax. Approved foreign investors can also enjoy a company tax holiday of up to 8 years;

* The regulations relating to foreign participation in equity are flexible. In many instances there can be 100 percent foreign ownership;

* There are no difficulties in securing approval for foreign workers, ranging from labourers to managers;

* The costs of utilities are among the lowest in the region;

* The local market, while relatively small, is lucrative and most overseas investors will encounter little or no local competition;

* The living conditions in Brunei Darussalam are among the best and most secure in the region.

* Above all else, His Majesty's Government genuinely welcomes foreign investment in almost any enterprise and will ensure that you receive speedy, efficient and practical assistance with all your enquries.

INFRASTRUCTURE

The country's infrastructure is well developed and ready to cater for the needs of the new and vigorous economic activities under the current economic diversification programme.

The country's two main ports, at Muara and Kuala Belait, offer direct shipping to Hong Kong, Singapore and several other Asian destinations. Muara, the deep-water port, 29 kilometers from the capital, was opened in 1973 and has since been considerably developed. There is 12,542 sq. metres of warehouse space and 6.225 sq. meters in transit sheds. Container yards have been increased in size and a container freight station handles unstuffing operations.

The recently expanded Brunei International Airport at Bandar Seri Begawan included the expansion of both passenger and cargo facilities to meet an expected substantial increase in demand. The new terminal, designed to handle 1.5 million passengers and 50,000 tonnes of cargo a year, is expected to meet demand until the end of the decade.

For additional analytical, business and investment opportunities information, please contact Global Investment & Business Center, USA at (703) 370-8082. Fax: (703) 370-8083. E-mail: ibpusa3@gmail.com Global Business and Investment Info Databank - www.ibpus.com

The 2,000-kilometre road network serving the entire country is being expanded and modernised. A main highway runs the entire length of the country's coastline. It conveniently links Muara, the port entry point at one end, to Belait, the oil-production centre, at the western end of the state.

TELECOMMUNICATIONS

Brunei Darussalam has one of the best telecommunication systems in South-East Asia and has major plans for improving it further. With an estimated population of about 270,000, the rate of telephone availability is currently 1 telephone for every 3 persons. And this is being continually upgraded.

There are two earth satellite stations providing direct telephone, telex and facsimile links to most parts of the world. Several systems currently in operation serving the country include an analogue telephone exchange, fibre-optic cable links with Singapore and Manila, a packet switching exchange for access to high speed computer bases overseas, cellular mobile telephone and paging system. Direct telephone links are available to the remotest parts of the country through microwave and solar-powered telephones.

ECONOMY

Brunei Darussalam's economy is dominated by the oil and liquified natural gas industries and Government expenditure patterns. Brunei Darussalam's exports consist of three major commodities, namely: crude oil, petroleum products and liquified natural gas. Exports are destined mainly for Japan, the United States and ASEAN countries.

The second most important industry is the construction industry. This is directly the result of increased investment by the Government in development and infrastructure projects within the current series of five-year National Development Plans.

Brunei Darussalam has entered a new phase of development in its drive towards economic diversification from dependence on the oil and liquified natural gas-based economy. It is encouraging to note that the contribution from the non-oil and gas-based sector of the economy, as reflected in the contribution to GDP (Statistical Year Report 1991), has continued to increase. The private sector (other than the oil and natural gas sector) contributes 24.31 percent compared to 46.43 percent of the oil and natural gas sector. Moreover the total number of establishments (registered) in the private sector has increased from 3,591 in 1986 to 4,749 in 1990, a significant increase of 32.2 percent.

This encouraging trend was initiated by the Government's moves to diversify the economy and to promote the development of the private sector as a means to attain this goal. This strategy was solidly backed-up by the implementation of the Investment Incentive Act in 1975 and the formation of the Ministry of Industry and Primary Resources in 1989.

The Government has very large foreign reserves and no foreign debt. Brunei Darussalam is, in fact, a significant international investor. The Brunei Investment Agency (BIA), formed in 1983, is entrusted with the management of the foreign reserves.

EMPLOYMENT

The Government sector is the largest employer, providing jobs for more than half the working population. The rest largely worked for Brunei Shell Petroleum Sdn. Bhd. and Royal Brunei Airlines.

In 1992 the number of employees in the private sector has increased to 61,761 from 53,613 in 1990. Of the total, 47,125 (76.3%) are foreign workers.

The small size of the indigenous work-force and the locals preference for public sector employment is a major constraint to development. Foreign workers have helped to ease labour shortages and make up over a third of the workforce. Regulations and procedures on recruitment of foreign workers are straight-forward and Government's assistance are readily available in securing approval for foreign workers ranging from labourers to executive managers.

FINANCE - POLICIES AND REGULATIONS

Although Brunei Darussalam has no central bank, the Ministry of Finance through the Treasury, the Currency Board and the Brunei Investment Agency exercises most of the functions of a central bank. Brunei Darussalam's monetary policy has been determined by linking the Brunei Darussalam's dollar to the Singapore dollar and there is parity between the two. The Ministry of Finance feels that the Monetary Authority of Singapore exercises sufficient caution and such a link will not have detrimental effects on the economies of either country. At the same time, this agreement is not seen as inhibiting the management of the domestic economy.

CURRENCY

Currency matters are the responsibility of the Brunei Darussalam Currency Board. It is responsible for the issuing and redemption of State banknotes and coins and the supervision of the banks. The setting up of a Central Monetary Authority is under consideration.

Money supply growth is presently around 20 percent per annum. The ratio of external assets to demand liabilities is around 110 percent - considerably more than the 70 percent laid down by the Board's governing Act.

EXCHANGE CONTROLS

There is no foreign exchange control. Banks permit non-resident account to be maintained and there is no restriction on borrowing by non-residents.

BANKING AND INSURANCE

There are currently eight commercial banks providing full banking services in the country. Two of these are locally incorporated. International banks such as Citibank, Hongkong and Shanghai Bank and Standard Chartered Bank have been operating branches in the state for decades. The financial sector also includes a number of locally incorporated and international finance and insurance companies. Interest rates are set by the Association of Banks. The authorities have been preparing to implement a comprehensive financial regulatory system via the proposed new Banking Act. The establishment of a development bank is also under consideration.

ECONOMIC DEVELOPMENT BOARD

The Economic Development Board is responsible for directly assisting local businessmen by providing loans at favourable rates of interest for start-up and expansion of their business. The scheme provides loans for up to a maximum amount of B$1.5 million at 4 percent interest rate repayable up to a maximum period not exceeding 12 years.

ONE-STOP AGENCY

As the focal point for all industrial development, the Ministry of Industry and Primary Resources coordinates all industrial development activities. For investments in Brunei Darussalam, the Ministry is a One-Stop Agency.

It is remarkably easy to start an industry in Brunei Darussalam. A totally private development which does not require Government facilities needs only the approval to start. Those requiring Government facilities and assistance need only deal with the Ministry, which will liaise with other agencies and expedite applications.

The Ministry realizes the importance of time frames and clear decision making processes to your business. The entire procedure has only four stages:-

a) Approval of the concept

b) Approval of firm proposal

c) Approval of physical plans

d) Approval to operate

In all four stages, the Ministry of Industry and Primary Resources is your contact as a One-Stop Agency. In Brunei Darussalam, we make it easy and look forward to being Your Profitable Partner. We invite you to invest in Brunei Darussalam as a Partner in Success. Please contact the Ministry of Industry and Primary Resources directly - we are ready and available to help.

CORPORATE INVESTMENTS

Semaun Holding Sendirian Berhad was incorporated as a Private Limited Company under the Brunei Darussalam's Companies Act on 8 December 1994. It serves as an investment and trading arm of the Ministry in enhancing economic diversification programs of Brunei Darussalam.

Semaun Holdings Sendirian Berhad can be contacted at the following address:

Unit 2.02, Block D, 2nd Floor
Yayasan Sultan Haji Hassanal Bolkiah Complex
Jalan Pretty
Bandar Seri Begawan BS8711
Brunei Darussalam
E-mail address: semaun@brunet.bn
Web3.asia.com.sg/brunei/semaun.html

MINISTRY OF INDUSTRY MISSION

Semaun Holdings's mission is to spearhead industrial and commercial development through direct investment in key industrial sectors in the interest of Brunei Darussalam.

The purpose of setting up Semaun Holdings is to accelerate industrial and commercial development in Brunei Darussalam and as well as to generate opportunities for active participation of Brunei citizen.

OBJECTIVES

Semaun Holding's objectives were established by taking into consideration the need to set up projects, which have high productivity level contributing to the national Gross Domestic product (GDP). This will be done through the transfer of technologies and utilise this technologies to improve productivity which will then be resulted in continuous growth and competitiveness of the company.

The setting up of new industrial sectors will generate employment opportunities for locals and as well as increase the technological expertise of Bruneians.

Semaun Holdings will lead and provide management support and control to enterprises that are willing to venture into strategic sectors. If necessary, Semaun Holdings will form partnership or joint ventures.

Semaun Holdings play as leading role in enhancing competitiveness and as well as to secure market for industrial productions and to ensure the concern of Islam particularly in food sectors.

CORPORATE OBJECTIVES FOR 1999

Integrated poultry projects
Food manufacturing and processing
Computer software development
Design of electronic components
Development of Technology Park
Silica based manufacturing
Steel rolling mills
Warehousing / Regional Distribution Centre
Commercial mushroom production
Local product outlet

MINISTRY ROLE

In order to carry out these objectives, Semaun Holdings plays an important role in Brunei Darussalam's economic development through the:

- Creation and expansion of existing industrial commercial activities.
- Introduction of new technologies to Bruneian companies.
- Provision of Joint-Venture partnership with foreign investors and suitable (emerging) local and foreign companies.

    Industrial and commercial strategic alliances with leading international companies.

SCOPE OF OPERATIONS

Semaun Holdings invests in business, trading and commercial enterprises including services, manufacturing, agriculture, fishery, forestry, industry and mining activities in Brunei Darussalam. Participation in related investment activities and opportunities outside the country is also a consideration.

BUSINESS SECTORS

Semaun Holdings currently targets a variety of business sectors with strong investment potential highlighting food, high-tech manufacturing and services.

FOOD SECTOR

Halal Food Processing and Manufacturing
Integrated Poultry Projects
Integrated Fisheries Projects
Local Product Outlet
Commercial Mushroom Production

HIGH- TECH MANUFACTURING

Biotechnology from Natural Resources
Silica Based Product Processing and Manufacturing
Semiconductor Related Business
Value-added Products Based On Oil and Gas Related Industries and Semiconductors Related Business
Manufacture of Computer Hardware and Software
Design of Electronic Components
Steel Rolling Mill
Industrial Estate Management

SERVICES

Tourism and Related Services
Distribution and Warehouse Facilities
Transshipments

PHILOSOPHY

Our investment philosophy highlights our first priority to invest within the country in areas of strategic importance and not in direct competition within the local private sector.
As a high profile company, the strategy employed by Semaun Holdings can be broadly grouped under three main categories:

i.   Direct investment in high-technology, high value-added industrial and commercial ventures.
ii. Investment in Research and Development leading to commercialization.
iii. Investment in overseas companies to facilitate expansion and growth of local ventures.

MECHANISM

- Wholly owned.
- New Joint-Venture companies.

  Equity investment in existing or emerging companies.

JOINT VENTURES

In 1996, Semaun Holdings through its subsidiary company, SemaunPrim Sendirian Berhad signed a joint-venture agreement with Eiwa Enterprises Company Limited, one of the producer of Peneaus Japonicus Prawn in Japan. Seiwa Corporation Sendirian Berhad was formed with present objectives summarised as follows:

- Ensure continuity supply of Tiger Shrimp and Seabass Fry for local requirement.
- Production of 0.8 million Seabass Fry (Day 60) meeting about 15 % of local requirement.
- Production of 15 million Shrimp Fry (PL 20) per annum.

In the same year, Semaun Seafood Sendirian Berhad was formed between SemaunPrim Sendirian Berhad, SinSinBun Pte Ltd (Singapore) and Koperasi Perikanan Brunei Berhad. The formation of Semaun Seafood is to carry out activities such as capture fishery and production of high commercial value and processed seafood products for domestic and export market and to utilise low value fish for production of Surimi, to process halal seafood and value added seafood product.

In 1997, another joint-venture agreement signed between SemaunPrim Sendirian Berhad and Baiduri Holdings Sendirian Berhad to carry out cage culture of groupers and other high commercial value fish and marine life. Under SeaGro Sendirian Berhad for domestic and export market.

Also in 1997, Semaun Holdings Sendirian Berhad together with Global Expertise SA, a British Photovoltaic technology resource corporation had formed a Joint-Venture company named Solar Tech Systems (B) Sendirian Berhad to be a Photovoltaic (solar electric) module manufacturer company based in Brunei Darussalam.

The main objective of the company is to produce Photovoltaic panels for local and export market. The company has a combined output capacity per year of one and a half megawatts of Solar Electric Power.

TRAVEL TO BRUNEI

US STATE DEPARTMENT SUGGESTIONS

COUNTRY DESCRIPTION: Brunei (known formally as the State of Brunei Darussalam) is a small Islamic Sultanate on the north coast of the island of Borneo. The capital, Bandar Seri Begawan, is the only major city. Tourist facilities are good, and generally available.

ENTRY REQUIREMENTS: For information about entry requirements, travelers may consult the Consular Section of the Embassy of the State of Brunei Darussalam, Suite 300, 2600 Virginia Ave., N.W. Washington, D.C. 20037; tel. (202) 342-0159.

MEDICAL FACILITIES: Adequate public and private hospitals and medical services are available in Brunei. Medical care clinics do not require deposits usually, but insist upon payment in full at time of treatment, and may require proof of ability to pay prior to treating or discharging a foreigner. U.S. medical insurance is not always valid outside the United States, and may not be accepted by health providers in Brunei. Travelers may wish to check with their health insurance providers regarding whether their U.S. policy applies overseas. The Medicare/ Medicaid program does not provide payment of medical services outside the United States. Supplemental medical insurance with specific overseas coverage, including provision for medical evacuation may be useful. Travel agents or insurance providers often have information about such programs. Useful information on medical emergencies abroad is provided in the Department of State, Bureau of Consular Affairs' brochure *Medical Information for Americans Traveling Abroad*, available via our home page and autofax service. For additional health information, the international travelers hotline of the Centers for Disease Control and Prevention may be reached at 1-877-FYI-TRIP (1-877-394-8747), via the CDC autofax service at 1-888-CDC-FAXX (1-888-232-3299), or via the CDC home page on the Internet: http://www.cdc.gov.

INFORMATION ON CRIME: The crime rate in Brunei is low, and violent crime is rare. The loss or theft abroad of a U.S. passport should be reported immediately to the local police and to the U.S. Embassy. Useful information on guarding valuables and protecting personal security while traveling abroad is provided in the Department of State pamphlet, *A Safe Trip Abroad*. It is available from the Superintendent of Documents, U.S. Government Printing Office, Washington, D.C. 20402 or via the Internet at http://www.access.gpo.gov /su_docs.

CRIMINAL PENALTIES: While in a foreign country, a U.S. citizen is subject to that country's laws and regulations, which sometimes differ significantly from those in the United States and do not afford the protections available to the individual under U.S. law. Penalties for breaking the law can be more severe than in the United States for similar offenses. Persons violating the law, even unknowingly, may be expelled, arrested or imprisoned. The trafficking in and the illegal importation of controlled drugs are very serious offenses in Brunei. Brunei has a mandatory death penalty for many narcotics offenses. Under the current law, possession of heroin and morphine derivatives of more than 15 grams, and cannabis of more than 20 grams, carries the death sentence. Possession of lesser amounts carries a minimum twenty-year jail term and caning.

AVIATION OVERSIGHT: The U.S. Federal Aviation Administration (FAA) has assessed the Government of Brunei's Civil Aviation Authority as Category 1 - in compliance with international aviation safety standards for oversight of Brunei's air carrier operations. For further information, travelers may contact the Department of Transportation within the U.S. at 1-800-322-7873, or visit the FAA's Internet website at http://www.faa.gov/avr/iasa/index.htm. The U.S. Department of Defense (DOD) separately assesses some foreign air carriers for suitability as official providers of air services.

For information regarding the DOD policy on specific carriers, travelers may contact DOD at 618-256-4801.

ROAD SAFETY: Roads are generally good and most vehicles are new and well-maintained. However, vehicular accidents are now one of the leading causes of death in Brunei. Possibly due to excessive speed, tropical torrential rains, or driver carelessness, Brunei suffers a very high traffic accident rate.

CUSTOMS INFORMATION: More detailed information concerning regulations and procedures governing items that may be brought into Brunei is available from the Embassy of the State of Brunei Darussalam in the United States.

Registration/Embassy Location: U.S. citizens living in or visiting Brunei are encouraged to register in person or via telephone with the U.S. Embassy in Bandar Seri Begawan and to obtain updated information on travel and security within the country. The U.S Embassy is located on the third floor, Teck Guan Plaza, Jalan Sultan, in the capital city of Bandar Seri Begawan. The mailing address is American Embassy PSC 470 (BSB), FPO AP, 96534; the telephone number is (673)(2) 229-670; the fax number is (673) (2) 225-293.

Brunei-Muara

On her state visit to Brunei in September of 1998, Her Majesty Queen Elizabeth II of Britain made a tour of the Kampung Ayer in the capital a part of her busy itinerary. Made up of numerous communities, and home to some 30,000 people, the Kampung Ayer ("Villages on Water") is certainly the most well-known of all attractions in the country.

Kampung Ayer has been around for a very long time. When Antonio Pigafetta visited the country in the mid-16th century; Kampung Ayer was already a well-established, "home to some 25,000 families," according to Pigafetta. It was the hub for governance, business and social life in Brunei at that time.

The Kampung Ayer of today retains many of its old-world features described by Pigafetta. Only now, its daily well being is overlooked by the chiefs of the many villages in the area. The Kampung has almost all the amenities available in other communities, such as schools, shops and mosques. The houses there are usually well equipped with the latest in modern technology.

For as low as $1, boatmen will ferry passengers along the breadth and length of the Brunei river.

River cruises aboard ferryboats can start at both ends of the Brunei river, one at the Muara side, at the Queen Elizabeth jetty (named after the reigning British queen after her first Brunei visit in 1972), and others at the various river boat taxi stations in the heart of town.

The journey from the other end of the river starts at Kota Batu, the 16th century capital. The upstream journey during the 10 miles per hour cruise passes an ancient landmark, the tomb of Brunei's fifth ruler, Sultan Bolkiah, the Singing Captain, under whose reign Brunei was a dominant power in the 15th century.

On one bank of the Brunei river is a newer relic, a British warship used dur-ing World War II, sheltered from the elements.

The ferry moves on to Kampong Ayer, the Venice of the East. During the 18th century, here lived the fisher-men, blacksmiths, kris (native sword) makers, brass artisans, nipa palm mat makers, pearl and oyster collectors, traders and goldsmiths.

A new Kampong Ayer has risen, settlements of concrete houses with glass windowpanes, and connected by cement bridges instead of the rickety, wooden catwalks.

Overlooking the old Kampong Ayer is the House of Twelve Roofs (Bum-bungan Dua Belas), built in 1906 and formerly the official home of the British resident. In the Kota Batu area on Jalan Residency is the Arts and Handicrafts Centre, where traditional arts and crafts have been revived.

But Kampung Ayer is only one of the many charms of Brunei that intrigue visitors to the country.

The Sultan Omar Ali Saifuddien Mosque in the heart of Bandar Seri Begawan continues to attract visitors fascinated by its majestic presence, and its role in the spiritual development of the Muslim citizens of the country. The mosque is practically synonymous with Brunei in general, and with the capital in particular.

Situated very close to the mosque is the public library with its attractive mural depicting Brunei's lifestyles in the 60s. The mural was done by one of Brunei's foremost artist, Pg Dato Hj Asmalee, formerly the director of Welfare, Youth and Sports, but now the country's ambassador to a neighbour-ing country.

Another landmark of the capital is the Yayasan Sultan Hj Hassanal Bolkiah commercial complex, across the road from the Sultan Omar Ah Saifuddien mosque. The newly estab-lished complex is the prime shopping centre in Brunei - four storeys of some of the premier big-name retailers in the region! There're outlets bran-dishing branded clothing, fast food, video games, books and many more. There's a supermarket in the Yayasan's west wing, and a food court on the east.

The Royal Regalia Building is a new addition to the attractions found in the capital. Within easy walking distance of all the hotels in the capital centre, the Royal Regalia Building houses artifacts used in royal cere-monies in the country. Foremost among the displays are the Royal Chariot, the gold and silver ceremonial armoury and the jewel-encrusted crowns used in coronation ceremonies.

Entrance is free, and visitors are expected to take off their shoes before entering. Opening hours are from 8.30am to 5.00pm daily except for Fridays, the Building opens from 9.00am until II.30am, and in the afternoon, from 2.30pm till 5.00pm.

Located next to the Royal Regalia Building is the Brunei History Centre. Drop by the centre and learn all about the genealogy and history of the sultans of Brunei, and members of the royal family. There is an exhibition area open to the public from 7.45 am to 12.l5pm, and l.30pm to 4.3Opm daily except for Fridays.

Across the road from the Brunei Hotel, is what is known throughout Borneo as the 'tamu.' A 'tamu' is a congregation of vendors selling farm produce and general items. If you are lucky, you can find valuable bargains among the potpourri of metalware and handicraft hawked by some peddlers.

The main Chinese temple in the country lies within sight of the 'tamu.' Its elaborately designed roof and loud red color of its outer walls make the temple stand out from among the more staid schemes of nearby buildings.

A visit during one of the many festivals that is observed at this sanctum of Taoist beliefs would be a celebration of colors, spectacle and smell. Another place of worship that should not be missed by visitors to Brunei is the Church of St Andrew's. The church, possibly the oldest in Brunei, is designed like an English country parish, complete with bells in the let fry. It lies within walking distance of the Royal Regalia Building.

If you are staying in a hotel or Bandar Seri Begawan, why not pay the nightly foodstalls a visit? The stalls are located at a site in front of Sheraton Hotel, and serve a wide variety of hawker fare cheap! A dollar worth of the fried noodles is enough to fill you up.

Check out the local burgers. They're as delicious as those you'll find in established fast food outlets. Or try out 'Roti John'-the Malay version of the Big Mac. Ask for 'goreng pisang' (banana fritters), 'begedil' (potato balls), or 'popiah' (meat rolls), in your jaunts to the sweetmeat stalls.

Outside the capital center, a worthwhile place to visit is the Jame' Asr Hassanil Bolkiah Mosque in Kiarong, about six kilometers away. This is a beautiful sanctuary for communication with God, a personal bequest from His Majesty the Sultan of Brunei himself for the people of the country.

More than just a place of worship, the Jame' Asr is also a center for learning. Classes teaching Islamic religious principles and practices are held there regularly, as do religious lectures. And every Friday morning, the lobbies of its vast edifice are filled with children studying the Quran.

A visit to the mosque is usually part of the itinerary of package tours to Brunei, but if not, visitors can make the necessary arrangement with local tour operators. Visitors wishing to come inside the mosque need to report to the officers on duty, at the security counter on the ground floor.

Further on, you will find the Jerudong Park Playground. Situated some 20 kms to the west of the capital, JP as it is popularly called, is a must-go place for visitors to the country. It has been described as "Brunei's first high-tech wonderland for people of all ages."

There are many amusement rides at the Jerudong Park Playground to cater to everyone's need.

For those who like to live life on the edge, you would be pleased to know that JP has THREE (that's right, three) roller coasters, each with different degrees of thrills (or insanity factors if you want).

'Pusing Lagi' takes riders up a crest almost six storeys high, and then takes them down a steep incline, before twisting and turning at breakneck speed, so much so you will regret the 'Roti John' you just had.

'Boomerang' is for people who would rather go for diabolical twists and turns, while 'Pony Express' is a ride for those newly-initiated to roller-coasters.

Other popular rides include the 'Condor', a very fast merry-go-round that takes you up some five stores high, the 'Aladdin' (a mechanical 'flying carpet'), 'Flashdance' (no dancing experience required), and the wildly swinging 'Pirate Ship'.

There is also a bumper car arena, only for children and youngsters though, a video arcade and tracks for skateboarding and carting. For those who prefer something more sedate, also available are a 'Merry-Go-Round', certainly the most beautiful this side of London, and the 'Simulator Tour' (virtual reality rides into the fantastic and the exotic). Try the up-tower rides, where you are taken up a tower 15 stores high, and given a superb view of the park, and the surrounding area.

For additional analytical, business and investment opportunities information, please contact Global Investment & Business Center, USA at (703) 370-8082. Fax: (703) 370-8083. E-mail: ibpusa3@gmail.com Global Business and Investment Info Databank - www.ibpus.com

Situated next to the playground is the 20-acre Jerudong Park Gardens, which is well-known for its concert class auditorium. This was where Michael Jackson had his performances some years back, drawing a record 60,000 people to a colorful extravaganza the first time he performed.

Whitney Houston was another megastar who has had performed here, as well as Stevie ("I Just Called To Say I Love You) Wonder and the wonderful Seal ("Kissed By A Rose").

And if all that running and riding gives you an appetite, there's good food to be found in the eating area next to the parking lot. Almost anything you could crave for is available, ranging from the local hawker spreads to international fast food fare.   If you're not doing anything on a Friday morning or late afternoon, take the no.55 purple bus to the end of its line at Jerudong Beach. Jerudong Beach on Fridays, especially around 9.00-10.00am, is a hive of activity as fishermen start landing their catch and customers rush to avail themselves of the freshest fish possible. The people you'll get to meet there are among the friendliest in the country, easy with the smile and always ready for the idle chatter.

But the place is more than just an informal fish market. Local fruits hang prominently from many of the stalls, and food stalls sell take-outs to cater to hungry visitors. Swim in the calm, waveless waters of the man-made cove, or try your luck fishing, if that is what you want to do. Just go around people watching.

 And if you need to go back to town, just board the purple bus to make the return journey.

The Bukit Shabbandar Forest Park is just the place to put those hiking legs to use. About ten minutes drive from the Jerudong Park Playground, the park is hectares upon hectares of greenery, dissected by tracks and paths for hiking, jogging and biking. While hiking, you can partake the wonders of the local forests - the rich diversity of its plant life, the exquisite charms and colors of the insects and reptiles that live within, and the symphony in the singing of the birds. Bukit Shahbandar Forest Park is just one of the 11 forest reserves in the country. To the east of Bandar Seri Begawan, about 6 kms into the Kota Batu area, visitors will find the Brunei Museum exhibits artifacts that archive the history of Negara Brunei Darussalam, both ancient and the relatively recent.

Well made cannons and kettles with their dragon motifs and elaborate patterns recall the glory days of the country -when Brunei was an important political and mercantile power in the region with territories that stretched that stretched all the way from Luzon Island in the Philippines to the whole western Borneo island.

There are exhibits which depict the traditional lifestyles of the various communities in the country, plus displays on the local flora and fauna. The exhibit by the local petroleum company Brunei Shell, illustrates the history on the discovery of oil in the country, and the commodity's significant role in economy of Brunei.

The Museum is open every day except Mondays from 9.00am till 5.00pm. On Fridays however, there is a scheduled prayer break from 11.30am until 2.30pm.

 And situated downhill of the Brunei Museum is the Malay Technology Museum, which, as its name implies, houses the technological tools utilised by the Malays in ancient times.

A government booklet describes it as offering the "the visitor an intriguing insight into the lifestyle of the people of Brunei in by-gone eras". The Technology Museum is open daily, except Tuesdays, from 9.00 am till 5.00 pm. with a 3-hour midday prayer break on Fridays. Entrance is free.

For additional analytical, business and investment opportunities information, please contact Global Investment & Business Center, USA at (703) 370-8082. Fax: (703) 370-8083. E-mail: ibpusa3@gmail.com Global Business and Investment Info Databank - www.ibpus.com

There is an "Asean Square" in Persiaran Damuan which is located on a stretch between Jalan Tutong and the bank of the Brunei River about 4.5km from the capital. The "Asean Square" has on permanent display the work of a chosen sculptor themed Harmony in Diversity from each of the Asean member countries.

HOLIDAYS

Brunei Darussalam's vision is to promote the country as a unique tourist destination and gateway to tourism excellence in South East Asia. The objectives are to create international awareness of Brunei Darussalam as a holiday destination; to maximize earings of foreign exchange and make tourism as one of the main contributor to GDP. In addition, it will create employment opportunities.

The country offers a wide variety of attractive places to be visited and experienced. The rainforest and National Parks are rich in flora and fauna. Its most magnificent mosques, water village (traditional and historic houses on stilts), rich culture and Jerudong Theme Park are among the uniqueness of Brunei Darussalam.

The government is now actively promoting tourism as an important part of its economic diversification. It would like to see a target of 1 million-visitor arrival by the year 2000. From January to August 1999, the statistic recorded 405,532 visitors visited Brunei Darussalam.

National Day Celebration

The nation celebrates this joyous occasion on the 23rd of February and the people usually prepare themselves two months beforehand. Schoolchildren, private sector representatives and civil servants work hand-in-hand rehearsing their part in flash card displays and other colourful crowd formations. In addition mass prayers and reading of Surah Yaasin are held at mosques throughout the country.

Fasting Month (Ramadhan)

Ramadhan is a holy month for all Muslims. This marks the beginning of the period of fasting - abstinence from food, drink and other material comforts from dawn to dusk. During this month, religious activities are held at mosques and *suraus* throughout the country

Hari Raya Aidilfitri

Hari Raya is a time for celebration after the end of the fasting month of Ramadhan. In the early part of the first day, prayers are held at every mosque in the country. Families get together to seek forgiveness from the elders and loved ones. You will see Bruneians decked-out in their traditional garb visiting relatives and friends.

Special festive dishes are made especially for Hari Raya including satay (beef, chicken or mutton kebabs), ketupat or lontong (rice cakes in coconut or banana leaves), rendang (spicy marinated beef) and other tantalizing cuisines. In these auspicious occassion Istana Nurul Iman was open to the public as well as to visitors for 3 days. This provides the nation and other visitors the opportunity to meet His Majesty and other members of the Royal Family, in order to wish them a Selamat Hari Raya Aidilfitri.

Royal Brunei Armed Forces Day

31st of May marks the commemoration of the Royal Brunei Armed Forces formation day. The occassion is celebrated with military parades, artillery displays, parachuting and exhibitions.

Hari Raya Aidiladha

This is also known as Hari Raya Korban. Sacrifices of goats and cows are practiced to commemorate the Islamic historical event of Prophet Ibrahim S.A.W. The meat is then distributed among relatives, friends and the less fortunates.

His Majesty the Sultan's Birthday

This is one of the most important events in the national calendar with activities and festivities taking place nationwide. Celebrated on 15th July, this event begins with mass prayer throughout the country. On this occassion, His Majesty the Sultan delivers a 'titah' or royal address followed by investiture ceremony held at the Istana Nurul Iman. The event is also marked with gatherings at the four districts where His Majesty meets and gets together with his subjects.

Birthday of the Prophet Muhammad

In Brunei Darussalam, this occasion is known as the Mauludin Nabi S.A.W. Muslims throughout the country honour this event. Readings from the Holy Koran - the Muslim Holy Book, and an address on Islam from officials of the Ministry of Religious Affairs marks the beginning of this auspicious occasion. His Majesty the Sultan also gives a royal address and with other members of the Royal family, leads a procession on foot through the main streets of Bandar Seri Begawan. Religious functions, lectures and other activities are also held to celebrate this important occasion nationwide.

Chinese New Year

Celebrated by the Chinese community, this festival lasts for two weeks. It begins with a reunion dinner on the eve of the Lunar New Year to encourage closer rapport between family members. For the next two week, families visit one another bringing with them oranges to symbolize longevity and good fortune. Traditional cookies and food are aplenty during this festivity. Unmarried young people and children will receive 'angpow' or little red packets with money inside, a symbolic gesture of good luck, wealth and health.

Christmas Day

Throughout the world, 25th of December marks Christmas day, a significant day for all Christians. Christmas is nevertheless a joyous and colourful celebration enjoyed by Christians throughout the country.

Teachers' Day

Teachers' Day is celebrated on every 23rd September in recognition of the good deeds of the teachers to the community, religion and the country. It is celebrated in commemoration of the birthday of the late Sultan Haji Omar 'Ali Saifuddien Saadul Khairi Waddien, the 28th Sultan of Brunei for his contribution in the field of education including religious education. On this occassion, three awards are given away namely, Meritorious Teacher's Award, Outstanding Teacher's Award and *"Guru Tua"* Award.

For additional analytical, business and investment opportunities information, please contact Global Investment & Business Center, USA at (703) 370-8082. Fax: (703) 370-8083. E-mail: ibpusa3@gmail.com Global Business and Investment Info Databank - www.ibpus.com

Public Service Day

The date 29th September is observed as the Public Service Day with the objective to uphold the aspiration of the Government of His Majesty the Sultan and Yang Di-Pertuan of Brunei Darussalam towards creating an efficient, clean, sincere and honest public service. The Public Service Day commemorates the promulgation of the first written Constitution in Brunei Darussalam. The Public Service Day is celebrated with the presentation of the meritorious service award to Ministries and Government Departments.

PUBLIC HOLIDAYS

1 January	New Year's Day
8 January	* Hari Raya Aidilfitri
5 February	Chinese New Year
23 February	National Day
16 Mac	* Hari Raya Aidiladha
6 April	Muslim Holy Month of Hijiriah
31 May	Royal Brunei Armed Forces Day
15 Jun	The Birthday of Prophet Muhammad S.A.W.
15 July	The Birthday of His Majesty Sultan Haji Hassanal Bolkiah Mu'izzaddin Waddaulah, Sultan and Yang Di-Pertuan of Brunei Darussalam
25 October	* Israk Mikraj
27 November	* First Day of Ramadhan (Muslim fasting month)
13 December	Anniversary of The Revelation of the Quran
25 December	Christmas
27 December	* Hari Raya Aidilfitri

BUSINESS CUSTOMS

Customs & Traditions:	Brunei Darussalam possess a long heritage of traditions and customs, behavioural traits and forms of address. Muslims observe religious rites and rituals, which is woven into the lifestyle of Bruneian Malays. Breach of Malay conduct can be liable to prosecution in Islamic courts.
Social Protocol for non-Muslims:	It is customary for Bruneians to eat with their fingers rather than use forks and spoons. Always use the right hand when eating. It is polite to accept even just a little food and drink when offered. When refusing anything that is being offered, it is polite to touch the plate lightly with the right hand . As the left hand is considered unclean, one should use one's right hand to give and receive things. Bruneians sit on the floor, especially when there's a fairly large gathering of people. It is considered feminine to sit on the floor with a woman's legs tucked to one side, and equally polite for men to sit with folded legs crossed at the ankles. It's rude for anyone to sit on the floor with the legs stretched out in front, especially if someone is sitting in front. It is considered impolite to eat or drink while walking about in public except at picnics

For additional analytical, business and investment opportunities information,
please contact Global Investment & Business Center, USA
at (703) 370-8082. Fax: (703) 370-8083. E-mail: ibpusa3@gmail.com
Global Business and Investment Info Databank - www.ibpus.com

or fairs.

During the Islamic fasting (Puasa) month, Muslims do not take any food from sunrise to sundown. It would be inconsiderate to eat and drink in their presence during this period.

It is not customary for Muslims to shake hands with members of the opposite sex. Public display of affection such as kissing and hugging are seen to be in bad taste. Casual physical contact with the opposite sex will make Muslims feel uncomfortable.

In the relationship between sexes, Islam enforces strict legislation. If a non-Muslim is found in the company of a Muslim of the opposite sex in a secluded place rather than where there are a lot of people, he/she could be persecuted.

If you are found committing 'khalwat' that is seen in a compromising position with a person of the opposite sex who is a Muslim, you could be deported.

When walking in front of people, especially the elderly and those senior in rank or position, it is a gesture of courtesy and respect for one to bend down slightly, as if one is bowing, except this time side way to the person or persons in front of whom one is passing. One of the arms should be positioned straight downwards along the side of the body.

Leaning on a table with someone seated on it especially if he/she is an official or colleague in an office is considered rude.

Resting one's feet on the table or chair is seen as overbearing. So is sitting on the table while speaking to another person who is seated behind it. To touch or pat someone, including children, on the head is regarded as extremely disrespectful.

The polite way of beckoning at someone is by using all four fingers of the right hand with the palm down and motioning them towards yourself. It is considered extremely impolite to beckon at someone with the index finger.

For additional analytical, business and investment opportunities information,
please contact Global Investment & Business Center, USA
at (703) 370-8082. Fax: (703) 370-8083. E-mail: ibpusa3@gmail.com
Global Business and Investment Info Databank - www.ibpus.com

SUPPLEMENTS

IMPORTANT LAWS OF BRUNEI

ACT / ORDER	CHAPTER / NOTIFICATION NO.	DATE OF COMMENCEMENT	STATUS
ADMIRALTY JURISDICTION ACT [2000 Ed.]	CAP. 179	01-10-1996	
ADOPTION OF CHILDREN ORDER 2001	S 16/2001	26-03-2001	
AGRICULTURAL PESTS AND NOXIOUS PLANTS ACT [1984 Ed.]	CAP. 43	01-08-1971	
AIR NAVIGATION ACT [1984 Ed., Amended by S 21/97, S 41/00, S 42/00, Repealed by S 63/06 - Civil Aviation Order]	CAP. 113	01-03-1978	REPEALED w.e.f. 20-05-06
AIRPORT PASSENGER SERVICE CHARGE ACT [2000 Ed.]	CAP. 188	01-05-1999	
ANTI-TERRORISM (FINANCIAL AND OTHER MEASURES) ACT [2008 Ed.]	CAP. 197	14-06-2002	
ANTIQUITIES AND TREASURE TROVE ACT [2002 Ed.]	CAP. 31	01-01-1967	
APPLICATION OF LAWS ACT [2009 Ed.]	CAP. 2	25-04-1951	
ARBITRATION ACT [1999 Ed.]	CAP. 173	24-04-1994	
ARBITRATION ORDER, 2009	S 34/2009		not yet in force
ARMS AND EXPLOSIVES ACT [2002 Ed.]	CAP. 58	08-04-1927	
ASIAN DEVELOPMENT BANK ACT [2009 Ed.]	CAP. 201	25-04-2006	
AUDIT ACT [1986 Ed., Amended by S 39/03]	CAP. 152	01-01-1960	
AUTHORITY FOR INFO-COMMUNICATIONS TECHNOLOGY INDUSTRY OF BRUNEI DARUSSALAM ORDER 2001 [Amended by S 13/03, S 35/03]	S 39/2001	01-01-2003	
BANISHMENT ACT [1984 Ed.]	CAP. 20	31-12-1918	
BANKERS' BOOKS (EVIDENCE) ACT [1984 Ed., Amended by S 29/93, Repealed by S 13/06]	CAP. 107	17-04-1939	REPEALED w.e.f. 12-02-06
BANKING ACT [2002 Ed., Repealed by S 45/06 - Banking Order]	CAP. 95	01-01-1957	REPEALED w.e.f. 04-03-06
BANKING ORDER, 2006	S 45/2006	04-03-2006	
BANKRUPTCY ACT [1984 Ed., Amended by S 12/96, S 52/00]	CAP. 67	01-01-1957	
BILLS OF EXCHANGE ACT [1999 Ed.]	CAP. 172	03-05-1994	
BILLS OF SALE ACT [1984 Ed.]	CAP. 70	16-01-1958	
BIOLOGICAL WEAPONS ACT [1984 Ed.]	CAP. 87	11-04-1975	
BIRTHS AND DEATHS REGISTRATION ACT [1984 Ed.]	CAP. 79	01-01-1923	

BISHOP OF BORNEO (INCORPORATION) ACT [1984 Ed.]	CAP. 88	25-04-1951	
BRETTON WOODS AGREEMENT ACT [2000 Ed.]	CAP. 176	30-09-1995	
BROADCASTING ACT [2000 Ed., Corrigendum S 41/07]	CAP. 180	15-03-1997	
BRUNEI ECONOMIC DEVELOPMENT BOARD ACT [2003 Ed., Amended by S 11/03]	CAP. 104	11-04-1975	
BRUNEI FISHERY LIMITS ACT [1984 Ed., Amended by S 25/09]	CAP. 130	01-01-1983	
BRUNEI INVESTMENT AGENCY ACT [2002 Ed., Amended by S 14/03, S 64/04, S 15/08, S 78/08]	CAP. 137	01-07-1983	
BRUNEI MALAY SILVERSMITHS GUILD (INCORPORATION) ACT [1984 Ed.]	CAP. 115	15-07-1959	
BRUNEI NATIONAL ARCHIVES ACT [1984 Ed.]	CAP. 116	01-08-1981	
BRUNEI NATIONAL PETROLEUM COMPANY SENDIRIAN BERHAD ORDER 2002 [Amended by S 6/2003, S 12/2003]	S 6/2002	05-01-2002	
BRUNEI NATIONALITY ACT [2002 Ed., Amended by S 55/2002]	CAP. 15	01-01-1962	
BUFFALOES ACT [1984 Ed.]	CAP. 59	01-01-1909	
BURIAL GROUNDS ACT [1984 Ed.]	CAP. 49	01-01-1932	
BUSINESS NAMES ACT [1984 Ed., Amended by S 30/88]	CAP. 92	01-03-1958	
CENSORSHIP OF FILMS AND PUBLIC ENTERTAINMENTS ACT [2002 Ed.]	CAP. 69	21-08-1962	
CENSUS ACT [2003 Ed.]	CAP. 78	07-06-1947	
CENTRE FOR STRATEGIC AND POLICY STUDIES ORDER, 2006	S 64/2006	01-07-2006	
CHILD CARE CENTRES ORDER 2006	S 37/06	04-03-2006	
CHILDREN AND YOUNG PERSONS ORDER, 2006 [Corrigendum S 24/06, Amended by S 60/08]	S 9/2006		not yet in force
CHILDREN ORDER 2000 [Amended by S 84/00, S 48/03]	S 64/2000	01-09-2000	
CHINESE MARRIAGE ACT [1984 Ed., Amended by S 44/89]	CAP. 126	31-07-1955	
CIVIL AVIATION ORDER, 2006	S 63/2006	20-05-2006	
COIN (IMPORT AND EXPORT) ACT [1984 Ed.]	CAP. 33	01-01-1909	
COMMISSIONS OF ENQUIRY ACT [1984 Ed., Amended by S 35/05]]	CAP. 9	28-04-1962	
COMMISSIONERS FOR OATHS ACT [1999 Ed.]	CAP. 169	26-08-1993	
COMMON GAMING HOUSES ACT [2002 Ed., Amended by S 20/08]	CAP. 28	01-01-1921	
COMPANIES ACT [1984 Ed., Amended by S 26/98, S 23/99, S 69/01, S 10/03, S 45/06, S 96/08]	CAP. 39	01-01-1957	

COMPULSORY EDUCATION ORDER, 2007	S 56/2007	24-11-2007	
COMPUTER MISUSE ACT [2007 Ed.]	CAP. 194	21-06-2000	
CONSTITUTION OF BRUNEI DARUSSALAM [2004 Ed., Amended by S 14/06] Article 8A, 9(2), 9(4), 9(5) - suspended by S 15/06 w.e.f. 21/02/06	CONST. I	29-09-1959	
CONSTITUTION [FINANCIAL PROCEDURE] ORDER [2004 Ed., Amended by S 14/08, S 36/08]	CONST. III	01-01-1960	
CONSULAR RELATIONS ACT [1984 Ed.]	CAP. 118	01-01-1984	
CONTINENTAL SHELF PROCLAMATION [1984 Ed.]	SUP. II		
CONTRACTS ACT [1984 Ed., Amended by S 60/02]	CAP. 106	17-04-1939	
CO-OPERATIVE SOCIETIES ACT [1984 Ed.]	CAP. 84	01-07-1975	
COPYRIGHT ORDER 1999	S 14/2000	01-05-2000	
CRIMINAL CONDUCT (RECOVERY OF PROCEEDS) ORDER 2000 [Amended by S 30/07]	S 52/2000	01-07-2000	
CRIMINAL LAW (PREVENTIVE DETENTION) ACT [2008 Ed.]	CAP. 150	26-11-1984	
CRIMINAL PROCEDURE CODE [2001 Ed., Amended by S 63/02, GN 273/02, S 62/04, S 32/05, S 6/06, S 9/06, S 4/07]	CAP. 7	01-05-1952	S 6/06 & S 9/06 not yet in force
CRIMINALS REGISTRATION ORDER, 2008	S 42/2008	01-04-2008	
CURRENCY ACT [1984 Ed., Repealed by S 16/04 - Currency and Monetary Order]	CAP. 32	Please refer Act	REPEALED w.e.f. 01-02-04
CURRENCY AND MONETARY ORDER 2004 [Corrigendum S 71/04; Amended by S 59/05, S 39/07]	S 16/2004	01-02-2004	
CUSTOMS ACT [1984 Ed., Amended by S 23/89, S 82/00, S 52/01, S 39/06, Repealed by S 39/06 - Customs Order]	CAP. 36	01-01-1955	REPEALED w.e.f. 04-03-06
CUSTOMS ORDER, 2006 [Amended by S 98/08]	S 39/06	04-03-2006	
DANA PENGIRAN MUDA MAHKOTA AL-MUHTADEE BILLAH FOR ORPHANS ACT [2000 Ed.]	CAP. 185	25-08-1998	
DEBTORS ACT [2008 Ed.]	CAP. 195	16-10-2000	
DEFAMATION ACT [2000 Ed.]	CAP. 192	17-08-1999	
DESCRIPTION OF LAND (SURVEY PLANS) ACT [1984 Ed.]	CAP. 101	03-09-1962	
DEVELOPMENT FUND ACT [1984 Ed.]	CAP. 136	01-01-1960	
DIPLOMATIC PRIVILEGES (EXTENSION) ACT [1984 Ed.]	CAP. 85	02-12-1949	
DIPLOMATIC PRIVILEGES (VIENNA CONVENTION) ACT [1984 Ed.]	CAP. 117	01-09-1982	
DISAFFECTED AND DANGEROUS PERSONS ACT [1984 Ed.]	CAP. 111	29-07-1953	

DISASTER MANAGEMENT ORDER 2006	S 26/06	01-08-2006	
DISSOLUTION OF MARRIAGE ACT [1999 Ed.]	CAP. 165	29-04-1992	
DISTRESS ACT [2009 Ed.]	CAP. 199	16-10-2000	
DOGS ACT [1984 Ed., Amended by S 14/90]	CAP. 60	17-04-1939	
DRUG TRAFFICKING (RECOVERY OF PROCEEDS) ACT [2000 Ed., Amended by S 29/07]	CAP. 178	30-03-1996	
EDUCATION ORDER 2003 [Amended by S 86/06]	S 59/2003	20-12-2003	
EDUCATION (BRUNEI BOARD OF EXAMINATIONS) ACT [1984 Ed.]	CAP. 56	01-01-1975	
EDUCATION (NON-GOVERNMENT SCHOOLS) ACT [1984 Ed., Repealed by S 59/03 - Education Order]	CAP. 55	01-01-1953	REPEALED w.e.f. 20-12-03
ELECTION OFFENCES ACT [1984 Ed.]	CAP. 26	28-04-1962	
ELECTRICITY ACT [2003 Ed. Amended by S 68/05]	CAP. 71	05-03-1973	
ELECTRONIC TRANSACTION ACT [2008 Ed.]	CAP. 196	01-05-2001	except Part X
EMBLEMS AND NAMES (PREVENTION OF IMPROPER USE) ACT [1984 Ed.]	CAP. 94	18-01-1968	
EMERGENCY REGULATIONS ACT [1984 Ed.]	CAP. 21	21-02-1933	
EMPLOYMENT AGENCIES ORDER, 2004	S 84/2004	20-12-2004	
EMPLOYMENT INFORMATION ACT [1984 Ed.]	CAP. 99	15-05-1974	
EVIDENCE ACT [2002 Ed., Amended by S 1/06, S 13/06]	CAP. 108	17-04-1939	
EXCHANGE CONTROL ACT [1984 Ed., Repealed by S 70/00]	CAP. 141	01-01-1957	REPEALED w.e.f. 01-07-00
EXCISE ACT [1984 Ed., Repealed by S 40/06 - Excise Order]	CAP. 37	01-01-1925	REPEALED w.e.f. 04-03-06
EXCISE ORDER 2006	S 40/06	04-03-2006	
EXCLUSIVE ECONOMIC ZONE, Proclamation of	S 4/94	20-07-1993	
EXTRADITION (MALAYSIA AND SINGAPORE) ACT [1999 Ed.]	CAP. 154	19-05-84 [S] 01-11-83 [M]	
EXTRADITION ACT [1984 Ed., Repealed by S 10/06 - Extradition Order]	CAP. 8	09-12-1915	REPEALED w.e.f. 07-02-06
EXTRADITION ORDER 2006	S 10/06	07-02-2006	
FATAL ACCIDENTS AND PERSONAL INJURIES ACT [1999 Ed.]	CAP. 160	01-02-1991	
FINANCE COMPANIES ACT [2003 Ed., Amended by S 41/06]	CAP. 89	01-08-1973	
FINGERPRINTS ENACTMENT [Repealed by S 42/08 - Criminals Registration Order, 2008]	17 of 1956	01-01-1957	REPEALED w.e.f. 01-04-08

FIRE SERVICES ACT [2002 Ed., Amended by S 79/06] now become FIRE AND RESCUE w.e.f. 1/8/2006	CAP. 82	04-08-1966	
FISHERIES ACT [1984 Ed., Amended by S 20/02, Repealed by S 25/09 - Fisheries Order, 2009]	CAP. 61	05-03-1973	REPEALED w.e.f. 30-05-09
FISHERIES ORDER, 2009	S 25/2009	30-05-2009	
FOREST ACT [2002 Ed., Amended by S 47/07]	CAP. 46	30-10-1934	
GENEVA AND RED CROSS ACT [1984 Ed.]	CAP. 86	12-12-1938	
GENEVA CONVENTION ORDER, 2005	S 40/2005		not yet in force
GUARDIANSHIP OF INFANTS ACT [2000 Ed.]	CAP. 191	01-08-1999	
GURKHA RESERVE UNIT ACT [1984 Ed.]	CAP. 135	09-05-1981	
HALAL CERTIFICATE AND HALAL LABEL ORDER, 2005 [Amended by S 75/08]	S 39/2005	01-08-2008	
HALAL MEAT ACT [2000 Ed., Amended by GN 274/02]	CAP. 183	17-04-1999	
HIJACKING AND PROTECTION OF AIRCRAFT ORDER 2000	S 41/2000	24-05-2000	
HIRE PURCHASE ORDER, 2006	S 44/06	04-03-2006	
IMMIGRATION ACT [2006 Ed., Amended by S 34/07]	CAP. 17	01-07-1958	
INCOME TAX ACT [2003 Ed., Amended by S 51/08, S 52/08, S 13/09]	CAP. 35	31-12-1949	
INCOME TAX (PETROLEUM) ACT [2004 Ed.]	CAP. 119	18-12-1963	
INDUSTRIAL CO-ORDINATION ORDER 2001	S 44/2001	01-06-2001	
INDUSTRIAL DESIGNS ORDER 1999	S 7/2000	01-05-2000	
INFECTIOUS DISEASES ORDER 2003 [Amended by S 27/06]	S 34/2003	08-05-2003	
INSURANCE ORDER, 2006 [Amended by S 88/06, S 28/07, S 54/07]	S 48/2006	04-03-2006	
INTERMEDIATE COURTS ACT [1999 Ed., Amended by S 57/04, S 74/04, S 80/06]	CAP. 162	01-07-1991	
INTERNAL SECURITY ACT [2008 Ed.]	CAP. 133	01-04-1983	
INTERNATIONAL ARBITRATION ORDER, 2009	S 35/2009		not yet in force
INTERNATIONAL BANKING ORDER 2000 [Amended by S 9/01]	S 53/2000	01-07-2000	
INTERNATIONAL BUSINESS COMPANIES ORDER 2000 [Amended by S 37/03]	S 56/2000	01-07-2000	
INTERNATIONAL INSURANCE AND TAKAFUL ORDER 2002	S 43/2002	01-07-2002	
INTERNATIONAL LIMITED PARTNERSHIP ORDER 2000 [Amended by S 7/01]	S 45/2000	01-07-2000	

INTERNATIONAL TRUSTS ORDER 2000	S 55/2000	01-07-2000	
INTERNATIONALLY PROTECTED PERSONS ACT [1984 Ed.]	CAP. 16	08-07-1995	
INTERPRETATION AND GENERAL CLAUSES ACT [2006 Ed.]	CAP. 4	29-09-1959	
INTOXICATING SUBSTANCES ACT [1999 Ed., Amended by S 58/07]	CAP. 161	01-05-1992	
INVENTIONS ACT [1984 Ed., Amended by S 28/97]	CAP. 72	01-03-1952	
INVESTMENT INCENTIVES ACT [1984 Ed., Repealed by S 48/01 - Investment Incentives Order]	CAP. 97	01-05-1975	REPEALED w.e.f. 01-06-01
INVESTMENT INCENTIVES ORDER 2001	S 48/2001	01-06-2001	
ISLAMIC ADOPTION OF CHILDREN ORDER 2001	S 14/2001	26-03-2001	except section 3
ISLAMIC BANKING ACT [1999 Ed., Repealed by S 96/08 - Islamic Banking Order, 2008]	CAP. 168	02-12-1992	REPEALED w.e.f. 30-09-08
ISLAMIC BANKING ORDER, 2008	S 96/2008	30-09-2008	
ISLAMIC FAMILY LAW ORDER 1999 [Corrigenda S 42/04, Amended by S 17/05]	S 12/2000	26-03-2001	except section 3
KIDNAPPING ACT [1999 Ed.]	CAP. 164	22-02-1992	
KOLEJ UNIVERSITI PERGURUAN UGAMA SERI BEGAWAN ORDER, 2008	S 84/2008	30-08-2008	
LABOUR ACT [2002 Ed., Amended by GN 274/02, S 84/04]	CAP. 93	01-02-1955	
LAND ACQUISITION ACT [1984 Ed.]	CAP. 41	03-01-1949	
LAND CODE [1984 Ed., Amended by S 29/09]	CAP. 40	06-09-1909	
LAND CODE (STRATA) ACT [2000 Ed., Amended by S 28/09]	CAP. 189	01-07-2009	
LAW REFORM (CONTRIBUTORY NEGLIGENCE) ACT [1984 Ed., Repealed by S 4/91]	CAP. 53	25-04-1951	REPEALED w.e.f. 01-02-91
LAW REFORM (PERSONAL INJURIES) ACT [1984 Ed., Repealed by S 4/91]	CAP. 10	25-04-1951	REPEALED w.e.f. 01-02-91
LAW REVISION ACT [2001 Ed., Amended by S 93/00]	CAP. 1	01-01-1984	
LAYOUT DESIGNS ORDER 1999	S 8/2000	01-05-2000	
LEGAL PROFESSION ACT [2006 Ed.]	CAP. 132	01-01-1987	
LEGISLATIVE COUNCIL AND COUNCIL OF MINISTERS ACT (REMUNERATION AND PRIVILEGES) [1984 Ed., Amended by S 46/05, S 12/06]	CAP. 134	30-01-1965	
LEGITIMACY ORDER 2001	S 33/2001	21-04-2001	
LICENSED LAND SURVEYORS ACT [1984 Ed.]	CAP. 100	01-07-1980	
LIMITATION ACT [2000 Ed.]	CAP. 14	01-09-1991	

LUNACY ACT [1984 Ed.]	CAP. 48	09-07-1929	
MAINTENANCE ORDERS RECIPROCAL ENFORCEMENT ACT [2000 Ed.]	CAP. 175	25-02-1998	
MARITIME OFFENCES (SHIPS AND FIXED PLATFORMS) ORDER, 2007	S 61/2007	17-12-2007	
MARRIAGE ACT [1984 Ed., Amended by S 42/05]	CAP. 76	03-08-1948	
MARRIED WOMEN ACT [2000 Ed.]	CAP. 190	01-08-1999	
MEDICAL PRACTITIONERS AND DENTISTS ACT [1984 Ed., Amended by GN 273/02]	CAP. 112	29-07-1953	
MEDICINES ORDER, 2007	S 79/2007	01-01-2008	sec.1(2)(a) only
MERCHANDISE MARKS ACT [1984 Ed.]	CAP. 96	07-10-1953	
MERCHANT SHIPPING ACT [1984 Ed., Repealed by S 27/02 - Merchant Shipping Order]	CAP. 145	01-09-1984	REPEALED w.e.f. 16-05-02
MERCHANT SHIPPING ORDER, 2002 [Amended by S 23/09]	S 27/2002	16-05-2002	
MERCHANT SHIPPING (CIVIL LIABILITY AND COMPENSATION FOR OIL POLLUTION) ORDER, 2008	S 54/2008	17-04-2008	
MIDWIVES ACT [1984 Ed., Amended by S 47/02]	CAP. 139	01-01-1959	
MINING ACT [1984 Ed.]	CAP. 42	04-03-1920	
MINOR OFFENCES ACT [1984 Ed., Amended by S 26/90, S 43/98, S 89/06, S 82/08]	CAP. 30	29-07-1929	
MISCELLANEOUS LICENCES ACT [1984 Ed., Amended by S 43/08, S 85/08]	CAP. 127	01-01-1983	
MISUSE OF DRUGS ACT [2001 Ed., Amended by S 7/2002, GN 273/02, S 59/07, S 5/08]	CAP. 27	01-07-1978	
MONEY CHANGING AND REMITTANCE BUSINESS ACT [1999 Ed.]	CAP. 174	01-01-1995	
MONEY LAUNDERING ORDER 2000	S 44/2000	01-07-2000	
MONEYLENDERS ACT [1984 Ed., Amended by S 53/00, S 45/06]	CAP. 62	01-01-1922	
MONOPOLIES ACT [2003 Ed.]	CAP. 73	13-12-1932	
MOTOR VEHICLES INSURANCE (THIRD PARTY RISKS) ACT [1984 Ed., Amended by S 28/98, S 48/08 (corrig)]	CAP. 90	28-02-1950	
MUNICIPAL BOARDS ACT [1984 Ed.]	CAP. 57	01-01-1921	
MUTUAL ASSISTANCE IN CRIMINAL MATTERS ORDER, 2005	S 7/2005	01-01-2006	
MUTUAL FUNDS ORDER 2001	S 18/2001	01-01-2001	
NATIONAL BANK OF BRUNEI BERHAD; NATIONAL FINANCE SENDIRIAN BERHAD ACT [1999 Ed.]	CAP. 156	19-11-1986	
NATIONAL REGISTRATION ACT [2002 Ed.]	CAP. 19	01-03-1965	

NEWSPAPERS ACT [2002 Ed., Amended by S 36/05, S 86/08]	CAP. 105	01-01-1959	
NORTH BORNEO (DEFINITION BOUNDARIES) ORDER IN COUNCIL 1958 [1984 Ed.]	Sup. III		
NURSES REGISTRATION ACT [1984 Ed.]	CAP. 140	01-01-1968	
OATHS AND AFFIRMATIONS ACT [2001 Ed.]	CAP. 3	08-09-1958	
OFFENDERS (PROBATION AND COMMUNITY SERVICE) ORDER, 2006 [Amended by S 80/08]	S 6/2006		not yet in force
OFFICIAL SECRETS ACT [1988 Ed., Amended by S 52/05]	CAP. 153	02-01-1940	
OLD AGE AND DISABILITY PENSIONS ACT [1984 Ed., Amended by GN 273/02, GN 649/03, S 38/08]	CAP. 18	01-01-1955	
PASSPORTS ACT [1984 Ed., Amended by S 6/86, S 2/00, S 44/03, S 24/04, S 54/05, S 33/07]	CAP. 146	14-12-1983	
PATENTS ORDER, 1999	S 42/99		not yet in force
PAWNBROKERS ACT [1984 Ed., Repealed by S 41/05 - Pawnbrokers Order]	CAP. 63	01-01-1920	REPEALED w.e.f. 01-08-05
PAWNBROKERS ORDER 2002 [Amended by S 41/05]	S 60/2002	01-08-2005	
PENAL CODE [2001 Ed.]	CAP. 22	01-05-1952	
PENSIONS ACT [1984 Ed., Amended S 23/87, S 37/08]	CAP. 38	01-03-1959	
PERBADANAN TABUNG AMANAH ISLAM BRUNEI ACT [1999 Ed., Amended by S 15/03, S 29/04]	CAP. 163	29-09-1991	
PERSATUAN BULAN SABIT MERAH NEGARA BRUNEI DARUSSALAM (INCORPORATION) ACT [1999 Ed., Amended by S 40/05]	CAP. 159	28-11-1999	S 40/05 not yet in force
PETROLEUM MINING ACT [2002 Ed.]	CAP. 44	18-11-1963	
PETROLEUM (PIPE-LINES) ACT [1984 Ed.]	CAP. 45	04-03-1920	
PHARMACISTS REGISTRATION ORDER 2001	S 21/2001	01-07-2001	
POISONS ACT [1984 Ed., Amended by S 16/96, S 28/01]	CAP. 114	01-07-1957	
PORTS ACT [1984 Ed., Amended by S 17/88, S 26/02, S 18/05]	CAP. 144	01-01-1986	
POST OFFICE ACT [1984 Ed., Amended by S 17/97]	CAP. 52	01-05-1988	
POWERS OF ATTORNEY ACT [2002 Ed.]	CAP. 13	01-01-1922	
PRESERVATION OF BOOKS ACT [1984 Ed.]	CAP. 125	18-01-1967	
PREVENTION OF CORRUPTION ACT [2002 Ed.]	CAP. 131	01-01-1982	
PREVENTION OF POLLUTION OF THE SEA ORDER, 2005	S 18/2005	28-03-2005	
PRICE CONTROL ACT [2002 Ed.]	CAP. 142	13-03-1974	

PRIME MINISTER'S INCORPORATION ORDER 1984 [Amended the Constitution (Mentri Besar Incorporation) Order 1960 (S 55/60)]	S 5/84	01-01-1984	
PRISONS ACT [1984 Ed., Amended by S 12/89]	CAP. 51	01-07-1979	
PROBATE AND ADMINISTRATION ACT [1984 Ed.]	CAP. 11	01-02-1956	
PROTECTED AREAS AND PROTECTED PLACES ACT [1984 Ed.]	CAP. 147	01-12-1983	
PUBLIC ENTERTAINMENT ACT [2000 Ed.]	CAP. 181	01-06-1997	
PUBLIC HEALTH (FOOD) ACT [2000 Ed., Amended by S 73/00, S 64/02]	CAP. 182	01-01-2001	
PUBLIC OFFICERS (LIABILITIES) ACT [1984 Ed., Repealed by S 40/00]	CAP. 80	25-02-1929	REPEALED w.e.f. 24-05-00
PUBLIC ORDER ACT [2002 Ed., Amended by S 33/05]	CAP. 148	01-11-1983	
PUBLIC SERVICE COMMISSION ACT [1984 Ed.]	CAP. 83	01-01-1983	
QUARANTINE AND PREVENTION OF DISEASE ACT [1984 Ed., Repealed by S 34/03 - Infectious Diseases Order]	CAP. 47	09-08-1934	REPEALED w.e.f. 08-05-03
RECIPROCAL ENFORCEMENT OF FOREIGN JUDGMENTS ACT [2000 Ed.]	CAP. 177	27-03-1996	
REGISTERED AGENTS AND TRUSTEES LICENSING ORDER 2000	S 54/2000	01-07-2000	
REGISTRATION OF ADOPTIONS ACT [1984 Ed., Amended by S 15/01]	CAP. 123	01-01-1962	
REGISTRATION OF GUESTS ACT [1984 Ed.]	CAP. 122	01-07-1974	
REGISTRATION OF MARRIAGES ACT [2002 Ed.]	CAP. 124	01-01-1962	
RELIGIOUS COUNCIL AND KADIS COURTS ACT [1984 Ed., Amended by S 1/88, S 31/90, S 37/98, S 12/00, S 24/03, S 17/05, S 26/05]	CAP. 77	01-02-1956	
ROAD TRAFFIC ACT [2007 Ed., Amended by S 39/04, S 59/08]	CAP. 68	01-01-1956	S 39/04 not yet in force
ROYAL BRUNEI ARMED FORCES ACT [1984 Ed., Amended by S 2/06]	CAP. 149	01-01-1984	
ROYAL BRUNEI POLICE FORCE ACT [1984 Ed.]	CAP. 50	31-12-1983	
ROYAL ORDERS AND DECORATIONS [1984 Ed.]	Sup. V		
RUBBER DEALERS ACT [1984 Ed.]	CAP. 64	01-01-1921	
SALE OF GOODS ACT [1999 Ed.]	CAP. 170	03-05-1994	
SARAWAK (DEFINITION OF BOUNDARIES) ORDER IN COUNCIL 1958 [1984 Ed.]	Sup. IV		
SEAMEN'S UNEMPLOYMENT INDEMNITY ACT [1984 Ed.]	CAP. 75	02-10-1939	
SECOND-HAND DEALERS ACT [1984 Ed.]	CAP. 65	01-01-1934	

SECURITIES ORDER 2001 [Amended by S 33/02, S 43/05]	S 31/2001	01-03-2001	
SECURITY AGENCIES ACT [2000 Ed.]	CAP. 187	01-06-2000	
SEDITION ACT [1984 Ed., Amended by S 34/05]	CAP. 24	06-04-1948	
SMALL CLAIMS TRIBUNALS ORDER, 2006	S 81/2006		not yet in force
SOCIETIES ACT [1984 Ed., Repealed by S 1/05 - Societies Order]	CAP. 66	04-10-1948	REPEALED w.e.f. 04-01-05
SOCIETIES ORDER, 2005	S 1/2005	04-01-2005	
SPECIFIC RELIEF ACT [1984 Ed., Amended by S 59/04]	CAP. 109	17-04-1939	
STAMP ACT [2003 Ed.]	CAP. 34	01-01-1909	
STATISTICS ACT [1984 Ed.]	CAP. 81	01-08-1977	
STATUTORY DECLARATION ACT [1984 Ed.]	CAP. 12	11-01-1951	
STATUTORY FUNDS APPROPRIATION ENACTMENT 1959 [Amended by S 63/63, 7 of 1966, 19 of 1967, 4 of 1975, S 50/76, S 49/76, S 110/79, S 12/82, S 13/82, S 42/84, S 13/86, S 22/93, S 22/03, S 39/08]	9 of 1959	01-01-1960	
SUBORDINATE COURTS ACT [2001 Ed., Amended by S 56/04, S 73/04, S 9/06, S 60/08]	CAP. 6	01-01-1983	S 9/06 and S60/08 not yet in force
SUBSCRIPTION CONTROL ACT [1984 Ed.]	CAP. 91	15-12-1953	
SUCCESSION AND REGENCY PROCLAMATION 1959 [2004 Ed., Amended by S 16/06, S 78/06]	CONST. II	29-09-1959	
SUMMONSES AND WARRANTS (SPECIAL PROVISIONS) ACT [1999 Ed.]	CAP. 155	19-05-84 [S] 01-11-83 [M]	
SUNGAI LIANG AUTHORITY ACT [2009 Ed.]	CAP. 200	06-04-2007	
SUPREME COURT ACT [2001 Ed., Amended by S 55/04, S 61/04, S 72/04]	CAP. 5	16-09-1963	
SUPREME COURT (APPEALS TO PRIVY COUNCIL) ACT [1999 Ed., Amended by S 45/05]	CAP. 158	01-02-1990	
SUSTAINABILITY FUND ORDER, 2008	S 36/2008	11-03-2008	
SYARIAH COURTS ACT [2000 Ed., Amended by S 17/05]	CAP. 184	26-03-2001	
SYARIAH COURTS CIVIL PROCEDURE ORDER, 2005 [available in Malay text only] - PERINTAH ACARA MAL MAHKAMAH-MAHKAMAH SYARIAH, 2005	S 26/2005	06-04-2005	
SYARIAH COURTS EVIDENCE ORDER, 2001	S 63/2001	15-10-2001 except s.5	

- 253 -

SYARIAH FINANCIAL SUPERVISORY BOARD ORDER, 2006 [Amended by S 65/07]	S 5/2006	17-01-2006	
TABUNG AMANAH PEKERJA ACT [1999 Ed., Amended by S 9/99, S 9/00, S 16/03, S 2/07]	CAP. 167	01-01-1993	
TAKAFUL ORDER, 2008	S 100/2008	30-09-2008	
TELECOMMUNICATIONS ACT [1984 Ed. Repealed by S 38/01 - Telecommunication Order]	CAP. 54	01-12-1974	REPEALED w.e.f. 01-04-06
TELECOMMUNICATIONS ORDER 2001	S 38/2001	01-04-2006	
TELECOMMUNICATION SUCCESSOR COMPANY ORDER 2001 [Corrigendum S 25/06]	S 37/2001	01-04-2006	
TERRITORIAL WATERS OF BRUNEI ACT [2002 Ed.]	CAP. 138	10-02-1983	
TOBACCO ORDER 2005	S 49/2005	01-06-2008	
TOKYO CONVENTION ACT [2008 Ed.]	CAP. 198	24-05-2000	
TOWN AND COUNTRY PLANNING (DEVELOPMENT CONTROL) ACT [1984 Ed.]	CAP. 143	19-09-1972	
TRADE DISPUTES ACT [1984 Ed.]	CAP. 129	21-01-1962	
TRADE MARKS ACT [2000 Ed.]	CAP. 98	01-06-2000	
TRADE UNIONS ACT [1984 Ed.]	CAP. 128	20-01-1962	
TRAFFICKING AND SMUGGLING OF PERSONS ORDER, 2004	S 82/2004	20-12-2004	
TRANSFER OF FUNCTIONS OF THE MINISTER OF LAW ACT [2000 Ed.]	CAP. 186	16-09-1998	
TRAVEL AGENTS ACT [1984 Ed.]	CAP. 103	01-01-1982	
TREATY OF FRIENDSHIP AND CO-OPERATION [1984 Ed.]	SUP. I		
TRESPASS ON ROYAL PROPERTY ACT [1984 Ed.]	CAP. 23	01-01-1918	
UNDESIRABLE PUBLICATIONS ACT [1984 Ed., Amended by S 60/07]	CAP. 25	01-12-1986	
UNFAIR CONTRACTS TERMS ACT [1999 Ed.]	CAP. 171	18-06-1994	
UNIVERSITI BRUNEI DARUSSALAM ACT [1999 Ed., Amended by S 22/00, S 17/03, S 84/06]	CAP. 157	01-07-1988	
UNIVERSITI ISLAM SULTAN SHARIF ALI ORDER, 2008	S 71/2008	14-08-2008	
UNLAWFUL CARNAL KNOWLEDGE ACT [1984 Ed.]	CAP. 29	15-01-1938	
VALUERS AND ESTATE AGENTS ORDER, 2009	S 30/2009	01-07-2009	
VETERINARY SURGEONS ORDER, 2005	S 30/2005	02-06-2008	
VICAR APOSTOLIC OF KUCHING (INCORPORATION) ACT [1984 Ed.]	CAP. 110	11-08-1973	
WATER SUPPLY ACT [1984 Ed.]	CAP. 121	01-01-1968	

WEIGHTS AND MEASURES ACT [1986 Ed.]	CAP. 151	01-01-1987	
WILD FAUNA AND FLORA ORDER, 2007	S 77/2007	31-12-2007	
WILD LIFE PROTECTION ACT [1984 Ed.]	CAP. 102	01-08-1981	
WILLS ACT [2000 Ed.]	CAP. 193	21-10-1999	
WOMEN AND GIRLS PROTECTION ACT [1984 Ed., Amended by GN 649/03]	CAP. 120	19-04-1973	
WORKMEN'S COMPENSATION ACT [1984 Ed., Amended by GN 273/02]	CAP. 74	01-04-1957	
YAYASAN SULTAN HAJI HASSANAL BOLKIAH ACT [2008 Ed.]	CAP. 166	05-10-1992	

STRATEGIC GOVERNMENT CONTACT IN BRUNEY

Prime Minister's Office
E-Mail: PRO@jpm.gov.bn
Telephone: 673 - 2 - 229988
Fax: 673 - 2 - 241717
Telex: BU2727
Address:
Prime Minister's Office
Istana Nurul Iman
Bandar Seri Begawan BA1000

Audit Department
Prime Minister's Office
Jalan Menteri Besar
Bandar Seri Begawan BB 39 10
Brunei Darussalam
Telephone: (02) 380576
Facsimile: (02) 380679
E-mail: jabaudbd@brunet.bn

Information Department
Prime Minister's Office
Berakas Old Airport
Bandar Seri Begawan
BB 3510
Brunei Darussalam.
E-mail:- pelita@brunet.bn
Fax: 673 2 381004
Tel: 673 2 380527

Narcotics Control Bureau
Prime Minister's Office
Jalan Tungku Gadong
Bandar Seri Begawan BE 2110
Tel No: 02-448877 / 422479 / 422480 / 422481
Fax No: 02-422477
E-mail: ncb@brunet.bn

One-Stop Agency
The Ministry of Industry and Primary Resources
Bandar Seri Begawan 1220
Brunei Darussalam

Telefax: (02) 244811
Telex: MIPRS BU 2111
Cable: MIPRS BRUNEI

Head Policy and Administration Division
Ministry of Industry and Primary Resources
Jalan Menteri Besar, Bandar Seri Begawan 1220
Brunei Darussalam
Tel: (02) 382822

Secretary of Public Service Commission
Old Airport
Bandar Seri Begawan BB 3510
Tel No: 02-381961
E-mail: bplspa@brunet.bn

Semaun Holdings Sdn Bhd
Unit 2.02, Block D, 2nd Floor
Yayasan Sultan Haji Hassanal Bolkiah Complex
Jalan Pretty
Bandar Seri Begawan BS8711
Brunei Darussalam
E-mail address: semaun@brunet.bn

Department of Agriculture
Ministry of Industry & Primary Resources
BB3510
Brunei Darussalam

Telephone: + 673 2 380144
Fax: + 673 2 382226
Telex: PERT BU 2456

Land Transport Department
KM 6, Jalan Gadong,
Beribi BE1110,
Brunei Darussalam.
Tel : (673-2) 451979
Fax : (673-2) 424775
Email : latis@brunet.bn

FOREIGN MISSIONS

AUSTRALIA

Australian High Commission
(His Excellency Mr. Neal Patrick Davis - High
Commissioner)
4th flr Teck Guan Plaza, Jln Sultan
Bandar Seri Begawan BS8811
Brunei Darussalam
or
P.O. Box 2990
Bandar Seri Begawan, BS8675
Brunei Darussalam
Tel: 673 2 229435/6
Fax: 673 2 221652

AUSTRIA

Austrian Consulate General
No. 5 Taman Jubli, Spg 75,
Jalan Subok,
Bandar Seri Begawan BD2717
Brunei Darussalam
or
P.O. Box 1303,
Bandar Seri Begawan, BS8672
Brunei Darussalam
Tel : 673 2 261083
Email: austroko@brunet.bn

BANGLADESH

High Commission of People's Republic of Bangladesh
(His Excellency Mr. Muhammad Mumtaz
Hussain - High Commissioner)
AAR Villa, House No. 5,
Simpang 308, Jalan Lambak Kanan, Berakas,
BB1714

Brunei Darussalam
Tel: 673 2 394716
Fax: 673 2 394715

BELGIUM

Consulate of Belgium
2nd Floor, 146 Jln Pemancha
Bandar Seri Begawan BS8711
Brunei Darussalam
or
P.O.Box 65,
Bandar Seri Begawan, BS8670
Brunei Darussalam
Tel: 673 2 222298
Fax: 673 2 220895

BRITAIN

British High Commission
(His Excellency Mr. Stuart Laing - High
Commissioner)
Unit 2.01, Block D of Yayasan Sultan
Hassanal Bolkiah
Bandar Seri Begawan BS8711
Brunei Darussalam
or
P.O.Box 2197
Bandar Seri Begawan, BS8674
Brunei Darussalam
Tel: 673 2 222231
Fax: 673 2 226001

CAMBODIA

Royal Embassy of Cambodia
(His Highness Prince Sisowath Phandaravong
- Ambassador)
No. 8, Simpang 845
Kampong Tasek Meradun, Jalan Tutong,
BF1520
Brunei Darussalam
Tel: 673 2 650046
Fax: 673 2 650646

CANADA

High Commission of Canada
(His Excellency Mr. Neil Reeder - High
Commissioner)
Suite 51 - 52, Britannia House, Jalan Cator
Bandar Seri Begawan, BS8811
Brunei Darussalam

For additional analytical, business and investment opportunities information,
please contact Global Investment & Business Center, USA
at (703) 370-8082. Fax: (703) 370-8083. E-mail: ibpusa3@gmail.com
Global Business and Investment Info Databank - www.ibpus.com

Tel: 673 2 220043
Fax: 673 2 220040

CHINA

Embassy of People's Republic of China
(His Excellency Mr. Wang Jianli - Ambassador)
No. 1, 3 & 5, Simpang 462
Kampong Sungai Hanching,
Jln Muara, BC2115
Brunei Darussalam
or
P.O.Box 121
M.P.C, Berakas BB3577
Brunei Darussalam
Tel: 673 2 339609
Fax: 673 2 339612

DENMARK

Consulate of Denmark
Unit 6, Bangunan Hj Tahir,
Spg 103, Jln Gadong
Bandar Seri Begawan
Brunei Darussalam
or
P.O.Box 140
Bandar Seri Begawan, BS8670
Brunei Darussalam
Tel: 673 2 422050, 427525, 447559
Fax: 673 2 427526

FINLAND

Consulate of Finland
Bee Seng Shipping Company
No.7 1st Floor Sufri Complex
KM 2, Jalan Tutong
Bandar Seri Begawan, BA2111
Brunei Darussalam
or
P.O.Box 1777
Bandar Seri Begawan, BS8673
Brunei Darusslaam
Tel: 673 2 243847
Fax: 673 2 224495

FRANCE

Embassy of the Republic of France
(His Excelleny Mr. Jean Pierre Lafosse - Ambassador)

#306-310 Kompleks Jln Sultan,
3rd Floor, 51-55 Jln Sultan
Bandar Seri Begawan BS8811
Brunei Darussalam
or
P.O.Box 3027
Bandar Seri Begawan, BS8675
Brunei Darussalam
Tel: 673 2 220960 / 1
Fax: 673 2 243373

GERMANY

Embassy of the Federal Republic of Germany
(His Excellency Klaus-Peter Brandes - Ambassador)
6th flr, Wisma Raya Building
Lot 49-50, Jln Sultan
Bandar Seri Begawan, BS8811
Brunei Darussalam
or
P.O.Box 3050
Bandar Seri Begawan, BS8675
Brunei Darussalam
Tel: 673 2 225547 / 74
Fax: 673 2 225583

INDIA

High Commission of India
(His Excellency Mr. Dinesh K. Jain - High Commissioner)
Lot 14034, Spg 337,
Kampong Manggis, Jln Muara, BC3515
Brunei Darussalam
Tel: 673 2 339947 / 339751
Fax: 673 2 339783
Email: hicomind@brunet.bn

INDONESIA

Embassy of the Republic of Indonesia
(His Excellency Mr. Rahardjo Djojonegoro - Ambassador)
Lot 4498, Spg 528
Sungai Hanching Baru, Jln Muara, BC3013
Brunei Darussalam
or
P.O.Box 3013
Bandar Seri Begawan, BS8675
Brunei Darussalam

Tel: 673 2 330180 / 445
Fax: 673 2 330646

IRAN

Embassy of the Islamic Republic of Iran
No. 2, Lot 14570, Spg 13
Kampong Serusop, Jalan Berakas, BB2313
Brunei Darussalam
Tel: 673 2 330021 / 29
Fax: 673 2 331744

JAPAN

Embassy of Japan
(His Excellency Mr. Hajime Tsujimoto -
Ambassador)
No 1 & 3, Jalan Jawatan Dalam
Kampong Mabohai
Bandar Seri Begawan, BA1111
Brunei Darussalam
or
P.O.Box 3001
Bandar Seri Begawan, BS8675
Brunei Darussalam
Tel: 673 2 229265 / 229592, 237112 - 5
Fax: 673 2 229481

KOREA

Embassy of the Republic of Korea
(His Excellency Kim Ho-tae - Ambassador)
No.9, Lot 21652
Kg Beribi, Jln Gadong, BE1118
Brunei Darussalam
Tel: 673 2 650471 / 300, 652190
Fax: 673 2 650299

LAOS

Embassy of the Lao People's Democratic Republic
(His Excellency Mr. Ammone Singhavong -
Ambassador)
Lot. No. 19824, House No. 11
Simpang 480, Jalan Kebangsaan Lama
Off Jalan Muara, BC4115
Brunei Darussalam
or
P.O.Box 2826
Bandar Seri Begawan, BS8675
Brunei Darussalam

Tel: 673 2 345666
Fax: 673 2 345888

MALAYSIA

Malaysian High Commission
(His Excellency Wan Yusof Embong - High
Commissioner)
No.27 & 29, Simpang 396-39
Kampong Sungai Akar
Jalan Kebangsaan, BC4115
Brunei Darussalam
or
P.O.Box 2826
Bandar Seri Begawan, BS8675
Brunei Darussalam
Tel: 673 2 345652
Fax: 673 2 345654

MYANMAR

Embassy of the Union of Myanmar
(His Excellency U Than Tun - Ambassador)
No. 14, Lot 2185 / 46292
Simpang 212, Kampong Rimba, Gadong
BE3119
Brunei Darussalam
Tel: 673 2 450506 / 7
Fax: 673 2 451008

NETHERLANDS

Netherlands Consulate
c/o Brunei Shell Petroleum Co. Sdn Bhd
Seria KB3534
Brunei Darussalam
Tel: 673 3 372005, 373045

NEW ZEALAND

New Zealand Consulate
36A Seri Lambak Complex,
Jalan Berakas, BB1714
Brunei Darussalam
or
P.O.Box 2720
Bandar Seri Begawan, BS8675
Brunei Darusslam
Tel: 673 2 331612, 331010
Fax: 673 2 331612

NORWAY

For additional analytical, business and investment opportunities information,
please contact Global Investment & Business Center, USA
at (703) 370-8082. Fax: (703) 370-8083. E-mail: ibpusa3@gmail.com
Global Business and Investment Info Databank - www.ibpus.com

Royal Norwegian Consulate
Unit No. 407A - 410A
4th Floor, Wisma Jaya
Jalan Pemancha
Bandar Seri Begawan, BS8811
Brunei Darussalam
Tel: 673 2 239091 / 2 / 3 / 4
Fax: 673 2 239095/6

OMAN

Embassy of the Sultanate of Oman
(His Excellency Mr. Ahmad Moh,d Masoud Al-Riyami - Ambassador)
No.35 Simpang 100,
Jalan Tungku Link
Kampong Pengkalan, Gadong BE3719
Brunei Darussalam
or
P.O.Box 2875
Bandar Seri Begawan, BS8675
Brunei Darussalam
Tel: 673 2 446953 / 4 / 7 / 8
Fax: 673 2 449646

PAKISTAN

Pakistan High Commission
(His Excellency Major General (Rtd) Irshad Ullah Tarar - High Commission)
No.5 Kampong Sungai Akar
Jalan Kebangsaan, BC4115
Brunei Darussalam
Tel. 073 2 0334909, 330707
Fax: 673 2 334990

PHILIPPINES

Embassy of the Republic of Philippines
His Excellency Mr. Enrique A. Zaldivar - Ambassador)
Rm 1 & 2, 4th & 5th floor
Badiah Building, Mile 1 1/2 Jln Tutong
Brunei Darussalam, BA2111
or
P.O.Box 3025
Bandar Seri Begawan, BS8675
Brunei Darussalam
Tel: 673 2 241465 / 6
Fax: 673 2 237707

SAUDI ARABIA

Royal Embassy of Kingdom of Saudi Arabia
No. 1, Simpang 570
Kampong Salar
Jalan Muara, BU1429
Brunei Darusslam
Tel: 673 2 792821 / 2 / 3
Fax: 673 2 792826 / 7

SINGAPORE

Singapore High Commission
(His Excellency Tee Tua Ba - High Commissioner)
No. 8, Simpang, 74,
Jalan Subok, BD1717
Brunei Darussalam
or
P.O.Box 2159
Bandar Seri Begawan, BS8674
Brunei Darussalam
Tel: 673 2 227583 / 4 / 5
Fax: 673 2 220957

SWEDEN

Consulate of Sweden
Blk A, Unit 1, 2nd Floor
Abdul Razak Plaza,
Jalan Gadong,
Bandar Seri Begawan, BE3919
Brunei Darussalam
Tel: 673 2 448423, 444326
Fax: 673 2 448419

THAILAND

Royal Thai Embassy
(His Excellency Thinakorn Kanasuta - Ambassador
No. 2, Simpang 682,
Kampong Bunut, Jalan Tutong, BF1320
Brunei Darussalam
Tel: 673 2 653108 / 9
Fax: 673 2 262752

UNITED STATE OF AMERICA

Embassy of the United States of America
3rd Flr, Teck Guan Plaza,
Jalan Sultan
Bandar Seri Begawan BS8811
Brunei Darussalam

Tel: 673 2 229670
Fax: (02) 225293

VIETNAM

Embassy of the Socialist Republic of Vietnam
(His Excellency Tran Tien Vinh - Ambassador)
No. 10, Simpang 485
Kampong Sungai Hanching
Jalan Muara,BC2115
Brunei Darussalam
Tel: 673 2 343167 / 8
Fax: 673 2 343169

BRUNEI'S MISSIONS IN ASEAN, CHINA, JAPAN AND KOREA

CAMBODIA
Embassy of Brunei Darussalam
No : 237, Pasteur St. 51
Sangkat Boeung Keng Kang I
Khan Chamkar Mon
Phnom Penh
Kingdom of Cambodia
Tel : (855) 23211 457 & 23211 458
Fax : (855) 23211 456
E-Mail : Brunei@bigpond.com.kh

CHINA
Embassy of Brunei Darussalam
No. 3 Villa, Qijiayuan Diplomatic Compound
Chaoyang District
Beijing 100600
People's Republic of China 1000600
Tel : 86 (10) 6532 4093 - 6
Fax : 86 (10) 6532 4097
E-Mail : bdb@public.bta.net.cn

INDONESIA
Embassy of Brunei Darussalam
Wisma GKBI
 (Gabungan Koperasi Batik Indonesia)
Suite 1901, Jl. Jend. Sudirman No. 28
Jakarta 10210
Indonesia
Tel : 62 (21) 574 1437 - 39 / 574 1470 - 72
Fax : 62 (21) 574 1463

JAPAN
Embassy of Brunei Darussalam
5-2 Kitashinagawa 6-Chome
Shinagawa-ku

Tokyo 141
Japan
Tel : 81 (3) 3447 7997 / 9260
Fax : 81 (3) 344 79260

REPUBLIC OF KOREA
Embassy of Brunei Darussalam
7th Floor, Kwanghwamoon Building
211, Sejong-ro, Chongro-Ku
Seoul
Republic of Korea.
Tel : 82 (2) 399 3707 / 3708
Fax : 82 (2) 399 3709
E-Mail : kbrunei@chollian.net

LAOS
Embassy of Brunei Darussalam
No. 333 Unit 25 Ban Phonxay
Xaysettha District
Lanexang Avenue
Vientiane
Laos People's Democratic Republic
Tel : (856) 2141 6114 / 2141 4169
Fax : (856) 2141 6115
E-Mail : kbnbd@laonet.net

MALAYSIA
High Commission of Brunei Darussalam
Tingkat 8 Wisma Sin Heap Lee (SHL)
Jalan Tun Razak
50400 Kuala Lumpur
Malaysia.
Tel : 60 (3) 261 2828
Fax : 60 (3) 263 1302
E-Mail : Sjtnbdkl@tm.net.my

THE UNIION OF MYANMAR
Embassy of Brunei Darussalam
No : 51 Golden Valley
Bahan Township
Yangon
The Union of Myanmar.
Tel: 95 (1) 510 422
Fax: 95 (1) 512 854

PHILIPPINES
Embassy of Brunei Darussalam
11th Floor BPI Building
Ayala Avenue, Corner Paseo De Roxas
Makati City, Metro Manila
Philippines
Tel : 63 (2) 816 2836 - 8

Fax : 63 (2) 816 2876
E-Mail : kbnbdmnl@skynet.net

SINGAPORE
High Commission of Brunei Darussalam
325 Tanglin Road
Singapore 247955
Tel : (65) 733 9055
Fax : (65) 737 5275
E-Mail : comstbs@singnet.com.sg

THAILAND
Embassy of Brunei Darussalam
No. 132 Sukhumvit 23 Road
Watana District

Bangkok 10110
Thailand
Tel : 66 (2) 204 1476 - 9
Fax : 66 (2) 204 1486

VIETNAM
Embassy of Brunei Darussalam
No. 4 Thien Quang Street
Hai Ba Trung District
Hanoi
Vietnam
Tel : (84) 4 826 4816 / 4817 / 4818
Fax : (84) 4 822 2092
E-Mail : bruemviet@hotmail.com

FOOD AND RESTAURANTS

Brunei restaurants, including western style fast food centres, cater to a wide range of tastes and palates.
Visitors can also sample authentic local food offered at the tamu night market in the capital.
The market, along the Kianggeh river, is actually open from early morning. It takes on a special atmosphere at night when crowds throng its alleys to shop and eat at the lowest prices in town.
Tropical fruits like watermelon, papaya, mango and banana are also available.
Locals are fond of the Malay-style satay, bits of beef or chicken in a stick, cooked over low fire and dipped in a tangy peanut sauce.

Brunei's first Chinese halal restaurant is Emperor's Court, owned by Royal Brunei Catering, which caters to Cantonese and Western tastebuds.

A list of restaurants in the capital and Seria-Kuala Belait areas follows:
Bandar Seri Begawan
Aumrin Restaurant, 1 Bangunan Hasbullah, 4 Jalan Gadong
Airport Restaurant, Brunei International Airport
Coffoo Troo, Unit 3, top floor ,Mabohai Shopping Complex
Emperor's Court, 1st Floor, Wisma Haji Mohd Taha, Jalan Gadong
Excellent Taste, G5 Gadong Properties Centre, Jalan Gadong
Express Fast Food, 22/23 Jalan Sultan
Ghawar Restaurant, 3 Ground Floor Bang Hasbullah 4
Jade Garden Chinese Restaurant, Riverview Inn, Km 1 Jalan Gadong
Jolibee Family Restaurant, Utama Bowling Centre, Km 11/2 Jalan Tutong
Kentucky Fried Chicken (B) Sdn Bhd, G15-G16 Plaza Athirah
Lucky Restaurant, Umi Kalthum Building, Jalan Tutong
McDonald's Restaurant, 10-12 Block H, Abdul Razak Complex, Simpang 137, Gadong
Phongmun Restaurant, Nos. 56-60, 2nd Floor Teck Guan Plaza
Pizza Hut, Block J, Unit 2 & 3 Abdul Razak Complex
Pondok Sari Wangi, 12 Blk A, Abdul Razak Complex, Jalan Gadong
Popular Restaurant, 5, Ground floor, PAP Hajjah Norain Building
QR Restaurant, Blk C, Abdul Razak Complex, Jalan Gadong
Rainbow Restaurant, 110 Jalan Batu Bersurat, Gadong
Rasa Sayang Restaurant, 607 Bangunan Guru-Guru Melayu
Rose Garden Restaurant, 8 Blk C, Abdul Razak Complex, Jalan Gadong
Season's Restaurant, Gadong Centrepoint
SD Cafe, 6-7 Bangunan Hj Othman, Simpang 105, Jalan Gadong
Seri Kamayan Restaurant, 4 & 5 Bangunan Hj Tahir ,Simpang 103, Jalan Gadong

Seri Maradum Baru, Block C6, Abdul Razak Complex
Sugar Bun Fast Food, Lot 16397 Mabohai Complex, Jalan Kebangsaan
Schezuan's Dynasty Restaurant, Gadong Centrepoint
Swensen's Ice Cream and Fine Food Restaurant, 17-18 Ground Floor Bagunan Halimatul Sa'adiah, Gadong
Tenaga Restaurant, 6 1st Floor Bangunan Hasbollah 4
The Stadium Restaurant, Stadium Negara Hassanal Bolkiah
Tropicana Seafood Restaurant, Block 1 Ground Floor, Pang's Building,Muara
Kuala Belait/Seria
Belait Restaurant, Jalan Bunga Raya
Buccaneer Steak House, Lot 94 Jalan McKerron
Cottage Restaurant, 38 Jalan Pretty
Jolene Restaurant, 83,1st Jalan Bunga Raya
New China Restaurant, 39/40 3rd Floor, Ang's Building, Jalan Sultan Omar Ali, Seria
New Cheng Wah Restaurant, 14 Jalan Sultan Omar Ali, Seria
Orchid Room, B5, 1st Floor, Jalan Bunga Raya
Red Wing Restaurant, 12 Jalan Sultan Omar Ali, Seria
Tasty Cake Shop/Pretty Inn, 26 Jalan Sultan Omar Ali, Seria
Tasconi's Pizza, Simpang 19, Jalan Sungai Pandan

WHERE TO SHOP

For many travellers one of the pleasures of visiting another country is finding something of interest and value for one's self, family or friends. There are many shops in Brunei offering a wide variety of goods at competitive prices. These range from modern department stores to small market stalls where bargaining is still commonly practised.

Modern department stores are found in the major towns of Bandar Seri Begawan, Tutong, Kuala Belait and Seria. In addition to these departmental stores there is a wide variety of old-fashioned shophouses as well as more modern air-conditioned shops.

Most items ranging from the latest electronic goods and imported luxury goods to common household items and groceries can be conveniently found in these shops.

Traditional items that reflect the culture of Brunei like the brass cannon, kris and kain songket, better known as "jong sarat" are excellent souvenirs to bring home from a visit to the country. These can be purchased at the Arts and Handicrafts Centre which is located off Kota Batu, and also at the airport.

Before leaving Brunei make sure you stop by the Duty Free shops at the airport. These offer a wide range of luxury goods, garments, jewellery, writing instruments, perfumes, handicrafts, Brunei souvenirs, books and chocolates at very reasonable prices.

SHOPPING CENTRES

Hua Ho Department Store, Jln Gadong, Bandar Seri Begawan

Kota Mutiara Department Store, Bangunan Darussalam, Bandar Seri Begawan

Lai Lai Department Store, Mile 1 Jln Tutong, Bandar Seri Begawan

Millimewah Department Store (BSB), Bangunan Darussalam, Bandar Seri Begawan

For additional analytical, business and investment opportunities information,
please contact Global Investment & Business Center, USA
at (703) 370-8082. Fax: (703) 370-8083. E-mail: ibpusa3@gmail.com
Global Business and Investment Info Databank - www.ibpus.com

Millimewah Department Store (Tutong),Tutong

Millimewah Department Store (Seria), Seria

Princess Inn Department Store, Mile 1 Jln Tutong , Bandar Seri Begawan

Tiong Hin Superstore,Jln Muara, Bandar Seri Begawan

Megamart,Jln Gadong, Bandar Seri Begawan

Wisma Jaya Complex, Jln Pemancha, Bandar Seri Begawan

First Emporium & Supermarket, Mohammad Yussof Complex, Jln Kubah Makam DiRaja, Bandar Seri Begawan

Seria Plaza, Seria

Seaview Department Store, Jln Maulana, Kuala Belait

TRAVEL AGENTS

BANDAR SERI BEGAWAN

Antara Travel & Tours Sdn Bhd 02-448805/808
Anthony Tours & Travel Sdn Bhd 02-228668
Borneo Leisure Travel Sdn Bhd 02-223420
Brunei Travel Services Sdn Bhd 02-236006
Century Travel Centre Sdn Bhd 02-227296
Churiah Travel Service 02-224422
Darat Dan Laut 02-426321
Freme Travel Services Sdn Bhd 02-234277
Halim Tours & Travel Sdn Bhd 02-226688
Intan Travel & Trading Agencies 02-427340
Jasra Harrisons (B) Sdn Bhd 02-236675
JB Travel & Insurance Agencies 02-239132
JJ Tour Service (B) Sdn Bhd 02-224761
Ken Travel & Trading Sdn Bhd 02-223127
Mahasiswa Travel Service 02-243452
Oriental Travel Services 02-226464
Overseas Travel Services Sdn Bhd 02-445322
Sarawak Travel Service Sdn Bhd 02-223361
Seri Islamic Tours & Travel Sdn Bhd 02-243341
Straits Central Agencies (B) Sdn Bhd 02-229356
Sunshine Borneo Tours & Travel Sdn Bhd 02-441791
SMAS 02-234741
Travel Centre (B) Sdn Bhd 02-229601
Travel Trade Agencies Sdn Bhd 02-229601/228439
Tai Wah Travel Service Sdn Bhd 02-224015
Tenega Travel Agency Sdn Bhd 02-422974
Titian Travel & Tours Sdn Bhd 02-448742
Twelve Roofs / Perusahaan Hj. Asmakhan 02-340395
Wing On Travel & Trading Agencies 02-220536

Zizen Travel Agency Sdn Bhd 02-236991
Zura Travel Service Sdn Bhd 02-234738

KUALA BELAIT

Freme Travel Services Sdn Bhd 03-335025
Jasra Harrisons Sdn Bhd 03-335391
JJ Tour Service Sdn Bhd 03-334069
Limbang Travel Service Sdn Bhd 03-335275
Overseas Travel Service Sdn Bhd 03-222090
Southern Cross Travel Agencies Sdn Bhd 03-334642
Straits Central Agencies Sdn Bhd 03-334589
Usaha Royako Travel Agency 03-334768

SELECTED COMPANIES

- Advance Computer Supplier and Services
- AJYAD Publishing
- Akitek SAA Home Page
- Amalgamated Electronic Sdn. Bhd.
- Anthony Tours & Travel Agency
- Baharuddin & Associates Consulting Engineers
- Beseller Sdn Bhd Homepage
- BIT Computer Services
- BruDirect Business Centre
- Brunei Hotel
- Brupost
- CfBT Homepage
- Compunet Computer & Office Systems
- Dalplus Technologies, Brunei
- DN Private Investigation and Security Consultant
- DP Happy Video House
- Elite Computer Systems Sdn. Bhd.
- Fabrica Interior Furnishing Co
- Glamour Homepage
- HSBC
- HSE Engineering Sdn. Bhd.
- Indah Sejahtera Development & Services
- Insurans Islam Taib
- Interhouse Marketing Sdn. Bhd.
- International School Brunei
- IP and Company
- ISS Thomas Cowan Sdn. Bhd.
- Jerudong Park Medical Centre
- Kristal
- L & M Prestressing Sdn. Bhd.
- Megamas Training Company Sdn. Bhd.
- Mekar General Enterprise Homepage
- Micronet Computer School
- National Insurance Company Berhad
- Paotools Supplies & Services Co.
- Petar Perunding Sdn. Bhd.

- Petrel Jaya Sdn Bhd
- Phongmun Restaurant Homepage
- Poh Lee Trading Company
- Q-Carrier
- Sabli Group of Companies - Brunei Darussalam
- Scanmark Design Sdn Bhd
- SDS System (B) Sdn. Bhd.
- SEAMEO VOCTECH Homepage
- Singapore Airlines
- Sistem Komputer Alif Sdn Bhd
- SPCastro And Associates Sdn Bhd
- Sunshine Borneo Tour & Travel Sdn.Bhd.
- Survey Service Consultants
- Syabas Publishers
- Syarikat Suraya Insan
- Syarikat Intellisense Technology
- Tabung Amanah Islam Brunei
- Tang Sung Lee Sdn. Bhd.
- The Lodge Resort (In Brunei)
- Trinkets Enterprise
- Twelve Roofs / Perusahaan Hj. Asmakhan
- Unicraft Enterprises
- Utama Komunikasi

SEVENTH APEC FINANCE MINISTERS MEETING BANDAR SERI BEGAWAN, BRUNEI DARUSSALAM

Joint Ministerial Statement

Introduction

1. We, the Finance Ministers of Asia Pacific Economic Cooperation (APEC)1[1], met in Bandar Seri Begawan, Brunei Darussalam, to discuss the regional economy and measures to ensure the sustainable growth necessary for increased economic prosperity in our region.Representatives of the International Monetary Fund (IMF), the World Bank and the Asian Development Bank took part in our discussions.

2. The Deputy Sultan of Brunei Darussalam, His Royal Highness the Crown Prince, Prince Haji Al-Muhtadee Billah, granted an audience to the APEC Finance Ministers and Representatives of the International Financial Institutions (IFIs).His Royal Highness noted the improvements in the region's economic prospects, but stressed that APEC still had an important role in helping to build stronger foundations in the region.

3. We note that Brunei's theme for APEC 2000, "Delivering to the Community", reflects the fact that skills development continues to be of crucial importance for the regional economic recovery.It is essential that all the benefits of the revolution in information and communication technology be harnessed for the betterment of APEC member economies.

4. As the region's recovery from the 1997/98 financial crisis has gathered pace, the challenge of maximizing the benefits, and minimizing the risks, of technological change and closer economic integration has become more sharply etched. Taking full advantage of the significantly enhanced opportunities offered by globalization is fundamental to APEC's shared vision of stability, security and prosperity for our peoples. Experience around the world has demonstrated conclusively that growth is a key requirement for an economy to be able to raise incomes and reduce poverty. We therefore welcome the significant improvements in prospects for growth in the region since we last met at Langkawi in May 1999.We resolve to continue to pursue sound economic and financial policies and to carry out the structural reforms necessary to sustain this progress.We also reaffirm the importance of free and open trade and investment for sustainable growth.

5. But globalization may also increase our economies' susceptibility to external shocks and social dislocation.We need robust institutions and well trained people to ensure that the opportunities are fully exploited. We also need well designed social policies and programs if all our citizens, especially the least fortunate, are to share the benefits of increased economic prosperity.

6. Equally, if we are to take full advantage of the promise of technological change and the "new economy", we need a sustained commitment to structural policies which underpin flexible and dynamic national economies.

ECONOMIC AND FINANCIAL SITUATION

7. We are encouraged by the improvement in economic and social conditions in the economies affected by the crisis of 1997/98, underpinned by continuing strong demand in major export markets.In all of these economies recovery has depended on the extent to which a credible commitment to the implementation of structural reforms, especially in the financial and corporate sectors, has underpinned the steady return of investor confidence.

8. In the United States, the economic expansion concluded a record 113 months in August with remarkable absence of the type of inflationary pressures that typically accompany long expansions.However, a risk remains of inflation pressures emerging from a gap between the growth of demand and potential supply.In Japan a modest recovery appears to be underway, supported by strengthening corporate profitability and investment.However, the output gap is still large and inflation is negative.Increases in personal consumption are key for further recovery. China continues to grow at a robust pace.Economic conditions in other APEC economies have also improved significantly.

9. However, there is no room for complacency.Continued strengthening of macroeconomic fundamentals and pursuit of structural reform are needed in order to secure financial stability and sustainable economic growth in the region.Much remains to be done to implement crucial financial and corporate sector restructuring and to strengthen key domestic financial, economic and judicial institutions.It will also be important to restore the region's tradition of prudent fiscal management, while remaining vigilant towards inflation as well as the needs of the poor and the vulnerable.In economies where there is a risk of overheating, macroeconomic policy would need to be tightened in the context of a consistent monetary policy and exchange rate regime.We note the risks posed by oil price volatility to the world economic recovery and for developing economies that are heavily dependent on oil market conditions, and the need to stabilize prices at sustainable levels. In the light of rising world demand, we call for appropriate increases in supplies and other necessary measures to promote long-term price stability in the mutual interests of consumers and producers.

FORGING A STRONGER GLOBAL FINANCIAL SYSTEM

10.   Efforts to strengthen the international financial architecture have been intensified in the aftermath of the financial crisis.We welcome the progress that has been made since we met at Langkawi and urge continued implementation of reforms, including at a regional and national level.It is important to get the views of all economies in discussions on global financial issues, and APEC Finance Ministers have sought broader representation in this debate.In this regard, dialogue at the new forum of the G-20 is welcome.

11.   Progress has been made in developing international standards, codes and best practice guidelines in a wide range of areas, including regulation and supervision of banking, securities, and insurance; corporate governance; economic data dissemination; and transparency of monetary, financial and fiscal policies.In particular, we support the key standards identified by the Financial Stability Forum and encourage APEC economies to implement them in accordance with their circumstances and priorities.These standards will assist our efforts to evaluate and improve the legal, institutional and regulatory frameworks for our economies.In this regard, we urge focused and targeted technical assistance to assist countries in the implementation of key standards.

12.   We affirm the importance of and encourage participation in the IMF/World Bank Financial Sector Assessment Program (FSAP) and Reports on Observance of Standards and Codes (ROSC) to strengthen financial systems by assessing countries' implementation of key financial and economic policy standards.These processes will contribute to adapting the IMF's surveillance role and the World Bank's developmental role. Voluntary disclosure of ROSCs can serve to promote policy transparency while enabling more effective measurement of progress towards meeting key standards.We note the importance of basing these assessments on the substantive quality of policies taking account of the circumstances of each economy.

13.   It is imperative that the recommendations set out in the reports of the Financial Stability Forum (FSF) Working Groups on highly leveraged institutions (HLIs), Capital Flows and Offshore Financial Centers (OFCs) be implemented. We support the recommendations of better risk management by HLIs and their counterparties, better disclosure practices by HLIs and a review by foreign exchange market participants of existing good practice guidelines.We note that the FSF did not recommend direct regulation of HLIs at this stage but emphasized that it could be considered if, upon review, the implementation of the Report's recommendations did not adequately address the concerns identified. In the light of the growing importance of cross-border capital mobility we emphasize the significance of strengthening the collection, dissemination and publication of aggregate data on cross-border capital flows to cover both debt and non-debt flows.We also welcome recognition of the importance of managing economies' balance sheet risks, and encourage the rapid finalization of the draft IMF/World Bank guidelines for public debt and reserve management with special attention to the risk created by short-term foreign currency liabilities.Regarding OFCs, we urge the IMF, together with other relevant international bodies, to make concrete progress in its plan of action to conduct assessment of these jurisdictions' compliance with relevant international standards.We emphasize the importance of constructive engagement to assist economies to strengthen regulatory and supervisory frameworks.

14.   In addition, there is recognition in APEC that economies' integration with world capital markets requires exchange rate policies that are highly credible and consistent with broader economic and financial policies.In this regard, there have been movements towards a mix of exchange rate regimes and macroeconomic policies more compatible with stability and avoidance of financial crises.

15. Private sector participation in the prevention and resolution of crises remains a major challenge.We note the progress that has been made in developing a framework for appropriately involving private creditors for that purpose and we urge the IMF and other relevant bodies to continue their efforts in this field of endeavour.

16. We support the efforts of the IMF and its members to engage in a comprehensive review of its core facilities to enhance its effectiveness.In this context we hope that consensus will soon be reached to make contingency facilities operational. Efforts to improve program design should continue.We also endorse the work of the Multilateral Development Banks to increase their focus on programs and policies directed at reducing poverty. In addition we encourage the international community, including heavily indebted countries themselves, to facilitate the effective implementation of the enhanced HIPC initiative.

17. All the IFIs should continue their efforts to strengthen their own governance and accountability, and to improve transparency.We emphasize the importance of ensuring that representation on the Boards of the IMF and the World Bank and quota/share allocation appropriately reflect the current world economy.

18. We welcome the recent developments in the area of regional cooperation. In the Asian region, ASEAN+3 Finance Ministers agreed on closer cooperation to monitor capital flows, enhance regional surveillance and implement the "Chiang Mai Initiative" that enlarges existing swap arrangements and establishes a network of bilateral swaps.A similar swap arrangement, the North American Framework Agreement, already exists in North America.Cooperative financing arrangements at the regional level designed to complement resources provided by the IFIs in support of IMF programs can be effective in crisis prevention and resolution.We are pleased to note the good progress in negotiations between Singapore and New Zealand to conclude a Closer Economic Partnership.

BUILDING STRONGER FOUNDATIONS

19. Our long-term objective remains to build stronger foundations for sustainable growth in the region by further developing financial and capital markets.Through the APEC process we are building the capacity of our institutions and our labor forces to enable economies in the region to do so.Taken together, our work in APEC on capital flows, strengthening financial markets, corporate governance, insolvency regimes, and financial disclosure and accountability is therefore very timely.Details of the collaborative initiatives we have been pursuing in APEC, as well as new initiatives for the coming year, are contained in the Annex.

PROMOTING FREER AND MORE STABLE CAPITAL FLOWS

20. Fundamental to the development of reliable and efficient financial markets are sound and credible financial policies.In that regard, we endorse the policy conclusions of the Voluntary Action Plan for Promoting Freer and More Stable Capital Flows.In particular, we note that economies are likely to derive substantial benefits from opening to cross-border capital flows provided that sound and credible economic and financial policies are adopted, and robust structures are established to manage risks effectively.We therefore resolve to continue policy reforms that enable us to take advantage of the opportunities available in international capital markets.We will establish in APEC a voluntary policy dialogue on strengthening financial markets, particularly focusing on issues related to the implementation of international financial standards and codes, and we look forward to a report on the results of this initiative when we next meet.

STRENGTHENING FINANCIAL SYSTEMS

21. We need to be able to manage difficulties in our financial systems should they occur.We therefore instruct our Deputies to undertake a study of APEC economies' experiences in managing bank failures, with the goal of developing a set of recommendations based on case studies that illustrate the various lessons drawn from the management of bank failures in our region, and to report back to our next meeting.

22. Over the previous two years, APEC economies have made significant progress towards strengthening financial supervisory systems through the development of training programs for banking supervisors and securities regulators.Given the progress being made in this initiative, we will extend it for a further two years, focusing on more intensive work to assist national regulatory organizations to implement model curricula, and continued provision of regional courses.In addition, to improve the skills and knowledge of life insurance regulators in the region, we welcome Australia's offer to lead a three-year project on managing regulatory change in life insurance and pensions.

STRENGTHENING ECONOMIC AND CORPORATE GOVERNANCE

23. Sound economic and corporate governance will encourage the return of capital to the region.We welcome the efforts of the OECD and the World Bank to raise the awareness of and the commitment to corporate governance reforms in the region through Roundtable discussions.APEC will undertake a policy dialogue on strengthening corporate governance in this region, starting in early 2001.As part of these efforts, we note the importance of insolvency law reform, and we welcome Indonesia's offer to host a conference in early 2001 to build on the November 1999 conference in Australia and work carried out in other international forums on insolvency law reform.We will assess progress on these initiatives at our next meeting.

24. Financial transparency in the private sector is an important ingredient in risk management and sound corporate governance.We have formed a taskforce on company accounting and financial reporting to improve the quality of financial disclosure and auditing practices in APEC economies.

25. The development of good practices in APEC is facilitated by policy forums directed at experts and practitioners who are able to share experiences and explore common issues.We welcome the contribution to developing sound economic management made by the APEC forums on privatization, pension fund reform and public sector management, held since we last met.

26. An increased private sector role is an important strategy to achieve structural adjustment, particularly in emerging economies.We note the development of a network of public officials, through the Privatization Forum and its cooperation with the OECD Privatization Network, to support and strengthen the capabilities of APEC economies to involve the private sector in government enterprises and services.We also welcome the ongoing development by the Forum of a Compendium of Best Practices for Privatization.

27. We recognize the importance of strengthening transparency and disclosure standards for all market participants for the effective functioning of markets.In this regard, we look forward to the finalization of the report on the results of the survey of Credit Rating Agencies (CRAs) that has been undertaken.A Workshop will be held in Manila next month to discuss the results of the survey among representatives from APEC economies, multilateral financial institutions, CRAs and the investor community.

FIGHTING FINANCIAL CRIMES

28. We welcome the agreement to establish an APEC working group that would conduct a survey of the domestic legal and regulatory frameworks for fighting financial crime, building on work already completed by APEC members of the Asia/Pacific Group on Money Laundering (APG).We recognize the need for strong measures to combat money laundering, tax evasion, financial fraud and other criminal or unethical activities.We welcome the work of international groups in combating financial crimes, including the Asia/Pacific Group on Money Laundering (APG), and related efforts by the Financial Action Task Force on Money Laundering (FATF), the OECD, the FSF, and the Committee on Hemispheric Financial Issues (CHFI).In this respect we encourage the International Financial Institutions to work further with their members in developing sound financial and capital markets and good governance.

IMPROVING SOCIAL SAFETY NETS

29. The social impact of the crisis revealed the need for well-designed, flexible, targeted, and cost effective social safety net policies and programs to respond to the needs of the poor and vulnerable.The experiences in administering social safety nets of the APEC economies are the subject of an on-going study.Three main themes have emerged from this review so far.First, the need for adequate pre-crisis safety net planning.Second, the importance of accurate and timely information on the poor and vulnerable groups.Third, the need to have a range of instruments to ensure adequate targeting and coverage.On the basis of this study we will develop a set of guidelines for responsive and fiscally manageable social safety nets to present to APEC Leaders.

CREATING NEW OPPORTUNITIES WITH INFORMATION TECHNOLOGY

30. We recognize that information technology (IT) has the potential to increase economic growth.A stable, non-inflationary macroeconomic environment will help businesses and consumers exploit the advantages presented by IT.We note that IT lowers the costs and speeds up delivery of financial services products, thereby contributing to overall greater efficiency and convenience of the financial sector.In this regard, we call on economies to formulate and implement appropriate policies and arrangements to facilitate electronic financial transactions.We also support efforts by APEC member economies and the International Financial Institutions to ensure that the benefits of IT are as widely shared as possible.

31. We welcome the work by the APEC E-Commerce Steering Group, in conjunction with the Subcommittee on Customs Procedures, the Transportation Working Group and other related forums, for "Paperless Trading" as defined in APEC Blueprint for Action on Electronic Commerce.We agree that, building on work in other competent bodies, a working group on electronic financial transactions systems, consisting of financial experts from member economies, will be established to develop and implement programs to foster paperless trading in collaboration with the E-Commerce Steering Group.

32. We also welcome the progress made by the Sub-Committee on Customs Procedures (SCCP) towards trade facilitation, including the elevation of "Paperless Trading" and "Integrity" as new SCCP Collective Action Plans.We urge APEC customs authorities to enhance harmonization of customs data elements, taking into account the outcomes of the G-7 Experts' work.Reaffirming that trade facilitation and enforcement must be well coordinated, we encourage customs authorities to continue strengthening their cooperation.

ACHIEVING APEC'S VISION

33. We value the contribution of the private sector to our discussions. We welcomed the opportunity for a dialogue with the APEC Financiers' Group, the APEC Business Advisory Council's Financial Architecture Task Force and the Pacific Economic Cooperation Council. We note their views on strengthening economies against future crises, including their work on corporate governance, financial standards and private sector involvement in resolution of financial crises. We task our Deputies to work with the private sector to continue consideration of their recommendations with a view to incorporating them in our on-going work. ABAC will present its final recommendations to Leaders in November.

34. The APEC Seoul Forum on Shared Prosperity and Harmony was successfully held March 31st – April 1st, 2000. In this Forum, senior officials and distinguished scholars discussed policies to prevent the recurrence of economic crises and to alleviate economic and social disparities among APEC economies. We welcome the Forum and hope that this kind of policy dialogue will continue among APEC economies.

35. Effective co-ordination and management of work across the APEC process is important to achieving our goals. We endorse proposals from our Deputies to improve information sharing and coordination between APEC forums and within capitals, including on crosscutting issues. Building closer linkages across APEC's work programs will be made easier for the People's Republic of China with the alignment of the APEC Finance Ministers' process with the rest of the APEC process.

36. We would like to thank the people and Government of Brunei Darussalam for the hospitality extended to all delegations and the excellent arrangements they have made to make the 7th APEC Finance Ministers Meeting a success. We also thank the Co?Chairs of our meeting, Pehin Dato Abdul Rahman Taib of Brunei Darussalam and Hon Dr Michael Cullen of New Zealand.

37. APEC Finance Ministers will next meet in Suzhou, People's Republic of China, in September 2001.

APEC FINANCE MINISTERS COLLABORATIVE INITIATIVES

Voluntary Action Plan for Promoting Freer and More Stable Capital Flows: At the 1997 APEC Finance Ministers' Meeting in Cebu, Ministers agreed that Deputies would prepare a Voluntary Action Plan (VAP) for promoting the freer and more stable flow of capital in the APEC region. The objectives of the VAP include enhancing APEC economies' understanding of the benefits and risks associated with cross-border capital flows; developing a sound understanding of the policies needed to maximise the benefits and minimise the risks associated with cross-border capital flows; and encouraging the implementation of policies to promote robust and open economies in the APEC region.

The VAP is structured in two parts. Part 1 comprises a report analysing the benefits and risks associated with cross-border capital flows and the policies that can assist economies to derive maximum benefit from accessing international capital markets while minimising the risks. Part 2 of the VAP is intended to actively encourage the implementation of policies to promote robust and open economies within the APEC region through a process of policy dialogue. It is envisaged that this process will assist economies to implement key international standards and to explore approaches to the promotion of sound and efficient financial markets. The policy dialogue will be based on particular policy issues or international standards, depending on the priorities identified by economies. It is proposed that the first stage of policy dialogue occur in the second half of 2001.

Development of Domestic Bond Markets: This initiative was launched in 1998 to promote the development of domestic debt markets for more efficient financial intermediation within APEC economies and the global financial system.An initial survey of the state of economies' bond markets identified various impediments to their development.A workshop in Hong Kong, China in December 1998 recommended preparation of a compendium of sound practices and a website to serve as a resource center and facilitate information exchange.Another workshop held in Hong Kong, China in August 1999 finalized the "Compendium of Sound Practices: Guidelines to Facilitate the Development of Domestic Bond Markets in APEC Member Economies", which was published in September 1999.

Bank Failure Management: Recent international financial crises have highlighted the importance of sound domestic financial systems and the need for strong, safe and reliable supervisory and regulatory frameworks.Much of the work being undertaken regarding banking regulation and supervision has focused on ways to prevent bank failure and financial system distress.This initiative plans to address the issue of how to manage bank failures when they occur.A report on bank failure management will be prepared, based on how different economies, in different stages, faced financial sector instability and the results they obtained.The report will be presented to APEC Economic Leaders in 2001.

Financial Regulators Training Initiative:The Finance Ministers in 1998 endorsed the APEC financial regulator initiative.Supported by the ADB, this initiative has been steered by advisory groups of bank supervisors and securities regulators.In the first phase of this initiative, the Advisors sponsored an Action Plan for the training of the bank supervisors and securities regulators.This action plan has formed the basis of implementation of the training programs over 1998-2000.The major emphasis of this training initiative has been to develop sustainable and cost effective training process and standardized courses.Specialized training programs have been held to disseminate guidelines and best practices for management of the national training process and to impart training in bank supervision and regulation and securities regulation.The initiative has further encouraged cooperation between international and regional providers of training and among regulators and training providers.

The Finance Ministers have extended this initiative for a period of two years.The advisory groups are to meet in November 2000 to finalize the action plans for training of bank supervision and securities regulators for Phase 2.Carrying forward the work undertaken in Phase 1, Phase 2 is expected to broaden the scope of the training initiative in order to amplify and deepen its impact.In the banking sector, model courses and self study materials will be developed for banking regulations and supervision, credit and market analysis, bank examination, and treasury management and operations.Similarly, materials will be developed for primary and secondary markets, securities regulations and enforcement.These model courses will be prepared in line with the international best practices and will be disseminated through the website.To support the regional training programs, the ADB will be assisting, on a pilot basis, with national level training programs in Philippines, Indonesia and People's Republic of China.The ADB has subcontracted a bank supervision expert to coordinate the course material and training.Simultaneously, model courses will be developed for training regulators in primary and secondary market issues, and enforcement and investigation areas.

Managing Regulatory Change in Life Insurance and Pensions: In recent years, the life insurance industry has become an important component of financial systems in Asia, and there is potential for further growth.The industry can play a significant role in deepening domestic capital markets, better marshalling domestic savings to meet national objectives, and better developing self-financing, private safety nets.This new initiative aims to encourage a well-functioning life insurance industry in the region.Good prudential regulation would assist capital market stability and efficiency, while leaving the industry free to grow strongly.A series of targeted symposiums and training programs will be held over the coming three years to promote improved regulation and actuarial standards and to assess international best practices in risk management, disclosure and accountability.

Strengthening Corporate Governance in the APEC region: This initiative, launched by APEC Finance Ministers at their 1998 meeting in Kananaskis, aims to help member economies of APEC respond to the challenge of achieving global best practice in corporate governance.At their 1999 meeting in Langkawi, Ministers endorsed the recommendations of the report on Strengthening Corporate Governance in the APEC region, which identified the leading issues in Asian corporate governance.Following on from this report, a policy dialogue will be held in March 2001 to promote understanding of corporate governance issues in the region.

Insolvency Law: The Asian financial crisis highlighted weak enforcement and implementation of existing insolvency laws.In recent times measures have been introduced to substantially improve insolvency laws of many economies in the APEC region.The existence of sound insolvency laws will reduce uncertainty for investors and will further promote the process of free trade and investment liberalization.APEC Finance Ministers aim to raise awareness of the importance of establishing and implementing strong insolvency regimes in the region.Australia, in conjunction with the OECD and the World Bank, hosted a symposium on "Insolvency Systems in Asia – an Efficiency Perspective" in November 1999.The symposium was attended by policy makers, members of the judiciary, private sector practitioners, insolvency experts and academics from the region.Indonesia will host a follow-up symposium in early 2001.

Company Accounting and Financial Reporting Task Force: In the years leading up to the 1997/98 financial crisis, inadequate financial and accounting disclosures, auditing practices and regulatory enforcement played an important underlying role in contributing to weak market discipline.APEC Finance Ministers have established a Company Accounting and Financial Reporting Task Force to consider issues related to promoting high quality internationally acceptable standards of accounting and disclosure and auditing practices by business.The Task Force will report to Ministers in 2001.Chinese Taipei will host a workshop on the topic in 2001.

Supporting the Development of Credit Rating Agencies(CRAs) and Strengthening Disclosure Standards: APEC Finance Ministers launched this initiative at their 1997 meeting in Cebu in recognition of the important role CRAs play in developing capital markets in the region.Work on this initiative has progressed under the broader context of international financial architecture discussions, particularly in the area of strengthening transparency and disclosure standards by all market participants.Towards this end and to respond to APEC Economic Leaders' request for a review of the practices of international rating agencies, a survey was undertaken of the codes of conduct and practices currently in use by various CRAs.Interviews have been conducted among international and national CRAs operating in the APEC region on issues such as (a) transparency and accountability in the ratings process; (b) potential sources of conflicts of interest; (c) credibility and reliability of ratings; and (d) unsolicited ratings.A Workshop will be held next month in Manila, the results of which will be reported to APEC Leaders.

Workshop on Public Sector Management: As part of APEC's work on strengthening markets, including efforts to improve private and public sector governance, New Zealand hosted a Workshop on Public Sector Management in May 2000. Given the importance of the public sector in all APEC economies, improving the management of the public sector is central to improving the broader economic performance of member economies.The Workshop provided the opportunity to share reform experiences, effective practices, particularly in financial management and improving public sector productivity, successes and challenges.

Privatization Forum: Thailand hosted the inaugural meeting of the APEC Privatization Forum in November 1999, and Indonesia hosted the second meeting in May 2000.The Forum aims to share experiences and expertise on privatization, including governance and regulation of state enterprises.

For additional analytical, business and investment opportunities information,
please contact Global Investment & Business Center, USA
at (703) 370-8082. Fax: (703) 370-8083. E-mail: ibpusa3@gmail.com
Global Business and Investment Info Databank - www.ibpus.com

Third Regional Forum on Pension Fund Reform: Thailand hosted the Third Regional Forum on Pension Fund Reform in March 2000 following on from forums hosted by Mexico and Chile in 1998 and 1999 respectively.The Third Forum focused on the integration of social security, pension and provident funds together with supervisory and regulatory considerations.

Social Safety Nets: The social consequences of the Asian crisis and other economic and natural events have highlighted the importance of social safety nets as cornerstones of effective public policy.APEC Finance Ministers are seeking to establish a set of guidelines on the use and implementation of safety net policies and programs, taking into account recent economy experiences.Guidelines will be presented to APEC Economic Leaders at their meeting in November 2000.

APEC Initiative on Fighting Financial Crimes: At Bandar Seri Begawan, Ministers agreed that APEC can play a significant role in the fight against the abuse of the financial system.In this regard a collaborative initiative was launched which will conduct a survey of the adequacy of legal and regulatory frameworks in fighting financial crimes, building on work already completed by APEC members of the Asia-Pacific Group on Money Laundering (APG).Results of the survey will be reported to Ministers in 2001.It was further agreed to incorporate elements tied to detection and the combating of money laundering into the model curriculum being developed through the APEC Bank Supervisors Training Initiative, and to develop course content to address abuses of the financial system.The Working Group will promote a policy dialogue, as part of the VAP Part 2 initiative, on the FATF 40 Recommendations based on the APG mutual evaluation results.

Electronic Financial Transactions Systems: IT lowers the costs and speeds up delivery of financial services products, thereby contributing to overall greater efficiency and convenience of the financial sector.In the light of the growing importance attached to achieving "Paperless Trading" and as part of APEC's concerted initiatives towards that goal, Ministers agreed at Bandar Seri Begawan to launch a working group on electronic financial transactions systems.Building on the work of other competent bodies, the working group will formulate programs to foster the use of electronic means for conducting financial transactions.

The working group, consisting of financial experts from interested economies, will be co-chaired by Japan and Hong Kong, China.

TWELFTH APEC MINISTERIAL MEETING
Bandar Seri Begawan, Brunei Darussalam

JOINT STATEMENT

Introduction

1. Ministers from Australia; Brunei Darussalam; Canada; Chile; the People's Republic of China; Hong Kong, China; Indonesia; Japan; the Republic of Korea; Malaysia; Mexico; New Zealand; Peru; the Republic of the Philippines; Russia; Singapore; Chinese Taipei; Thailand; the United States of America; and Viet Nam participated in the Twelfth Asia-Pacific Economic Cooperation (APEC) Ministerial Meeting in Bandar Seri Begawan on 12-13 November 2000. The APEC Secretariat was present. The Association of South-East Asian Nations (ASEAN) Secretariat, the Pacific Economic Cooperation Council and the Pacific Island Forum attended as observers.

2. The meeting was Chaired by the Honourable Abdul Rahman Taib, Minister of Industry and Primary Resources, of Brunei Darussalam, and Her Royal Highness Princess Masna, Acting

For additional analytical, business and investment opportunities information,
please contact Global Investment & Business Center, USA
at (703) 370-8082. Fax: (703) 370-8083. E-mail: ibpusa3@gmail.com
Global Business and Investment Info Databank - www.ibpus.com

Minister of Foreign Affairs, of Brunei Darussalam. The main theme for APEC 2000, *Delivering to the Community,* signified the need for sustaining economic growth to raise incomes and reduce poverty in the region. Thus, the agenda of the meeting was organised in accordance with the three themes:

- Theme 1: Building Stronger Foundations,
- Theme 2: Creating New Opportunities, and
- Theme 3: Making APEC Matter More

3. Global and regional macroeconomic conditions have boosted the confidence for better prospects and economic outlook for the APEC region. However, economies should continue to reform and restructure in enhancing the sustainability of growth. The full realisation of the potential of economic growth depends on close cooperation between government and business, as well as among economies in harnessing vast opportunities presented by globalisation and APEC's commitment towards the open trading system. This potential for a huge increase in prosperity would require continuous efforts in strengthening the APEC cooperation agenda that would enable developing economies to participate more meaningfully in the globalised economy. In spite of the many achievements by APEC, much remains to be done. Against this backdrop of new opportunities and challenges, APEC Ministers met to discuss and advance regional economic cooperation for common prosperity in the APEC region.

BUILDING STRONGER FOUNDATIONS

4. Ministers reaffirmed their commitments to the Bogor goal of free and open trade and investment. After a decade of progress, Ministers considered that the years ahead offered APEC economies wide ranging opportunities for further growth that must be seized. However, there would be many challenges and APEC needed to explore more creative and efficient ways to prepare each of its members as they move towards the Bogor goal. APEC's shared goal of economic prosperity and social improvement would be made possible through building upon the solid foundations which APEC economies had laid over the last decade and through continued cooperation in building capacity. Such efforts would help economies realise their growth potential and transform that into higher living standards. It would also enhance APEC's ability to play a stronger leadership role in international fora and act as a force for growth in international markets.

TRADE AND INVESTMENT LIBERALISATION AND FACILITATION (TILF)

INDIVIDUAL ACTION PLANS

5. Ministers reaffirmed APEC's unique approach in advancing liberalisation and facilitation goals through the process of individual and collective actions.

6. Ministers commended the e-IAP initiative as an effective response to calls by business to make Individual Action Plans (IAPs) more transparent, specific and comprehensive. Ministers welcomed the work undertaken to improve the IAP mechanism through its transformation into an electronic medium to improve their usefulness and accessibility for the business community and policy makers. Ministers endorsed these landmark developments including the proposed 2000 IAP Format Guidelines for the new e-IAPs and concluded that the new format made the IAP system a more effective mechanism to reflect and encourage progress towards the Bogor Goals. Ministers expressed their appreciation for Microsoft Corporation's sponsorship of and contribution to the e-IAP system. This development together with the streamlining of the reporting requirements would enable the business

community to plan with more certainty and benefit more quickly from the liberalisation, facilitation and deregulation processes which APEC economies were undertaking to improve the business environment. Ministers recognised that the e-IAP system could be further refined based on experience with using the system and requested officials to report its progress to the Ministers Responsible for Trade (MRT) Meeting in 2001.

7. Ministers were encouraged by the improvements in IAPs submitted by economies in 2000 and by the firm commitment demonstrated by economies to progressively and continuously improve their individual plans to reach Bogor goals. Ministers commended those economies that had made use of the new electronic format this year and agreed for all members to use the new e-IAP system for their 2001 IAP submissions.

8. Ministers reiterated their support for the on-going process of peer reviews by which economies demonstrate their commitments to further improve their individual plans and provided an additional opportunity for members to conduct close consultations on how this would be done. Guided by the Osaka Action Agenda (OAA) principles, Ministers endorsed a set of recommendations to improve the rigour and profile of the peer review process which called for regular, focused and manageable peer reviews without compromising their voluntary nature. Ministers commended China, Indonesia, Mexico, Peru, Singapore, Chinese Taipei and Thailand for submitting their IAPs for peer reviews this year and welcomed the offer from Canada and Russia to do so in 2001. Ministers also took note of the participation of business in some of these peer reviews and welcomed this invitation on a voluntary basis in the peer review process.

9. Ministers acknowledged the importance of strengthening the foundation of APEC and of forging closer relationships with business and the community at large in their effort to achieve economic growth and equitable development through trade and economic cooperation. They agreed it was imperative for APEC to continually build upon its successes and ensure that its work remained relevant in order to face the emerging global challenges and take up new opportunities in the coming century. Ministers reaffirmed the decision made at the MRT Meeting in Darwin to adopt a comprehensive approach in reviewing and building upon the OAA guidelines. Ministers acknowledged the initial work undertaken thus far and instructed officials to finalise the work, taking into account the views of ABAC, and submit their recommendations to the MRT Meeting in 2001.

Collective Action Plans, including Early Voluntary Sectoral Liberalisation and Trade Facilitation

10. Ministers approved and endorsed the annual report of the Committee on Trade and Investment (CTI) and its recommendations. They noted the enhancement of Collective Action Plans (CAPs) and considered that the increased transparency of trade and investment policies would provide greater certainty and predictability for the business community and would result in lower transaction costs for business. Ministers endorsed and highlighted some key outcomes in 2000 which include:

- Expansion of the CAPs to intensify work on non-tariff measures (NTMs),

- Principles and Features of Good Practice for Technical Regulations and Information Notes, and

- Broadening of the CAPs to include "paperless trading" for customs procedures; and

- Completion of the APEC Policy Framework for work on services.

11. Ministers approved the priority areas proposed by the CTI for 2001 and called on officials to explore new ways of enhancing the effectiveness of the work programs. Ministers stressed the importance of working closely with the business community, including ABAC, in this process to ensure that APEC's work remained dynamic and relevant.

12. Taking into account the importance of ensuring stable investment flows into APEC region, Ministers welcomed Russia's offer to host the Third Investment Mart and Seventh Investment Symposium in Vladivostok in 2002.

EARLY VOLUNTARY SECTORAL LIBERALISATION

13. Ministers noted the many activities under the EVSL initiative, including a wide- range of surveys and sectoral seminars/workshops to progress the work on non-tariff measures (NTMs), facilitation and ECOTECH. In particular, Ministers welcomed the consolidation of the NTMs work programme and tasked the CTI to further develop additional collective actions on NTMs by the next Ministerial Meeting. Ministers also called on the relevant APEC fora to consider appropriate ECOTECH programmes to assist in this process.

14. Ministers also welcomed progress made in 2000 in the APEC Auto Dialogue, and encouraged further such progress at the next Dialogue in Thailand. Ministers welcomed the initiative to establish a Chemical Dialogue comprising government and industry representatives. Such public-private sector dialogues were important for improving the mutual understanding of key imperatives for the development of future policy and for enhancing the competitiveness of the industry.

TRADE FACILITATION

15. Ministers reviewed recent APEC advances in improving trade and investment facilitation and agreed that this had immediate benefits for business and was taking APEC economies toward the goal of free and open trade and investment. Ministers noted the accomplishments in the work on the rapid exchange of information and increased transparency in testing and certification requirements in the region, APEC Business Travel Card, launch of the *BizAPEC.com* website, *APEC: Getting Results for Business* and the *2000 SCCP Blueprint: Meeting the Challenges of Modern Business Environment*. Ministers requested APEC fora to continue this work and explore new areas and ways of taking it forward because of the direct benefit it has in reducing transactions costs for business and consumers.

16. Ministers agreed that trade facilitation must remain a priority issue. They welcomed initial work on developing a set of non-binding principles on trade facilitation and instructed officials to complete this work and report it for the consideration of Ministers Responsible for Trade in June 2001. Ministers noted that the work on the non-binding principles on trade facilitation could also be a useful contribution to the WTO. Ministers recognised the outcome of an APEC Workshop on Trade Facilitation in the Asia-Pacific and instructed officials to consider Canada's proposals on trade facilitation in the next year's process.

STRENGTHENING THE MULTILATERAL TRADING SYSTEM

17. Ministers expressed their firm commitment to open regionalism and strong support for the primacy of the multilateral trading system. They agreed that the system should respond to the needs of the globalised economy of the 21st Century and that trade liberalisation under WTO rules is a dynamic force for accelerating growth and development. Ministers also agreed that better

communication of the importance of the WTO in fostering growth in the global economy would broaden support for further trade liberalisation.

18. Ministers reiterated their commitment to building the capacity of developing economies to implement WTO agreements and to more fully participate in the multilateral trading system. They endorsed the strategic APEC plan as a basis for concerted action to enhance capacity for full participation in the WTO and agreed on the importance of implementation as early as possible. They welcomed the fact that this strategic plan was tailored to offer specific programmes to respond to individual needs. They also decided that both developed and developing members would prioritize as appropriate the plan in the developmental programmes, and that priority should be given in allocating the APEC TILF fund to finance possible programmes in accordance with the established TILF approval process. Ministers also decided that members would pursue collaboration with relevant international organizations such as the World Bank and the Asian Development Bank in implementing this plan.

19. Ministers reaffirmed their strong commitment to the launch of a new round of multilateral trade negotiations at the earliest opportunity. They agreed that the successful and expeditious launch of a new round requires an agenda that is balanced and sufficiently broad-based to respond to the interests and concerns of all WTO members. With this in mind, they called on delegations in Geneva to agree on an agenda in 2001 and urged all WTO members to muster the political will and exercise flexibility. Ministers also commended the confidence-building measures adopted in the WTO, including those on market access for least-developed countries and those addressing concerns over aspects of the implementation of WTO agreements. They committed to seriously address all issues relating to implementation.

20. Ministers reaffirmed that the concerns of developing economies should be addressed through enhanced attention to the effective implementation of special and differential treatment and ongoing support for capacity building and technical assistance, so as to facilitate their ability to participate fully in the WTO.

21. Ministers welcomed the commencement in Geneva of the mandated negotiations on agriculture and services. Acknowledging the agreement reached by Ministers in Auckland last year concerning the negotiations on agriculture and services, they encouraged meaningful progress in these areas.

22. Ministers noted APEC's expertise in the areas of services and supported efforts to use that expertise to add impetus to the negotiations. They agreed on the importance to business of continuing to advance trade facilitation measures, including through the work of WTO services bodies. Ministers also recognized the contribution economic and technical cooperation could make to the WTO services negotiations.

23. Ministers urged all WTO members to contribute positively to the WTO preparatory work on industrial tariffs and other related areas, as part of the preparation for a new round, without prejudice to the overall agenda for negotiations.

24. Ministers reaffirmed their commitment to the APEC-wide moratorium on the imposition of customs duties on electronic transmissions until the next WTO Ministerial Conference. They acknowledged the importance of avoiding unnecessary measures restricting the use and development of electronic commerce and called for the establishment of an *ad hoc* analytical taskforce in the WTO that would examine how WTO rules are relevant to the evolution of electronic commerce.

For additional analytical, business and investment opportunities information, please contact Global Investment & Business Center, USA at (703) 370-8082. Fax: (703) 370-8083. E-mail: ibpusa3@gmail.com Global Business and Investment Info Databank - www.ibpus.com

25. Ministers noted the outcomes of the seminar that has been held in Peru to aid mutual understanding of investment and competition policy and welcomed the seminar to be held in the Philippines in November. They also noted APEC's existing analytical work on these issues.

26. Ministers also welcomed the offer by China to host a seminar on the implementation of TRIMS in September 2001.

27. Ministers welcomed the substantial progress that had been made in the WTO accession negotiations for China and urged the rapid completion of its accession negotiations. They also reiterated support for rapid accession to the WTO by Chinese Taipei and the advancement of the accession processes for Russia and Vietnam. Ministers supported an agreement that all acceding economies will participate in some capacity in a new round of WTO negotiations.

28. Ministers noted the progress that has been made in compiling a database on existing sub-regional trade agreements and bilateral investment treaties.

29. Ministers agreed that sub-regional and bilateral trade agreements should serve as building blocks for multilateral liberalisation in the WTO. They considered it essential that the existing and emerging sub-regional and bilateral trade agreements be consistent with WTO rules and disciplines. They believed that these agreements should be in line with APEC architecture and supportive of APEC goals and principles.

OPEN ECONOMIES DELIVERING TO PEOPLE: APEC'S DECADE OF PROGRESS

30. Ministers endorsed the report *Open Economies Delivering to People: APEC's Decade of Progress* prepared by Australia for the APEC Economic Leaders Meeting. The report concluded that by adopting open economic policies, combined with measures to improve international competitiveness and strengthen economic governance, APEC economies had achieved not only strong economic growth, but also substantial improvements in the lives of the people of the region. Ministers took particular note of the substantial inroads in alleviating poverty and creating large number of jobs during the past decade of open economic policies in the APEC region. Ministers also acknowledged that managing economic change required structural adjustment strategies including, where appropriate, the development of social safety nets.

31. Ministers concluded that the continued pursuit of open economic policies was essential to meet the aspirations of the people of the region and that APEC was well placed to help its members pursue open economic policies. Ministers therefore instructed officials to intensify work in relevant fora to assist economies pursue open economic policies, including with respect to institutional capacity-building and adopting strategies to manage change.

STRENGTHENING THE FUNCTIONING OF MARKETS

32. Ministers welcomed the significant contribution that APEC was making towards strengthening the functioning of markets in the region. They recognised that strong markets were a necessary complement to trade and investment liberalisation and facilitation in the pursuit of sustained economic growth. They also noted that the advent of the new economy had only served to underscore the importance of efficient, competitive and dynamic markets.

33. Ministers commended the progress report on the *APEC Road Map on Strengthening Markets*. The report was able to bring into focus APEC's substantial collective and individual efforts in addressing important market fundamentals. Further to these efforts and the elements of the *Road Map* that were identified in Auckland, Ministers endorsed:

- the *Cooperative Initiative on Regulatory Reform* being organised jointly with the OECD and aimed at building the capacities of economies to implement the *APEC Principles to Enhance Competition and Regulatory Reform*.

- the *Cooperation Framework for Strengthening Economic Legal Infrastructure*, which will initially focus on the areas of corporate law, competition policy as well as capacity and institutional building to develop good regulatory systems. The *APEC Symposium on Strengthening Economic Legal Infrastructure* held in Jakarta in July 2000 and co-organised by Indonesia, Japan and Australia provided the genesis for the Framework.

- the *Cooperation Program* in the area of *SME and New Business Support* based on the Evolving Cooperation Initiative, following two workshops held in Tokyo and Taipei in September 2000.

- the proposal to invite the Pacific Economic Cooperation Council (PECC) to develop ideas which APEC may consider furthering its work on improving economic and corporate governance in the region. In doing so Ministers commended the progress in the APEC Finance Ministers' *Initiative on Corporate Governance* and noted that future proposals should take into account the ongoing work in that forum.

34. Ministers also commended the progress APEC had made in implementing specific elements of the Road Map. Of particular note were the efforts being made to develop seamless and safe transportation systems, which were of importance for trade and the provision of basic services in the region. As such, Ministers welcomed the progress in implementing the recommendations for more competitive air services on a voluntary basis, including the proposals on widening and deepening the measures within APEC as well as a plurilateral arrangement among five like-minded economies to liberalise air services. Other initiatives included the seminar on *Strengthening Human Resources Development for Structural Reform* held in September 2000, hosted jointly by Japan and Brunei Darussalam on the issue of *Aligning Human Resources Development with Advancing Industrial Structure* and the *APEC Workshop on Public Sector Management*, organised by New Zealand and held in Singapore in May 2000, which provided a useful forum to exchange views and experiences on improving public sector effectiveness.

35. Ministers noted that increasingly APEC's work on strengthening markets needs to address the challenges of building relevant market infrastructure and institutions as well as strengthening human capacity. Ministers therefore instructed officials to report further progress on the Road Map in 2001, concentrating on these challenges and taking into account the new initiatives and proposals.

ECONOMIC AND ECOTECH ISSUES

SOM Sub-Committee on Economic and Technical Cooperation (ESC)

36. Ministers endorsed the SOM report on ECOTECH and its recommendations and conclusions. In advancing the APEC ECOTECH Agenda, Ministers stressed that ECOTECH projects should be more focused and properly prioritised. Ministers instructed the ESC in 2001 to develop further the Joint Activities/Dialogue sections of the OAA guidelines, building upon the review of the implementation of such guidelines. In re-affirming the importance of ECOTECH in achieving the Bogor Goals, Ministers called for a more focused and intensified action agenda. In this regard, Ministers instructed officials to consider the possibility of establishing IAPs on ECOTECH.

37. Recognising the need to improve project coordination, Ministers welcomed the establishment of the *ECOTECH Clearing House* and endorsed the revision to the *ECOTECH Weighting Matrix*. Ministers encouraged APEC fora to use the Clearing House electronic notice board facility to coordinate ECOTECH projects. Ministers also called for widening the participation in the ECOTECH projects and emphasised that the ESC should assume a more important role in APEC. In this regard, they instructed officials and APEC fora to communicate and publicise the benefits that APEC projects have brought to the quality of life of the people in the region, citing the publication on *Making APEC Matter More to People Through ECOTECH* as an example.

38. Ministers welcomed a report on the Regional Integration for Sustainable Economies (RISE), and committed to seek greater private sector involvement, as it would continue in China and Indonesia, and expand to cities in other economies.

39. Ministers welcomed the efforts to revitalise the *APEC Education Foundation* and urged economies to participate actively in the Foundation.

ECONOMIC COMMITTEE (EC)

40. Ministers endorsed the *Economic Committee's Report to Ministers for 2000* and noted the outcomes from the symposia organised by the EC for its research projects. They also welcomed the EC's report on the *Impacts of Higher Oil Prices on APEC Economies* and instructed the EC to continue to study this issue and to include the findings in the *2001 APEC Economic Outlook*.

41. Ministers endorsed the *2000 APEC Economic Outlook*. The report confirmed that the Asian crisis has been contained and that economic recovery was more prevalent in the APEC region. Ministers also endorsed the *APEC Economies beyond the Asian Crisis* report, which highlighted the major challenges of the new economy. Ministers further endorsed the *Towards Knowledge-Based Economies in APEC* report and its recommendations to establish a *Knowledge Clearing House*, to produce a menu of *Igniting Policies* for triggering the transition to KBE, and to include *KBE Status Indicators* In the *APEC Economic Outlook*. Ministers instructed the EC to identify recommendations that can be implemented through collective action and develop detailed plans of implementation in cooperation with APEC Secretariat and report to Ministers in their next meeting.

NEW INITIATIVE ON HUMAN CAPACITY BUILDING

42. The emergence of the new economy has created a new dimension for human capacity building. In this regard, Ministers reaffirmed the importance of human capacity building and instructed senior officials to prepare a human capacity building strategy that would define the objectives, priorities and principles for APEC to respond to the challenges of the new environment.

43. To support this process Ministers agreed that a special coordinating group of HRD representatives led by the ESC be established to share information towards improving the coordination and efficacy of APEC's human capacity building efforts as recommended by SOM. In particular, Ministers endorsed the recommendation to improve the reporting and public outreach of APEC's efforts in human capacity building by tasking the Coordinating Group to prepare annually a report on Human Capacity Building to Leaders and Ministers.

For additional analytical, business and investment opportunities information,
please contact Global Investment & Business Center, USA
at (703) 370-8082. Fax: (703) 370-8083. E-mail: ibpusa3@gmail.com
Global Business and Investment Info Databank - www.ibpus.com

Ministers welcome Brunei's offer to provide assistance for the publication of the first annual report.

44. Ministers acknowledge the significance of accelerating the adoption of information and communication technology (ICT) across the APEC fora in order to take advantage of the new opportunities and contributions it brings to delivery of education and training as well as in other aspects of capacity building. The work on human capacity building in the APEC region can be strengthened and be made more effective through the development of mechanisms to enhance partnerships among all stakeholders including business and workers. In this regard, Ministers encouraged APEC working groups to engage relevant non-government representatives and instructed officials to seek appropriate ways to engage them. Ministers welcomed the efforts by Brunei Darussalam and China to advance this initiative.

APEC Forum on Shared Prosperity and Harmony

45. Ministers welcomed the successful hosting of the *APEC Forum on Shared Prosperity and Harmony* held in Korea in 31 March – 1 April 2000. Among others, the Forum discussed measures to avoid recurrence of economic crisis and to bridge the economic and social disparity among economies. Ministers also welcomed the initiatives arising from the Forum and instructed officials and relevant fora to review them for implementation, as appropriate.

Sectoral Ministerial Meetings

46. Ministers welcomed the outcomes from the 2nd APEC Education Ministers Meeting (AEM) held in Singapore in April 2000. They agreed that economies should consider the key strategies recommended by the AEM in the development of education systems. Namely, the strategies identified were: (a) importance of IT as a core competency for learning and teaching in the future, (b) enhancement of the quality of teaching and teacher development, (c) cultivation of sound education management and exchanges in education within APEC, and (d) to promote a culture of active engagement among APEC economies in education to forge deeper understanding within the Asia-Pacific community and energise and enrich their continuing efforts for improving education at local and regional levels. Ministers instructed officials to develop an overall workplan in these strategic areas and that the Education Network of the HRDWG would coordinate implementation of the workplan. Ministers noted the decision of the AEM to meet once in every five years. Ministers also noted the progress on the initiative by Australia and New Zealand to identify measures affecting trade and investment in education services in the Asia Pacific region, and instructed officials to finalise the initiative this year including identifying potential areas for cooperation and to report to the MRT Meeting in 2001.

47. Ministers welcomed the outcomes from the Meeting of Ministers of Telecommunication and Information Industry (TELMIN) held in Cancun, Mexico in May 2000, in particular the adoption of the *Cancun Declaration*. Ministers noted the commitments on advancing the Asia Pacific Information Infrastructure (APII), Asia Pacific Information Society (APIS) and on implementation of the Reference Framework for Action in E-Commerce. Ministers also noted the role of TELMIN in promoting pro-competitive environment and cooperation with the business sector in broad areas.

48. Ministers acknowledged that SMEs were important for sustaining economic recovery and that APEC should respond to their needs in supporting the foundations for growth and creating new opportunities. They welcomed the outcomes from the SME Ministers Meeting held in Bandar Seri Begawan, Brunei Darussalam in June 2000 and encouraged APEC fora to advance the interests of SMEs in the areas of HRD, ICT, financing, and strategic alliances. In

this context, Ministers instructed officials and relevant fora to develop work programme in these specified areas, and joint with private sector in enhancing SMEs development. Ministers encouraged economies to consider opening up some of their domestic training programmes to participants from APEC economies on a voluntary basis and to include a list of trainers that are available for conducting training across the APEC region. Ministers acknowledged the New Business Partnership Initiative that facilitates commercial linkages between American SMEs and qualified business partners from interested APEC economies, and requested the US further develop the programme during 2001 and report to the SME Ministerial in Shanghai.

49. Ministers noted the outcomes from the first Tourism Ministerial Meeting in Seoul in July 2000 including the adoption of the *Seoul Declaration on APEC Tourism Charter*. In this respect, Ministers instructed officials to develop collective commitment for promoting tourism in the APEC region and report progress in 2001. Ministers also welcomed the deliverables on *Environmentally Sustainable Tourism*, *Establishment of a Tourism Information Network*, and *Tourism Satellite Account*, and instructed the Tourism Working Group to take actions to implement them.

50. Ministers welcomed the message from APEC Energy Ministers in the *Declaration* from their San Diego meeting on the central importance of energy to sustainable development and welcomed their commitment to a new implementation strategy. Ministers also noted the risks posed by oil market volatility to economic development and called for appropriate measures to promote greater long-term market stability in the mutual interests of consumers and producers. In this regard Ministers welcomed efforts by member economies this year to balance oil markets.

51. Ministers noted the report of the Senior Officials and in view of the importance of strengthening energy security in member economies, including achieving greater equilibrium between supply and demand, directed the Energy Working Group to continue its programs to improve the functioning of energy markets; energy efficiency and conservation; diversification of energy resources; renewable energy development and deployment; and explore the potential for alternative transport fuels, to alleviate pressure on the oil market. Ministers also noted the new initiative to develop and share information, on a voluntary basis, on the role that stocks could play as an option to respond to oil market disruptions.

52. In ensuring overall effectiveness of the APEC process, Ministers requested officials to undertake a review on the implementation of initiatives that were endorsed in APEC Sectoral Ministerial Meetings.

CREATING NEW OPPORTUNITIES

53. The revolution in ICT has transformed the ways of doing business in the region. This new economy presents both developed and developing APEC economies with many new and exciting opportunities for increasing economic growth. APEC has an important and expanding role as a catalyst for the necessary policy frameworks that would enable all APEC economies to maximize the potential benefits of these new opportunities.

NEW ECONOMY

54. The world economy is experiencing a trade and technological revolution with rapid growth in the Internet, thriving e-commerce and many other changes that are transforming the way business and trade is conducted. The efficiencies from the ICT revolution present many opportunities for both developed and developing economies to achieve higher growth and

realise better standards of living without igniting inflation. However, as discussed in the two EC's reports, *Towards Knowledge-Based Economies in APEC* and *APEC Economies beyond the Asian Crisis*, to fulfill much of these potential benefits would require an appropriate policy framework that encourages: strengthening the functioning of markets; openness to trade and investment; innovation and new enterprises; sound macroeconomic policy; education and lifelong learning; and the enabling role of information and telecommunications infrastructure. Ministers recognised the importance to the new economy of innovation in the software industry. In this context, they agreed that APEC should promote strong asset management practices to ensure legal and proper use of software and other IP assets by users. Ministers also requested officials to examine ways to enhance interaction among IT professionals, using existing APEC fora.

55. Ministers acknowledged that a digital divide could further widen social and economic disparities across the APEC region, and underlined the importance of ensuring that everyone in the APEC region has access to the opportunities presented by ICT networks. Ministers therefore called for improvement in access to affordable technology. The new economy is primarily driven by the business sector, therefore APEC needs to strengthen its relationship with the business community in ensuring that APEC's work remains relevant. In this regard, Ministers called for a public-private partnership to create digital opportunities and spread the benefits of the new economy throughout all segments of society. Ministers reaffirmed the vital linkages between education and maximisation of the potential of the new economy, stressing that as the region moves ahead no person should be left behind. As part of the efforts to reduce the digital divide, Ministers also reaffirmed the importance for all children in the region to have access to basic education.

56. Ministers welcomed the conclusions reached at the two APEC symposia on venture capital, which were the follow-ups of the endorsed proposal on *Economic Revitalisation through Start-Up Companies and Venture Capital,* held in Chinese Taipei this year and encouraged further work in this area. Ministers instructed officials to coordinate and package the various APEC initiatives that concerned with the new economy for the benefit of synergy. The following initiatives were endorsed by Ministers:

- the US proposal on *Readiness Evaluation Action Partnership,*

- Chinese Taipei's proposal on *Transforming the Digital Divide into a Digital Opportunity,* of which the phase I will be implemented in 2001

- Viet Nam's proposal to develop an *APEC Guide to Enact Legal Framework for Electronic Commerce,*

- Korea's proposal on *Cyber Education Cooperation,*

- Brunei's proposal on *Human Capacity Building in APEC- Meeting the needs of the 21st Century.*

- Singapore's proposal on *Use of Information Technology in a Learning Society,*

- Malaysia's proposal on a *Network of Skills Development Centers,* and

- the EC's project on KBE.

ELECTRONIC COMMERCE (E-COMMERCE)

57. E-Commerce is an important element for creating new opportunities that would benefit the communities in the APEC region. In welcoming the ongoing work on e-Commerce, Ministers emphasized the need to make progress in various other aspects such as capacity building, consumer protection, network security, favourable and compatible legal framework, and in the role of e-commerce in trade facilitation to gain full benefit from e-commerce.

58. In pursuing capacity building and helping SMEs to adopt e-commerce, Ministers endorsed a proposal on *APEC-Wide Action Plan to Support Use of Electronic Commerce by SMEs*. They also endorsed a symposium on *APEC High-level Symposium on E-Commerce and Paperless Trading* by China and Australia. Ministers commended the progress made in the *APEC E-Commerce Readiness Initiative* and acknowledged that 20 economies are participating in the initiative using the *APEC Electronic Commerce Readiness Guide*. Ministers encouraged all economies to make use of the results of Readiness Assessments to guide future policies and plan further work to enhance e-commerce readiness in their respective economies. Ministers also commended the efforts by the PECC in bringing together all interested parties to develop a comprehensive approach for training and education needs in e-commerce.

59. Recognizing the need to improve consumers' trust and confidence in e-commerce, Ministers endorsed a work programme leading to favourable as well as compatible legal and regulatory frameworks for consumer protection, electronic transactions documents and signatures across APEC. In this regard, Ministers welcomed work on legal framework for e-commerce and further workshops on e-government, authentication and network security, and current business models.

60. As e-commerce is becoming a mainstream activity across many sub-fora, Ministers urged the need for better coordination and collaboration. In this regard, Ministers instructed officials to work together with the Secretariat in updating the inventory on e-commerce activities and consider widening the scope of APEC's e-commerce work programme taking into account the relevant recommendations by the Electronic Commerce Steering Group (ECSG). Ministers also urged economies to promote participation of private sector in establishing interconnection and interoperation among the existing Electronic-Data-Interchange (EDI) systems respectively in each economy.

Making APEC Matter More

61. Ministers welcomed the efforts in 2000 to provide focus on the tangible benefits that were accruing to the people of the region. Through the overall theme, Delivering to the Community, APEC has ensured that its work program is more relevant and meaningful to its stakeholders.

INTERACTION WITH THE COMMUNITY

APEC PUBLIC OUTREACH/COMMUNICATING THE BENEFITS OF TRADE LIBERALISATION

62. Communicating the role of APEC and the benefits of trade liberalisation remains a key collective and individual task. Conscious of wider public interest in the work of APEC, Ministers also endorsed the establishment of an Ad-Hoc Study Group of Officials on APEC Interaction to consider how best to benefit from the interests, expertise and insight of our communities and requested Brunei Darussalam to lead the group. Recognising the importance of outreach activities, Ministers also noted the SOM's recommendations to Ministers for APEC to develop effective communication and outreach strategy with the assistance of an independent expert.

63. Recognising that close liaison with the private sector and other groups remains an important tool for achieving outcomes that are meaningful to our communities, particularly to business,

Ministers instructed officials to enhance interaction of APEC with the business community and other relevant stakeholders, where appropriate, as exemplified by the hosting of the *SME Business Forum* and *E-Trade Fair* parallel to the SME Ministerial in Bandar Seri Begawan.

BizAPEC.com

64. In view of the vast potential of E-commerce to promote and facilitate trade in the APEC region, Ministers welcomed and commended the development of the *bizAPEC.com* website, under the initiative of the *Improved APEC Internet Services for Business* and instructed officials and economies to publicise, maintain and update the website.

DIALOGUE WITH APEC BUSINESS ADVISORY COUNCIL (ABAC)

65. Ministers welcomed the ABAC Report to Leaders, *Facing Globalisation the APEC Way,* and its two major themes stressing the need to stay on track with the Trade and Investment Liberalisation and Facilitation agenda and the importance to be placed on giving substance to capacity building. Ministers also noted ABAC's emphasis on building stronger financial systems at the regional as well as national levels and agreed on the importance of sectoral government-business dialogue, as exemplified by the APEC Automotive Dialogue and the newly launched Chemical Dialogue. Ministers welcomed ABAC's overall emphasis on outreach. Ministers appreciated ABAC's continued support and encouragement, and instructed officials to review the implementation of ABAC's recommendations including the submissions this year.

SOCIAL IMPACT OF THE CRISIS

66. Ministers reiterated the importance of supporting the poor and vulnerable segments of the communities that were affected by the crisis and by the process of economic restructuring. In this respect, Ministers endorsed a proposal on the *Revitalisation of Social Safety Net Activities in APEC* by Korea and Thailand. They also agreed to establish an Ad-hoc Task Force on Strengthening APEC Social Safety Net for reviewing APEC's activities on social safety and forward recommendations to Ministers in 2001.

67. Ministers noted the further work by various APEC fora to strengthen social safety nets and to reduce the adverse impacts of the Asian crisis. This includes the establishment of the Australian-Thailand *Social Protection Facility* that focuses on providing capacity building assistance for the development of social policy and programme delivery. Ministers also noted the successful hosting of the *Third Regional Forum on Pension Fund Reform* held in Thailand in March 2000. The forum deliberated on the integration of social security, pension and provident funds as well as supervisory and regulatory matters. Ministers also welcomed the synthesis, submitted by Canada, of the report *The Poor at Risk's Economic Crisis in Southeast Asia.*

FRAMEWORK FOR INTEGRATION OF WOMEN

68. Ministers also recognised the significant contribution of women to economic development in the APEC region, particularly in the SME sector and endorsed the first SOM report on *Implementation of Framework for the Integration of Women in APEC* noting the significant progress in the implementation of the Framework. Ministers commended the *Gender Information Sessions* held in several APEC fora and instructed other APEC fora that have not held a Session to request one. In view of the fact that further work was needed to enhance women's participation in the APEC process, Ministers tasked APEC fora and encouraged

economies to fully implement all the recommendations of the SOM and more broadly to implement the *Framework.*

Youth

69. Ministers recognised the importance of youth as stakeholders in APEC and encouraged further promotion of their involvement by networking and strengthening their relationship through APEC activities. Ministers noted the *Bangkok APEC Youth Statement,* a key outcome from the forum *APEC Youth Networking: Youth Preparation for the APEC Society in the Next Millennium,* held in Bangkok in July 2000. Ministers noted the outcomes of the *APEC Conference on Eliminating the Worst Forms of Child Labor and Providing Educational Opportunities for Youth* held in Bangkok in October 2000, which included the recognition that child labour limited access to basic education. Ministers also noted the success of the 2nd *APEC Youth Science Festival* and welcomed the *APEC Youth Festival* that would be held in China in mid 2001. Ministers welcomed the successful hosting of the First APEC Youth Skills Camp in September 2000 in Ulsan, Korea. They also welcomed the *Town Hall Session with APEC Young Entrepreneurs,* held in Bandar Seri Begawan in June 2000 and a similar *Session* that would be held during the Leaders' Meeting in November. Ministers further welcomed the first *APEC Young Artists' Exhibition* that would be held during the APEC Business Summit and Canada's initiative to develop the *APEC Site for Kids - A Youth Outreach Initiative.*

APEC FOOD SYSTEM (AFS)

70. Ministers welcomed and endorsed the SOM report on the implementation of the AFS. They reaffirmed the importance of addressing the three areas of the AFS on rural infrastructure development, promotion of trade in food products, and dissemination of technological advances in food production and processing. Ministers encouraged economies and tasked fora to give priority to implementing the AFS recommendations through intensified activities in their areas of responsibility, and to provide reports annually on progress in implementation of the AFS recommendations.

Biotechnology

71. In recognition of the huge potential of biotechnology to contribute to food security through increased production, and to the development of sustainable farming practices, Ministers stressed the continuing importance of transparent and science-based approaches to risk assessments and risk management in the introduction and use of biotechnology products. Ministers recognised the importance of safe introduction and use of biotechnology products, and agreed that the development and application of biotechnology should take into consideration WTO rules, as well as consumers' interests in food safety and environmental quality. Ministers instructed the Agricultural Technical Cooperation Experts Group (ATCEG) to implement further technical cooperation programmes in biotechnology, including capacity building and exchange of information and to report on progress at the MRT Meeting in 2001. Ministers also encouraged close cooperation with other international fora and voluntary bodies, as appropriate, to enhance consumers' awareness on the benefits and risks of biotechnology products to facilitate the realisation of the potential benefits of this technology.

MANAGEMENT ISSUES

72. Ministers endorsed the SOM Chair's Report on the Review of APEC's Management Process and all its recommendations, particularly the *Criteria for the Establishment of New APEC Fora,* the *Mechanism for Delivering for Developing Greater Links Among APEC Fora* and their work programmes. Ministers also

noted the achievement of the 3-year management review process, led by Brunei Darussalam, New Zealand and Malaysia, including implementation of measures endorsed during the process. Ministers also noted the conclusion of the three-year management review process. They further noted the SOM's decisions to improve the management process and requested the SOM to continue streamlining APEC process on an ongoing basis.

73. Ministers noted the renaming of the Infrastructure Workshop (IWS) as Group on Economic Infrastructure (GEI). They also agreed to rename the ATCEG as Agricultural Technical Cooperation Working Group (ATCWG), and the PLGSME as Small & Medium Enterprises Working Group (SMEWG).

2001 BUDGET

74. Ministers endorsed the SOM Chair's Report on Budget Issues and approved the 2001 budget of US$7,661,920 and contribution of US$ 3,338,000 from member economies to the APEC Central Fund.

75. Ministers delegated authority to the Budget and Management Committee (BMC) to approve for immediate implementation of, but subject to satisfying the usual criteria and bearing in mind the need to maintain long-term budget sustainability, urgent projects that have not been submitted to Ministers/Officials for inclusion in the annual operational budget, and to make use of the uncommitted reserves accrued after June/July for urgent projects under the Operational Account.

APEC SECRETARIAT

76. Ministers endorsed the report of the Executive Director of the APEC Secretariat and welcomed the Secretariat's offer to work with the BMC on the APEC budget cycle, and appreciated the work and assistance of the Executive Director, Ambassador Serbini Ali and his staff.

STATEMENT BY OBSERVERS

77. Ministers noted the statements by the ASEAN Secretariat, PECC and Pacific Island Forum.

APEC 2001

78. Ministers thanked China for the briefing on preparations for the 13th APEC Ministerial Meeting and the Ninth APEC Economic Leaders Meeting in China on October 2001.

Future Meetings

79. Ministers thanked Mexico for the update on preparations for the 14th Ministerial Meeting in 2002. Thailand will host the Ministerial Meeting in 2003, to be followed by Chile in 2004 and Korea in 2005.

BASIC TITLES ON BRUNEI
IMPORTANT!
All publications are updated annually!
Please contact IBP, Inc. at ibpusa3@gmail.com for the latest ISBNs and additional information

TITLE
Brunei A "Spy" Guide - Strategic Information and Developments
Brunei A Spy" Guide"
Brunei Air Force Handbook
Brunei Air Force Handbook
Brunei Business and Investment Opportunities Yearbook

TITLE
Brunei Business and Investment Opportunities Yearbook
Brunei Business and Investment Opportunities Yearbook Volume 1 Strategic Information and Opportunities
Brunei Business and Investment Opportunities Yearbook Volume 2 Leading Export-Import, Business, Investment Opportunities and Projects
Brunei Business Intelligence Report - Practical Information, Opportunities, Contacts
Brunei Business Intelligence Report - Practical Information, Opportunities, Contacts
Brunei Business Law Handbook - Strategic Information and Basic Laws
Brunei Business Law Handbook - Strategic Information and Basic Laws
Brunei Business Law Handbook - Strategic Information and Basic Laws
Brunei Business Law Handbook - Strategic Information and Basic Laws
Brunei Business Law Handbook Volume 1 Srategic Information and Basic Laws
Brunei Business Success Guide - Basic Practical Information and Contacts
Brunei Company Laws and Regulations Handbook
Brunei Constitution and Citizenship Laws Handbook - Strategic Information and Basic Laws
Brunei Country Study Guide - Strategic Information and Developments
Brunei Country Study Guide - Strategic Information and Developments
Brunei Country Study Guide - Strategic Information and Developments Volume 1 Strategic Information and Developments
Brunei Criminal Laws, Regulations and Procedures Handbook - Strategic Information, Regulations, Procedures
Brunei Customs, Export-Import Regulations, Incentives and Procedures Handbook - Strategic, Practical Information, Regulations
Brunei Customs, Trade Regulations and Procedures Handbook
Brunei Customs, Trade Regulations and Procedures Handbook
Brunei Darussalam Investment, Trade Strategy and Agreements Handbook - Strategic Information and Basic Agreements
Brunei Diplomatic Handbook - Strategic Information and Developments
Brunei Diplomatic Handbook - Strategic Information and Developments
Brunei Ecology & Nature Protection Handbook
Brunei Ecology & Nature Protection Handbook
Brunei Ecology & Nature Protection Laws and Regulation Handbook
Brunei Electoral, Political Parties Laws and Regulations Handbook - Strategic Information, Regulations, Procedures
Brunei Energy Policy, Laws and Regulation Handbook
Brunei Energy Policy, Laws and Regulations Handbook
Brunei Energy Policy, Laws and Regulations Handbook
Brunei Energy Policy, Laws and Regulations Handbook - Strategic Information, Policy, Regulations
Brunei Export-Import Trade and Business Directory
Brunei Export-Import Trade and Business Directory
Brunei Foreign Policy and Government Guide
Brunei Foreign Policy and Government Guide
Brunei Immigration Laws and Regulations Handbook - Strategic Information and Basic Laws
Brunei Industrial and Business Directory
Brunei Industrial and Business Directory

TITLE
Brunei Investment and Business Guide - Strategic and Practical Information
Brunei Investment and Business Guide - Strategic and Practical Information
Brunei Investment and Business Guide - Strategic and Practical Information
Brunei Investment and Business Guide - Strategic and Practical Information
Brunei Investment and Business Guide Volume 2 Business, Investment Opportunities and Incentives
Brunei Investment and Business Profile - Basic Information and Contacts for Succesful investment and Business Activity
Brunei Investment and Trade Laws and Regulations Handbook
Brunei Labor Laws and Regulations Handbook - Strategic Information and Basic Laws
Brunei Land Ownership and Agriculture Laws Handbook
Brunei Mineral & Mining Sector Investment and Business Guide - Strategic and Practical Information
Brunei Mineral & Mining Sector Investment and Business Guide - Strategic and Practical Information
Brunei Mineral, Mining Sector Investment and Business Guide - Strategic Information and Regulations
Brunei Mining Laws and Regulations Handbook
Brunei Oil & Gas Sector Business & Investment Opportunities Yearbook
Brunei Oil & Gas Sector Business & Investment Opportunities Yearbook
Brunei Oil and Gas Exploration Laws and Regulation Handbook
Brunei Recent Economic and Political Developments Yearbook
Brunei Recent Economic and Political Developments Yearbook
Brunei Recent Economic and Political Developments Yearbook
Brunei Starting Business (Incorporating) in....Guide
Brunei Sultan Haji Hassanal Bolkiah Mu'izzaddin Waddaulah Handbook
Brunei Sultan Haji Hassanal Bolkiah Mu'izzaddin Waddaulah Handbook
Brunei Tax Guide
Brunei Tax Guide
Brunei Tax Guide Volume 1 Strategic Information and Basic Regulations
Brunei Taxation Laws and Regulations Handbook
Brunei Telecommunication Industry Business Opportunities Handbook
Brunei Telecommunication Industry Business Opportunities Handbook
Brunei: Doing Business and Investing in ... Guide Volume 1 Strategic, Practical Information, Regulations, Contacts
Brunei: How to Invest, Start and Run Profitable Business in Brunei Guide - Practical Information, Opportunities, Contacts

For additional analytical, business and investment opportunities information,
please contact Global Investment & Business Center, USA
at (703) 370-8082. Fax: (703) 370-8083. E-mail: ibpusa3@gmail.com
Global Business and Investment Info Databank - www.ibpus.com

INVESTMENT, TRADE STRATEGY AND AGREEMENTS HANDBOOK
STRATEGIC INFORMATION AND BASIC AGREEMENTSLIBRARY

Price: $99.95 Each
World Business Information Catalog: http://www.ibpus.com

TITLE
Afghanistan Investment, Trade Strategy and Agreements Handbook - Strategic Information and Basic Agreements
Albania Investment, Trade Strategy and Agreements Handbook - Strategic Information and Basic Agreements
Algeria Investment, Trade Strategy and Agreements Handbook - Strategic Information and Basic Agreements
Angola Investment, Trade Strategy and Agreements Handbook - Strategic Information and Basic Agreements
Antigua and Barbuda Investment, Trade Strategy and Agreements Handbook - Strategic Information and Basic Agreements
Argentina Investment, Trade Strategy and Agreements Handbook - Strategic Information and Basic Agreements
Armenia Investment, Trade Strategy and Agreements Handbook - Strategic Information and Basic Agreements
Australia Investment, Trade Strategy and Agreements Handbook - Strategic Information and Basic Agreements
Austria Investment, Trade Strategy and Agreements Handbook - Strategic Information and Basic Agreements
Azerbaijan Investment, Trade Strategy and Agreements Handbook - Strategic Information and Basic Agreements
Bahamas Investment, Trade Strategy and Agreements Handbook - Strategic Information and Basic Agreements
Bahrain Investment, Trade Strategy and Agreements Handbook - Strategic Information and Basic Agreements
Bangladesh Investment, Trade Strategy and Agreements Handbook - Strategic Information and Basic Agreements
Barbados Investment, Trade Strategy and Agreements Handbook - Strategic Information and Basic Agreements
Belarus Investment, Trade Strategy and Agreements Handbook - Strategic Information and Basic Agreements
Belgium Investment, Trade Strategy and Agreements Handbook - Strategic Information and Basic Agreements
Belize Investment, Trade Strategy and Agreements Handbook - Strategic Information and Basic Agreements
Benin Investment, Trade Strategy and Agreements Handbook - Strategic Information and Basic Agreements
Bolivia Investment, Trade Strategy and Agreements Handbook - Strategic Information and Basic Agreements
Bosnia and Herzegovina Investment, Trade Strategy and Agreements Handbook - Strategic Information and Basic Agreements
Botswana Investment, Trade Strategy and Agreements Handbook - Strategic Information and Basic Agreements
Brazil Investment, Trade Strategy and Agreements Handbook - Strategic Information and Basic Agreements
Brunei Darussalam Investment, Trade Strategy and Agreements Handbook - Strategic Information and Basic Agreements
Bulgaria Investment, Trade Strategy and Agreements Handbook - Strategic Information and Basic Agreements
Burkina Faso Investment, Trade Strategy and Agreements Handbook - Strategic Information and Basic Agreements
Burundi Investment, Trade Strategy and Agreements Handbook - Strategic Information and Basic Agreements
Cambodia Investment, Trade Strategy and Agreements Handbook - Strategic Information and Basic Agreements
Cameroon Investment, Trade Strategy and Agreements Handbook - Strategic Information and Basic Agreements
Canada Investment, Trade Strategy and Agreements Handbook - Strategic Information and Basic Agreements
Cape Verde Investment, Trade Strategy and Agreements Handbook - Strategic Information and Basic Agreements
Central African Republic Investment, Trade Strategy and Agreements Handbook - Strategic Information and Basic Agreements
Chad Investment, Trade Strategy and Agreements Handbook - Strategic Information and Basic Agreements
Chile Investment, Trade Strategy and Agreements Handbook - Strategic Information and Basic Agreements
China Investment, Trade Strategy and Agreements Handbook - Strategic Information and Basic Agreements
Colombia Investment, Trade Strategy and Agreements Handbook - Strategic Information and Basic Agreements
Comoros Investment, Trade Strategy and Agreements Handbook - Strategic Information and Basic Agreements
Congo Investment, Trade Strategy and Agreements Handbook - Strategic Information and Basic Agreements

TITLE
Congo, Democratic Republic of the Investment, Trade Strategy and Agreements Handbook - Strategic Information and Basic Agreements
Costa Rica Investment, Trade Strategy and Agreements Handbook - Strategic Information and Basic Agreements
Côte d'Ivoire Investment, Trade Strategy and Agreements Handbook - Strategic Information and Basic Agreements
Croatia Investment, Trade Strategy and Agreements Handbook - Strategic Information and Basic Agreements
Cuba Investment, Trade Strategy and Agreements Handbook - Strategic Information and Basic Agreements
Cyprus Investment, Trade Strategy and Agreements Handbook - Strategic Information and Basic Agreements
Czech Republic Investment, Trade Strategy and Agreements Handbook - Strategic Information and Basic Agreements
Denmark Investment, Trade Strategy and Agreements Handbook - Strategic Information and Basic Agreements
Djibouti Investment, Trade Strategy and Agreements Handbook - Strategic Information and Basic Agreements
Dominica Investment, Trade Strategy and Agreements Handbook - Strategic Information and Basic Agreements
Dominican Republic Investment, Trade Strategy and Agreements Handbook - Strategic Information and Basic Agreements
Ecuador Investment, Trade Strategy and Agreements Handbook - Strategic Information and Basic Agreements
Egypt Investment, Trade Strategy and Agreements Handbook - Strategic Information and Basic Agreements
El Salvador Investment, Trade Strategy and Agreements Handbook - Strategic Information and Basic Agreements
Equatorial Guinea Investment, Trade Strategy and Agreements Handbook - Strategic Information and Basic Agreements
Eritrea Investment, Trade Strategy and Agreements Handbook - Strategic Information and Basic Agreements
Estonia Investment, Trade Strategy and Agreements Handbook - Strategic Information and Basic Agreements
Ethiopia Investment, Trade Strategy and Agreements Handbook - Strategic Information and Basic Agreements
Finland Investment, Trade Strategy and Agreements Handbook - Strategic Information and Basic Agreements
France Investment, Trade Strategy and Agreements Handbook - Strategic Information and Basic Agreements
Gabon Investment, Trade Strategy and Agreements Handbook - Strategic Information and Basic Agreements
Gambia Investment, Trade Strategy and Agreements Handbook - Strategic Information and Basic Agreements
Georgia Investment, Trade Strategy and Agreements Handbook - Strategic Information and Basic Agreements
Germany Investment, Trade Strategy and Agreements Handbook - Strategic Information and Basic Agreements
Ghana Investment, Trade Strategy and Agreements Handbook - Strategic Information and Basic Agreements
Greece Investment, Trade Strategy and Agreements Handbook - Strategic Information and Basic Agreements
Grenada Investment, Trade Strategy and Agreements Handbook - Strategic Information and Basic Agreements
Guatemala Investment, Trade Strategy and Agreements Handbook - Strategic Information and Basic Agreements
Guinea Investment, Trade Strategy and Agreements Handbook - Strategic Information and Basic Agreements
Guinea-Bissau Investment, Trade Strategy and Agreements Handbook - Strategic Information and Basic Agreements
Guyana Investment, Trade Strategy and Agreements Handbook - Strategic Information and Basic Agreements
Haiti Investment, Trade Strategy and Agreements Handbook - Strategic Information and Basic Agreements
Honduras Investment, Trade Strategy and Agreements Handbook - Strategic Information and Basic Agreements
Hong Kong, China SAR Investment, Trade Strategy and Agreements Handbook - Strategic Information and Basic Agreements
Hungary Investment, Trade Strategy and Agreements Handbook - Strategic Information and Basic Agreements
Iceland Investment, Trade Strategy and Agreements Handbook - Strategic Information and Basic Agreements
India Investment, Trade Strategy and Agreements Handbook - Strategic Information and Basic Agreements
Indonesia Investment, Trade Strategy and Agreements Handbook - Strategic Information and Basic Agreements
Iran, Islamic Republic of Investment, Trade Strategy and Agreements Handbook - Strategic Information and Basic Agreements
Iraq Investment, Trade Strategy and Agreements Handbook - Strategic Information and Basic Agreements
Israel Investment, Trade Strategy and Agreements Handbook - Strategic Information and Basic Agreements
Italy Investment, Trade Strategy and Agreements Handbook - Strategic Information and Basic Agreements
Jamaica Investment, Trade Strategy and Agreements Handbook - Strategic Information and Basic Agreements
Japan Investment, Trade Strategy and Agreements Handbook - Strategic Information and Basic Agreements
Jordan Investment, Trade Strategy and Agreements Handbook - Strategic Information and Basic Agreements
Kazakhstan Investment, Trade Strategy and Agreements Handbook - Strategic Information and Basic Agreements
Kenya Investment, Trade Strategy and Agreements Handbook - Strategic Information and Basic Agreements
Korea, Dem. People's Rep. of Investment, Trade Strategy and Agreements Handbook - Strategic Information and Basic Agreements
Korea, Republic of Investment, Trade Strategy and Agreements Handbook - Strategic Information and Basic Agreements

TITLE
Kuwait Investment, Trade Strategy and Agreements Handbook - Strategic Information and Basic Agreements
Kyrgyzstan Investment, Trade Strategy and Agreements Handbook - Strategic Information and Basic Agreements
Lao People's Democratic Republic Investment, Trade Strategy and Agreements Handbook - Strategic Information and Basic Agreements
Latvia Investment, Trade Strategy and Agreements Handbook - Strategic Information and Basic Agreements
Lebanon Investment, Trade Strategy and Agreements Handbook - Strategic Information and Basic Agreements
Lesotho Investment, Trade Strategy and Agreements Handbook - Strategic Information and Basic Agreements
Liberia Investment, Trade Strategy and Agreements Handbook - Strategic Information and Basic Agreements
Libya Investment, Trade Strategy and Agreements Handbook - Strategic Information and Basic Agreements
Lithuania Investment, Trade Strategy and Agreements Handbook - Strategic Information and Basic Agreements
Luxembourg Investment, Trade Strategy and Agreements Handbook - Strategic Information and Basic Agreements
Macao, China SAR Investment, Trade Strategy and Agreements Handbook - Strategic Information and Basic Agreements
Macedonia, The former Yugoslav Republic of Investment, Trade Strategy and Agreements Handbook - Strategic Information and Basic Agreements
Madagascar Investment, Trade Strategy and Agreements Handbook - Strategic Information and Basic Agreements
Malawi Investment, Trade Strategy and Agreements Handbook - Strategic Information and Basic Agreements
Malaysia Investment, Trade Strategy and Agreements Handbook - Strategic Information and Basic Agreements
Mali Investment, Trade Strategy and Agreements Handbook - Strategic Information and Basic Agreements
Malta Investment, Trade Strategy and Agreements Handbook - Strategic Information and Basic Agreements
Marshall Islands Investment, Trade Strategy and Agreements Handbook - Strategic Information and Basic Agreements
Mauritania Investment, Trade Strategy and Agreements Handbook - Strategic Information and Basic Agreements
Mauritius Investment, Trade Strategy and Agreements Handbook - Strategic Information and Basic Agreements
Mexico Investment, Trade Strategy and Agreements Handbook - Strategic Information and Basic Agreements
Moldova, Republic of Investment, Trade Strategy and Agreements Handbook - Strategic Information and Basic Agreements
Mongolia Investment, Trade Strategy and Agreements Handbook - Strategic Information and Basic Agreements
Montenegro Investment, Trade Strategy and Agreements Handbook - Strategic Information and Basic Agreements
Morocco Investment, Trade Strategy and Agreements Handbook - Strategic Information and Basic Agreements
Mozambique Investment, Trade Strategy and Agreements Handbook - Strategic Information and Basic Agreements
Myanmar Investment, Trade Strategy and Agreements Handbook - Strategic Information and Basic Agreements
Namibia Investment, Trade Strategy and Agreements Handbook - Strategic Information and Basic Agreements
Nepal Investment, Trade Strategy and Agreements Handbook - Strategic Information and Basic Agreements
Netherlands Investment, Trade Strategy and Agreements Handbook - Strategic Information and Basic Agreements
New Zealand Investment, Trade Strategy and Agreements Handbook - Strategic Information and Basic Agreements
Nicaragua Investment, Trade Strategy and Agreements Handbook - Strategic Information and Basic Agreements
Niger Investment, Trade Strategy and Agreements Handbook - Strategic Information and Basic Agreements
Nigeria Investment, Trade Strategy and Agreements Handbook - Strategic Information and Basic Agreements
Norway Investment, Trade Strategy and Agreements Handbook - Strategic Information and Basic Agreements
Occupied Palestinian territory Investment, Trade Strategy and Agreements Handbook - Strategic Information and Basic Agreements
Oman Investment, Trade Strategy and Agreements Handbook - Strategic Information and Basic Agreements
Pakistan Investment, Trade Strategy and Agreements Handbook - Strategic Information and Basic Agreements
Panama Investment, Trade Strategy and Agreements Handbook - Strategic Information and Basic Agreements
Papua New Guinea Investment, Trade Strategy and Agreements Handbook - Strategic Information and Basic Agreements
Paraguay Investment, Trade Strategy and Agreements Handbook - Strategic Information and Basic Agreements
Peru Investment, Trade Strategy and Agreements Handbook - Strategic Information and Basic Agreements
Philippines Investment, Trade Strategy and Agreements Handbook - Strategic Information and Basic Agreements
Poland Investment, Trade Strategy and Agreements Handbook - Strategic Information and Basic Agreements
Portugal Investment, Trade Strategy and Agreements Handbook - Strategic Information and Basic Agreements
Qatar Investment, Trade Strategy and Agreements Handbook - Strategic Information and Basic Agreements
Romania Investment, Trade Strategy and Agreements Handbook - Strategic Information and Basic Agreements
Russian Federation Investment, Trade Strategy and Agreements Handbook - Strategic Information and Basic Agreements
Rwanda Investment, Trade Strategy and Agreements Handbook - Strategic Information and Basic Agreements
Saint Lucia Investment, Trade Strategy and Agreements Handbook - Strategic Information and Basic Agreements

TITLE
Saint Vincent and the Grenadines Investment, Trade Strategy and Agreements Handbook - Strategic Information and Basic Agreements
San Marino Investment, Trade Strategy and Agreements Handbook - Strategic Information and Basic Agreements
Sao Tome and Principe Investment, Trade Strategy and Agreements Handbook - Strategic Information and Basic Agreements
Saudi Arabia Investment, Trade Strategy and Agreements Handbook - Strategic Information and Basic Agreements
Senegal Investment, Trade Strategy and Agreements Handbook - Strategic Information and Basic Agreements
Serbia Investment, Trade Strategy and Agreements Handbook - Strategic Information and Basic Agreements
Seychelles Investment, Trade Strategy and Agreements Handbook - Strategic Information and Basic Agreements
Sierra Leone Investment, Trade Strategy and Agreements Handbook - Strategic Information and Basic Agreements
Singapore Investment, Trade Strategy and Agreements Handbook - Strategic Information and Basic Agreements
Slovakia Investment, Trade Strategy and Agreements Handbook - Strategic Information and Basic Agreements
Slovenia Investment, Trade Strategy and Agreements Handbook - Strategic Information and Basic Agreements
Somalia Investment, Trade Strategy and Agreements Handbook - Strategic Information and Basic Agreements
South Africa Investment, Trade Strategy and Agreements Handbook - Strategic Information and Basic Agreements
Spain Investment, Trade Strategy and Agreements Handbook - Strategic Information and Basic Agreements
Sri Lanka Investment, Trade Strategy and Agreements Handbook - Strategic Information and Basic Agreements
Sudan Investment, Trade Strategy and Agreements Handbook - Strategic Information and Basic Agreements
Suriname Investment, Trade Strategy and Agreements Handbook - Strategic Information and Basic Agreements
Swaziland Investment, Trade Strategy and Agreements Handbook - Strategic Information and Basic Agreements
Sweden Investment, Trade Strategy and Agreements Handbook - Strategic Information and Basic Agreements
Switzerland Investment, Trade Strategy and Agreements Handbook - Strategic Information and Basic Agreements
Syrian Arab Republic Investment, Trade Strategy and Agreements Handbook - Strategic Information and Basic Agreements
Taiwan Province of China Investment, Trade Strategy and Agreements Handbook - Strategic Information and Basic Agreements
Tajikistan Investment, Trade Strategy and Agreements Handbook - Strategic Information and Basic Agreements
Tanzania, United Republic of Investment, Trade Strategy and Agreements Handbook - Strategic Information and Basic Agreements
Thailand Investment, Trade Strategy and Agreements Handbook - Strategic Information and Basic Agreements
Timor-Leste Investment, Trade Strategy and Agreements Handbook - Strategic Information and Basic Agreements
Togo Investment, Trade Strategy and Agreements Handbook - Strategic Information and Basic Agreements
Tonga Investment, Trade Strategy and Agreements Handbook - Strategic Information and Basic Agreements
Trinidad and Tobago Investment, Trade Strategy and Agreements Handbook - Strategic Information and Basic Agreements
Tunisia Investment, Trade Strategy and Agreements Handbook - Strategic Information and Basic Agreements
Turkey Investment, Trade Strategy and Agreements Handbook - Strategic Information and Basic Agreements
Turkmenistan Investment, Trade Strategy and Agreements Handbook - Strategic Information and Basic Agreements
Uganda Investment, Trade Strategy and Agreements Handbook - Strategic Information and Basic Agreements
Ukraine Investment, Trade Strategy and Agreements Handbook - Strategic Information and Basic Agreements
United Arab Emirates Investment, Trade Strategy and Agreements Handbook - Strategic Information and Basic Agreements
United Kingdom Investment, Trade Strategy and Agreements Handbook - Strategic Information and Basic Agreements
United States of America Investment, Trade Strategy and Agreements Handbook - Strategic Information and Basic Agreements
Uruguay Investment, Trade Strategy and Agreements Handbook - Strategic Information and Basic Agreements
Uzbekistan Investment, Trade Strategy and Agreements Handbook - Strategic Information and Basic Agreements
Vanuatu Investment, Trade Strategy and Agreements Handbook - Strategic Information and Basic Agreements
Venezuela, Bolivarian Republic of Investment, Trade Strategy and Agreements Handbook - Strategic Information and Basic Agreements
Viet Nam Investment, Trade Strategy and Agreements Handbook - Strategic Information and Basic Agreements
Yemen Investment, Trade Strategy and Agreements Handbook - Strategic Information and Basic Agreements
Zambia Investment, Trade Strategy and Agreements Handbook - Strategic Information and Basic Agreements
Zimbabwe Investment, Trade Strategy and Agreements Handbook - Strategic Information and Basic Agreements
ACP (African, Caribbean and Pacific Group of States) Trade and Investment Agreements Handbook - Strategic

TITLE
Information and Basic Agreements
ANCOM (Andean Community) Trade and Investment Agreements Handbook - Strategic Information and Basic Agreements
ASEAN (Association of South-East Asian Nations) Trade and Investment Agreements Handbook - Strategic Information and Basic Agreements
AU (African Union) Trade and Investment Agreements Handbook - Strategic Information and Basic Agreements
BIMSTEC (Bay of Bengal Initiative for Multi-Sector Technical and Economic Cooperation) Trade and Investment Agreements Handbook - Strategic Information and Basic Agreements
BLEU (Belgium-Luxembourg Economic Union) Trade and Investment Agreements Handbook - Strategic Information and Basic Agreements
CACM (Central American Common Market) Trade and Investment Agreements Handbook - Strategic Information and Basic Agreements
CARICOM (Caribbean Community) Trade and Investment Agreements Handbook - Strategic Information and Basic Agreements
CEFTA (Central European Free Trade Agreement) Trade and Investment Agreements Handbook - Strategic Information and Basic Agreements
CEMAC (Economic and Monetary Community of Central Africa) Trade and Investment Agreements Handbook - Strategic Information and Basic Agreements
CEPGL (Economic Community of the Great Lakes Countries) Trade and Investment Agreements Handbook - Strategic Information and Basic Agreements
COMESA (Common Market for Eastern and Southern Africa) Trade and Investment Agreements Handbook - Strategic Information and Basic Agreements
EAC (East African Community) Trade and Investment Agreements Handbook - Strategic Information and Basic Agreements
ECCAS (Economic Community of Central African States) Trade and Investment Agreements Handbook - Strategic Information and Basic Agreements
ECO (Economic Cooperation Organization) Trade and Investment Agreements Handbook - Strategic Information and Basic Agreements
ECOWAS (Economic Community of West African States) Trade and Investment Agreements Handbook - Strategic Information and Basic Agreements
EFTA (European Free Trade Association) Trade and Investment Agreements Handbook - Strategic Information and Basic Agreements
Energy Charter Treaty members Trade and Investment Agreements Handbook - Strategic Information and Basic Agreements
ESA (Eastern and Southern Africa) Trade and Investment Agreements Handbook - Strategic Information and Basic Agreements
EU (European Union) Trade and Investment Agreements Handbook - Strategic Information and Basic Agreements
Eurasian Economic Union Trade and Investment Agreements Handbook - Strategic Information and Basic Agreements
Gulf Cooperation Council Trade and Investment Agreements Handbook - Strategic Information and Basic Agreements
Latin American Integration Association Trade and Investment Agreements Handbook - Strategic Information and Basic Agreements
League of Arab States Trade and Investment Agreements Handbook - Strategic Information and Basic Agreements
Mercado Común Sudamericano (MERCOSUR - Economic Community Consisting of Argentina, Brazil, Paraguay, and Urugua) Trade and Investment Agreements Handbook - Strategic Information and Basic Agreements
OCT (Overseas Countries and Territories) Trade and Investment Agreements Handbook - Strategic Information and Basic Agreements
Organization of the Islamic Conference Trade and Investment Agreements Handbook - Strategic Information and Basic Agreements
Southern African Customs Union Trade and Investment Agreements Handbook - Strategic Information and Basic Agreements
Southern African Development Community Trade and Investment Agreements Handbook - Strategic Information and Basic Agreements
South Asian Free Trade Area Accord Trade and Investment Agreements Handbook - Strategic Information and Basic Agreements
South Pacific Regional Trade and Economic Cooperation Agreement Trade and Investment Agreements Handbook - Strategic Information and Basic Agreements
Arab Maghreb Union Trade and Investment Agreements Handbook - Strategic Information and Basic Agreements
West African Economic and Monetary Union Trade and Investment Agreements Handbook - Strategic Information and